1 MONTH OF
FREE
READING

at

www.ForgottenBooks.com

By purchasing this book you are eligible for one month membership to ForgottenBooks.com, giving you unlimited access to our entire collection of over 1,000,000 titles via our web site and mobile apps.

To claim your free month visit:

www.forgottenbooks.com/free238979

ISBN 978-0-666-32523-5
PIBN 10238979

RECORDS

OF THE

American Catholic Historical Society

OF

PHILADELPHIA

Volume XXIX

PUBLISHED BY THE SOCIETY

1918

ST REV. EDMOND F. PRENDERGAST, D. D.

ARCHBISHOP OF PHILADELPHIA

BORN MAY 5, 1843

ORDAINED NOVEMBER 17, 1865

CONSECRATED BISHOP FEBRUARY 24, 1897

APPOINTED ARCHBISHOP MAY 27, 1911

DIED FEBRUARY 26, 1918

ARCHBISHOP PRENDERGAST

THIS issue of the RECORDS had gone to press ere the shadow of the death of our venerated and beloved Archbishop had been cast upon the Archdiocese.

There is time but to note the sad occurrence and to offer a little tribute of affectionate respect to the memory of one who among his manifold cares and duties still found time to aid with his approval and encouragement the American Catholic Historical Society. A more adequate account of him and his work will appear in our June number.

Archbishop Prendergast will be sadly missed in the lives of his priests and people and in the direction of the great affairs which had come within his jurisdiction, but above any personal sense of sorrow is that essentially Catholic feeling of separation from our local chief Shepherd and Bishop of our souls.

As the mind ranges back through the centuries there is however a compensation, a deep interior satisfaction in the thought that another link has been completed in the Apostolic chain which, reaching out in all directions to the uttermost parts of the earth, binds them to the feet of Peter.

We know that the succession will continue and that others will carry on what our late Archbishop was summoned to relinquish; but we know also that his achievements have set a high mark of successful accomplishment and that his simple, modest, holy life, lofty ideals and intensity of purpose will furnish an undying example and inspiration to those who come after him. The record of his administration of his great office will constitute a most valuable and illuminating chapter in the history of the Archdiocese and of the Church in America.

RECORDS OF THE

AMERICAN CATHOLIC HISTORICAL SOCIETY

| VOL. XXIX | MARCH, 1918 | NO. 1 |

ADDRESS OF THE PRESIDENT OF THE SOCIETY

AT THE ANNUAL MEETING, DECEMBER, 1917

It has been the annual custom of the President of this Society to present a summary of its work and needs, leaving the details to be supplied by the report of the Board.

A review of some of the Presidents' addresses taken at random through a period of years shows that they have devoted considerable space to an exposition of the objects of the Society, of the value of those objects, and of the extent and worth of the work hitherto accomplished. All of this has been rehearsed so often and so well that it will not be repeated on this occasion. On these matters I will content myself with the simple reminder that the aim of the Society is, and that its work has been, to collect, classify, preserve, and make known the facts of American Catholic history. This in its nature involves the collection of a library of books and manuscripts and historical records and documents pertaining to American Catholic history; the creation of a storehouse of authenticated information, including primarily as far as possible original sources of historical data.

To many it would doubtless seem a loss of time to urge the importance of a study of history, and yet in this age there are more persons who question its value than the casual observer would imagine. The proof of this is the indifference of the average successful man of business to any history except such fragments as he picks up in the journals and periodicals of the day. He finds he does not need it in his business, and that for his leisure there are other less laborious and more diverting occupations than its study.

Of what use is history? It preserves the continuity of the mental processes of the race; fortifies its traditions and establishes a connection with the past which tends to develop the racial consciousness of universal brotherhood, of a common origin and a common destiny. Likewise it engenders a national spirit, and by the example of noble deeds creates a sentiment of generous rivalry with the past and a determination to hold fast to the best in what has been so laboriously won. The ever present interest of man in man leads to a study of his thoughts, motives, and actions, to the end that, understanding others, he may the better understand himself. The result is the acquisition of wisdom from knowledge and the cultivation of an ardent spirit of devotion to ideals; of a spirit to abolish evil and to preserve and improve his heritage.

We know from experience that these ends are only partially attained; that human nature is weak and wayward. and that even brilliant minds become possessed of fantastic notions by which honest persons innocently mislead the unthinking and which dishonest persons use to advance their own selfish interests. There is, however, hardly an expedient or experiment in politics that has not its prototype in the past, and not a single cure for the ills that a man brings on himself that the Church has not offered and urged for two thousand years. These are weighty reasons, then, for the study of history, which fails in its primary object unless it is written with an eye single to the truth. It must be accurate, comprehensive, and sympathetically under standing of circumstances; of the interpretative atmosphere and setting of facts; above all it must be impartial and full of the essential elements that have constituted the life which it portrays. This is to make the experience of the past available for the present.

Now, chief of the influences among all nations and all people has been religion, whose appeal lies both to the mind and heart. Man's feelings largely determine many of his most important acts. " Let me write the ballads of a people and I care not who makes their laws " is only less fundamental than, " Let me know the religion of a people and I will give you the inspiration for their ballads and indeed for all their literature and arts." Unfortunately ignorance and prejudice, sometimes in good faith but at other times maliciously, distort and pervert the facts of history, and the fruit of their union (for prejudice is ever wedded to ignorance) is injustice. The more involved the emotions become in the subject, the greater the liability to untruth and the consequent unfairness. We know from experience that the average historian is incapable of doing justice to a religion unless he knows it from the inside, (and it might be said from his own inside) ; but he can impartially state the concrete facts of a situation even if he does not understand them. It is for the expert in these matters to supply both the facts and their interpretation.

The foregoing is a mere outline of the advantages and of the responsibilities of history considered simply as a record of the past; but sacred history has a far wider and deeper significance. Here the whole principle of development is different. Instead of being a chronicle of events springing from the unstable, ever-changing, passionate longings and convictions of the human heart and mind, it is the record of the slow unfolding of divine purposes in the application of

the doctrines and the expounding of the principles contained
in one immutable deposit of faith committed to the Apostles
two thousand years ago. To the eye of the impartial outside observer the obvious facts of the Church are its duration, its wonderful organization, its extension throughout
the world, its power; its contributions to education in the
preservation of literature, the accumulation of liberties and
the foundation and support of schools, colleges and uni-
versities; its immense charities; its beautiful edifices; its
unfailing, consistent record of upholding lawful authority;
its firm stand against all the vagaries of the unbalanced
intellect that would undermine the sacred rights of the
individual and the foundations of society. Associated with
these and many other evidences of the Church's existence
and work have been alas, in all ages, the deplorable effects
of individual human weakness. This is the material from
which the unprejudiced non-Catholic historian makes up
his picture of the Church. Of its interior life—its doctrine,
its Sacraments, the foundations of its claims, its theology
and philosophy, its ideals, its motives, missions and great
purposes—he knows little or nothing; and yet it is by these
that its visible activities are to be interpreted.

Its history therefore is the record of a divine revelation
and dispensation to the human race, every essential part of
which is of the greatest moment and must be preserved and
promulgated. It is all of super-vital interest to mankind.
Does any Christian entertain a doubt of the relative importance of the words that came from the mouth of Homer
or those that fell from the lips of our Lord; of the writings
of Herodotus or those of St. Paul? The object of preserving the evidences of Catholic Christianity is the salvation
of the soul of man and transcends in importance the facts
of profane history by so much as redemption and immortality transcend the passing events of time.

The purpose of collating, guarding, and making known

the Christian heritage is therefore not simply or primarily to draw a lesson for the present from the past, but to preserve in its entirety the unfolding of God's mercies to mankind in order that the operations of the Divine Spirit may be witnessed at all times to all parts of the world, and all parts of the world witness thereto. In this large, spiritual sense the history of the early missions to this continent is of infinitely more value to the human race than the history of the growth and application of any mere social or political theories, because the God-given fruits of these we have and enjoy, whether or not we know their history (and who can say that he knows it accurately or more than partially?); whereas the missions were the fulfilling of the command to go teach all nations, and so constitute a part of that record whereby we have proof of one of the marks of the Church, its universality, and are made one with her servants and martyrs whose blood has ever been its seed.

I hope this idea is clear. Secular events are necessarily mere mutations as changeable as the ideas, convictions, emotions and whims of the mind and heart of man; fragmentary and largely unrelated. While, from the seething of this vast cauldron of human energies, results must ensue, they are composite, vague, imperfect, and different in different places and times according to the accidents of antecedents and environment. On the other hand, the activities of the Church throughout the ages are all intimately connected with and find their motive in the one, unchangeable revelation which was committed to it twenty centuries ago. Both together, therefore, constitute a single record. Portions of this are of course at times lost, but in the main and in so far as it relates to the mission of the Church it has been preserved.

This thought of the oneness of the history of the Church obliterates the importance of time as a factor in its duration, by identifying its life with the age of the deposit of faith

and the ever present deposit of faith at all times with its
life. The unfolding of the dispensation is felt through all
the ramifications of its growth, from its visible head to the
last soul that has been born into new life, and so gives value
not only to the larger aspects of the record but also even
to the parochial and individual contributions thereto.

Not that the account was intended to include, or could
include, all individual effort. That vast record is being kept
in the Book of Life, and its relations to the great commit-
ment will be made known at the last day—

> " Liber scriptus proferetur,
> In quo totum continetur
> Unde mundus judicetur; "

but it is practicable that so much of it shall be known in
each age and preserved for all ages as may be necessary to
distinguish the divine from the human and give effect to
our Lord's words. " By their fruits ye shall know them."
Even the small events of Catholic annals have their place
and value as a part of the great record; still more so those
which have helped to determine, and are determining, the
religious future of the nations of a vast continent.

We now see the importance of the work in which this
Society is engaged. It is a matter of profound regret to the
Board that it seems to be so little understood and receives
such inadequate support. We are living in times when every
day makes history on a large scale. The whole civilized
world is torn and bleeding; and we know that only a divine
voice can quiet the tumult and a divine hand heal the wounds.

We are witnessing the Vicar of Christ with the impar-
tiality his position demands praying for peace while his
spiritual children in all countries are either engaged in the
conflict or are girding themselves for war. It is plain that
both are taking an active part in the great events. Our own
beloved country is involved in the awful cataclysm. Her

sons are gathering to the colors by the hundreds of thousands, and we are reliably informed that with less than 20% of the population more than 30% of the volunteer organizations are Catholics. This is the living proof that true religion and patriotism go hand in hand. But it means, if the war continue for a year or two, that many Catholic hearts will mourn and the prospects of Catholic families will suffer for the loss of Catholic young men. I say this in no critical spirit. What we want in this country is a united citizenship, unrent by factions; and if the Catholic youth is setting an example of patriotism, we rejoice. But we want it to be known that they are making their sacrifice not for themselves alone but for the cause; for all. A record is being made. It will be the duty of this Society to see that it shall be preserved and made known.

In conclusion I wish to thank the Board for their faithful and valuable assistance in the management of the Society's affairs, and to ask every one to make a special effort to obtain new members. The Society must rely for its main support on its membership, and unless we replenish its ranks, and especially from among the youth of our people, we shall find in the course of a few years that the roll has dwindled to such an extent through natural causes as to preclude the possibility of continuing the work.

JAMES M. WILLCOX.

REPORT OF THE BOARD OF MANAGERS, AMERICAN CATHOLIC HISTORICAL SOCIETY, PHILADELPHIA, FOR 1917

The Board of Managers, in bringing to a close the work of the American Catholic Historical Society for the year 1917, feels confident that the term has been marked by achievements of permanent value that will add much to the Society's future welfare and efficiency.

A survey of the year's labors will show that plans, some of which were initiated in a previous year, have been carried to a high point of excellence, which has resulted in a systematizing of the various forces of the Society for performing the great work for which the Society was instituted, and for which it has continued to struggle.

THE RECORDS, under the editorial management of the Rev. Joseph J. Murphy, D. D., have admirably reflected the mission of the Society to assemble, to preserve and to publish the historical facts relating to this continent. An examination of the four numbers issued demonstrates the care and good judgment which have been exercised in the preparation of this quarterly publication of the Society.

The memoir of the Right Rev. John W. Shanahan, D. D., third Bishop of Harrisburg, by the Right Rev. Monsignor Maurice M. Hassett, D. D., V. G., published in the March number of THE RECORDS, was reprinted in pamphlet form for distribution in the Harrisburg diocese.

In keeping with the zeal he has ever displayed for his sacred office and in attestation of his patriotic solicitude for the welfare, spiritual and temporal, of the men who are preparing to fight the nation's battles abroad, the Rev. William J. Lallou, for two years President of this Society, is acting as chaplain to the soldiers at Camp Hancock, Augusta, Georgia. Father Lallou says: " It is real missionary work and its high character makes one forget the inconveniences involved in attending to it."

At this meeting, which brings to a close the first year of the presidency of Mr. James M. Willcox, the Board wishes to acknowledge the great debt it owes to Mr. Willcox for his work for the Society. He has given his services unremittingly and has accomplished results that must have a favorable influence upon all the future labors of the Society.

The Society has had the services of Miss Mary Z. Cruice as Librarian since June 1, 1917. Miss Cruice has devoted much of her time to the task of bringing order to the great mass of papers, magazines and books which have come into the possession of the Society during many years. While much has been accomplished in the six months, this special branch of work has only been entered upon. There are thousands of papers, periodicals and books that need attention. To make them of use they must be sorted, classified and labeled. Many of these papers are of considerable value and are worth preserving as original records for the use of future historians of our country. One example of the invaluable character of the Society's collection may be found in the D'Orlic-Rodrigue papers, some of which have been arranged for publication in THE RECORDS by Miss Jane Campbell.

Failure to do all that is possible to take care of this store of material would be an irremediable blunder. The Board is pleased to report that many members of the Society understand the importance of this work and have given prompt and generous response to the Library Committee's request for pecuniary support in the undertaking.

Members of the Society and others are invited to visit the headquarters at 715 Spruce Street to make themselves acquainted with the work in progress.

The following new members were received during the year:

The Rev. F. J. Purtell,
The Rev. Francis E. Tourscher, O.S.A.,
Mr. C. D. Terry,
Mr. William J. Brady,

Mr. John F. Gonlin,
Mr. Thomas Hughes Kelley,
Mr. James G. Hughes.

A list of members who died during 1917 follows:

His Eminence Cardinal Diomede Falconio,
Mr. Z. P. Bresseau (Life member),
Mr. J. Burleigh,
Mr. Michael Murphy (Life member),
Rt. Rev. Monsiegneur J. J. Koch, D. D.,
Rev. James A. Dalton,
Mr. Simon J. Martin (Life member),
Rt. Rev. James A. McFaul, D. D.,
Miss Eleanor C. Donnelly,
Most Rev. Archbishop Kennedy,

Rev. W. A. McDonald,
Rev. William P. Masterson,
Mrs. Joseph Lonergan,
General Edward Morrell,
Hon. Morris Dallett,
Mr. Hugh J. Fagin,
James Brady,
T. M. Daly,
Hon. J. P. McNichol,
John D. Crimmins.

Having completed the publication of the Index to the *American Catholic Historical Researches* from 1884 to 1912, which work has been given the most cordial reception by librarians throughout the country and by these who own sets of the *Researches,* the Board, at the suggestion of Dr. Flick, has taken up the matter of preparing an index to the *Records.*

At the March, 1917, meeting President Willcox appointed a publicity Committee to keep the public informed of the Society's purposes and activities. The Committee, consisting of Mr. E. J. Galbally, chairman, the Rev. F. P. Siegfried, the Rev. Wm. J. Lallou, Miss Jane Campbell and Dr. L. F. Flick, has issued a pamphlet which has been widely circulated and has furnished much information of the Sociey's work to the newspapers of the city.

On November 28 the Society held a smoker in its Hall and entertained many guests. There was at the same time a reception to the Rt. Rev. Bishop P. R. McDevitt, a former

President of the Society, who made an address upon the misinterpretation by Violet Oakley of certain historic events in her paintings in the Governor's reception room at the Capitol in Harrisburg. The reasons for the objections made by Catholics to the spirit of these paintings were clearly stated by Bishop McDevitt, whose address, it is hoped, the Board may be privileged to publish in the RECORDS, for its historical and literary value.

Miss Jane Campbell arranged an afternoon reception for the ladies of the Society and their friends which was well attended. Miss Campbell represented the Society at a meeting of the Pennsylvania Federation of Historical Societies at Harrisburg early in the year.

A statement of the financial operations of the Society for the year is appended hereto.

P. A. KINSLEY, *Secretary.*

REPORT OF LIBRARIAN

Your Librarian presents her annual report. During the year just closed 199 volumes and 107 pamphlets have been added to the shelves. All the pamphlets were donated, some of the volumes were presented, the rest were purchased, for the sum of $284.58. 796 volumes, mostly newspapers and magazines, have been bound, the price for binding being $681.40.

Shelves for periodicals, made of North Carolina pine and white pine, were erected in the third floor, west room, for $298. It is a very satisfactory piece of work, well done, and a much-needed addition to the library.

The work of collating the old newspapers, putting each volume in a temporary cardboard case, marking on the case the numbers missing, was completed. These had been placed on floors of the second story rooms. The periodicals and church calendars which had been in the attic, without arrangement, were collated and placed on the floor of the third story back room. The newspapers, of which there were 352 titles, were carried to the third floor and placed in alphabetical order, chronologically arranged under each title. They filled the shelves in the third floor, east room and one side of the double case in the third floor, west room. The periodicals, of which there were 835 titles, were then arranged in alphabetical order and by date under the title; the church calendars, of which there were calendars from 134 churches, were given the same arrangement. They have been placed on the remaining shelves in the third floor, west room—first the periodicals in one alphabet, followed by the church calendars in a separate alphabet. There are still a number of unused shelves which gives room for growth. In arranging the newspapers many duplicates were found. These were rolled together by title, and a slip was attached stating what numbers were in the roll. These were all put in the third floor back attic.

There have been serveral donations of the *American Catholic Historical Researches.* Mr. Engel presented 94 numbers; Dr. Flick has presented 15 numbers and two volumes; the Rev. Martin I. J. Griffin of St. Paul, thirty numbers; and the Very Rev. Dr. T. C. Middleton, O. S. A. two numbers. We purchased from Father Schroeder, St. Joseph's Priory, Somerset, O., 20 complete vols. and 25 odd numbers for $64. Mr. Engel also presented a complete set of the *Records of the Americon Catholic Historical Society* and Dr. Flick sent several numbers of the RECORDS.

The gifts of the year which seem to be of particular value are:

From Mr. Gregory B. Keen: a volume of manuscript letters from Archbishop Kenrick of Baltimore to Professor and Mrs. George Allen, also a life-size portrait of Professor Allen of the University of Pennsylvania.

From Miss Jane Campbell: papers and manuscript letters in regard to the Stack-O'Hara case, also a number of papers and documents relative to the Scull case.

From Dr. Flick, Dr. Walsh, Dr. McCarthy, Mr. Willcox, and Mr. Kinsley: a valuable incunabulum, " Origen against Celsus ", first book published by George Herolt, Rome, 1481.

From Father Tourscher of Villanova: "Diary of the Rt. Rev. Francis Patrick Kenrick."

The donations to the Binding Fund for the year have been $366.50: to the Special Library Fund, $775.

The hall of the Society has been loaned to various Catholic organizations, 47 times.

Your Librarian regrets more has not been accomplished in the year just ending, but trusts that in the coming year there will be twice as much work done.

Respectfully submitted,

MARY Z. CRUICE, *Librarian.*

STATEMENT OF RECEIPTS AND EXPENSES FOR THE YEAR ENDING NOVEMBER 30, 1917.

RECEIPTS.

Dues from Active Members	$1871.00		
Dues from Contributing Members .	12.00		
Dues from Life Members	100.00		
		$1983.00	
Subscriptions to RECORDS	$589.45		
Advertisements in RECORDS	194.32		
Sale of RECORDS	85.75		
Sale of *Researches*	8.00		
Sale of Index to *Researches*	240.15		
		$1117.67	
Subscriptions to Special Library Fund	$775.00		
Subscriptions to Binding Fund	366.50		
Subscriptions to Endowment Fund	10.00		
Donations, St. Vincent's Aid	100.00		
St. Francis County House	100.00		
Other donations	11.00		
For binding two copies of Index ..	1.80		
Subscription to Reception	199.50		
Memorial Care Fund	48.28		
Interest on bonds, Endowment Fund	190.00		
Interest on bond, Life Membership Fund	45.00		
Interest on deposit, General Fund .	28.51		
Interest on deposit, Life Membership Fund	8.74		
Interest on deposit, Endowment Fund	6.42		
Interest on deposit, Memorial Care Fund	17.61		
		$1608.36	$5009.03
Balance Dec. 1, 1916			1113.00
			$6122.03

EXPENSES.

Account of Committee on Hall:

Interest on mortgage	$154.00
Water rent	12.00
Coal	114.00

Gas	8.60	
Insurance on contents	60.00	
Ice	2.87	
Repairs	19.55	
Cleaning and house supplies	192.30	
Painting	35.00	
Building shelves on 3d floor, west	298.00	
		$896.32

Account of Committee on Publication:

Printing RECORDS	$855.62	
Printing Index to *Researches*	572.22	
Binding 3 cop. of Index	3.30	
Printing pamphlets	55.72	
Copying manuscript	10.00	
Expressage on RECORDS	5.67	
Commission on advertisements ..	5.55	
		$1508.08

Accounts of Committee on Library:

Books and magazines	$334.55	
Cards and supplies	14.89	
Binding newspapers & magazines	681.40	
		$1030.84

Account of Secretary:

Printing, postage & stationery ..	$218.64		
Addressing wrappers	9.30		
Notary fees	1.00		
Engrossing & framing resolutions to Bishop McDevitt	30.00		
Dues in Federation of Hist. Society	4.00		
Telephone service	47.50		
Reception expenses	115.55		
Salaries, Editor	150.00		
Librarian, 6 months ...	600.00		
Clerk	600.00		
Librarian's Assistants ..	635.00		
		$2410.99	$5846.23
Transfer to Life Membership Fund			108.74
Transfer to Endowment Fund			16.42
Transfer to Memorial Care Fund ..			65.89
			$6037.28

Balance in GENERAL FUND, Dec. 1, 1917	$84.75

SUMMARY OF RESOURCES.

ENDOWMENT FUND $4091.92
     Invested in bonds $3900.00
         Balance 191.92

LIFE MEMBERSHIP FUND $1408.74
     Invested in a bond $1000.00
         Balance 408.74

MEMORIAL CARE FUND (de la Roche Legacy) $571.18

SPECIAL LIBRARY FUND $344.50

BINDING FUND $99.10

INDEX TO CATHOLIC HISTORICAL RESEARCHES $7.93

GENERAL FUND $84.75

SOME PAINTINGS IN THE CAPITOL BUILDING, HARRISBURG, PA.

AN ADDRESS BEFORE THE AMERICAN CATHOLIC HISTORICAL
SOCIETY, PHILADELPHIA, 28 NOVEMBER, 1917

BY THE RIGHT REVEREND PHILIP R. McDEVITT, D.D.
BISHOP OF HARRISBURG

The Capitol building at Harrisburg, Pennsylvania, is
burdened with an unenviable notoriety, because of the
reputed scandals which were associated with the completion of the interior.   Be the truth of the charges of cor-
ruption what they may, the fact remains that the interior
of the structure is of exquisite beauty, not surpassed and
perhaps rarely matched in any public building in America.
The imposing dome, the superb stairway, the splendid
assembly halls, the richly and highly finished reception
rooms, the glorious paintings by one of America's greatest artists, Edwin A. Abbey, make the Capitol rather a
home of art than a hall of legislation.

While the sense of the beautiful is charmed with the
splendors of painting and architecture, the sense of historical truth is grossly offended by certain pictures in a
group entitled " The Founding of the 'State of Liberty
Spiritual', representing The Triumph of the Idea of
Liberty of Conscience in 'The Holy Experiment of
Pennsylvania'."

The paintings, eighteen in number, are placed in the
frieze of the Governor's reception room.   The artist is
Miss Violet Oakley, who recently completed another

series of pictures for the Senate Chamber of the Capitol.
The following are the titles given to the various scenes
by Miss Oakley herself in a pamphlet of which she is the
writer.

1. William Tyndale printing his Translation of the Bible
into English at Cologne.

2. Smuggling the first volumes of the New Testament into
England.

3. The burning of the books at Oxford in the attempt to
stop the "New Learning."

4. The execution of William Tyndale at Vilvorde.

5. The Answer to Tyndale's prayer.   Henry VIII granting
permission that the complete translation is "to be sold and
read of every person without danger of any ordinance hitherto
granted to the contrary."

6. Anne Askew before the Lord Chancellor.

7. Culmination of all Intolerance and Persecution in the
Civil War,—Development of the Puritan Idea.

8. George Fox on his Mount of Vision.

9. The lad William Penn—stirred by his own Vision of
Light, and consecrated to God's service.

10. Penn meets the Quaker Thought in the field-preaching
at Oxford.   He turns from the world to listen to its message.

11. Admiral Sir William Penn denouncing and turning his
Son from Home, because of his Sympathy with the despised
set of Quakers.

12. Penn's Arrest while preaching at meeting.

13. Penn examined by the Lieutenant of the Tower of London, condemned to imprisonment in Newgate.

14. Writing in Prison, "The Great Case of Liberty of Conscience."

15. Having been liberated, Penn seeks to free other Friends
imprisoned.

16. Penn's Vision.

17. The Charter of Pennsylvania receives the King's Sig-
nature, March 4th, 1681.

18. Penn's First Sight of the Shores of Pennsylvania.

My few remarks this evening will dwell upon three of these eighteen representations.

The first picture bears the title: "William Tyndale printing his Translation of the Bible into English at Cologne." The second is called: "Smuggling the First Volumes of the New Testament into England." The third is: "The burning of the Books at Oxford in the attempt to stop thereby the New Learning."

Since all three scenes refer to the activities of William Tyndale, a short sketch of his stormy career will afford a better understanding of the significance of what the artist has placed on canvas. William Tyndale, or, as he is sometimes called, William Hutchins, was born in Gloucestershire, in the west of England, towards the close of the 15th century. He was educated at Oxford and Cambridge, and became a member of the Franciscan Order. After his ordination, attracted by the doctrines of Luther, he left England and went to Germany. He met Luther and, possibly with his encouragement and assistance, began a translation of the New Testament into English. When the work was finished, it was printed secretly at Cologne, Germany. Then copies of the book were smuggled into England. Some of these copies were seized by the authorities and burned. These facts, as far as the Bible is concerned, are embodied in the three paintings just mentioned.

The facts themselves are undeniable. The offence against historical truth is not in the facts, but in the inferences or the conclusions which the mass of non-Catholics, after having seen the pictures, draw from the facts.

The common and almost invariable impression which non-Catholics visiting the Capitol bear away, is that at the close of the 15th and the beginning of the 16th century an intolerant and arrogant hierarchy, supported by tyrannical civil powers, deliberately kept the Bible from

the people, for fear that its sublime truths might dispel
ignorance and superstition, and thereby shatter ecclesiastical domination; that this same sacerdotal influence
visited condign punishment upon those who dared bring
the Sacred Book to the knowledge of the oppressed
masses; that William Tyndale from his love of the Revealed Word of God fled to Germany, where, unmolested,
he might print the New Testament; that when his work
was done, he smuggled the precious volumes into England, but alas! failed to keep them from falling into the
hands of his enemies, who forthwith committed the
priceless translation to the flames.

These stirring events, which owe their inception to
William Tyndale, mark, in the opinion of the artist, Miss
Oakley, the beginning of "The Founding of the 'State
of Liberty Spiritual'," for she says in her pamphlet: "The
Foundation of the State of Pennsylvania was laid deep
in the characters of the men who founded it and the
condition of thought of the times in which they lived,
suffered, endured, and finally triumphed."

I might take up in detail each picture. The inference
from the first picture, namely, that Tyndale was compelled to go to Germany in order to have his translation
of the New Testament printed, because the ecclesiastical
and civil authorities would not allow the Bible to be
printed in England, is wholly and totally unwarranted.
He went to Germany because the authorities in England
deemed it a duty to the public to prevent him printing
a Bible which in their estimation perverted and distorted
the true reading of the Holy Scriptures.

The inference from the second picture, namely, that
Tyndale was forced to smuggle the New Testament into
England, because the authorities feared that in its sacred
pages the people would learn the pure, simple and un-
diluted truth of God's word, is likewise wholly unwar-

ranted. The smuggling of the Tyndale translation of the Bible into England was necessary for the same reason that the printing of this false version of the Sacred Book in a foreign country was necessary.

The inference from the third picture, namely, that the Bible was burned because the Church hated the New Learning, which found its deepest inspiration in the New Testament, completes a trinity of false, illogical, unwarranted, and unhistorical conclusions. The books were burned for the same reasons that forced Tyndale to go to Germany for his printer and then to smuggle his translation of the New Testament into England.

The simple proofs that the inferences drawn by the unthinking and the ignorant from these pictures are false, are found, first, in the undeniable historical fact that the Bible in English existed in England long before Tyndale's time; secondly, in the attitude of the Church towards the Bible during the centuries before Tyndale published his version of the New Testament.

The proofs which show that the Bible in English existed in England before Tyndale's day may be found in Cardinal Gasquet's *Eve of the Reformation.* This eminent historian devotes a chapter of his invaluable book to the discussion of the Bible in English before the Reformation. Using as his authority the published works of Sir Thomas More, Chancellor of England, and the most distinguished layman of Europe in the sixteenth century, the Cardinal proves conclusively that the Bible was translated into the English tongue long before the days of Wycliffe and Tyndale, and that the deeply entrenched and long established charge, so commonly repeated at Luther centenary celebrations, about the Catholic Church, in the days of Luther and Tyndale, forbidding the laity to read the Sacred Scriptures, is a baseless accusation.

The authority of Sir Thomas More on this subject of
the Bible in Tyndale's time is singularly convincing and
trustworthy, because he took upon himself the specific
duty to refute the extravagant charges of Tyndale that
the Church forbade the circulation of the Bible among
the people.

The saintly Chancellor of England, by reason of his
position, piety and learning, surely deserves as much
respect as Tyndale or any other reformer. Says Cardinal
Gasquet:

It is very commonly believed that until the influence of
Cranmer had made itself felt, the ecclesiastical authorities
continued to maintain the traditionally hostile attitude of the
English Church towards the English Bible. In proof of this,
writers point to the condemnation of the translation issued by
Tyndale, and the wholesale destruction of all copies of this,
the first printed edition of the English New Testament.

It may not be without profit to point out that the existence
of any determination on the part of the Church to prevent the
circulation of vernacular Bibles in the fifteenth century has
been hitherto too hastily assumed.

Those who were living during that period may be fairly
considered the most fitting interpreters of the prohibition of
Archbishop Arundel, which has been so frequently adduced
as sufficient evidence of this supposed uncompromising hostility to what is now called "the open Bible."

The terms of the Archbishop's monition do not on examination bear the meaning usually put upon them ; and should
the language be considered by some obscure, there is absolute
evidence of the possession of vernacular Bibles by Catholics
of undoubted orthodoxy with, at the very least, the tacit
consent of the ecclesiastical authorities. . .

*   *   *   *   *   *   *   *

That a Catholic version, or some version viewed as Catholic and orthodox by those who lived in the sixteenth century,
really existed does not admit of any doubt at all on the dis-

tinct testimony of Sir Thomas More. It will be readily admitted that he was no ordinary witness.

*   *   *   *   *   *   *   *

Some quotations from Sir Thomas More's works will illustrate his belief better than any lengthy exposition. It is unnecessary, he says, to defend the law prohibiting any English version of the Bible, "for there is none such indeed. There is of truth a constitution which speaks of this matter, but nothing of such fashion. For you shall understand that the great arch-heretic, whereas the whole Bible was long before his days by virtuous and well learned men translated into the English tongue, and by good and godly people and with devotion and soberness well and reverently read, took upon himself to translate it anew. In this translation he purposely corrupted the holy text, maliciously planting in it such words, as might in the reader's ears serve to prove such heresies as he 'went about' to sow. These he not only set forth with his own translation of the Bible, but also with certain prologues and glosses he made upon it, and he so managed this matter, assigning probable and likely reasons suitable for lay and unlearned people, that he corrupted in his time many folk in this realm.

" After it was seen what harm the people took from the translation, prologues and glosses of Wycliffe and also of some others, who after him helped to set forth his sect for that cause, and also for as much as it is dangerous to translate the text of Scripture out of one tongue into another, as St. Jerome testifieth, since in translating it is hard to keep the same sentence whole (i. e. the exact meaning): it was, I say, for these causes, at a Council held at Oxford, ordered under great penalties that no one might henceforth translate (the Scripture) into English, or any other language, on his own authority, in a book, booklet, or tract, and that no one might read openly or secretly any such book, booklet or treatise newly made in the time of the said John Wycliffe, or since, or should be made any time after, till the same translation had been approved by the diocesan, or, if need should require, by a Provincial Council.

"This is the law that so many have so long spoken about, and so few have all this time sought to look whether they say the truth or not. For I hope you see in this law nothing unreasonable, since it neither forbids good translations to be read that were already made of old before Wycliffe's time, nor condemns his because it was new, but because it was 'naught.' Neither does it prohibit new translations to be made, but provides that if they are badly made, they shall not be read till they are thoroughly examined and corrected, unless, indeed, they are such translations as Wycliffe and Tyndale made, which the malicious mind of the translator has handled in such a way, that it were labor lost to try and correct them."[1]

Again says Cardinal Gasquet:

This absolute denial of any attitude of hostility on the part of the Church to the translated Bible is reiterated in many parts of Sir Thomas More's English works. When upon the condemnation of Tyndale's Testament, the author pointed to this fact as proof of the determination of the clergy to keep the Word of God from the people, More replied at considerable length. He showed how the ground of the condemnation had nothing whatever to do with any anxiety upon the part of ecclesiastics to keep the Scriptures from the lay people, but was entirely based upon the falsity of Tyndale's translation itself. "He pretends," says Sir Thomas More, "that the Church makes some (statutes) openly and directly against the Word of God, as in that statute whereby they have condemned the New Testament. Now, in truth, there is no such statute made. For, as for the New Testament, if he mean the Testament of Christ, it is not condemned nor forbidden. But there is forbidden a false English translation of the New Testament newly forged by Tyndale, altered and changed in matters of great weight in order maliciously to set forth against Christ's true doctrine, Tyndale's anti-Christian heresies. Therefore, that book is condemned, as it is well

[1] Gasquet, *The Eve of the Reformation*, pp. 208, 209, 210.

worthy to be, and the condemnation thereof is neither openly nor privily, directly, nor indirectly, against the 'Word of God.' " [1]

The direct testimony of Sir Thomas More, that the Bible in English existed in England before Tyndale's translation, and that the Church condemned neither the publication of the Bible nor the reading of the Bible, but only the printing and use of corrupted versions, is more than sufficient to shatter the historical value of those Capitol pictures. But they are deserving of condemnation not only because they distort the history of the Church in regard to the Bible, but also because they present a wholly false view of the character of William Tyndale, who, in the fervent imagination of Miss Oakley, was the harbinger of liberty and freedom. That Tyndale is undeserving of such high commendation may be learned from his writings and from his character, especially in contrast with that of Sir Thomas More, his uncompromising opponent.

In 1528, Tyndale published *The Obedience of a Christian Man*. The nature of this book is best unfolded by James Gairdner in *A History of the English Church in the Sixteenth Century from Henry VIII to Mary* (pp. 126, 127). Dr. Gairdner, who is not a Catholic, says that the book "was secretly introduced to the King's (Henry VIII) notice and gave him real satisfaction." On reading it, Henry VIII declared: "This book is for me and all kings to read." Dr. Gairdner continues:

Coming from Henry, the sentiment was not unnatural, for a more thorough-going treatise in favor of absolutism it would be difficult to find ; moreover, it contained abuse of the clergy to Henry's heart's content. It showed that obedience was right from children to parents, from servants to masters, from

---

[1] *Ibid.*, pp. 214–215.

subjects to kings. But a king was in this world without law ; he might do right or wrong as he pleased and was accountable only to God. Even an evil king was a great benefit to his realm. On the other hand, the Pope's authority was founded upon jugglery ; cardinals and bishops had no right to obedience, and men might lawfully break any oaths which they had made to them. Such were the main principles set forth in this treatise of Tyndale's. It removed positively the only restraint on despotism that men could see in that day. What wonder that the Church denounced as heretical a book so expressly composed in defense of " the right divine of Kings to govern wrong "?

After weighing these sentiments which sanction autocratic rule, one might see in his mind's eye Sir Thomas More and William Tyndale. Looking at both men after four centuries, we may ask who deserves a place in the temple of honor which a great Commonwealth has erected—Tyndale, whose political principles were eagerly accepted by the ruffianly tyrant, Henry VIII, because he saw in them the sanction for his tyranny and brutalities, or Sir Thomas More, who went bravely to the scaffold rather than do the bidding of a monster whose name is synonymous with sensuality, tyranny, and cruelty?

The statements and arguments of Sir Thomas More as to the character and the purpose of the legislation of the Church in regard to the Bible, are substantiated and strengthened by the simple fact that the Catholic Church, if she had wished to keep the Sacred Book from the people for fear of their gaining a knowledge of the mighty truths contained therein, could have done so in a more effective way than by passing restrictive laws against the popular reading of the Holy Scriptures. Practically the sole guardian for centuries of the Revealed Word of God, she could have easily destroyed, had she desired to do so, almost every trace of authentic copies of the Bible.   But as a matter of historic record, the Church guarded the precious treasures with a solicitous care which even Miss Oakley, in spite of her limited knowledge of true history, acknowledges, when she confesses that the Bible was "preserved through the centuries by the devout and patient hands of the monks, scribes, and illuminators."

Sufficient has already been said to show the unhistorical character of these paintings, but one more proof emphasizes the injustice which they perpetuate against the Church of the ages.   This proof, indirect it is true, is found in the fact that the history of the Bible in England in pre-Reformation days is substantially the same as the history of the Bible in Germany before the time of Luther.   The evidence is overwhelming that in Germany the Bible was printed in the vulgar tongue and widely circulated among the masses of the people.   The place which the Bible held in Germany in pre-Reformation times may be inferred from the illuminating testimony which one of Germany's great historians, Johannes Janssen, adduces in his classic work, *History of the German People*. This justly celebrated authority makes clear in the chapter, "Elementary Schools and Religious Education of the People" [1] that the Bible played a notable part in the religious life of the people of Germany. He says :

The number of translations both of single books of the Old and New Testaments, as well as of the complete Bible, was indeed very great.   We have evidence of twenty-two editions of the Psalms with German translations up to 1509, and of twenty-five German versions of the Gospels and Epistles up to 1518.   Between this period and the Reformation, at least

[1] *Op cit.*, chap. i, vol. i.

fourteen complete editions of the Bible were published in
High German, and five in the Low German dialect.

*   *   *   *   *   *   *   *

By the beginning of the sixteenth century a sort of German "Vulgate" had crystallized into shape.

Like the German catechisms and manuals of devotion generally, these Bibles were illustrated with numerous woodcuts, in order, as the publisher of the Cologne Bible expressed it, "that the people might be the more readily induced to a diligent study of Holy Writ." We have a mass of evidence to show that this was the prevailing motive in this extensive multiplication of copies of the Scriptures.

In the light of such truths it is high time for the disappearance from popular belief of the absurd calumnies that the German people hardly suspected the existence of the Bible until Martin Luther, by a happy accident, discovered a complete copy of the Scriptures in the University in which he was a student, and that the English people knew little of the Sacred Scriptures until Wycliffe and Tyndale braved death that the Sacred Book might become the possession of the masses of their countrymen.[1]

The perversion of the true history of the attitude of the Church towards the Bible is not, however, the only indictment against the pictorial creations of Miss Oakley.

[1] "It was in his [Luther's] twentieth year, he tells us, that he first saw a complete copy of the Scriptures in the university library at Erfurt. He had hitherto supposed they embraced only the lessons read in the public service, and was delighted to find much that was quite unfamiliar to him. His ignorance, it may be remarked, though not exceptional, was his own fault. The notion that Bible reading was frowned upon by the ecclesiastical authorities of that age is quite unfounded. To be sure, it was not considered part of a Christian's duty, as it is in many Protestant Churches, and few homes possessed a copy of the Scriptures; but they were read regularly in church, and the study of the Bible was no more prohibited to university students of that day than of this, and was probably as little practised then as now." *Martin Luther, The Man and His Work*, by Arthur Cushman McGiffert, p. 35.

They insinuate an invidious and unwarranted comparison which reflects unjustly on the times gone by. The inference which they convey is accepted by many who pass through the Governor's reception room and who believe with complacent satisfaction that the Tyndale scenes, if for the moment they are accepted as true and typical of a superstitious, ignorant and intolerant age, could not be re-enacted in our times, when the fruition of the "Holy Experiment" and of other struggles for liberty is seen in its choicest flowering in the great Republic of the New World.

The question might be asked whether or not this self-satisfied and self-sufficient assumption of superiority of the present over the past finds any foundation in fact. Let it be admitted that the times preceding the Great Reformation were narrow, intolerant and bent on the persecution of those who dared worship God according to the dictates of their conscience. On the other hand is it at all certain that modern times have improved immeasurably beyond the past, in the principles which underlie persecution of any kind?

The world of the present claims that mighty progress has been made in religious toleration since the days of Wycliffe, Tyndale, and other reputed heroes of the revolt against Catholic Christianity. Perhaps it may be conceded that men to-day are broad and tolerant in their attitude towards those who differ from them in matters of religious belief, and that persecution for adherence to a definite religious doctrine is no longer sanctioned by enlightened public opinion. But is the toleration of the present the result of a cordial and widespread recognition of the principle of toleration in all its bearings? Is it the fruit of a conviction that every man should be permitted to follow his individual religious belief without let or hindrance, or is it the inevitable consequence of want in men's souls of a strong religious sentiment, and of the absence of fixed and definite notions as to the truth of certain religious teachings and the falsity and destructiveness of others? The judgment may be expressed that, if the world to-day felt religious truth as deeply as did the world in the days of Tyndale, there would be reason to fear many a repetition of the persecutions which we now look back upon as conclusive evidence of a dark and superstitious age.

The justification for expressing this statement is that our much-vaunted policy of toleration is radically modified or is wholly abrogated whenever we find ourselves in conditions that affect us profoundly either as individuals or as a nation. We face such conditions to-day and we find that our cherished policy of absolute freedom of thought, word, and act totally breaks down. Before the United States entered into the world conflict, it was accepted beyond question that the freedom of the press and freedom of speech were priceless rights which a free people should maintain unimpaired. But roused to a high degree of patriotic fervor and enthusiasm, because of a great national danger, we put aside the high and supposedly irrevocable claims of free speech and a free press; we declare that " free speech does not mean freedom to say anything one pleases at any time one pleases; " [1] we adopt a policy which takes cognizance of the opinions, words and conduct of every citizen; we visit condign punishment upon those individuals who give evidence of disloyalty, and we demand of all citizens a cordial and sympathetic support of the government in the mighty task it has undertaken. No relaxation of this discipline is made in favor of those who claim that their hostile attitude to the war or their merely passive resist-

[1] *Outlook*, 19 Dec. 1917.

ance is based upon religious grounds. That this departure from the traditions of generations brings serious consequences is seen in the summary treatment which a
community accords to those individuals who have dared
express an opinion which is construed as wanting in
the truly American spirit. *The Public Ledger* of
Philadelphia says in this connection:" A high-minded
Quaker in Coatesville who 'is alleged to have doubted
the atrocities of the Germans ', but who declared, 'I am
not pro-German, but merely following my religious be-
liefs which I feel I am entitled to hold', was asked to
leave the town as soon as possible." [1] Again, the Rev.
Herbert Bigelow, about to address a meeting at Newport,
Kentucky, was seized by a band of masked men, taken
into the woods and beaten with a horse-whip. The
victim of this treatment is called by the *Detroit Free
Press* " An Ohio Socialist, pacifist spouter." "So far
as we have heard," says the same paper," the victim is
the only one complaining." [2]

These outrages, it need hardly be said, were not committed by the responsible civil authorities. Nevertheless
the government itself, in the effort to bring about a uni-
fication of public sentiment in regard to the war, has
deemed it wise at times to suppress newspapers or re-
strict their circulation, and at all times to exercise a
censorship over all printed matter. Editors, publishers,
and all other citizens understand clearly that they cannot
express opinions which in the judgment of the civil
authorities tend to lessen in the slightest measure the
patriotic sentiments of the masses and thereby weaken
the efficiency of the government in its great undertaking.

I need hardly say that I am not expressing any criti-

[1] *Public Ledger*, 14 Nov. 1917.
[2] Cf. *The New Republic*, 10 Nov. 1917.

cism of the wisdom, lawfulness, or necessity on the part
of the government in regulating the Press by taking
measures against those whose words or conduct tend to
weaken the successful carrying on of the present war.
Every government has a right and a duty to protect itself against elements that endanger its welfare. There
comes a time when individual opinion cannot hold against
the decision of the supreme civil authority. To grant
that any citizen may determine the extent of his loyalty
to the government, or to say that the government should
permit absolute and unqualified freedom of speech and
conduct, simply because the individual claims, on religious or on any other grounds, the inviolable right to
think and act as he pleases, would be to introduce into
the commonwealth anarchy pure and simple.

My purpose in dwelling upon the state of public
opinion to-day and the repressive measures of the government which in times of peace would be considered
acts of tyranny, is to show a parallel between the present
and the past, and to point out that the civil authorities
in every nation at war base their treatment of pacifists,
traitors, and seditious publications upon precisely the
same principles that the civil and ecclesiastical authorities of the sixteenth century used in dealing with Tyndale
and his distorted version of the New Testament.

The preservation of the peace of a nation is a prime
duty of the civil authorities. Whoever disturbs that
peace renders himself liable to the punishment of the law.
When Tyndale and others like him provoked disorder,
the civil and ecclesiastical law took action against them.
That such proceedings were justified is amply clear
from the history of the times. On this point, Dr.
Gairdner remarks:

For we must remember, when reading More's attacks on

Tyndale, that the arguments of biblical devotees encouraged a spirit of irreverence and profanity which not only shocked the devout Catholic world, but was really dangerous to society. Crucifixes and other images were spoken of as "idols"; their destruction even by private hands was a work of piety, and if men got hanged for such enterprise, they were martyrs. Lollardy prompted men to outrage the consecrated host itself.[1]

Moreover, in those days, according to Dr. Gairdner, "heresy was regarded as an evil weed which even humane men like Sir Thomas More considered it necessary to stamp out at all costs."[2]

Unhappily human nature is so constituted that few individuals are rarely consistent in judging deeds or policies when these are bound up with religious, racial, or political issues. If men were always consistent, they would see that if Tyndale, and others of his class, are heroes and martyrs, then syndicalists, anarchists, pacifists, and the anti-war advocates, of to-day, who claim that they are following the dictates of conscience, should be placed in the same category; and that if it is right for the government to-day to regulate and suppress publications of a certain character and to take action against individuals, for the reason that in the judgment of the police both the publications and the individuals are a menace to the commonwealth, surely it was hardly wrong for the civil authorities of the sixteenth century to treat in the same manner Tyndale and his translations of the Bible, when in their estimation author and translation threatened the peace and welfare of the nation. We justify the radical measures of the government to-day by saying that newspapers and individuals fall under the

[1] *A History of the English Church in the Sixteenth Century from Henry VIII to Mary*, p. 190.

[2] *Ibid*, p. 92.

law's displeasure when they fail to see the difference
between liberty and license, and to recognize that liberty
is a sacred and inviolable right which every properly constituted government respects and guards, but that license
is an abuse of liberty which every efficient government
punishes with fine, imprisonment, or death.

Since this is our defence of the severity of the government which is now accepted as a matter of wise public
policy, why should we be unwilling to admit that the
ecclesiastical and civil rulers of past ages had precisely
the same view of liberty and license, and that when they
burned spurious translations of the Holy Scriptures or
punished the translators in question, their intention was
to check license and not to suppress liberty, to maintain
peace in the country and not to destroy the Bible or to
keep its saving truths from the people?

If, however, we refuse to admit that the authorities of
of the sixteenth century were moved by right principles
in burning Tyndale's translation of the Bible and in
punishing the translator, at least we should hesitate to
condemn them in unmeasured language, for the simple
reason that too often the boasted toleration of our generation, and indeed of every generation during the past
four hundred years, is honored in the breach rather than
the observance.

Perhaps the admission is made unwillingly and regret-
fully, yet it can hardly be denied, that the action of the
government in its repressive legislation and especially
the conduct of private citizens towards all those who are
known or are thought to be lacking in true patriotism,
shatter completely the theory, eloquently defended in
normal times, that all men should have unrestricted liberty to think, speak or act as they please.

So thoroughly has public opinion and public policy
departed from its former ideals in this question of liberty

that it is quite possible, when the story of these stirring times is told by the dispassionate historian in the generations to come, that a condemnation hardly less severe than that which these Capitol pictures attempt to pronounce upon the fifteenth and sixteenth centuries for intolerance, may be uttered against the nations now engaged in a struggle for national existence, because of their regulation or suppression or punishment of the slightest evidence of want of patriotism and loyalty.

These pictures, both for their perversion of history and their violation of the right of a great religious denomination to fair treatment in any public building, should be placed side by side with another flagrant distortion of truth, a monument which insults the State of Pennsylvania, established by Penn, and the city of Philadelphia, founded by him. I refer to the statue of the Puritan on City Hall Square, Philadelphia. This gigantic figure might be looked for down in Massachusetts, the land of the Puritan. But the last place in the broad world where one should expect to find it would be in Philadelphia. None the less, there stands this bronze embodiment of the Puritan spirit in the very heart of Penn's city, under the shadow of Penn's statue, in the home of the Quaker, whom the Puritan hunted with a ferocity that was not surpassed in the sixteenth-century persecutions.

In conclusion, I should say that, before these pictures were hung in the Capitol, Mr. Walter George Smith, as President of the Federated Catholic Societies of Pennsylvania, and Mr. James A. Flaherty, the head of the Knights of Columbus, lodged a strong and dignified protest against the acceptance by the State of the objectionable paintings for the Capitol: "Taken as a whole, they violate the truth of history and, even if they were true, they are in themselves improper subjects for decoration of a public building". Alas! the protest was in vain. Hence to-day the State of Pennsylvania, by its official sanction, as the late Rev. H. G. Ganns, who wrote an illuminating pamphlet upon the Capitol paintings, said, " places counterfeit historical data in circulation and in this case all the more dangerous and pernicious since civil authority in a way constitutes itself an official clearing house."

BISHOP FLAGET'S DIARY

BY REV. W. J. HOWLETT

It was in the year 1811 that Bishop Flaget took possession of his See of Bardstown in Kentucky, with jurisdiction
over Tennessee, Ohio, Michigan, Indiana, Illinois and the
balance of the great Northwest. It was a wild diocese, with
only a few parts settled, and the principal portions of his
civilized flock gathered in settlements in the country at no
great distance from Bardstown. Yet, these portions were
not so closely drawn together that he could build a church
and take up his residence in his episcopal village until eight
years later.

During this time Bishop Flaget lived literally in the forests, and often, like his few priests, as a lone missionary
attending to the wants of the settlers. His first year was
spent in a rough log cabin at St. Stephen's—now the Mother
House of the Sisters of Loretto—the nearest village being
Bardstown, about fifteen miles distant by bridle-path
through the woods. Most of this time he had no priest with
him, and only met one when he went to his seminary at St.
Thomas', twelve miles away, to the Dominicans of St
Rose's, ten miles, or as he was visited by one of his missionaries.

For many years he kept a diary, or daily record of his
work, his travels, weather conditions, etc. It was a con-
cise history of his life at that time, and was made use of by
Bishop Spalding when writing his *Life of Bishop Flaget* in
1852. Only one year (1812) of this diary is now known
to exist, and that lies before me now. It is leather-bound,
3½x6, and the cover is well-worn, as if carried much in

the pocket. It contains fifty-two leaves of strong paper, unruled, and to each day about one inch of space is allowed. The entries are in French, in bold, fairly formed letters, and the black ink shows but little signs of fading. The record is complete and continuous up to November 16th, when he was in Baltimore, and then begins a narrative account of his journey to that city in the company of Father Badin. Some desultory notes and heads of sermons make up the rest of the book. A feature of the book is, that at the end of each day's entry he adds a number of detached letters, the significance of which is not clear, but they might easily stand for the initials of words of prayer or pious ejaculations. Often we find the combination S. A. P. D. M., which might mean, *Seigneur, ayez pitié de moi*, (Lord have mercy on me), and D. S. L., *Dieu soit loué*, (God be praised), both of which would accord well with the text.

The only English page in it is a document written later— a Bill of Sale for a slave. It reads as follows:

"BILL OF SALE.

"Know all men by these presents, that I, B. J. Flaget, of Nelson County and State of Kentucky, have, for and in consideration of the value of four hundred dollars in hand paid, the rct. of which I do hereby acknowledge, have bargained and sold, and do by these presents bargain, sell and deliver unto N. R., of the Cty. and State aforesaid, One Negroe Girl named Henney, about 16 or 17 years. Whom said Negroe I will forever warrant and defend unto the said N. R., his heirs, and from me, my heirs, and from the claim or claims of any person or persons whatsoever.

"Given under my hand and seal this twenty first day of April, 1815.

"B. J. FLAGET.   (*Seal.*)"

Negro slavery was a national institution then, and existed long afterwards in New England, the Middle States, and every state of the Middle West. In Kentucky, as in all the South, it was looked upon as a necessary condition, and ministers of every denomination were slave-holders. Of the Catholic laity, however, and for stronger reasons, of the priests and institutions, it must be said that they treated their slaves in a kindly manner, and instructed them in religion and kept them up to its practices. When forced to sell them, it was to such as would give them like care. An old Sister of Loretto, now living, knew the same negro girl Henney when she was an old woman and belonged to the Wathen family, and a more pious old soul did not belong to the congregation of Calvary, in Marion county, Ky. Many of the Catholic churches and institutions of Kentucky in the early days had lands given to them for their support, and slaves were used for field work and the rougher work of the household.

The Diary opens at St. Michael's Church at Fairfield, Ky:

JANUARY, 1812.

Wednesday, January 1, 1812.—I published to-day at the high mass my opinion on the subject of Mr. B—n and the lands. Weather cold and cloudy. S. R. P. M.

Thursday, Jan. 2.—One single person agrees with my opinion. Pride restrains the others. Confessions until 2 o'clock P. M. Started at 3 to go to Mr. Gwynn's. Weather fine, cold. S. R. P. M.

Friday, Jan. 3.—Dinner at the seminary, supper at St. Stephen's—14 miles. Weather gloomy and very cold. P. D. R. J. M. J.

Saturday, Jan. 4.—Three confessions. 27 miles to go to Clear Creek with Mr. N—x. Weather very fine but cold. R. P. F. C.

Sunday, Eve of Epiphany, Jan. 5.—Confessions all day. Mass at one o'clock P. M. Sermon. Weather cloudy and moderate. C. C. D. A. P. D. M. S.

Monday, Jan. 6.—Confessions, mass, sermon till 1½ P. M. Slept at Mr. Dant's—19 miles. Weather fine and mild. R. G. S. R. A. D.

Tuesday, Jan. 7.—Long conversation with Mr. Dant on the subject of the convent for girls. Return to St. Stephen's —9 miles. Notes taken with Mr. Badin upon the principal events since my arrival. Fine weather. R. J. M. J.

Wednesday, Jan. 8.—Letters to the Bishops of Boston, Phil'a, Neale, The Abp. of Quebec. Letters of Vicar General. Fine weather in the forenoon, wind towards evening. S. R. B. T.

Thursday, Jan. 9.—Difficulties concerning my jurisdiction to examine. Important visits. Trip to seminary—10 miles. Fine weather. R. D.

Friday, Jan. 10.—Meeting of the directors of my Cathedral, which was missed. Visit to a professed infidel, who has lost his mind, and in his ravings sometimes calls for a priest. Distance 14 miles. Weather fine. D. V.

Saturday, Jan. 11.—Conversation with Mr. David about the seminary, the convent and cases of conscience. Go to St. Stephen's,—10 miles. Weather cloudy. R. A. S.

Sunday, Jan. 12.—Confessions till one o'clock, mass, Father Flynn preached. Trip to Dant's,—12 miles. Snow, very cold. R. F. L. S.

Monday, Jan. 13.—Confessions till one o'clock P. M. No mass for lack of a chalice. Weather fine and mild. R. D. D. S. A. P. D. M.

Tuesday, Jan. 14.—Confessions, mass, till 11 o'clock A. M. Went to Bardstown to baptize the son of Mr. Saunders; his name is B. J. Flaget. From Bardstown to the seminary; in all 15 miles. Weather superb, and wind S-W. R. F. D. G.

Wednesday, Jan. 15.—Letters to Messrs. Olivier, Savine, Marie J. Erection of a dormitory for the seminarians. Snow. Started at 9 P. M. to see Mrs. Merryman. Weather very cold.

Thursday, Jan. 16.—Returned at 9 o'clock A. M.—14 miles. Started at one o'clock for St. Stephen's,—10 miles. Weather fine but cold. F & R. D. G.

Friday, Jan. 17.—Confessions and mass till one o'clock. Snow all day. Feel sad; incapable of application. D. E. S. A. P. D. M.

Saturday, Jan. 18.—Confessions and mass till one o'clock P. M. Rain most all day. Preparations for the instruction of tomorrow. S. R. D. S. L.

Sunday, Jan. 19.—Very violent thunderstorm last night about 9 o'clock. Today confessions, mass preaching till two o'clock P. M. After that, to McAtee's,—7 miles. Weather fine in the morning, cloudy in the evening. G. G. A. R. A. D.

Monday, Jan. 20.—Confessions, instruction, marriage, visits to sick all day. Slept at Mr. Hagan's,—2 miles. Wind N-W. Extremely cold. P. E. R. D. S. L.

Tuesday, Jan. 21.—Administered Mesdames Hagan and O'Bryan. Returned to Mr. McAtee's,—5 miles. Went to administer the daughter of Mr. Bowling,—12 miles. Weather very cold and clear. F. S. D. S. L.

Wednesday, Jan. 22.—Ministry till 1 o'clock P. M. Left for St. Stephen's,—5 miles. Weather fine and milder. R. M. M. M.

Thursday, Jan. 23.—Another earthquake at quarter to nine. Duration 4 or 5 seconds. Study all day, or write letters. Rain, snow, sleet. P. R. D. G.

Friday, Jan. 24.—A few confessions, letters, study. Rainy weather, thawing, moderating. T. R. S. J. M. J.

Saturday, Jan. 25.—Study, wind south, weather rainy. Arrival of Mr. Badin from Lexington. Interesting conversation with Mr. N—x. T. M. M. D.

Sunday, Jan. 26.—Confessions, preaching till noon. Dinner at St. Stephen's. Thawing. Heaviness of body and spirit. L. S. M. M. D.

Monday, Jan. 27.—Agricultural Society with Mr. B.

Many callers. Letters. Weather fine and mild. D. M. M. D.

Tuesday, Jan. 28.—Received several visitors, among them Mr. Hill. Letters for Baltimore and France. Weather like spring. R. S. L. S. J.

Wednesday, Jan. 29.—Rain this morning. To the seminary,—10 miles, and to Mr. Seams, sick, —11 miles. Weather mild and fine. R. D. G.

Thursday, Jan. 30.—Visit two sick persons., — fine weather. Return to St. Stephen's,—10 miles. D. E. S. A. P. D. M.

Friday, Jan. 31.—Confessions and mass till half-past two P. M. Weather very mild but cloudy. R. F. D. S. L.

This diary for the month presents a great deal of sameness—confessions, mass, sermons, sick-calls and weather conditions. It shows his life to be that of a missionary, and it speaks well for the faith of the people, who crowd around his confessional, listen to his instructions, and hear his daily mass said at any convenient hour between ten and two o'clock. Sundays are not special days, but incidents only in his ordinary work. On sick-calls he was prompt, and they were not few, nor all in the vicinity of his home. In the absence of other priests he even went as far as Bardstown on sick-calls, and thus spared Father David to his work of the seminary. His mode of travel was on horseback, and it is doubtful if any of his priests owned a gig. It is certain that such a conveyance would have been of but very little use to any of them, for most of the roads were merely paths through the forests, where no wheeled vehicle could pass. Time has changed many things since then, but not all, for there are parts yet in this oldest diocese of the West where the people are as primitive as in the early days, good roads as rare, and where the priest has more than one county in his mission, which he travels over on horseback with his mass vestments in his saddlebags.

In this vicinity there were a number of small churches, where only a few years before mass was said in private houses. The first of these was Holy Cross, four miles from St. Stephen's, on Pottinger's Creek. The first Catholic chapel in Kentucky was built there in 1792, on the land of Basil Hayden by Rev. Wm. de Rohan, then the only priest in Kentucky. Henry Norris hewed the logs of which it was made, and no doubt all the Catholics of the settlement helped to put them in place. The deed to the church and two acres of land was made May 1, 1798, by Basil Hayden to Wm. Bald, Bernard Cissell, Charles Payne and Wm. Brewer, and their heirs, for the use of the Roman Catholic Church forever. This was the first Board of Trustees of any Catholic church in Kentucky, and Bishop Flaget was not without some trouble from their meddling in matters of his right.

Another chapel was St. Joseph's, near Bardstown. Mass had been said at the house of Thomas Gwynn when there was no chapel, but Dr. George Hart, a pioneer Catholic of Harrodsburg, in 1774, and later of Bardstown, gave 2¾ acres of ground for a church and cemetery,—it is used still for a cemetery by the Catholics of Bardstown. On this land a church was built in 1799 by Father Salmon. Wm. Coomes, who came to Harrodsburg with Dr. Hart, and also to the vicinity of Bardstown, offered a tract of land three miles northeast of Bardstown for a church, but upon the condition that he and his descendants to the fourth generation would be freed from the obligation of contributing anything for church purposes. Father Salmon advised Bishop Carroll not to accept the offer, for said he; " he has ten children, & they may be increased to a hundred families in forty years." The wife of Wm. Coomes opened at Harrodsburg the first school in Kentucky. The Rev. Charles I. Coomes was their grandson. St. Michael's Church was built by Father Nerinckx on Cox's Creek, where mass was said at the house of Clement Gardiner, who gave the ground for the church. St. Ann's, on Cartwright's Creek, was built by Father Badin, after he had said mass for some years at the house of Thomas Hill. This was assigned to the Dominican Fathers at a later date, and is now the parish of St. Rose. On Hardin's Creek mass was said at the home of Henry Hagan, but Father Salmon built St. Charles' Church in 1799, and on the Rolling Fork mass was said at the house of Robert Abell until Father Fournier opened a small oratory, and Father Nerinckx built Holy Mary's in 1806. As a charge these places were not attended by Bishop Flaget, for Father Chabrat was at St. Michael's, Father David was at St. Thomas', near Bardstown, Father Flynn was at Holy Cross, Father Nerinckx had St. Charles' and Holy Mary's, although most of his time was spent on missions in the western part of the State, and Father Badin was still nominal pastor here, but at present building churches at Louisville and Lexington. These visited their churches as they could, and Bishop Flaget made occasional visits to them, going this year as far as St. Clare's in Hardin County, about thirty miles distant.

One circumstance worried Bishop Flaget at this time, and for long afterwards, and this was the question of the church lands in Kentucky. His first entry in the diary of this year indicates it. Before the appointment of Bishop Flaget several tracts of land had been secured to the Church by gift or purchase, and the titles to some of them were in the name of Father Badin. Some of these properties were encumbered with conditions that Father Badin felt himself bound to fulfil personally, and some with debts occasioned by their purchase or by improvements upon them. For these Father Badin felt a personal liability, and he had a deeper interest where he had advanced money of his own in securing and improving these properties. Left to his management he saw these properties gradually emerging from these obligations, and freeing him from personal liability.

Bishop Flaget asked that all these lands be transferred to himself as the responsible head of the diocese. Upon the terms of transfer they could not agree. At first the Bishop wanted no terms; his office as bishop he thought a sufficient guaranty that justice would be done, but Father Badin would not be satisfied without special stipulations assuring the carrying out of all conditions. Also he believed that until certain conditions were fulfilled he could not legally make the transfer. There was some truth in this contention, and legal opinions supported him in the position. For many years this question was the cause of a more or less marked estrangement between the Bishop and Father Badin. Mutual friends tried to bring them together, but failed; the case was taken to Baltimore and laid before Archbishop Carroll, but without settlement; the Bishop threatened excommunication, but was afraid to put it into execution lest Father Badin's friends would cause a schism. The matter was taken to Rome by the Bishop in 1816, and probably settled, for the property was turned over to the Bishop, and Father Badin was not held for any liabilities or conditions.

No real break came between them, but Father Badin resigned his mission of Louisville and retired temporarily to St. Stephen's. It is not even known if this was the cause of his resignation, but his retirement came at this time, and two years later he went to Europe, where he remained eight years. Yet during his absence he did what he could for the Diocese of Bardstown and for Bishop Flaget, and his letters, while showing his grievance, express great regard for the Bishop. Upon his return he accepted no charge in the Diocese of Bardstown, but came and went with the good will of all. For some years he labored among the

Indians on the shores of Lake Michigan, under the jurisdiction of the Bishops of Ohio and Indiana. There he secured a tract of land which, upon conditions readily accepted, he donated to the Bishop of Vincennes, and later designated to the Fathers of the Holy Cross. Their magnificent University of Notre Dame is on Father Badin's gift, and his bones lie there under a chapel specially erected to his memory. He died in Cincinnati in 1853, and was buried under the Cathedral there, but a few years ago his remains were removed to Notre Dame.

Already we see the Bishop solicitous for a Cathedral church and holding meetings of committees for it, but he was not destined to see it up and in service for some years. Its dedication took place on August 8, 1819.

FEBRUARY, 1812.

Saturday, Feb. 1, 1812.—Confessions till 2½ P. M. After dinner confession of Mrs. Beams, Protestant. Weather superb. Letter from Baltimore. D. R. J. M. J.

Sunday, Feb. 2.—Confessions, preaching, mass, till 1 o'clock P. M. Went to the seminary. The students were in retreat. Weather dark and rainy. 10 miles. R. F. C. D. G.

Monday, Feb. 3.—Renovation of the Baptismal and Clerical Promises. Little exhortation before the ceremony. Conversation about these good children; they have made a good retreat; appear fervent; it is a great satisfaction. Weather rainy, but fine later. R. D.

Tuesday, Feb. 4.—At the seminary till two o'clock P. M. Visited a sick lady,—20 miles. In danger of losing eyes and life. Weather dreary. V. D. *par.*

Wednesday, Feb. 5.—Weather very cold but clear. Went 16 miles to seminary. Spoke to a young Protestant man who wants to become a Catholic. R. D. S. L.

Thursday, Feb. 6.—Went to Bardstown. Disagreeable

discussion about the Cathedral and useless. Discouraged.
Slept at Mr. Gwynn's,—5 miles. Weather fine and mild.
D. D. S. P. P. M.

Friday, Feb. 7.—Another earthquake at 3½ A. M.
Duration five minutes according to Mr. B———n. Heavy
snow. Went 15 miles. S. R. D. S. L.

Saturday, Feb. 8.—Another earthquake yesterday about
10 o'clock P. M. Confessions, mass, till 2½ P. M. Fine
weather. Ten miles to visit some sick persons. R. S. S.
S. A. J.

Sunday, Feb. 9.—Officiated at St. Charles'. Confessions, mass, preaching till 2½ P. M. Monday, Wednesday and Saturday, days of abstinence,—20 miles; weather
mild and very fine. U. P. D. D. P. P. F.

Monday, Feb. 10.—Officiated at St. Charles' from 7
o'clock A. M. till 6 o'clock P. M. Weather very fine, and
very mild towards evening. Relation of the effects of the
earthquake. Went to the Little Meadows,—9 miles. A.
R. D. S. B.

Tuesday, Feb. 11.—From Mr. Elder's to Holy Mary,
5 miles. Confessions till 7 o'clock P. M. Snow, towards
evening fine. D. B. S. A. P. D. M.

Ash-Wednesday, Feb. 12.—Confessions, mass, instructions till 3 o'clock P. M. From Holy Mary to Mr. Lucas',
—10 miles. Weather very mild. R. S. D. S. L.

Thursday, Feb. 13.—Services, dinner, till three o'clock
P. M. From Mr. Lucas' to St. Stephen's,—12 miles.
Weather rainy and night very dark. T. F. F.

Friday, Feb. 14.—Confessions, mass, till 3 P. M.
Weather cloudy in the morning and fine in the evening.
Very interesting conversation with Mr. Nerinckx about
his missions. R. D. P. F.

Saturday, Feb. 15.—Confessions, mass till 3 o'clock P. M.
Spoke to Mr. Moore about Mr. Maxwell, jr., Charles Dr.
&c. Weather very fine, but cold. R. T.

Sunday, Feb. 16.—Received a letter from Father Urbain ——— Dubois, Despada, Bruté. Went to the seminary, 10 miles. Weather mild, overcast. R. D. P. F.

Monday, Feb. 17.—Answered Father Urbain, wrote to Mr. Demun, to Mr. Olivier; gave a letter of exchange to Mr. Wickliffe. 6 miles. Weather very fine. P. D. R. M. D.

Tuesday, Feb. 18.—Conversation about the Synod. Left for St. Stephen's, 10 miles. Weather clear and cold. Conversation with Mr. Nerinckx upon the same subject. R. S. D. S. L.

Wednesday, Feb. 19.—This morning very cold and gloomy, finer after dinner. Afternoon employed in preparing my palace for the Synod. R. S. E. D. C. aD.

Thursday, Feb. 20.—Conference composed of 8 ecclesiastics and the Bishop. Several points decided after a discourse upon the subjects, the mass of the Holy Ghost and the *Veni Creator*. Grand weather. P. G. F. D. S. L.

Friday, Feb. 21.—Confessions all the morning. Sharp worry over Mr. Nerinckx who wants to leave me. Unfortunate conversation with Mr. B—n. Superb weather, P. M. T. R. P. F. M. M. D.

Saturday, Feb. 22.—Confessions till 2 o'clock P. M. Two young Protestant women went to confession. Weather cloudy and rainy. R. P. I. M. M. D.

Sunday, Feb. 23.—Confessions, sermon, mass, till 11 A. M. Weather mild and rainy, towards evening violent wind from the west. M. R. F. P. T. D. S. L.

Monday, Feb. 24.—All the forenoon to myself for prayer, study, writing. After dinner started to Mr. Hayden's, but turned back because my horse went lame. Weather cloudy and cold. R. P. D. S. L.

Tuesday, Feb. 25.—In retreat. Fine weather. F. C. R. J. M. J.

Wednesday, Feb. 26.—Ditto. Weather good. R. S. J. M. J. D. G.

Thursday, Feb. 27.—Ditto.

Friday, Feb. 28.—Retreat. Weather superb; wind .S-W. Conversation on the church property unsatisfactory. T. M. S. D. S. L.

Saturday, Feb. 29.—Weather very fine, warm wind from the south. 12 miles. Confessions six hours running. M. P. P. F.

A great portion of these daily entries have little interest now beyond the fact that they are the jottings of Bishop Flaget. They note his ordinary work, which alone was heavy, his visits to his seminary of St. Thomas, his consolations there as an offset to his occasional worries about the church property, his cathedral, etc. We find him this month (Feb. 20) holding his little quasi-synod, the first in the West, with eight priests, who, probably, were Fathers David, Badin, Nerinckx, Flynn, Chabrat of the diocesan clergy, and the Dominicans of St. Rose'. A touch of humor is seen in his note of the preparation of his "palace" for the occasion,—a palace sixteen feet square, of rough logs hastily cut to provide him a shelter upon his arrival in Kentucky.

At this conference missionary districts were defined and missionaries assigned to them, as Bishop Spalding tells us, and the western district, extending from Washington county to Union county, was assigned to Father Nerinckx. It is no wonder that Bishop Flaget experienced some sharp worries when this missionary told him of his desire to leave Kentucky and go farther west. This, however, he did not do until twelve years later. In the meantime he yielded to the solicitations of Bishop Flaget and attended to his large territory, founded the Sisters of Loretto, and made two very successful trips to Europe in the interests of Bishop Flaget and the Diocese of Bardstown. While attending to others Bishop Flaget, also, does not neglect himself, but makes his own private retreat at his little palace.

MARCH, 1812.

Sunday, March 1.—From six in the morning till eight in the evening constantly employed in the holy ministry, except one hour for dinner. Weather cold but superb. P. F. R. D. G.

Monday, March 2.—Confessions, mass sermon, till a quarter to two P. M. After dinner visited a sick man, ten miles. Weather cold but very fine. R. P. D. S. L.

Tuesday, March 3.—Weather very fine but very sharp. Made 16 miles. R. P. J. M. J.

Wednesday, March 4.—Went to the seminary, where I spent the night. Twelve miles. Conversation about the cathedral, plans, etc. D. D. M. M. D.

Thursday, March 5.—Went to Bardstown with Mr. B—n. Received a letter * from Mr. Bruté. Sad session upon the subject of my cathedral. It is necessary to suffer. *Fiat, fiat!* Weather cloudy. R. P. F. A. C.

Friday, March 6.—Extremely painful conversation with Mr. B——n. It requires all charity possible to believe him in good faith in his proceedings. From Mr. Gwynn's to the seminary; from the seminary to St. Stephen's,—18 miles. Weather very fine. Trouble of spirit. R. C. B. O. M. Sr.

Saturday, March 7.—Confessions part of the day. P. P. ch. R. P. F. P.

Sunday, March 8.—Confessions, instructions, mass, till 6 P. M. Fourteen miles. Weather very mild, wind south —in the evening N-W and cold. R. P. E. A. O. M. S.

Monday, March 9.—Wrote a letter to Mde Fournier. Thoughts on the property of the church. Weather superb. R. P. D. S. L.

Tuesday, March 10. — Weather dark and gloomy, yet mild. Went to the seminary,—10 miles. Great consolation in this house. P. R. P. P. O. M. D.

* (Destruction of S. S.)

Wednesday, March 11. — Visit to a sick woman, — 12 miles. Spent the night at Mr. Dant's. Weather mild and rainy. Conversation upon the convent for girls. R. S. M. Bn. M. R. A. L. P.

Thursday, March 12.—From Mr. Dant's to Bardstown, —12 miles. Spoke to a contractor,—little show for a cathedral. Received a (letter) from the church wardens of Vincennes, and from Gov. Harrison $250. Weather very mild. Slept at the seminary,—3 miles. R. P. F. D. S. L.

Friday, March 13.—From the seminary to St. Stephen's, —10 miles. Confessions till 2 o'clock P. M. Conversation with Mr. Nerinckx about his missions. Weather very fine. A. G. V. R. P. T. D. S. L.

Saturday, March 14.—Confessions till one o'clock P. M. Then, after dinner, visits to sick, 9 miles. Confessions at Mr. McAtee's. Returned home, 9 miles; storm, weather rainy and dark. Special protection of M. B. R. S. L. A. D. S. A. P. D. M.

Sunday, March 15.—Confessions, mass, sermons, till 2 o'clock P. M. Visit 2 sick,—6 miles. Weather mild, rainy. O. H. R. P. F. S. A. P. D. M.

Monday, March 16.—Violent storm during the night. Sick call, 8 miles. Went to the seminary. Weather overcast and mild. Always a fresh pleasure to come to this house. R. P. D. S. L.

Tuesday, March 17.—Cloudy and cold. Interesting conversation with Mr. David. Answers to Gov. Harrison and the Churchwardens. R. P. D. G.

Wednesday, March 18.—Fine weather. Traveled 10 miles. Retreat at St. Stephen's. D. AND R. P. F. M. M. D.

Thursday, March 19.—St. Joseph, my patron, pray for all the friends who have thought of me! Fine weather. Retreat all day. Confession of a sick person. R. S. D. D. S. D. M. M. D.

Friday, March 20.—Confessions a part of the day. Visit to a sick woman,—5 miles. Confessions till 8 P. M. Fine weather. R. P. T. D. G. P. M. S.

Saturday, March 21.—Return from sick call,—5 miles. Confessions till noon. Conversation with Mr. Blair, Protestant. Fine in the morning, rainy afternoon. R. P. T. P. D.

Sunday, March 22.—Confessions, instructions, mass, at St. Stephen's a good part of the day. Weather cold, snow. Study. Indifferent conversation with Mr. B——n. R. D. B. P. D. S. L.

Monday, March 23.—Weather cold and overcast in the morning, fine towards evening. Study. Retired, called to a sick girl,—6 miles. To bed at midnight. S. S. R. C. A. L. V. D. D. M. M. D.

Tuesday, March 24.—Confessions in the morning. Weather superb. Visit a sick man, 16 miles. Sent a letter to Mr. B——n upon the affair of the property. To me his sentiments look suspicious. R. P. U. A. D. D. S. L.

Wednesday, March 25.—Confessions, instructions, mass, till 2 P. M. Weather superb. Study in the evening. R. P. F. T. S. A. P. D. M.

Thursday, March 26. — Confessions, mass, instructions till one o'clock. Visited a young Protestant lady who is sick,—6 miles. Weather very mild, south wind. T. F. R. P. F. T. M. M. D.

(Good) Friday, March 27.—Weather extremely dark and gloomy. Rain part of the day; a few confessions; no ceremony; sadness——and meditation. R. D. S. D. S. L.

Saturday, March 28.—Confessions, mass, instructions till one o'clock. Fine weather, cold for the season. Disagreeable conversation with Mr. Flynn, ——— B. H. A. D'E. R. P. F.

(Easter) Sunday, March 29.—Fine weather, but cold for the season. Confessions, mass, instructions till one o'clock P. M. Catechism for 1st Communion. Friendly interview with Mr. B——n;· nothing yet decided. R. S. D. S. L.

Monday, March 30.—Confessions, mass, instructions till one o'clock P. M. Visit two sick persons,—17 miles. Weather very fine, but cold. Frequent thoughts of Mr. B. A. D'E. T. S. A. P. D. M.

Tuesday, March 31. — Received a letter from Mr. B. analogous to his character, at the bottom consoling. Went to the seminary,—10 miles. Weather very fine. A. D'E. P. D.

APRIL, 1812.

Wednesday, April 1. — Conversation with Mr. David about the seminary; extremely encouraging. Little instruction to the seminarians. Visit to a sick woman,—13 miles. Returned to St. Stephen's. Weather very fine and mild. E. A. R. P. F. M. M. D.

Thursday, April 2.—Conversation with Father Wilson about Mr. XX. Quite disturbed and indignant,—17 miles. Weather rainy in the forenoon, fine in the afternoon. P. C. L. Ch. F. R. P. F.

Friday, April 3.—Confessions all the morning. Sent an answer to Mr. XX. Received a letter from Mgr. de Boston, one from Mr. Bruté, one from Mr. Garnier. Robert Abell at the seminary. Eight masses for Mr. D. Very fine. E. T. R. D. S. L.

Saturday, April 4.—Catechism, conf., mass till three o'clock P. M. Six miles. Unpleasant conversation with Mr. XX; deep grief. Very fine weather. Unexpected change; in the end Mr. XX. and I understand each other. D. S. L. G. T. d'E. S. aD.

Sunday, April 5.—Confessions, mass, instructions till one o'clock. Very fine weather, strong wind S. W. Retired to my room; visited by Mr. XX., an icy look upon his face: I don't know why. R. D. P. F. P. C. S. S. M.

Monday, April 6.—Gloomy weather. A marriage to perform. Mr. Newton, a saintly man, died at midnight. Started to Mr. Steve Hayden's, eight miles. Weather fine and mild. L. R. D. S. A. P. D. M.

Tuesday, April 7.—Confessions, instructions, mass till one o'clock. Weather overcast. Letter to the Nuncio of Rio J. Useless conversation. D. D'E. R. P. F. M. M. D.

Wednesday, April 8.—Confessions, mass, catechism till 12 o'clock. Went to seminary, eight miles. Weather mild and cloudy. Preside at the lectures of the seminarians. Gave some *interiors*. P. C. L. C. R. P. F. E. D. S. P. M.

Thursday, April 9.—All day at the seminary. Letter to Mr. John Olivier; sent his deed. Retreat. P. D. T. N. S. P. Q. L. S. A. P. D. M.

Weather mild and cloudy; the seminarians happy. I had a talk with Mr. Chabrat. J. F. int.

Friday, April 10.—From the seminary to St. Stephen's. Confessions till 11 A. M.,—10 miles. Weather fine till evening, then dark, cold and rainy. T. E. P. to Mr. B—n; fear for the future. D. S. L.

Saturday, April 11.—Went to sick,—14 miles. Confessions, mass till one o'clock. Weather very cold for the season. Sleet this morning; wind N. W. Letter to Mr. B—n who *l'a b-n m-e. Elle e.p.a.l.f.* A'd. E. S. A. P. D. M.

Sunday, April 12.—Went to Holy Cross. Disappointed. Father Flynn had preached there. Dinner at 3 o'clock P. M. Went to sick, 16 miles; weather very cold, ice quite thick. R. S. D. S. L.

Monday, April 13.—Went to Mr. Lucas', 11 miles. Confessions and catechism. Weather cold, ice thick, wind N. W. Confessions till 9 P. M. P. R. D. S. L.

Tuesday, April 14.—Confessions, instructions, mass till 2 o'clock P. M. Went to St. Stephen's,—11 miles. Partial reconciliation with Mr. B—n. Burn his letters. Conversation about a very singular energumen. Agreeable evening. D. R. D. S. L.

. Wednesday, April 15.—To the seminary,—10 miles. Weather very warm. (entry vague) Seminarians happy; I am glad. G. P. D. L. A. G. A. D.

Thursday, April 16.—From the seminary to St. Stephen's, —10 miles. Weather stormy and rainy in the forenoon, afternoon rather fine. T. M. R. P. F. S. P. M.

Friday, April 17.—Messrs. David and Chabrat went with me to visit the energumen. Story of the father of the child about holy water, the beads, scapular, etc. Violent convulsions, but not decisive. Weather stormy, rainy. Returned to St. Thomas' with Messrs. D. & Ch. 10 miles. Frightful thunder; it fell quite near to us T. E. but P. D. L. S. P. M.

Saturday, April 18.—Began my retreat; the affair of Mr. B——n comes to my mind often. Weather stormy, thunder. E. S. E. M.

Sunday, April 19.—Weather very stormy, thunder. Retreat; a little more composed in mind. Satisfaction of the seminarians. God is very good; I desire to love Him and make Him loved. R. P. Dn. P. M. S.

Monday, April 20.—Clear and cold. Retreat continued, int. D. S. L.

Tuesday, April 21.—Retreat; warm weather. G. C. D. S. L.

Wednesday, April 22. — Fine weather, warm. Very agreeable retreat. Sickcalls,—10 miles. Reflections on the property of the church. U. A. D. S. A. P. D. M.

Thursday, April 23.—Frightful effects of the storm which I saw with my own eyes,—8 miles. Said mass at St. Stephen's. Went to St. Rose' on account of the affair of Mr. XX,—18 miles. Fine weather; visit of Mr. Fenwick. P. F. S. M. Bn. R. P. F. D. S. L.

Friday, April 24.—Confessions till 2 P. M. Indifferent conversation with Mr. B.; deep pain in the heart. Received several letters from Baltimore by Mr. Cambron. T. A. D. E. S. A. P. D. M. Beautiful weather.

Saturday, April 25.—Confessions from 5 A. M. till 12. Very fine weather; wind in the south. Confessions in the afternoon. Gave $10 to Father Flynn as mass stipends. R. P. F. M. M. D.

Sunday, April 26.—Confessions, mass, sermon at St. Charles' till half past four P. M. Weather very fine. Arrive at St. Stephen's at 7 P. M. 14 miles. R. P. D. S. L.

Monday, April 27.—All day at St. Stephen's; A marriage to perform; a few confessions to hear. Very fine weather. Visited by Mr. Flynn and Edward Fenwick. P. R. D. S. L.

Tuesday, April 28. — Long conversation with Mr. Ed. Fenwick about Mr. B—n. Went to St. Thomas'. Very fine and very warm weather. R. S. S. A. P. D. M.

Wednesday, April 29.—Letter to Mr. XX. Great sadness and disgust; weakness of mind and body; distracted and dissipated. R. P. F. M. M. D.

Thursday, April 30.—From the seminary to Bardstown for my letter of exchange of $121. Six miles. From the seminary to St. Stephen's; storm, rain; 10 miles. R. P. T. S. A. P. D. M.

Traveled in four months almost 800 miles.

Bishop Flaget at this time could not do much for his diocese. No doubt he gave Confirmation many times during his little trips to the churches and missions, and perhaps planned for other churches in settlements that he visited, but his larger plans for the diocese seem to have been waiting the solution of his difficulties with Father Badin, and the building of his cathedral. Yet the poverty of the people, and the privations incident to pioneer conditions were formidable obstacles to progress. However, he had his seminary, on which he founded strong hopes, and in which he took a pardonable pride. It was small, but it was fighting its way to the front under the sole care of Father David, who was a host in himself, and was beginning to draw around him some of the sons of the settlers. On the 3rd of April Bishop Flaget notes the entrance of Robert Abell, that old warhorse of Catholicity in Kentucky, whose name will never be forgotten. His work covered Kentucky, extended into Tennessee and Indiana; it began in the real missionary days, went through the formation period, and ended in 1873, when the Diocese of Louisville held high rank among the prosperous dioceses of America.

The Abells were prominent among the early settlers of Kentucky,—perhaps more so than their illustrious kinsmen, the Spaldings, whose name at a later date become a name to conjure by. Let us hope that the day of the latter is not past forever, but will revive to live and share the luster of the Abell fame, which is still an actuality in Kentucky, and promises to remain so for many years yet.

Bishop Flaget thought of schools, and we find him conferring with Mr. Dant upon the question of a convent for girls. The idea was not new, nor was Mr. Dant's interest in it of recent date. Both Father Badin and Father Nerinckx entertained the same idea and tried to put it into working shape. Father Nerinckx had hopes of founding a convent in 1805, and both he and Father Badin went so for in 1808 as to put up a building for that purpose. An unfortunate fire destroyed the building, and with it all their means and immediate prospects for a convent. A brother of the Mr. Dant here mentioned gave 100 acres of land upon which this building was erected, and this Mr. Dant later gave his land where a convent was built in 1816. The first tract is now a part of the holdings of Loretto, and the second is the home of the Trappists of Gethsemani. Mr. Dant had several children, and he wished to have them cared for as a consideration of his gift. We suppose they were properly reared and educated, for the Dants are now very prominent and respected in the neighborhood, and a village and railroad station near by is named for them. No priest of the name has as yet come from the family in Kentucky, but the gentler sex has given several consecrated members to God's service. A Miss Dant, as Sister Rosanna, was among the first of the Sisters of Loretto to go to New Mexico in 1852, and she labored there and edified the community until her holy death in 1916.

While Bishop Flaget was consulting with Mr. Dant, Providence was at work elsewhere with Father Nerinckx, who was opening a little school at St. Charles'. This small beginning was the nucleus of the Sisters of Loretto at the Foot of the Cross, and so silently did it crystallize into form that Bishop Flaget makes no mention of it on April 26, when he officiated there, although Father Nerinckx assigns April 25 as its birthday. Later in the year we shall find him noticing them.

We know nothing definite about his energumen. Whether it was a case of possession, or merely a form of epilepsy no one knows, nor to what family the afflicted individual belonged. Mr. Gwynn and Mr. Saunders were members of the Bardstown church. The former lived about two miles from the village, near the present site of Nazareth Convent, and the latter was a hat maker and resided in Bardstown. One of Mr. Gwynn's daughters married a Mr. Alexius Hagan, and was the mother of the Rev. Alfred Hagan of the diocese of Louisville. Mr. Gwynn died at the home of this daughter in 1830. Mr. Saunders sold to Bishop Flaget for a nominal price the ground upon which he built his cathedral in Bardstown, and he also gave him a portion of the land now used as a cemetery. He died at Bardstown, Jan. 4, 1839. A daughter of his was married to Mr. James McGill, a brother of the Rev. John McGill, later Bishop of Richmond.

We see that Bishop Flaget kept in touch with his brethren of the hierarchy and of St. Sulpice, also with high church dignitaries, as he seemed to have correspondence with the Nuncio at Rio Janeiro. With Governor Harrison of Vincennes there was some arrangement by which the government paid a certain sum for the services of a priest to attend the Indians and others attached to that Post. Fathers Badin and Nerinckx visited Vincennes, and Father Donatian Olivier was there for a time with Bishop Flaget in 1814.

(To be continued.)

ELEANOR C. DONNELLY

BY HONOR WALSH.

(*Concluded.*)

At one time, Ignatius Donnelly was more generally known than his sister Eleanor, but, as was expressed in an *Evening Bulletin* editorial at the time of our poet's death, her title to immortality is much more credible than any claim which could be put forward for her more widely advertised brother:

It is much to be feared that not many readers are aware of the loss to poetry occasioned by the death of Eleanor C. Donnelly, who passed away in her old age at West Chester, in the village where she was born.

In this generation we read a good deal of poetry, but forget the poet. The time has passed when perhaps a dozen men and women provided all this sort of mental pabulum, and their names were household words. Miss Donnelly wrote many volumes of verses, some of which reached the true heights of poetic inspiration. Every day some of her poems are quoted without the slightest knowledge of the author.

No one would pretend that she belonged in the brighter stars of the American Galaxy of Poets, and yet she had fine sentiment, excellent diction, and always a love for the more beautiful and the better things of life.

She had no patience with the anarchistic notion which prevails in these days, which considers rhythm a crime and form a disease. Like all true poets, she felt that meter was of the very essence of poetic form, and that through this medium alone could she express such inspirations as were within her.

It is a pity that she was known through so much of her life as only the sister of her brother, Ignatius Donnelly, who made a great stir by his advocacy of the Baconian theory of the authorship of Shakespeare's dramas, and who left little behind him that is of constructive value. Much of the brother's success—such as it was—was due to the devotion of his sister, and although she was more modest in her appeals to fame, her writing will endure when his controversy over the Bard of all Time is forgotten.

The sole error in this notable secular tribute to Eleanor Donnelly's genius, is in accrediting her nativity to West Chester instead of to Philadelphia.

Ignatius and Eleanor were not the only talented members of the Donnelly family. The five daughters of Philip Carroll and Catherine Gavin Donnelly were exceptionally brilliant women. All were musical, literary artistic; all had the social graces in an eminent degree, but as time went on, the aging sisters turned to their one genius like worshipers at a shrine. In their later years, they delighted to bask in Eleanor's starlight: their devotion to her, as indicated in a former chapter, was inexpressibly touching.

" I always sleep in Eleanor's room," the then septuagenarian Philipanna confided to the present writer ten years ago; " Sometimes she wakes after midnight and sits straight up. She says not a word; neither do I, but I arise, light two candles at her desk, arrange paper and pencil and retire again. In the morning there is a poem completed—sometimes two."

" And you never say anything? "

" Oh no—that might break the spell! " explained Philipanna, in tones of hushed solemnity.

As before stated, the other sisters attended to all business matters and to domestic management, in the years of housekeeping; thus, surrounded by loving care,

and wholly enfranchised from "the drudgery of detail,"
Eleanor Donnelly was free to devote all her time to her
indubitable gift of song.   That gift was laid unreservedly
at the feet of the All-Giver.   In later years the venerable
poet was asked why, with her ready facility, she had not
become a regular contributor to secular literature.

"It never occurred to me," she answered; "you see,
I write entirely from a Catholic point of view, and, years
ago, subconsciously, I dedicated my lifework to the
service of the Church.   If I should deliberately forsake
the path I chose so long since, I should feel, well—almost
sacrilegious.   As for fame, if a line of mine helps some
struggling soul, or if my hymns shall be sung by the
children after I have left the world, that, to me, would
be finer than anything the world could do to honor my
memory."

Narrow?—"Narrow, but deep," in the Bensonian
phrase.   After all, what would Catholic literature be,
but for the souls dedicated to its necessarily intensive
cultivation.

The Church, to whose service that long and fruitful
life had been dedicated, honored our dead poet as no
woman was ever honored before in this Archdiocese:

In the old convent at Villa Maria at West Chester, attended by the Bon Secours nuns whom she had brought
to Philadelphia, and in the presence of the Sisters of the
Immaculate Heart of Mary, whose guest she had been
for so many semi-cloistral years; fortified by the rites of
our Holy Mother Church, and praying fervently to her
last articulate word, Eleanor Donnelly died in the morning of April 30th, the feast of her Dominican patron, St.
Catherine of Siena.   She was robed in the white habit
of a Dominican tertiary and placed in a tiny casket, none
too small for the frail little shell which had encased so
great a soul.

On Friday morning, May 4, the feast of St. Monica, Solemn Requiem Mass was celebrated in the convent chapel at Villa Maria, where every morning while she was still able to walk, our valiant little saint had knelt to receive the Bread of Life. The celebrant was Rev. Philip E. Donahue, the Rev. Robert J. Tracy, S.J., was deacon, the Rev. Augustin J. Schulte sub-deacon, and the Rev. Francis X. Wastl master of ceremonies. In the sanctuary were the Right Rev. Monsignor Nevin F. Fisher, the Very. Rev. Samuel B. Spalding, the Revs. George T. Montague, Michael H. Gormley, Edward G. Dohan, O.S.A., and John A. Nugent, O.S.A. The music was·rendered by the novices of the Community and by the boys from St. Aloysius' Academy, which is connected with the convent. Before and after the mass, our poet's own sweet hymns to the Sacred Heart were sung by the choir of sincere mourners.

In the sermon delivered by Father Tracy, the other-worldliness of the poet was emphasized:

She might have courted the favor and the applause of a more shallow world with songs that lift the heart lightly and thoughtlessly for a time over the rough ways of life. She might have sung of themes that please a world whose thoughts and pleasures are, at the best, but worldly thoughts and pleasures. She might have sung lofty themes, for the world will listen to lofty themes that still are worldly : but no, her aim was higher than all this. Her aim was the glory of God in her own life and in the lives of others, and she touched on things of the world, she sang of things of the world only as they could help her to attain to that sublime object of her life.

Although Peter F. Kernan, Esq., Miss Donnelly's life-long friend and her executor, was averse to a public funeral, believing that because of the poet's age and the passing away of so many of her contemporaries, personal interest would not be evinced to any great extent, he was prevailed upon to agree to an arrangement which the Philadelphia Catholic public seemed to expect.

From West Chester the remains were taken to the Pennsylvania Station, Philadelphia. The little group of mourners included, besides the Sisters, of the Immaculate Heart of Mary, and the Sisters of Bon Secours, Mr. Kernan, his sister, Mrs. Camblos and her family, Judge Cassidy, his sister and niece, also the present writer and her "Sonshine." Among the relatives present were Mrs. Giltinan, a daughter of Ignatius Donnelly, her son, and Mrs. Hoover, a beloved step-daughter of Eleanor's sister, Agnes Donnelly Kilpatrick. Among the flowers which covered the casket were a great mass of St. Joseph's lilies from Mr. Kernan, white and red roses and palms from the Sisters, from the relatives, and the Cassidy family, and a wreath of heartsease from "Sonshine." From Broad Street Station the cortege proceeded in automobiles to the Cathedral of Sts. Peter and Paul in Logan Square.

Long before 3 o'clock, the appointed hour for the obsequies in the Cathedral, great throngs of people had arrived, and when the actual funeral procession came, it was almost impossible to move up the central aisle, for by that time all the available seats had been taken and all standing room was occupied. The presence of these thousands of admirers of Eleanor Donnelly, from every walk of life, was a notable tribute to the memory of the dead, and to the influence she had exerted throughout her grace-gifted life. Every local religious Order was represented in the congregation, and many of the Sister teachers had taken groups of advanced pupils to the funeral of the Catholic poet who had been famous for more than half a century.

His Grace, the Most Rev. Archbishop Prendergast, performed the absolution of the body, and the Right Rev. Mgr. Hugh T. Henry, LL. D., Litt. D., delivered the panegyric. Hundreds of priests were in the sanctuary. Among the prelates present were the Right Rev. Philip R. McDevitt, D. D., Bishop of Harrisburg, the Right Rev. Mgr. Henry T. Drumgoole, LL. D. the Right Rev. Nevin F. Fisher, the Right Rev. Mgr. William F. Kieran, D. D., the Right Rev. Mgr. Michael J. Crane, the Right Rev. Mgr. James P. Turner, D. D., and the Very Rev. Edmund J. Fitzmaurice, D. D., V. G.

Monsignor Henry, a close personal friend of Miss Donnelly, spoke most eloquently of the saintly poet, taking for his text these words from Wisdom iii, 1–3:

The souls of the just are in the hand of God, and the torment of death shall not touch them. In the sight of the unwise they seemed to die ; and their departure was taken for misery ; and their going away from us, for utter destruction. But they are in peace.

Following the obsequies, the little casket was opened, and the venerable poet lay in state while the great congregation of mourners filed by to look for once, and for the last time, upon the face of their beloved dead.

It was a day of drenching weather—"happy is the corpse that the rain rains on." When the casket had been covered and returned to the hearse the funeral wended its way through the downpour to historic St. Mary's Churchyard where Commodore Barry and other Catholics of Revolutionary times are entombed. Beside the open vault of the Donnelly family the final blessing was given by the Rev. Jeremiah J. Mahon. With him were the Right Rev. Mgr. Antonio Isoleri and her former pastor the Rev. Daniel I. McDermott, her cousin the Rev. E. J. Curran and her devoted friends

Father Wastl, Father Montague, Father Donohue and the Rev. V. F. O'Donnell, O. P., besides the Sisters and the other mourners who had accompanied their lamented friend all the way to her last earthly home. Eleanor Donnelly's fame was not confined to her native land. Many of her poems have been translated into French, Italian and German. Several years ago, thirty of her books were placed in the British Museum. Among the volumes still in print are:

Out of Sweet Solitude . . . . Poems
Legend of the Best Beloved . . . . Poems
Domus Dei . . . . Poems
Crowned with Stars . . . . Poems
Children of the Golden Sheaf . . . . Poems
Rhyme of the Friar Stephen . . . . Poems
Prince Ragnal. . . . . · . . . Poems
Christmas Carols
Poems
A Tuscan Magdalen, etc. . . . . Poems
A Garland of Festival Songs (versified from the
    German).
Hymns of the Sacred Heart.   Vol. I.
Hymns of the Sacred Heart.   Vol. II.
Our Birthday Banquet (both prose and verse)
Little Rhymes for Little Readers . . . . Poems
Blessed Youth . . . . Poems
Petronilla . . . . Fiction
A Klondike Picnic . . . . Fiction
Storm-Bound . . . . Fiction
Amy's Music Box . . . . Fiction and verse
A Lost Christmas Tree . . . . Fiction and verse
Lot Leslie's Folks . . . . Fiction
Miss Varney's Experience . . . . Fiction
Memoir of Rev. Felix J. Barbelin, S.J. . . . . . Biography
Life of Sister Gonzaga Grace . . . . Biography
Pearls from the Casket of the Sacred Heart . . . . Compilation
Liguori Leaflets . . . . Compilation
Holy and Wholesome Thoughts on Purgatory . . Trans. and Comp.
Girlhood's Handbook of Women . . . . Compilation
A Lapland Flower (from the French) . . . . . . Translation
The Conversion of St. Augustine and other Poems Poems
The Secret of the Statue . . . . Poems

The last named book, also the last published, appeared during the second term of ex-President Roosevelt and was dedicated to that strenuous executive.

A vast quantity of Eleanor Donnelly's work remains, uncollected. In justice to her memory, and while that memory is still alive among the people whom she loved and who loved her, a representative collection of her best poems should be made for the spiritual benefit of future generations and for the permanent enrichment of Catholic literature.

In this sketch of our lamented friend and fellow-member, no attempt is made to give a critical estimate of her various writings in verse and prose — writings which cover a period of seventy years, from her ninth to her seventy-ninth birthday. For appraisals of her literary achievements, the reader is referred to an eloquent tribute in the *Catholic World*, of June 1917, by the Rev. Thomas M. Schwertner, O. P., S. T. L., and to an article by the present writer in *America*, week of May 19th, 1917.

NOTE.—In a former chapter, it was stated that Miss Donnelly left but one nephew. There are still living *four* nephews—two sons of John Donnelly in Minnesota and two sons of Agnes Donnelly Kilpatrick in Pennsylvania. Three nieces also survived our poet.

SAN DOMINGO REFUGEES IN PHILADELPHIA.

COMPILED FROM THE ORIGINAL D'ORLIC–RODRIGUE PAPERS BY JANE CAMPBELL.

(*Continued.*)

WILLIAM RODRIGUE.

In 1830 William Rodrigue went to Northumberland, Pennsylvania, as directed by the following letter:

NORTHUMBERLAND, *15 June, 1830.*

MR. WILLIAM RODRIGUE,
Sir:

You will proceed as early as your services as Assistant Engineer on the W. Branch division of the Penna. Canal be dispensed with and make an accurate survey of the said W. Branch division of the Canal, and make a plot of the same showing the quantity of land occupied by the Canal and owned by each individual, as also that portion which may be included in — Banks, and the procurement of materials for the construction of said canal and not previously paid for. You will employ two men as chain carriers and not more. The superintendent in the said division is herely requested to furnish the funds necessary to effect the object.

MITCHELL, C. C.

While William Rodrigue was in Northumberland, his brother was also in the same town, and they were both on the most friendly terms with the family of Dr. Samuel Jackson.

Evelina had paid a visit to these friends of her brothers,

and several letters from Dr. and Mrs. Jackson show the regard felt by them for their young guest.

Letter from Dr. S. Jackson to Mr. Andre Rodrigue:

NORTHUMBERLAND, *July, 1830.*

Dear Sir:

It has always proved both a pleasant and profitable thing for me, in this remote situation, to have the company of your good children. I thank you kindly and so does Mrs. J. for sending Evelina to us. We should have persuaded her to stay longer for many reasons, but your parental anxiety seemed almost to command our silence on this particular point.

We take great pleasure in contributing every little that is in our feeble hands to the comfort of your sons, and I am sure that in no way could we have done this so effectively as by inviting one of their sisters. If the Dr. or Wm. remain here till next summer we may hope to see one or more of you in our little group, but if this should not be the case and there should be nothing to tempt any of you across the mountains, we shall have at least the continual pleasure of anticipating the making of your acquaintance in Philadelphia. It is possible we may return thither before we die.

Respectfully your frd and servt.

S. JACKSON.

Letter from Mrs. Samuel Jackson to Miss Aline Rodrigue:

NORTHUMBERLAND, *July 22, 1830.*

My dear Miss Rodrigue:

The time has come for us to give up your sister, and I can enter with your feelings of anxiety on account of her journey. The gentleman who has taken charge of her is unexceptionable and such a person as I should be quite willing to confide a daughter to; an old maiden Lady completes the group and I hope you will receive her in good health and spirits. I presume she has enjoyed herself while with us. I am sure she has been much gratified with the society of her brothers, and

it has afforded us much pleasure to be able to contribute to
their happiness. I hope you will give up the supposition of
trespassing, concerning which you have written to Evelina.
We have never felt her the least burden, but have received
her in that kind of family way which I hope has precluded
everything like ceremony; my wish was that she should feel
herself at home.

My health has not been quite at my usual standard, since
we have had the pleasure of her company and our house being
in an unfinished state, has prevented our promoting much en-
tertainment with the ladies in the neighborhood, but I am
happy to say our Evelina has not appeared to want society.
Had it been consistent with the happiness of her friends, we
should have been glad to have had her stay at least until the
warm weather was over, but the anxiety of your father combined with your own delicate health, makes me willing she
should join you in your retreat from the dust and heat of the
city.

I shall consider it among the pleasant occurrences of my
life that I have formed an acquaintance with your family and
therefore hope that you and Evelina will not forget me but
let me hear from you, which I can assure you, my dear Miss
Rodrigue, will always give great pleasure to your

Affectionate friend,
E. B. Jackson.

William Rodrigue's work on the canal was now nearing
completion.

Northumberland, *Aug. 12, 1830.*

Resolved, unanimously that the appointment made by J.
Ryan, Superintendent on the N. Branch Canal of W. Rodrigue
to make a survey of said Canal, be and the same is hereby
confirmed, and that the said Rodrigue be allowed three dollars
for every day actually engaged in the performance of said
duty and the sum of one dollar per day shall be allowed for
each man necessarily employed to aid him in the same.

Resolved, further that the said W. Rodrigue shall state upon oath to the Superintendent of said division the number of days himself and hands have actually been engaged in performing said duty and that he be required to complete the same on or before the 25th instant.

Extract from the journal of the Board.

Signed—R. SHUNK, *Sec.*

W. RODRIGUE,

HARRISBURG, *December 30, 1830.*

Dear Sir:

I hasten to inform you that the Board of Canal Commissioners have this day adopted a resolution directing the Superintendent upon the West Branch division to pay you one hundred and forty-seven dollars for 49 days service subsequent to the 25th August last in making a draft of the W. Branch Canal and land adjoining. I have sent a copy of the resolution to Mr. Bull directed to him at Milton.

I am yours respectfully,
Sign—R. SHUNK.

COMMONWEALTH OF PA.

DR. TO WM. RODRIGUE.

For services rendered in surveying damages of West Branch division of Penna. Canal from 23d June to 25th of August both days inclusive at $3.00 per day $192.00. Deduct for absence 6 day $18.00—$174.00.

NORTHUMBERLAND COUNTY.

Personally appeared before me, the subscriber, one of the Justices of the Peace in and for said county, Wm. Rodrigue who being duly. affirmed according to law saith' that the above account is correct and that he has been actually employed for the time set forth in said account in the service of the Commonwealth.

W. RODRIGUE.

Affirmed and Subscribed before me this 2d day of February, 1830.

JOHN WHEATLEY.

COMMONWEALTH OF PA.

DR. TO WM. RODRIGUE.

For services rendered in surveying, calculating and drafting map of damages of West Branch division, Pa. Canal from 23d June to 2d of November 1830—both days inclusive 133 @ $3.00 per day $399.00 deduct 20 days for absence $60.00 —$339.00.

64 days to 25th August at $3.00	192.00
49 days since 25th August as granted by Board of Canal Commission	147.00
	339.00

To the Board of Canal Commissioners of Pennsylvania.

The undersigned beg leave respectfully to state that they are personally or by reputation acquainted with William Rodrigue, one of the engineers under Mr. Rawle on the West Branch of the Susquehanna and they believe him to be a faithful and well qualified officer, extremely diligent and attentive to his duties, and that the public service would sustain a loss by his removal. They therefore pray that he may be continued in a situation in which he has given, as we believe, universal satisfaction. We beg leave further to state that the political character of Mr. Rodrigue is in accordance with that of the great majority of Pennsylvanians and of the Union, and that therefore no obstacle can arise to his continuance on that score.

(Signed) James Hopkins; Charles Pleasants; John Cowden; M. Taggart; Lewis Hobart; C. Woods & Co., W. B. Chapman; James Kay; Geo. A. Snyder; Samuel Jackson; Israel Pleasants; L. B. Stoughton; John Hepburn.

(*Note.* Pennsylvania was at this time Democratic, and remained so until about 1856, although the Wilmot Proviso set it partly on the way to a change of politics. The negro vote however during the Civil War, turned the scale and made it a Republican State).

Letter from Dr. Jackson to Mr. Andre Rodrigue:

November 22, 1830.

Dear Sir:

The time has too soon arrived when we are obliged to part with our good children. They have been a great comfort to us during the last two and one-third years, and I cannot be too grateful to you for making them such as they are. The Dr. has gone away in better spirits than I expected. His position will be very respectable and I have no doubt he will be comfortable in it. I did all in my power to persuade him to settle in Philadelphia but in vain. He may, however, yet return to you when he shall have acquired more years, experience and learning to fit him for competition in the grand sphere of action. He is wise beyond his years and you have been careful to teach him the whole routine of the *savoir-vivre,* so that he will be respected whenever he goes among genteel people.

It is now almost a question whether we shall ever see again our dear, amiable and good Evelina among us; and as to Aline, whom everybody has taught us almost to reverence, we presume there will be nothing to tempt her across the mountains. You cannot conceive how glad we should be to see any of you under our humble roof.

Let me thank you once more, dear Sir, for all the comfort we have received from the society of your good children.

I pray you give my love to Evelina and her sister and consider me with sincere respect,

Your affect. frd. & servt,
SAMUEL JACKSON.

Letter from Dr. Jackson to Mr. Andre Rodrigue:

NORTHUMBERLAND, *Feb. 14, 1831.*

My dear Sir:

I had intended to write very fully by Wm. both to you and my dear friend Evelina, but I put it off till the last day, when I find myself so very unwell with riding in the cold night and with the loss of sleep that I must really plead an utter inability.

The time has now come when we must part with the last of your dear good children (William) and I do assure you it is not without the deepest regret that we see him obliged to turn his back on Northumberland; and such are the feelings of all his acquaintances in this vicinity. The greatest comfort I have in seeing him go is this — that he will find friends and happiness wherever he goes—with such a mind have you endowed him.

He has been so very bad with a cough and oppression on his breast that I did not think it prudent for him to set out sooner on his long and cold journey.

We shall always be desirous of hearing from you. Mrs. Jackson joins me in sentiments of sincere affection and esteem for all your family.

Your very affectionate & obt. servt.,
S. JACKSON.

P. S. I am sorry to hear that the Dr. is not satisfied with the place he has chosen. It may prove a useful trial of his patience and fortitude. He and I are both believers in the utility of " works of supererogation." These he may now perform toward those poor people, and if he attend them with a benevolent mind he will find a reward that is better than silver or gold. A good man once said " the poor are my best patients, for God is their paymaster ".

One of the most important architectural works of William Rodrigue was the building of the Church of St. John the Evangelist, on Thirteenth Street, north of Chestnut Street, Philadelphia.

The church was dedicated on April 8, 1832, and the *National Gazette*, a newspaper published in Philadelphia, in its issue of April 10 of the same year records the fact as follows:

The new Catholic Church of St. John, on Thirteenth Street, was thronged on Sunday for the purpose of witnessing the ceremony of its consecration (dedication?). An able and eloquent sermon was delivered on the occasion by Rev. Dr. Power of New York, and a collection made with a view of obtaining funds for the completion of the edifice. It is one which greatly adorns our city and reflects the highest credit upon its architect, whom we understand to be Mr. Rodrigue.

Everything about it is beautiful, and though its inferiority of size prevents it from producing as imposing an effect as the Cathedral of Baltimore, yet for elegance and execution, it may safely challenge a comparison with that of any other church in the country. The concourse in it on Sunday consisted in great part of ladies and gentlemen of other religious denominations than the Catholic, and the spectacle altogether was uncommonly brilliant.

In the issue of the same paper of April 12 it was announced:

We are requested to state that for the gratification of the public, St. John's Church on Thirteenth Street will be open every day this week from twelve to two o'clock.

William Rodrigue, at the beginning of the year 1833, was surveying in Schuylkill County, Pa.

Broad Mountain Post Office,
Schuylkill Co.,
Jan. 12, 1833.

William Rodrigue, Esq.,
Dear Sir:

I am now prepared to commence the surveys for a continuation of the Little Schuylkill Rail Road, as soon as you can join me.

I wish you, on receipt of this, to call at Young's (the mathematical instrument maker in Front or 2d street) and ask for a double telescope German Compass, which was some time since left there by one of my assistants for repairs. I presume they have been made. If they have not, then I wish you to have them effected without delay, and to bring up the instrument in the stage with the chains' and pins, stationery, etc., which I requested you to purchase.

As you will probably be able to take your seat in the stage of Thursday, I will make my arrangements to meet you at Port Clinton. . . . . . .

The stage for Port Clinton leaves the Swan on Race Street every morning at 3 o'clock and reaches Port Clinton the same evening.

Very truly yours,

M. ROBINSON.

LETTER FROM PETER S. DUPONCEAU TO WILLIAM RODRIGUE.

PHILADELPHIA, *August 29, 1833.*

Dear Sir:

The bearer Mr. Charles Renad is an emigrant from Switzerland, recommended to me by General Lafayette. He was in his own country " Géographe de premiere Afse ". He wishes to know what chance there is for him in this country in the exercise of his profession, after he shall have learned the English language, which he intends to set about immediately, and thinks he can compass in a few months.

Knowing of no person, more capable than yourself to give him information on the subject of his prospects, I take the liberty of addressing him to you, with the request that you will give him the best information and advice in your power.

I am respectfully my dear Sir, your most obedient humble servt.

PETER S. DU PONCEAU.

LETTERS FROM REV. JOHN HUGHES.

Mr. Rodrigue and his children had intimate friends among quite prominent people and were on most friendly terms with many of the clergy, especially those stationed at the Church of St. John the Evangelist on Thirteenth Street in Philadelphia.

One of the very dear friends of the family was Rev. John Hughes, afterwards Archbishop of New York. Indeed they became closely connected; for William Rodrigue married Margaret Hughes, the sister of the Archbishop, and many of the letters in the collection were written by him, as for instance the following:

Letter from Rev. John Hughes to Andre Rodrigue in Philadelphia:

CHAMBERSBURG, *Oct. 12, 1830.*

My dear Friend:

In taking leave of you I calculated on a briefer absence, and imagining that I would be the bearer of my own thoughts, I did not think it would be necessary to address you by letter. However, in consequence of the different arrangement that has been made for me, I feel it due to your friendship and that of my two nieces to address you a few lines. The crisis of the Bishop's disease had passed away before I arrived, and altho' he had not required in his letter that I should come, yet it was evident that he expected me, having authorized a spy to peep into the stage as it passed. If he could, he would have returned with me and proceeded no farther, but as he could not, he determined that I should accompany him the rest of his journey. We set out to-morrow for Bedford, where we will be next Sunday; thence to Pittsburgh, and return by what they call the Northern route, by Ebensburg, Huntingdon and Harrisburg, etc. I am sorry that Northumberland does not lie in our way, that I might have the pleasure of seeing your sons and bringing you their love. I hope to be at home about the 10th of November . . . .

My sister, who is by my side, unites with me in love to you all. The arrangement which will keep me so long from Philadelphia will prevent her from going at all this autumn. But even if this were not the case, the delicate state of my mother's health would scarcely permit her absence. She would scarcely consent to leave her mother at this time on any account, and indeed I would be the last to advise it, and the more so, as everything in your excellent family would reproach her if she was wanting in the filial devotion which a child owes to a loved parent.

I remain your affectionate and sincere friend and servant,

JOHN HUGHES.

Letter from Rev. John Hughes to Miss A. Rodrigue:

FREDERICK, *June 28, 1831.*

My dear Aline:

I received yours of the 22d instant at the College on Saturday evening and would have answered it yesterday had it not been that I was engaged to preach in the forenoon and had to come to this place, a distance of twenty-one miles, after dinner. I do not mean to allow the building to trouble me until I return, and the only thing on that subject I have to regret is the accident to which your anxiety for its progress has exposed you. You must be cautious and not attempt to walk too soon. . . . I must now give you an account of my journey.

Leaving Philadelphia at 2 o'clock, I got into Harrisburg about a quarter past 12 the following night, and without going to bed, started after a delay of nearly an hour. We arrived at Chambersburg about 12 o'clock on Tuesday, and had the consolation to find all well, and rejoiced as you may suppose to see me. . . . We started from Chambersburg on Wednesday morning and arrived at the Sisterhood about 5 o'clock in the afternoon, whence I left and went to find my own quarters at the College. We stayed there until yesterday and arrived here about seven. The surprise was almost too sudden for poor Mary Angela.[1] The sister who sent for her did not tell her anything, and when she came in and saw me, she knelt down to receive my blessing, but was so overcome by the rush of feelings that she was unable to stand until I had to raise her.

I will not be in Philadelphia until after next Sunday as it will not be in my power to start from Emmetsburg until after Thursday.

Give my love to your father and all friends.

Always your affectionate friend in Christ,

JOHN HUGHES.

[1] Sister Mary Angela was a sister of Rev. John Hughes.

Dr. William E. Horner.

Another specially intimate friend of the family was Dr. William E. Horner, professor of Anatomy in the University of Pennsylvania.   In fact the relations of his whole family were very close, especially with Aline.

Dear Miss Aline:

Having some paper to spare after my business with your father, I have taken the liberty of devoting the remainder of the sheet to yourself.   Our little party has got on bravely so far.   Elizabeth has improved in health and strength and so has Josephine.[2]   The former has not complained on any occasion till yesterday, when the effects of confinement in a warm room at Delaware City the preceding night, and the navigation of the Bay to this place, were perceptible in her feeling much out of sorts (to use a good but not a very classical expression). The roaring of the breakers just under our windows at night discomposed her so, that if a steam boat had been at hand, she was almost ready to sail forthwith to the city.   A sound night's rest has, however, restored her to herself, and the really majestic ocean scenery, which she enjoys, has now exalted in her that pleasure and sentiment of enjoyment which it seldom fails to impart.   I now hear no more of going off so abruptly and she will probably give the allotted time to her visit.

Mrs. Hughes and Elizabeth are seated together at table . . . we all regret that you do not participate in our enjoyment. There is one equally esteemed by us all, the Rev. Mr. Hughes, the want of whose company we cannot but regret.   Tell him I hope still to see him here and that there is room to spare, so that he need not fear on that account . . . Josephine went into the sea this morning and was terribly frightened at the breakers; she was dragged into it like a little martyr going to the stake, and implored by every consideration she could master to be excused; she got into my arms and entreated to be taken out again.   I, however, kept her in till she had her quantum

---

[2] Josephine was, a few years later, a pupil at the Rodrigue School.

of sousing. I trust that the next time she will have more fortitude. She declared that there was a little girl drowned, for
she saw the ladies, searching with their arms under the water,
for her. She went to sleep shortly after and on waking had
forgotten all her troubles.

I am with every sentiment of regard in which I am joined
by Elizabeth,

Yours, etc.

W. E. HORNER.

DR. ARISTIDE RODRIGUE.

Dr. Aristide was now settled in Philipsburg and kept up
an active correspondence with his family.

Extract from a letter from Dr. Aristide Rodrigue to his
sister Evelina.

PHILIPSBURG, *Nov. 10, 1832.*

. . . The Bishop has been here to consecrate the church in
Clearfield. I accompanied him over the mountain for 16 miles.
He is a very pleasant and fine man, whose manners are extremely engaging, and who cannot fail to make every one his
friend. He must have thought me a rough blade, for he saw
me in all my roughness when I went across the mountain with
him. I carried my gun on my shoulder, as I am in the habit
of doing in order to kill game I shot him some pheasants,
unfortunately it was Friday, and he could not eat them for
some days. . . . Have you read Mr. Vigne's *Six Months in
America*? If not, I advise you to do so. I knew him, he is a
well educated, polished gentleman, and his work on America
the best that has yet appeared. Mrs. Trollope has written an
excellent caricature of the 'Americans, with which you might
be pleased as you would be with a book of caricatures.

Adieu, Your affectionate brother,

A. R.

Extract from a letter of Dr. Aristide Rodrigue to his sister:

PHILIPSBURG, *Nov. 21, 1832.*

You will see by my letter to my father, my dear Aline, that I propose paying you a visit some time in December. It will depend on circumstances when I shall come. You may, there-fore, expect me to drop in one of these days very suddenly, and like Paul Pry, say, "I hope I don't intrude." . . . The book which I recommended you to read was Vigne's *Six Months in America.*[3] He is the least prejudiced Englishman who has written about America, but still you may be able to perceive the John Bull who thinks there is nothing better, to say the least, than the English. I think if there exists the bump of Egotism, it would be found more frequently on their heads than on those of any other nation. It is a great pity, for there are really some worthy men of that nation.

I saw with a great deal of regret the death of Dr. Spurzheim,

---

[3] *Six Months in America* by Godfrey T. Vigne, Esq. Published in 1832.

After a laudatory description of Pratt's garden at Lemon Hill in the present Fairmount Park, and of the Water Works, and the beauti-fully wooded banks of the Schuylkill, the author adds—"In a very few years this fine scene is destined to be unnatured. By this time a railroad is commenced which will run from Philadelphia to Columbia, a distance of eighty-two miles. It will then join the Pennsylvania Canal, which has been finished nearly all the way from the Eastern side of the Alleghany Mountains." Again Vigne writes "The society in Philadelphia is the very best in the United States."

Vigne wrote thus of Philipsburg—"It is rapidly increasing under the advantages of English superintendence. It contains about 800 in-habitants in the town and environs. It is almost exclusively the prop-erty of one Englishman, who is master of nearly 70,000 acres in this part of the country. While I partook of his hospitality I was agreebly surprised by the circle of English society which I found collected under his roof. Several English people have made Philipsburg their place of residence. Its advantages consist in a remarkably healthy situation on the western slope of the Alleghanies, where the decent is so gradual as to be hardly perceptible. An easy and constant com-munication with Philadelphia and Pittsburg on the Ohio, excellent trout fishing and shooting in the forest, a very cheap market (a sheep or deer can be bought for a dollar) and excellent medical advice. Un-cleared land may be purchased at one, two or three dollars an acre."

the celebrated Phrenologist. Science has lost a truly eminent advocate, especially that branch of Physiology which is destined some day to become the foundation of correct and useful education.

Adieu, my dear sister,

Your brother,

ARISTIDE.

HUGHES-BRECKENRIDGE CONTROVERSY.

Extract from a letter written by Dr. Aristide Rodrigue to his sister from Philipsburg:

PHILIPSBURG, *Feb. 19, 1833.*

. . . Evelina tells me that you are keeping the correspondence between Mr. Hughes and Breckenridge [4] for me. You need not, for I receive the *Catholic Herald.* If he cannot answer better than he has, he had better give it up. I would advise him to study Locke and Abercombie *On the Mind,* for none that have made those authors their study, will ever consider his mode of discussion orthodox. I remember once meeting with a Protestant clergyman, of the same cast, finding him too prejudiced to discuss the Catholic questions, I took him upon natural religion, and with the aid of a little philosophical, and

[4] There are many allusions in these letters to the famous controversies between Rev. John Hughes, afterward Archbishop of New York, and Rev. John Breckenridge, a well known Presbyterian clergyman, commenced in 1830, on the question " Is the Protestant Religion the Religion of Christ ? " The controversy was carried on in the newspapers for a number of months and attracted wide attention among both Protestants and Catholics. So great was the interest excited that it was ultimately published in a pamphlet which had an immense circulation.

In 1834 Mr. Breckenridge tried again to batter down the bulwarks of the Catholic Religion, and challenged Rev. Mr. Hughes to debate the question " Is the Roman Catholic Religion, in any or in all its principles and doctrines, inimical to civil or religious liberty ?" Again did the Rev. Mr. Hughes come forward as the champion of truth. This debate was also published in book form and had a wide circle of readers.

I may add, metaphysical, reasoning, I made him confess himself a Deist, and then a Materialist. . . .

Your affectionate brother,

ARISTIDE.

Extract of a letter from William Rodrigue to his sister, Aline:

READING, *Feb. 28, 1833.*

My dear Aline:

. . . I wish you to tell Mr. Hughes that I did not receive the 7th No. of the *Herald*, and that I am very much pleased with the manner he drubs that " Blackbridge."

Tell Miss Hughes . . . last Sunday I was at church here. They sit like at Quaker Meeting, the men on one side and the women on the other. Mr. McCarty, the priest here, received me very well and would have taken me to Mrs. Smith, but as Mr. Robinson was in town I had no time to go.

I kiss you with all my heart.

Your brother and Friend,

W. RODRIGUE.

Extract from a letter written by Dr. Aristide Rodrigue to his sister:

PHILIPSBURG, *March 20, 1833.*

I do not know, my dear sister Aline, whether I have a letter of yours to answer, nevertheless, I take the opportunity of Mr. Potter's visit to Philadelphia to write to you. You will perceive by my letter to my father the impossibility of my leaving this place at present; it seems to me almost impossible to pay you a visit, but I am determined that nothing shall prevent me between this and next fall. Summer is approaching and we have less sickness at that time than at any other. You know there is no other physician for fifty miles whom my friends would send for in case I should be absent, indeed, I could not recommend any under these circumstances. I cannot think of going to Philadelphia when so many formidable diseases are raging through the country.

I still run over with pleasure, to read I have no time, the controversy between Mr. Hughes and Breckenridge. I look upon Mr. Hughes' last communication, No. 5, as a master-piece, just suited to the generality of Protestant readers. I think Breckenridge will not be fond of his allies hereafter. I commenced his answer, but cannot say that it is at all a refutation; I have as yet read but the commencement. I have no doubt but that this controversy will do Rev. Breckenridge no good, but still it will have its effects upon his people, the unprejudiced will be convinced of their errors, and the bigotted will bite their lips in mortification at finding their scientific parson and his favorite opinions so decidedly and ably overthrown.

I look upon Mr. Bracouler of New York as far superior in talents to Mr. Breckenridge. Rev. Mr. Power will have more difficulty with him, for he gives notice he will stop at nothing. If you do not receive the whole of their communications, I can supply you with them. I must send the editor of the *Catholic Herald* $5.00 in order to have the pamphlet form. I want to distribute them in this country. When men pretend to exercise their reason, when they make their reason paramount to all other light and be guided only by the evidence of their senses, as these people only pretend, there is nothing easier than to make materialists of them, or rather, to force them in their reasoning and arguments, as to acknowledge either Deism or Materialism. I do not see why our clergy, or any other persons competent should not offer to meet them on such grounds, for at present they are laboring under the disadvantage of these quacks, holding forth to the world that it is for the liberty of conscience and reason that they are contending, and yet they so subtly arrange their arguments, that a superficial observer would pass them unnoticed.

You must not think from either the above or what follows, that I am a Materialist. No, I assure you, I firmly believe all the Roman Catholic Church teaches. Abercrombie on *The Faculty of the Mind* was placed by a parson in my hands. I read it and made notes on it; read it subject to the same laws and rules which he lays down in his chapter on " Manner of Reasoning ", and from his own premises and his own laws of reason, I proved conclusively that he should be a materialist. My notes are extant. I only say this to prove that although Abercrombie is looked upon as one of the great heads of the day, yet when he trusts to his own reason, he falls into error and may be refuted by his own words.

Yours brother,

ARISTIDE.

ANTIDOTE FOR SNAKE BITES.

Letters from Dr. Aristide Rodrigue to his brother William Rodrigue.

PHILIPSBURG, June 23, 1833.

My dear Brother:

The last time I wrote to you I could not say much in consequence of the disability of my arm, which is now completely recovered, by, as you will say, a very strange though not less effectual remedy, namely, grubbing and wheeling which I had to do to level the yard for my back building.

Should you be bitten at any time by a venomous serpent apply immediately a ligature of common twine which will cut deep in the surrounding skin, I mean, which will imprint deep without cutting through, immediately above the wound, then apply your cupping glass over the bite and after concentrating the poison by the application of the glass for five minutes, remove the bitten part with a knife, then re-apply your cup, having previously well washed the parts. Do this frequently, after which apply a compress dipped in some stimulating substance such as whiskey, camphor, horse-radish or anything of that nature which may be at hand, not forgetting to drink freely of any kind of stimulant, not to produce intoxication, but sufficient to excite the system and brain. The great danger in all these poisoned wounds is, that from the depressed state of the system, either from fear or any other cause, sickness, etc., the poison acts with redoubled energy and virulence, nature herself shows us that to relieve any individual she creates a fever, and happy it is for him, for if it continues any time, the animal recovers. The Indians use the different snake roots all of which are strong and diffusable stimulants. Be sure to make the wound suppurate, eat moderately, so that digestion be well performed and drink moderately also, that is after the immediate danger is over, for whilst the poison is supposed to be in the system, I should recommend freely, you must bear in mind that it must not be followed by the depression subsequent to intoxication, and likewise, that the action of the cup is not merely to extract the poison. Let no advice from any physician induce you to heal up the wound without first making it matter. I have never yet been able to obtain an authenticated death from the bite of the copper, though great injury has followed the introduction of the poison.

You do not tell me where you are next bound to or what you are going to do. I recommend you to save all the money you can and speculate a little in property in this part of the country. There are several good town lots in the most eligible part of this place which will have to be sold at public sale, which you know is cash. $600.00 would probably buy them; they are both just across from my house. . . . If you have any leisure time come and see me. I am making arrangements to go the whole hog in keeping bachelor's hall; I find it quite as expensive the way I live, without any comfort or satisfaction. Would you ask Dr. Horner if he could obtain the favor of any chemist of eminence in the city to analyze some bituminous coal. I find there is such a prejudice against it that I cannot have it done.

Adieu,
Your brother,
ARISTIDE.

Extract from a humorous letter from Dr. Aristide to his sister, narrating the difficulties experienced by a country doctor in collecting his fees:

PHILIPSBURG, *June 23, 1833.*

My dear Sister Evelina:

I am going to give you all the particulars of what I am doing with myself, for you do write considerably well to me, so here's a Roland for an Oliver.

In the first place the people here that owe me money can't or wont pay. I meet a man whose life I have probably saved, and he says " I am sorry, Doctor, but by the Laurel Hills (the name of mountains in the neighborhood) I've not seen the best side of a dollar this long time, God help me, I haven't got a cent." . . .

Then some honest man will come and say, " Doctor, I can't pay your bill just now, but I've a couple of sucking pigs I can spare, or some board shingles, or perhaps some eggs or chickens ", perhaps a bit of an old hog or some such like. What can I do, either take these things or do as they do in France, but when I'm in Turkey, I like to do as the Turkies do, so I take them and do the best I can with them and trade them off for something else and so I get along.

Well, the consequence is, I'll send to your city of steady habits for a black waiter, who will keep my bachelor's hall, who will cook, roast, etc., etc., as soon as I can convert my pigs into money.

I will be down to see you and buy myself a stock of provisions, for coffee sells here, 30 cents a lb., and other things in the same way. I've built an addition of 14 feet by 24 to my log house; the new building will be my kitchen. Next summer I will have my garden in order, and then I'll be more comfortable, but the trouble, the vexations and the dear knows what, make me send the country practice to the four winds of heaven.

I can't get any one to dig the side of a hill for my kitchen to be level. I've been obliged to do a great deal of it myself. I've now an old Frenchman at work . . . July 4. You will find a great difference of date between my letters and their receipt in consequence of the scarlet fever and putrid sore throat breaking out here, which has kept me too engaged to close my letter.   I have the misfortune to announce the death of Henry, oldest son of Mr. Philips, who fell a victim to putrid sore throat. . . .

Your Brother,

Aristide.

BOOK REVIEWS.

THE QUEST OF EL DORADO—THE MOST ROMANTIC EPISODE
IN THE HISTORY OF SOUTH AMERICAN CONQUEST. By The
Reverend J. A. Zahm, C.S.C., Ph.D. (H. J. Mozans.) D.
Appleton and Company, New York. 1917. Illustrated with
34 engravings and maps. 261 pp.

"Where can it be—this land of *El Dorado*?" sings Poe.
Wistful is the poet's answer: "Over the mountains of the
moon, down the valley of the shadow." *El Dorado,* to the
average reader, evokes a dim vision of romance and gold somewhere in tropical America. Who of us knows that *El Dorado*
meant originally a man, rather than a place? How many are
aware that the quest of *El Dorado* lasted over two centuries,
enlisted the genius of three peoples—Spain, Germany, England
—and cost thousands of lives, besides untold wealth? These
facts, brought out by Father Zahm in his illuminating book
The Quest of El Dorado, may well surprise the reader *to*
whom *El Dorado* is but a playful phrase, born of fancy and
unrelated to history.

This modest volume is mainly a reproduction of a series
of articles written in 1912 for the *Pan-American Bulletin.*
The sources are chiefly ancient Spanish chronicles, notably the
sixteenth-century writings of Padre Simon, the poet-priest
Castellanos, Fra Carvajal, and Vasquez: the last three actual
participants in the quest. Curious old engravings enrich the
volume, while the routes of the Doradoists are traced in maps.

Who and what was *El Dorado*? In 1535 a roving Indian
in Quito told Belalcazar, Pizarro's lieutenant, the story of the
gilded cacique, or chieftain. Anointed with resinous gum and
covered from head to foot with powdered gold, a certain ruler
was wont to make oblation on a raft in a certain lake (reputed
to be Guatavitá, near Bogotá). Rich votive offerings of gold,
emerald, etc, were consigned to the depths of the lake as a

propitiatory offering to the gods. Several variants of this legend occur, but all are in substantial agreement: they revolve about a chieftain powdered with gold, whence *El Dorado*— "the gilded one". By degrees the name was extended to the sacred lakes, then to the province of this ruler, so that the quest of *El Dorado* presently broadened into a search for the mysterious gold-bearing land of the gilded chief. It is interesting to learn from Father Zahm that many attempts have been made by treasure-hunters to drain Lake Guatavitá; indeed, an English concessionaire is now engaged in probing the bed of the lake for the storied gold.

Belacazar led the long procession of Conquistadores in their fruitless quest of the Gilded Man and his earthly paradise. The highly dramatic episode of Belalcazar's encounter in the wilderness with two rival explorers, Quesada and Federmann, is sketched by Father Zahm in an appendix. Next to enter the lists was Gonzalo Pizarro. With an elaborate equipment he started from Quito in February, 1541, to achieve *El Dorado,* but retired in defeat after sixteen months of fearful suffering. A geographical contribution of major importance—the discovery of the Amazon by Orellana, an officer of the party, helped to redeem the hapless venture.

There followed quickly one expedition upon another: Fernan Quesada from Bogotá, the German Von Hutten from Venezuela, Ursua from Peru, Chaves from far-off Paraguay, Proveda, Gonzalo Quesada, Berrio. Hostile Indians, mutiny, disease, famine, death were the allied forces with which they were unable to cope, and failure was writ large over all their efforts.

Ever more feverish became the quest and now the Old World joined the hunt. De Silva left Spain in 1569 with six hundred nobles and plebeians. Undaunted by defeat he returned to Spain; tried again, failed again. De Vera now attacked the fascinating problem. He went to Spain for no more than three hundred men, but the glittering mirage was potent enough to entice two thousand men, women and children from the mother country into that mysterious land of gold—and death. Complete disaster bore its message to Spain and thenceforth enthusiasm flickered out in the romantic breast of the Don.

The scene shifts and the brilliant figure of Sir Walter Raleigh flashes upon the stage. Well versed in Spanish lore, he deemed the quest not a Quixotic venture but " feasible and certain ". Fully equipped, he sailed from Plymouth in February, 1595, and arrived at Trinidad. To protect his base he burned the Spanish settlement of San José, murdered the guard, conciliated the Indians with wine and money, then started up the Orinoco on his search for the rainbow's end. Six months found Raleigh back in England, an object of derision. Twenty-one years later this dauntless Argonaut again sought the land that beckoned, but failed to enter therein, so that, sick and disheartened, he crept back home to face the ridicule of the crowd and finally the ax of the headsman.

Men continued to pursue this *ignis fatuus* of *El Dorado*. An expedition was sent out in 1775 by the Governor of Spanish Guiana, of which only one person survived. This practically ended the quest. The taunting challenge of the Gilded King was disregarded thereafter, although to-day, in parts of Venezuela and Colombia, the old belief still lingers.

Most modern historians are severe in their estimate of these visionaries. Father Zahm, however, is sympathetic. And rightly so. For, with the news of Aztec and Incan opulence still ringing throughout the land, no further discovery of fabulous wealth was deemed impossible. Benign, too, is our author's interpretation of motives. Not merely the *auri sacra fames*, but the imperious call of adventure, and patriotism as well, urged on these pathfinders to deeds of valor and endurance that compel unbounded admiration. And though their quest, as we now know, was the quest of a chimera, still it led to incidental discoveries of solid scientific worth. Important contributions were made to geography, ethnography and natural history; moreover the trail was blazed in the stern jungle for the missionary and his story of the Cross.

Father Zahm's admirable book has the cardinal merit of increasing in interest as it goes on. The volume is superbly printed; the illustrations are happily chosen; many of them entertaining, all helpful. Some of the route maps, however, are rather too small for close inspection; again, one notes with regret the omission of a large, serviceable map of South America.

The author has given us an absorbing study, but he modestly awaits "an exhaustive and authoritative work on the subject, one which shall embody the results of the most recent researches in Spain and Latin America." Very true, but something more is demanded; the theme of the Quest is of Odyssean size and calls for an epic frame as its final setting. May we not indulge the hope that some day a Homer of the Spanish New World will give in stately procession of sonorous measures adequate expression to the yearning charm, the profound pathos of this quest of the Unattainable.

T. C. B.

THE LIFE AND LETTERS OF SISTER ST. FRANCIS XAVIER (Irma Le Fer de la Motte), of the Sisters of Providence of Saint Mary-of-the-Woods, Indiana. By one of her Sisters, Mme. Clémentine de la Corbinière. Translated from the French by the Sisters of Providence. Revised and enlarged edition. B. Herder Book Co., St. Louis and London. 1917. Pp. xxix and 416. Price $2.25.

Irma Le Fer de la Motte, in religion Sister St. Francis Xavier, one of the first members of the Congregation of the Sisters of Providence of Saint Mary-of-the-Woods, Indiana, was born at a place called Fours-à-Chaux, near the town of Saint Servan in Brittany, April 15, 1816. There was nothing very remarkable in the first years of her childhood. Like many children, she was capricious and wilful, vain of her appearance and sprightly wit, had a hasty temper and was given to day-dreaming. But these faults were by God's grace happily amended under the salutary corrections of pious parents and wise directors. Her education, save for a short time spent at a private school at Saint Servan, was conducted by her relations at home at Fours-à-Chaux and at the homestead of her paternal grandmother at Lorette, some distance from

Saint Servan on the road leading from Rennes and Dinan to Saint Malo.

Concerning this period of Irma's life, Léon Auboneau, a French Catholic writer of the last century, in his introduction to the original French edition of the present work, tells us that "at Lorette the domestic chaplin, Abbé Cardonnet, was both the friend of the family and the instructor of the children. Irma placed herself under his direction and received from him special light and great help in the choice of her missionary career. The religious life was no part of Irma's early plans. She was full of zeal and ardor, but tenacious of her independence; and though she wished to travel to distant lands to help souls deprived of the light of faith, she had no idea of doing this under rule. Her plan was to devote herself to the foreign missions, to teach school, to dedicate herself to the service of the sick—in a word, to give up her whole being to do it as she pleased, more freely even than when she lived in the bosom of her family" (pp. xxi, xxiii).

From her childhood, she had entered into and aided much in sustaining and developing apostolic work at Saint Servan and in the neighborhood of Lorette. She was an eager reader of the *Nouvelles Recus des Missions*, the original name of the *Annals of the Propagation of the Faith*, which gave strange accounts of the American Missions. "Cannibals were reported to be among the flocks of the newly-erected dioceses. Vincennes, which was to be the realization of Irma's dreams, was only a post in the midst of a savage people, who still retained an exalted idea of the early Catholic missionaries, and refused to receive among them any Protestant ministers. 'We know from our ancestors', they said, 'that the ministers of the Great Spirit wear black gowns and do not marry'" (p. xxiii).

Brittany had a large share in the American apostolate. Simon Bruté de Rémur, the first Bishop of Vincennes, his successor De La Hailandière and some of their priests were natives of Brittany. The account of their life and labors in Indiana as told by the "Annals" and the sermons of the Abbé Carret, a missionary apostolic, helped to foster and strengthen Irma's growing vocation. The Abbé Cardonnet and Father Besnoin, a Jesuit, advised her to enter religion. Father Besnoin ended his talk with her by saying, "You will go to the missions to convert the little savages." At length Irma, convinced that her vocation was first to be a religious and afterwards, if it pleased God, a missionary sister, applied for permission to enter the motherhouse of the Sisters of Providence at Ruillé-sur-Loire.

The Congregation of the Sisters of Providence of Ruillé-sur-Loire was a society of teaching sisters, devoted also to various works of mercy and charity and founded by the Abbé Dujarie, Curé of Ruillé (Sarthe) in the diocese of Le Mans in Brittany. Abbé Dujarie was also the founder of the Brothers of St. Joseph, united afterwards to the society of missionary priests called the Congregation of the Holy Cross, of which the Abbé Antoine Moreau was the founder and first Superior General. These two societies and the Eudist Fathers were destined by God to be His instruments with Bishop Bruté's missionaries in the evangelization of the vast diocese of Vincennes, which at the time of its foundation comprised the states of Indiana and Illinois. When Bishop Bruté died, his successor, Mgr. De La Hailandière prevailed on the Eudists to establish a theological seminary at Vincennes, drew Father Sorin and the Fathers of the Holy Cross to begin the work now flourishing at Notre Dame, and brought the Sisters of Providence into Indiana from France.

When Mother Theodore Guérin and her small band of six Sisters of Providence of the new foundation came from Brittany into the diocese of Vincennes in the year 1840, they were not located, as they expected to be, in the episcopal city, but were sent some miles out into a densely wooded country, where only after long years of privations and sufferings were they able, through the Divine Providence, to lay and perfect the foundation of what is now one of the glories of the West, the great teaching society of the Sisters of Providence of Saint Mary-of-the-Woods, Indiana.

With this digression, for which we ask the kind forbearance of our readers, and returning to Sister St. Francis Xavier, the

Irma of our sketch, we find from her biography that, after taking the veil at Ruillé in 1840, in the autumn of the same year she obtained her heart's desire and was sent to complete her novitiate in the new foundation in Indiana. There she remained to become the first mistress of novices of the society and the most prominent member of her sisterhood after its saintly foundress, Mother Guérin. Sister St. Francis Xavier died in 1856. For some years before her death, God blessed the sacrifices which she had made, in departing from her family and country, with the companionship in religion of her young sister Elvire, who became Sister Mary Joseph in the Sisterhood in 1852. Elvire le Fer de la Motte succeeded her sister as mistress of novices at St. Mary-of-the-woods and died in 1881.

The whole story of the beautiful life of Sister St. Francis and her interesting family at the ideal homes of Fours-à-Chaux and Lorette and the early trials and sufferings of the Sisters of Providence of Saint Mary-of-the-Woods, Indiana, is told in a very interesting way, chiefly through Irma's letters, in the present work compiled in French by Irma's sisters, Mme. Clémentine de la Corbinière. Her Life and Letters show that Sister St. Francis Xavier was a type of what the true religious ought to be—humble, obedient, self-sacrificing, and full of zeal for the glory of God and the salvation of souls. The translation of the original edition of this book was made by Sister Mary Joseph shortly before her death and published in 1882. The translation of the present edition was made by the Sisters of Providence. The Sisters and the publishers are to be congratulated on the merits of a very well written, a very readable, a very well printed, and a very well bound volume. We feel sure that all its readers will find it of spiritual as well as historical interest.

J. E. Colclough.

The Commonwealth of Pennsylvania. By Thomas Kilby Smith ; The Encyclopedia Press, Inc., New York.

A scholarly contribution to the histories of the States of the nation is this by Thomas Kilby Smith, a member of the

Philadelphia bar. The introduction is by Walter George Smith, President of the American Bar Association, and a former President of the AMERICAN CATHOLIC HISTORICAL SOCIETY.·

The author has departed from the customary method of writing a history. While he treats of events that may not be omitted in any chronology of the State, he especially gives attention to these events in their relation to sociological, industrial and political conditions. What Green did for England, George Kilby Smith has done for Pennsylvania on a more limited but none the less important scale. A bare statement of events unilluminated by collateral studies of governing conditions is nothing but a mere skeleton of history. Mr. Smith does more than articulate dry bones. With scholarly analysis, discriminating appraisement, and judicial keenness of vision he presents a living record of the beginnings and the development of the Commonwealth: the formation of counties, the manners and customs of the people, the state's finances, resources and religion. He reviews the educational systems, public and parochial, and the achievements of the people in art, science and literature. Especially important is the chapter on religion, wherein Mr. Smith treats of the organization of religious bodies, state legislation affecting religion, the status of church law in civil courts, church property, and the seal of the confessional. Mr. Smith has performed a valuable service to the whole nation in preparing this history.

NOTE.—Owing to lack of space in this number we are obliged to defer the publication of the review of Mr. Frank H. Severance's NIAGARA: AN OLD FRONTIER OF FRANCE, and also of the second volume of Richard D'Arles' work on ACADIE.

Another important review held over for next issue is HISTORY OF THE SOCIETY OF JESUS IN NORTH AMERICA. VOL. II. By the Rev. Thomas Hughes, S. J.

Chapter XIX of the LIFE OF BISHOP CONWELL will be published in the June number.

THE MOST REVEREND DENNIS J. DOUGHERTY, D. D.
Archbishop of Philadelphia

THE MOST REVEREND DENNIS J. DOUGHERTY, D.D.,
ARCHBISHOP OF PHILADELPHIA.

The American Catholic Historical Society with joy and deep reverence pays homage to the new Metropolitan of our Archdiocese.

His Grace studied the sacred sciences in Rome, where pulsates the heart of the Catholic Church, where the greatness and majesty of the Spouse of Christ are more fully realized than anywhere else, whence her world-wide spiritual empire is surveyed and directed, where the command of Christ, "Go ye and teach all nations," is heard to-day by the bishops, the successors of the Apostles. Years ago, at the bidding of the Vicar of Christ, the brilliant young Professor of St. Charles Seminary, Overbrook, went forth to the far-away Philippine Islands, where he has left the impress of his zeal and energy in the two dioceses of Nueva Segovia and Jaro, which he successively ruled with conspicuous success.

And now, coming from the important Diocese of Buffalo, he is welcomed back to his home, for he is a son of this Archdiocese, succeeding a noble line of illustrious and saintly predecessors, who have been makers of history in this part of the republic, and many of whose labors and great achievements have been and are being published in the RECORDS of this Society.

His Grace, who has already been a maker of history in the Far East, will, with characteristic zeal, take up the work of his predecessors in this Metropolitan See, where the polyglot Catholic population vividly reminds one of the first Pentecost day, and, true shepherd of our souls, will still farther extend the Kingdom of Christ in the great State of Pennsylvania.

AD MULTOS ANNOS!

RECORDS OF THE

AMERICAN CATHOLIC HISTORICAL SOCIETY

| VOL. XXIX | JUNE, 1918 | NO. 2 |

MISSIONARY JOURNEYS IN ALASKA

A Letter of Father Philip I. Delon, S.J., to Very Rev.
Richard A. Gleeson, S.J.

ST. MARY'S MISSION, ⎫
AKULARAK, MAY 29, 1916. ⎰

REV. DEAR FR. PROVINCIAL:

P. C.

It is a year since I came to the "land of promise", and
your Reverence has doubtless been waiting for some account
of myself. I have long since intended to send you a few
notes about my winter trips, but the short summer season
has kept me so constantly on the go that I have not even had
the time to begin my story.

To-day, I find myself stranded out on the shore of the
Bering Sea, at one of the many fishing camps which our
native Eskimos set up every summer all along the Alaskan
coast. I came down here from Akularak in a row-boat,
three days ago. The trip was made partly by rowing, and
partly with an occasional spurt of an Evinrude motor. The
latter, however, bucked and kicked all the way down, so that

my arms are both stiff and slightly swollen from the continual cranking-up of that little cranky engine. To-day, a strong headwind and rainstorm keep me at a little village, which the natives call " Nunam Ikkoa ", the " End of the Earth ". So that your Reverence will receive what few people have ever had, a letter from the " End of the Earth".

The Akularak district depending upon St. Mary's Mission is large enough for a diocese; but as it is little better than a wilderness, the total population is scarcely that of the average country parish in the western United States. I have visited all of the seventy or eighty villages of the district, with the exception of a few; and making a mental census of the people, I have counted 1375 souls. My estimate is probably too low, but the total number certainly does not reach 2000. If you have a good map of Alaska at hand, you can form a very fair idea of this district by drawing a north and south line from the Yukon to the Kuskokwim River at about 163 degrees west longitude. The irregular polygon to the west of that line bounded by the Yukon on the north, the Bering Sea on the west, and the Kuskokwim on the south (with the exception of the triangle south of Vancouver Island), is what we call up here among ourselves the " Akularak " district. Vast as it is, with an area of some 15,000 square miles, there is only one inhabitant to every ten or twelve square miles. Your Reverence may judge from this the huge task that falls to the lot of the missionary when he starts out to visit his scattered flock. As the whole country along the coast is a swamp, covered with a perfect network of rivers, sloughs, lakes and ponds, there is no question of ever seeing a road in summer from village to village. However, we have quite a lay-out of winter roads, or better, winter trails. These are usually the direct and shortest routes from one village to another, and lead you over tundra, rivers, lakes, brush and bushes. As everything is deep in the snow, and even the brushwood is almost entirely covered, the traveller is frequently unable to tell whether he is going over land, or lake, or river; besides, one not thoroughly familiar with a particular locality may find it rather difficult at times to know for certain whether he is heading for his destination or whether he has already passed one side of it; for the landmarks are so few, so uncertain and so much alike in character, that one may be easily mistaken for another. But let me not worry your Reverence with general and random talk about the place; perhaps you will rather prefer a few notes about one of my long trips this last winter.

Of all the winter trips with sled and dogs, the one to Tununa, Vancouver Island, is the most eventful of all; it certainly was for me this year. Being a total stranger to the place, to the people and the customs of the country, I was looking forward to it with a feeling of anticipation mingled with some anxiety as to how it would turn out. It is a long trip, requiring about three weeks of continual traveling. As it not unfrequently happens that one has to pass the night in a cold hovel, or sometimes in the open air, we have to take plenty of warm clothing and must also have aboard the sled enough food to keep us alive during the entire trip, as the native hospitality does not, except on a few occasions, extend to the giving of food to the missionary. Like St. Paul, the latter feels more satisfied when he can say that he is not a burden to those to whom he announces the Gospel of salvation. But what loads down our sled the most is the fish that we have to take along to feed our dogs. Of course in many villages someone will be found whose stock of frozen or smoked fish is sufficiently large to permit him to sell us enough for one dog-feed, but in just as many places we may be told that nobody has a fish to sell; that they have scarcely enough for themselves. The standard coin, the legal tender of the traffic among the coast Eskimos, is tea and chewing leaf-tobacco; so a bag of tea and a few pounds of the precious weed are carefully laid at the bottom of the sled; my guide and I have both our bedding, my own consisting of two common grey blankets and a sort of quilt made of skins of muskrat. It takes about seventy skins to make a full-sized quilt, the bellies of the animals being sewed together on one side of the quilt, and the backs forming the other side. About half a dozen pairs of boots are also needed for such a trip, as we must be prepared for very cold and for very wet weather. Then there is my chapel. Special care is necessary to protect the mass wine from freezing, for as the holy sacrifice is the chief, I might say the only, consolation of the missionary on these long journeys, it would be a great misfortune indeed if the bottle should break. To insure safety, I usually take two or three little bottles, half a pint in each, and wrap them up carefully in separate packages. One tablespoonful is considered a liberal amount for each mass, out on the trail.

MARCH 15 was the day I had determined on to begin my trip. That morning, the minimum thermometer registered a temperature of 28 below zero, Fahrenheit. Fortunately, there was no wind, so the cold would not be keenly felt. The entire village around the mission gathered to see us go; the children also viewing our departure, and wishing Godspeed. Our sled is heavily loaded indeed, each of our dogs has a full 100 pounds to pull; the trail is only fair, having been badly broken by soft weather a few weeks before, and having been but little travelled since that time. Two out of the nine dogs got "knocked out" shortly after starting. After five hours, we find a chance traveller going to the mission, and we send one of our dogs back, keeping but eight for the trip; only about five or six of these can be relied on for steady work. Eleven hours brings us to our first stopping place, a village of three houses. We pick out the largest one, bring in our bedding and enough bread for a couple of meals, cook a little rice and canned meat on the family stove, boil a little tea, and after this most appetizing repast, I recite aloud the night prayers for the entire household, and we stretch ourselves on the floor to enjoy a welcome night's rest.

MARCH 16. Rise at about five o'clock, say mass on an improvised altar, and set out southward. We pass several small villages on the way, stop about noon for a little lunch. It consists of frozen bread or frozen hardtack with a cup of hot tea which we get out of our thermo-vacuum bottle. It was only at 7 o'clock in the evening that we reached a little village of three houses at the foot of the Kúsilwak Mountains. These mountains may not be more than 2,000 or 3,000 feet high, but as they are the only break in the monotonous evenness of tundra from the coast to about 100 miles inland, they are visible from every point of the compass on a clear day. They are to the traveller on his winter trail what a lighthouse beacon is to the mariner at sea. As long as we can catch sight of the snow-covered Kúsilwak standing out in conspicuous whiteness against the dark horizon, we know which course to take, or at least we can tell where we are. In this village I found a little girl twelve years old, who had been at our mission school for some time and had there made her first communion. She was glad to be able to receive our Lord again; it was the first and only time thus far that I had administered the Sacraments.

MARCH 17. Early in the day we arrive at Chinígmint, where we expected to add to our little party the company of an Indian who has in former years frequently accompanied Father Treca on his trip to Tunúna. What was our disappointment when we find out that George is not going on his annual trading expedition this year! My guide does not feel sure of the way, but we have to go ahead, and shall do so, relying upon Divine Providence and the good angels to protect us on the journey.

MARCH 18. Saturday, the day which all devout clients of Mary love to select to begin any difficult enterprise. We place our trip under the special care of that Blessed Mother. No matter what may happen to us, we know she will be with us. We do indeed feel rather uneasy, for we now are venturing beyond the well-known and well-beaten trails that lie within two days' journey from the mission. The sun shines brightly, the cold weather makes our dogs lively; they are always at their best when the thermometer is about twenty degrees below zero, Fahrenheit, then no matter how long they keep running, they never get overheated and are able to maintain a brisk trot for hours without any apparent fatigue. With the aid of the compass, we head to the southeast, but towards noon we begin to doubt; we are in a trackless waste, flocks of ptarmigans fly off as we approach; numerous fox tracks and mink tracks and tracks of other animals valued for their fur keep our dogs sprightly with expectation for their fresh scent; but just the same, we are off the right trail, and though we take our bearings frequently, we fear we have left our destination to the side, and are almost tempted to retrace our steps. At sundown, as we lost all hope of reaching any village that day, we make for a far-away cluster of brush wood, intending to pass the night there. It is full moon, and its rays light up an immaculate white landscape, a bright, cloudless sky; everything so still that you cannot even breathe without a plainly audible sound. Our dogs are so exhausted that they lie down at once without so much as caring to have their harness taken off; we feed them their ration of dry fish, they curl up in the snow and go to sleep. As for ourselves, we try to build a fire, but cannot succeed in boiling enough melted snow for even a cup of tea. A handful or two of crumbs of " pilot bread," often called " hard tack," a box of sardines, the contents of which are so frozen that I have to chip them up with the prong of a fork, constitute my royal supper. A hole is soon dug in the snow, using the snowshoes in lieu of a shovel, and a few sticks thrown in to prevent direct contact with the snow. I open up my bag of blankets, put on my fur parkey, and try to wrap the blankets around me, so I may at least keep from freezing. After a couple of hours, I began to feel my limbs getting numb with the cold. After vainly trying to restore circulation I was compelled to crawl out of my blankets and look around for a hard mound of snow, where I began to execute a dance that would baffle accompaniment by the best orchestra. I jigged and clogged around for fifteen or twenty minutes, and feeling I was again alive in every part of my body, I sought my blankets once more, but the cold was too intense, and I could but say a few ejaculations and make a practical application of the fifth point of the meditation " De propriis peccatis ".

MARCH 19, SUNDAY. No mass of course; but after a crust of frozen bread and a few handfuls of snow in lieu of coffee, we strike out to the southward. After a couple of hours, our good angels led us on to the track of a lone huntsman who was already out with his rifle in search of fox or arctic hare. It was not long before we reached a little village of two houses, where we soon forgot the hardships of the previous day. Here, two little babies were waiting for the priest to make them children of our Heavenly Father. Here I came upon a new style of native dwelling: a low-roofed, miserable hovel about twelve feet square; in the centre, a pit about two-and-a-half feet deep, was the sink and dumping ground for the refuse of the house; there anyone had to descend who wanted to enjoy the privilege of standing erect. That is where I placed myself to perform the baptism of the latest arrival of the family whom the mother held on her lap, seated or rather squatted on the higher ground which served for a bed. We set out once more after dinner, and in about three hours we came to

Al'archarak, where only one family was then living: two mud huts, the roof partly caved in, were the only evidence of a larger number of people having once lived in that village. Here a seven-year-old boy, who had repeatedly been withheld from baptism by his father, was now permitted to receive that Sacrament, to the exceeding great joy of the little fellow, who seemed willing to jerk his head off in answering " Yes ", " I renounce ", " I believe ", " I wish it ", during the baptism ceremony. I named him Daniel Joseph. The house was a miserable dugout, about nine feet square. A small sheet-iron stove was set in the left-hand corner just behind the door; alongside of it, in the very centre of the dwelling, was a pool of water, the dump hole for the extra water from the kitchen utensils. A few sticks of brush were laid over that miniature pool; over that I spread my blankets, still moist from the preceding night's moonlight dew. My head was right up against the door, through the cracks of which the cool outside air was whistling its way into the interior. To protect myself, I put on my fur cap, and was soon asleep. The rest of the floor space had to serve for the inmates of the house and my guide. We were ten persons in that little dwelling. The next morning I said mass under the window or skylight which, according to the custom of the country, is set in the centre of the roof. The family was squatted right around; they could kneel, but could not stand up owing to the low roof. I myself could scarcely turn around for the " Dominus vobiscum ". Yet, as I found out many times later on that same trip, that was a comparatively comfortabe position in which to say mass. Many times since, I have said mass in places where I could not hold myself erect.

MARCH 20. After breakfast of rolled oats and tea, we set out to the southward again. Three and a half hours bring us to Kégetmint, a two or three house hamlet, where we had to stop over night, for the next village was too far for us to reach it that same day. Here, as in every place I visited, the morning and night prayers were recited in at least one house, the one I was staying in. Frequently, if I was physically fit to do it, I would go to the various houses in succession, and recite evening prayers aloud in the Eskimo language. No one ever joined in, for, except in the immediate vicinity of the mission, no one knows any prayers.

MARCH 21, TUESDAY. I got up at 3.30 A. M., and immediately prepared for my mass, which I celebrated on the family stove as an altar. Owing to the great ignorance of the family as regards the mass, and even the essentials of salvation, I thought it better to say the mass privately before the inmates would wake up; besides, we had to make an early start, and by insisting on material attendance at mass, I would lose at least one hour of precious time. I performed one baptism before leaving, and towards noon I passed by a village where I made another angel out of a poor mortal baby.

The whole of this day had a great geological interest for me. We were passing through a volcanic region. Everything being deeply set in the snow, we could not notice all the evidence of former volcanic activity, but there were several very plain, unmistakable crater-mouths rising not more than a couple of hundred feet above the plain. It looked as though there must have been here formerly a chain of mountains, every peak a volcano, and that some upheaval had caused a subsidence of the whole country round. This is not at all unlikely, as it is certain from the old traditions among the natives that the sea once covered this entire district, and from the formation of the ground it is evident that we are now living on a vast iceberg covered or overlaid with a layer of silt. Nowhere can we dig more than two or three feet, even at the height of summer, without striking solid ice or solid frozen ground. And any hole made beneath the surface will immediately fill with seepage water, up to the top. The tundra is, in reality, but little different from a swamp; it is overgrown with a thick layer of moss, its roots deep in the oozy, marshy soil, and when a person steps on it he will invariably sink down to the water beneath. The slope of the ground seems to have no effect in draining the soil, as the ice underneath prevents the surface water from soaking in, and the bog-like compactness of the surface soil holds the water wherever it may happen to gather.

In the afternoon our trail led us past several ledges of rock cropping out about six feet above the snow. As I had not seen a rock or a stone, nor even a small pebble since coming to Alaska, I could not resist the temptation to go and see what kind of rock that was. I found it like the volcanic rocks around Spokane, cellular, slaggy, scoriáceous lava. I chipped off a piece to keep as a specimen. Towards evening we sighted far ahead a slender column of smoke rising from the limitless field of snow about us: It was the so-called village of Nannaváronak. It consists of just one house; a flight of steps cut into the hard snow leading from the outside to an underground passage about two and a half feet wide and three feet high. I crawl along, dragging my baggage behind me till I come upon a pack of dogs that are curled up together, seeking protection from the cold. I know then that I am near the inner door of the dwelling. I grope along carefully, not to hurt the feelings of the animals, feel about for the grass mat that hangs over the entrance, push it aside with my head and shoulders, and make my appearance in the midst of the family, mute with astonishment and waiting for a few words from the intruder to reveal his identity. A warm " chamai l" (welcome) is given me when they find out the successor of Father Treca. A few sticks of green wood brought from many miles away are put into the stove, and we soon have a kettle of hot water, into which we throw a pinch of tea leaves. My guide and I take about one cup each, and the rest goes to regale the members of the family, who drink cup after cup till the supply of hot water in the house is exhausted. Here, too, a little baby was awaiting the saving waters of baptism. As usual, I teach the children how to bless themselves, make them and their parents recite a few prayers, and go to rest.

MARCH 22. Built up an altar out of some boxes, placed my suit case on top, and after ascertaining there was no danger of toppling over, I celebrated mass near the hot stove, in the centre of the house, under the skylight, water dripping all around me from the melted snow and frost around the window. Our trail to-day led over a most dreary waste, not a sign of life anywhere around. A cold north wind on our backs; the glaring sun in our eyes, causing the dogs to sweat, and depriving them of their strength; the sled runners sinking deep into the soft snow; no chance to sit down; it's walking all day. About noon we stop for lunch, squatted behind the sled, seeking shelter from the cold north wind. Early in the day we catch sight of the Tunúna Mountains on Vancouver Island, the end of our journey; two more days will bring us there. At Katwára-mint, where we arrived after a very tedious trip, one of our dogs went through the window of one of the two houses in the village. The wonder to me is that the accident did not happen oftener, for as the houses are buried under the snow, the roof is frequently on the level with the trail that we have to follow to reach the place. I myself have often been afraid of " dropping in " while making my visits to all the families of the villages I visited. Here I found about fifteen people, all claiming to have been baptised by our Fathers. An old man is pretty near the grave, judging from his age and a bad cold. I give him an instruction on the principal articles of the faith, prepare him for death as well as I can by stammering the little Eskimo that I know, and give him Extreme Unction.

MARCH 23. Six hours of travel on a cross-country road brought us to the next stopping place. About halfway we were met by Loska, the old friend of our first Fathers on the Bering Coast. With three sleds and three teams of dogs, he was going up to the Yukon to trade, and bring back flour and tea, which he had been without for several months. This meeting was a great disappointment to both of us, more so to me. For we had expected to revictual ourselves at Tunúna before starting back, and now it looked rather as though we might have to part with some of the scanty provisions that were still left in our sled. On our way, we stopped at a one-house village for dinner. A little six-months-old baby was there, and I was permitted to baptize it. Here, as in many other houses, the skylight was a block of clear ice fitted into the opening in the roof. The heat from within had hollowed out the block in the shape of a cone; a fresh block had already been prepared, and was ready to serve the purpose as soon as the other one would be melted through. Of course, you may readily imagine the condition of the floor within from the continual dripping of the melted ice: it was a pool of mud. These windows or skylights are usually made of the intestines of the seal or of the white whale, thoroughly dried and sewed together in strips. These diaphragms, though not transparent, are highly translucent, and transmit more light to every part of the house than several lateral windows usually do. At Kayaliuwigmint I performed five baptisms and went through the daily, ever-new routine of gathering the children together, teaching them the sign of the cross and a few short prayers, such as " My God, have mercy on me ", " I love thee ", " I am sorry for my sins ". If I could only succeed in inducing these poor people to pray thus every day, I am sure that many would find mercy before God; but few there are who pray at all. Oh! for the means to stay in one village for a couple of months at a time. Then, we might lay the foundation at least for a solid instruction in the elements of the faith; and after a few years the name of God and of our Blessed Redeemer would be in honor among them. For that we would need to have a house of our own so as to be independent of everybody, and so that we could freely preach to whoever would come to listen to us. That would mean quite an expense at the start, and also every year, to bring thither the needed provisions and furnishings to make the dwelling habitable.

MARCH 24, FRIDAY. This morning the weather is threatening, the sky overcast, snow falling lightly, the north wind blows and the snow is drifting. We start all the same, guided solely by our compass. We pass by two abandoned villages; the inhabitants have already gone to their spring camps on the seashore to hunt seal. We lunch in the shelter of one of them, and after a short run we come to the frozen sea. Here in places the trail is very rough; it requires a quick eye and strong muscle to keep the sled from turning over. We make another stop at the village of Niluluwára-mint, where I baptize a little child; and at 7.30 P. M. we reach the village of Tunúna, where several of our Fathers resided for a number of years, from the year 1889. The people here receive us with great jubilation, though taken somewhat aback at not seeing their old missionary, Father Treca. All hands got busy fixing up a little room for us in Loska's house; we have a warm supper of rice and fish, and having said night prayers in common, we go to sleep, with an "at home" feeling that we have not had since leaving the mission.

MARCH 25, FEAST OF THE ANNUNCIATION. Large attendance at mass, about thirty persons; but the people, having been without resident priest for twenty years, have forgotten their prayers. I announce confessions for the afternoon, and spend the rest of the morning instructing the children. Twenty confessions heard in the afternoon.

MARCH 26, THIRD SUNDAY IN LENT. Morning prayers before mass as usual, followed by the prayers in preparation for holy communion. Twenty communions! Deo Gratias! This is the only place on the coast where there are people admitted to holy communion, except, of course, in the villages near the mission. At ten o'clock I start for a visit of a couple of villages on the south coast of the island. I had only one baptism in the first one, but in the second I had the happiness of regenerating fifteen little ones, twelve girls and three boys. At this latter spring-village, Upnarkilramint, many people gather from far away inland to hunt the seal at the breaking-up of the ice. These amphibious animals remain, indeed, in the water the greater part of the time, but they frequently climb up on the ice blocks or ice floes and there remain for a long time, especially when the sun is shining. The huntsman, or, better, fisherman, in hiding behind some mound of ice or snow, has then a good chance to secure his prize, which he does by means of a rifle, or maybe with the more primitive weapon of a bow and arrow.

All the people in this village appeared to me very well disposed; all seemed very anxious to have their children baptised.

MARCH 27. After mass and instruction I returned to Tunúna over the mountain trail. Fortunately the sled was almost empty, otherwise it would have been impossible for the dogs to follow the steep trail. I caught a bad cold the day before, and so now I was not able to teach the children as I had planned to do. However, I managed to prepare a young couple for the wedding ceremony to take place the next morning.

MARCH 28. Mass at 5 o'clock. About 7 o'clock we are ready to start on our homeward journey. In spite of the fog and wind, we say farewell to the villagers all assembled to see us off, and are soon picking our way amid the many heavy blocks of rough ice that the west winds have crushed up against the shore of the island. A few minutes later we make a stop at a little hut built up on the steep slope, at the edge of the cliff, about 200 feet above the level of the sea. This is, really, in many respects, the poorest dwelling I have been in so far. It is only about eight feet square, and six or seven persons are living in it; the roof is so low that, small as I am, I can find no place where I can stand erect, so I have to sit down to confer baptism. The stove used by these poor people is an ordinary kettle or stew-pan, eight inches in diameter, turned upside down over two pieces of rock; a small hole has been punched through the upturned bottom of the pan, and a two-inch stove-pipe made of old pieces of tin roughly joined together leads the smoke up through the roof. The smoke-stack is just about three feet high. Like most native dwellings in this section, the floor is wet and soggy and filthy, for it is not only the dump for the fish skins and bones from the dinner dish, but it is also the family cuspidor. It is always a puzzle to find a place sufficiently free from grime and dirt in which to lay and spread out my baptismal outfit; hence it is not long before everything is soiled and needs renewal. Having finished the ceremony, I give the mother a " miraculous medal " on a blue string to hang around the child's neck. Then I must leave them a certificate of baptism with the name given by me to the baby. And the following year, when I come around again, they are pretty sure to pull that slip of paper out of some crack in the wall, and ask me to tell them again what the child's Christian name is. The task of writing out that little slip is not an easy one, and develops sometimes into a ludicrous and provoking performance. You begin by asking the baby's Indian name; nobody knows; they have not yet given him a name. You insist, saying that you must know it to write it in the certificate. Finally, after every old crony in the house has made her suggestion, a name is given which in all probability will soon be changed to another. Then you suggest a Christian name, with which they are usually satisfied. Next, you must find out the names of the parents. It is a funny sight to see the look of amazement on the father's face when you ask him his name. Sure, he " does not know ", meaning he " does not want to tell "; for all the natives on the coast are just ashamed to pronounce their own name aloud; so he asks some one of the bystanders to speak out his name, or maybe one of them volunteers of his own accord. It may be a toothless old woman or a fat-tongued young boy who thus constitutes himself an information bureau; no matter how indistinct their pronunciation of the name, you have to make the best of it and write it down phonetically the best way you can.

But I have made a long digression. We are only a couple of miles from Tunúna and we have about 200 or 250 more to make before we reach home. The fog is thick around the island; close to the shore the ice blocks are jammed together to a height of ten, twenty, sometimes thirty feet. Thinking he might gain time, my guide tries to round off the cape without hugging the shore, but soon we are at sea both literally and figuratively. It is evident that we are far out from land; for a few minutes the fog lifts, and with my glasses I descry some abandoned huts away off to the right; our trail should have led us alongside of them. The wisest plan would be to make straight for them; but the guide, along with many qualities that are good, has a stubborn head; he must attempt another short cut. It is no easy matter to keep one's bearing in a fog, unless one keeps his compass in his hand almost constantly. We keep zigzagging to the right and to the left, till finally, as the shades of night were about to hide from our gaze even the frozen waste on which we stood, we came upon a deserted cluster of huts. All are partly caved in save one. My guide lifts the trap-door from the window in the centre of the roof, lets himself down, and from the interior has soon burrowed a passage through the mound of snow that blocks the entrance. We have to crawl through this tunnel on our hands and knees, but we are thankful and fortunate to find such a good shelter. We fix ourselves quite comfortably, and after our usual supper of rice and canned meat, we say our night prayers and lie down to rest. A square block of hard snow is set over the entrance; so there is no danger of draft.

MARCH 29. Early the next morning I say mass, using my suit-case and the mess-box as an altar. Then I wake up my guide. We make an early start, taking a northeasterly direction. Soon we come upon a fresh trail, which we agree to follow. This decision made us lose four precious hours; for having followed it first one way, then the other, we found that the man was lost, and had slept the night before in the shelter of a drift of snow. We once more strike out for the northeast, and at nightfall we have the comfortable satisfaction of reaching Nrufkartule. Here I perform two baptisms, give the usual instructions in the catechism, prayers and singing, say night prayers, and go to sleep amidst a heap of fish, partly frozen, partly rotten. Early, before the family awakes, I say mass in the little corner that had been allotted to me for the night; I stack up my blankets, place my suit-case on top of them, say a fervent prayer to the Angels of the Eucharist to keep that improvised altar steady, and celebrate the holy sacrifice.

MARCH 30. We are ready for an early start, but the wind is cold, the snow is drifting. The villagers tell us it is not safe to venture out, so we spend a day here, resting up our dogs; and I profit by it to give a few more instructions on the essentials of the Faith. In the afternoon of this day, the man whose trail we had followed the day before arrived at the village, thoroughly exhausted. Though belonging to the next village, Kaialinwigmiut, he had lost his way going to Tunúna. He had slept twice outside, and only after the fog lifted was he able to take his bearings and retrace his steps.

MARCH 31. The soft, deep snow affords but a miserable trail: I walk the first three hours on snowshoes ahead of the dogs; the rest of the day I walk behind the sled, holding on to the handle-bars. I never thought I could have stood it so well. But I walked eleven hours without ever sitting down, except for a few minutes during which we stopped for lunch. At one time my foot broke through a crack in the snow, and seeing water in the hole, I stopped to taste it; it was salty. So then we had gone too far west. That was the conclusion I at least came to. After fruitlessly scanning the horizon for signs of a village, we were overtaken by darkness. Once more we had to spend the night in the open air. This time I constructed a scientific Pullman berth for myself. Selecting the leeward side of an ice block, I dug a trench in the snow, using the frying-pan as a shovel. I hewed out a pillow at the head, and made the grave (it looked indeed like one) about two feet wide and two feet deep, and my exact length. Stretching my cassock over it with the snowshoes as a supporting rack, I crawled into it, and passed a tolerably restful night, though I awoke a dozen of times from the violent coughing that had stuck to me since my stay in Tunúna.

APRIL 1, SATURDAY. No mass, of course. After several hours plodding along in a northwesterly direction, came upon a few sticks of driftwood sticking above the snow. We stopped, and my guide proceeded to break them up and build a fire to make a little tea. As for myself, I was so tired that I lay down on the top of the sled, and for a few minutes was sound asleep. Several cups of hot tea proved to be a welcome restorative to both of us; we set out feeling much refreshed, and soon struck a trail that led us to a little village of two or three houses. There being no children to baptize, we pushed right on to Kasúnok, which we reached four hours later, at seven o'clock in the evening. This is a large village of about a dozen houses and over 100 souls. Though most of them belong, nominally at least, to our Church, they are very backward in their knowledge of it. Here the Khazim, at once the club-house and city-hall of the village, is our hotel for the night. I go to sleep stretched on the elevated platform that corresponds to the first gallery of a modern auditorium. The Khazim is known to be the largest on the coast, and can accommodate a couple of hundred people. I remember hearing read in the refectory, during my novitiate days at Desmet, a description of this very Khazim from the pen of Father Barnum. This pen-picture has remained vividly impressed on my mind; and now that I found myself on the very spot, I took special pleasure and delight in verifying all its details. The entrance to the Khazim is through a hole in the ground about thirty feet away in what we might call the vestibule; you let yourself down or jump down through that opening, thence you crawl along the underground tunnel till you come to the exit, or better the ingress hole, in the centre of the floor of the Khazim. You bob up through that hole, place your hands on the walrus tusks which are set into the planks one on each side of the hole, and spring into the midst of the gathering without any ceremony whatever. A few words of salutation from you will evoke a warm welcome from all those who recognize you; for though they have seen but little of the Catholic priest, having met him but occasionally, they have learned to love and respect him.

What a pity that we have no missionary residing here! To many of these people we have not yet given a fair chance to know the Christian faith. An occasional visit, usually a hurried one in the course of a trip to a distant point, a few words of instruction about God, the necessity of salvation, the commandments of God, and the Apostles' Creed, that is all that they have received of the Gospel. But from one year to another, all those things would be forgotten. Yet with the exceedingly great difficulties of bringing provisions and other things to the missionary who would be thus isolated, one can readily see the well-nigh impossible task of imparting to these people a thorough knowledge of the Faith. Really the problem seems to baffle solution, unless we want to submit to a very great expense in money, and simultaneously to a lavishly generous supply of men knowing the language of the natives THOROUGHLY, and willing to bury themselves in this frozen, barren wilderness. The missionary should be well equipped with every material necessity, so that he would never have any money transaction or trade dealings with the natives. For experience has shown us here that the moment that the priest has to meddle with the material, his spiritual authority will wane. To some of our experienced old missionaries here, it also appears equally certain that even the making of gifts, be they food or clothing, is in the end prejudicial to the spiritual interests of the people, for the majority of them seem willing to submit to any hardship, to do anything, to secure a little donation; and thus the missionary can no longer be sure of their sincerity. To go no farther than this very mission of Akularak for an instance in point: no less than one mile away from here is a village in which there are about a dozen people admitted to communion. To encourage or better facilitate their attendance at the Holy Table the custom was started of giving them a piece of bread and a pinch of tea leaves after mass on Sunday so they would not be obliged to return fasting to their homes, and that they might remain for the second mass.

As we had strong reasons to suspect that their fervent attendance at weekly communion was due more to the piece of bread than to a spiritual motive, we stopped giving anything. The result has been: no communion, and sometimes no attendance at mass. It is really discouraging to see such things. After nearly thirty years which our Fathers have devoted to their instruction, trying to instil into their minds a proper appreciation of spiritual and heavenly things, there do not apear to be adequate returns for all that has been done. Of course I only speak of this district of Akularak, for I know nothing of other parts of Alaska. But again I have trespassed with my long digression. We are still at Kasunok, and I have unwittingly changed the scene to Akularak.

APRIL 2. As we had arrived late the night before, I postponed the conferring of baptism to the following morning. This naturally delayed our departure for Naporearamiut, or as we know it among ourselves Eskinok. This is by far the largest and most populous village of this entire coast. There are twenty-five houses and about 200 souls. Uncle Sam has established here a public school which he maintains at a very great expense. But we were not to reach our destination the day of our departure from Kasunok. When we reached the seashore, on the southern side of Hooper Bay, which we had to cross, we found ourselves confronted with an apparently impassable barrier of huge blocks of ice extending far out beyond the visible horizon. There was no question of circling around the bay by keeping on the mainland; that would have meant a good two days' journey. So we pushed ahead, making our way the best we could through that forest of icy pyramids. One of us went ahead, trying to pick out the easiest and least dangerous openings; the other held the sled, to keep it from upsetting. But many a time one runner would sink into the soft snow. The sled would then capsize or turn a somersault, and it would be a few minutes before the dogs would be once more on the go. When finally we emerged quit unexpectedly into a fairly clear field of ice, we took our bearings and headed northwest. That course was straight into the teeth of a cold wind which we had to face the rest of the day. Our dogs, worn out by the unusual and continual exertions of that day, soon began to give evidence of their exhaustion: some of them would throw themselves down and curl up as they do when sleeping, and would let themselves be dragged along. As we were expecting every moment to come in sight of the village, we forced them on, but night came on, a heavy fog began to settle on the bay. There was nothing better to do than to camp out for the fourth time during this trip. We gave to each dog its allowance of one dry smoked salmon; we threw everything out of the sled: and as there was no snow in which to dig a bed, nor blocks of ice behind which to seek shelter, we settled down in the sled itself, one at each end, but the wind found us out, for it had access to our blankets from every direction. We shook ourselves up early, and continuing our march in the same direction, we soon descried the little mound on which are clustered the houses of the village, and beyond them the tar-papered school-house.

APRIL 3. It took us about two hours more to reach the place. We received a noisy welcome from those dirty-faced, seal-oil-reeking Eskimos, all of whom at once accompanied us to the school-house. I got a hearty reception from the public-school teacher, the Rev. John S. Calkins, a Methodist clergyman, belonging to the Northern Montana Conference of that church. He and his wife made our stay in the village most pleasant. I had a package of mail from the States for them, which was the best sort of an introduction for me to have: but there was really no need of an introduction, for hospitality is one of the universally practised Alaskan virtues, especially when white people meet so far from the centres of civilized life. A holiday was at once called for the schools; he gave me the freedom of the place, and after a most appetizing warm breakfast, I found already waiting for me in the school-room an instruction class of more than fifty children, and a large number of adults. The afternoon was spent in making the rounds of the village and baptizing the babies born during the year. There were fourteen in all. The next morning I blessed the marriage of a young Christian couple. The morals of the village are at a rather low ebb: a large number of the girls attending school are married; some of them have changed husbands several times.

APRIL 4. I said mass at 5.30, which was well attended, after which I gave my usual instruction, teaching my hearers some ejaculations which, with God's infinite mercy, might suffice to bring their souls to salvation, if death were to overtake them. We were ready for an early start, but snow was falling heavily, and drifting under the force of a violent wind. A blizzard seemed to be brooding. We both had become decidedly timid about venturing out without a trail in this unknown waste in a thick fog. So we decided to wait till the next day. This permitted me to " take things in ". From what I saw and heard, I concluded that, though we are baptizing the children, they are growing up more like pagans or Methodists than Catholics.

APRIL 5. We were almost entirely out of provisions, and had still several days' journey ahead of us. The Rev. Calkins and his wife very generously revictualed us with bread, tea, rice, meat, etc. The only way I know of to show them my gratitude is to offer up prayers for them. I have done so many times since. *Retribuat eis Dominus!*

Passing a little village on the way, where I baptized an infant, we arrived in the evening at the camp of the reindeer herders at the foot of the Eskinok Mountains. The chief herder, a pupil of the Protestant School at Unalaklit, gave me a hindquarter of reindeer that he had just butchered. The herd of reindeer, 500 in number, had just been brought to the camp; I had thus a splendid opportunity to gratify my desire of seeing reindeer, for I had not yet seen any since coming to Alaska.

APRIL 6. A slow climb to the southern slope of the Eskinok Mountains, and a dangerous tumbling-down on the other side brought us to the house of a white man, whom the lure of the fur trade had kept in this wilderness for a number of years. He, too, adds some gifts to our stock of provisions, besides making me a present of a pair of water boots. I was in great need of them, for the snow had now become very soft, and the heat of the foot was sufficient to melt it, so that the sealskin boots would soon become thoroughly soaked. Later in the day when the temperature falls, the boots freeze stiff, and one may suffer greatly from the results of keeping these boots on for a long time. In the afternoon we reached the village of Kotmiut. From there on till we reached the mission, two days later, there were no incidents worth mentioning: we were twelve hours on the go the first day, and on April 8, the last day of our long trip of twenty days, we travelled thirteen hours without more than a few minutes' stop for lunch. The dogs were all exhausted, but they knew they were near home and bore up well under the strain.

Your Reverence may wonder what I think about during those long hours of travelling in a perfect wilderness. Well, I just try not to lose my time; I say my Rosary, during which I invariably recite several hundred Hail Marys. The Holy Names and a few of the more familiar ejaculations frequently repeated help to keep the mind from wandering about. But travelling in a sled is not like riding in a railway car. You can never relax your attention. If you are behind the sled, you have to guide it, keep it steady: if you are riding on it, you must be ready for a shock or a jerk any minute; just when you least expect it one of the runners may hit a chunk of ice, and the sled may upset or you may be thrown off. So you must hold yourself on and be ready to hang on firmly at the critical moment.

On the evening of Saturday, April 8, we reached the mission, to the great relief of every one, for they were beginning to think we had met with some accident. Never before had the Tunúna trip taken so long. This was due in great measure to the exhausted condition of our team of dogs: we walked practically the whole distance back from Tunúna, about 250 miles. So we said a heartfelt *Deo Gratias* when we reached home again. During this trip I performed fifty-six baptisms, blessed two marriages, gave one Extreme Unction, heard twenty-three confessions, and gave twenty-five communions. Apart from the number of baptisms, you see, Reverend Father Provincial, how little, comparatively, a missionary can do in these long, laborious and expensive winter trips. Many times, indeed, ere coming to Alaska, have I, in one single afternoon, done, outwardly at least, more spiritual work than I did during these twenty-five days of hardship, except, as I said, the number of baptisms. But that very excess of baptisms and its disproportion to the other spiritual ministrations is the very thing that betrays the meagre results of our missionary exertions up to this time. As long as we are allowed to baptize the new-born infants, no priest can have the heart to refuse to confer the sacrament; the very child that would be denied that grace might be the one to die that year before the priest makes his rounds again. We tell the people that no one can enter heaven without baptism: as none of them want to be excluded from that blissful place, they have all, or mostly all, submitted to the rite of baptism; but therein lies the danger, that they may think it is sufficient to be baptized in order to be saved. And if we tell them it is not enough, that does not help matters unless we can impart to them the necessary instruction about their faith and their duties.

Now, the difficulty of instructing these people, as Christians should be instructed, is one that baffles solution, at least according to our present means and method. Let me suppose for a minute that your Reverence has been granted a vacation from your arduous duties and that you are accompanying one of us here in Akularak on one of our missionary excursions. You arrive at a village at nightfall; it will take over an hour before you can refresh yourself with a cup of tea and a warm supper. You feel you were in great need of it, for since your breakfast early this morning at some far-off village you have had only a piece of frozen bread or frozen crackers, with a slice of frozen meat (maybe), and a cup of tea from your thermo-vacuum bottle. Well, while you are eating supper the entire village may come, one by one, to watch your appetite. The children, used to their frugal fare of smoked fish, are wistfully watching the bread, the rice or beans, the butter which you and your Eskimo guide (this latter especially) are fast putting out of sight. You know that to these poor children of the Arctic a slice of bread mean much more enjoyment than a handful of chocolate candy does to a white child; but you have to steel your heart against the strong instinct of giving at once a slice to each: at the most, all you can prudently afford is to give them the broken pieces and crumbs when your guide is through eating. You cannot carry bread enough for everybody, nor can you be a walking bakery.

Very little work can be done before bedtime. If you have a great facility in the use of Eskimo, you may tell the inmates of the house about the purpose of God in creating them and what they must do to be saved. But, first of all, you should try to give them some notion of the real nature of God, for their concept of the Supreme Being is of the grossest and most grotesque nature. Their minds are exceedingly limited in their capacity, far more so probably than that of the negro in Africa. Their constant, daily fare of fish does not seem to produce a large quantity of gray matter in their brains. So you must look out lest you give them more than *one* idea at a time. And you have to repeat your brief instruction many times over before you feel certain that you are properly understood. The next day, after Mass—let us suppose you are able to stay at least one day—you devote entirely to spiritual work around the village. Early in the morning, perhaps even before Mass, the men have gone out to visit their fish-traps, out in the lakes and creeks within many miles around; or maybe they have gone out for a sled load of brushwood (in some instances they have to go five or ten miles for green brush); or maybe they have gone to make the rounds of their traps for wild animals, fox, mink, lynx, squirrel, muskrat, wolf, wolverine, bear; or again, maybe they have gone out hunting for some of those animals, or for rabbit, arctic hare, or ptarmigan. At any rate, they will probably be back only late in the afternoon. So the women and the children and a few old men alone remain. At about 11 o'clock the many little chores about an Eskimo house are about done, and maybe you can interest the people in their souls. But where are you going to gather them? If you find a house big enough, the chances are that the occupants of it are not popular in the village, and the rest would rather go to some one else's house. Or maybe some of them are at loggerheads with the rest, and will not go to anybody else's house. This, however, is not so much of a difficulty as to find a house large enough to accommodate your hearers, for every house is usually barely sufficiently large to afford comfortable elbow room to the members of the household. When the men are back from the wild prairie in the afternoon or evening, the same difficulty is greatly increased. If the houses were too small for the women alone, how can there be room enough for the men in addition to the women? But maybe the Khazim is the proper place to try and hold your instruction classes in? Sometimes it may be decent enough, but any one who has tried it, or any one who is personally acquainted with the details of life in the Khazim, will tell you of a hundred difficulties besetting such an undertaking. It would be just about as easy to secure an attentive audience on Market Street, in front of the ferry, as to expect to be listened to during the day in the Khazim in an Eskimo village, except occasionally. In the evening, at what hour you can never tell, things are a little better; but in the winter there is a dance ever so often, and if one has been arranged for the day you happen to arrive in the village, or for the day on which you intend to give an instruction, you simply have to give up your plan. So the day has passed, and in spite of all your good will you feel you have done but little. Had you a house of your own, those more interested would no doubt linger around, even when others would go to their pleasure, and you might thus sow a few more grains of good seed. You would be free at all hours of the day, not depending upon the domestic program of any particular family, nor upon the whimsical appointments of the promoters of the dances in the Khazim. Of course, it would take quite a sum of money to have in each village a log house built that would shelter you from the Alaskan cold. There is no timber here, you must rely upon the driftwood that comes down from the Upper Yukon. After you have built the house, you must be ready to transport it elsewhere the following year. Since my coming here, a little over a year ago, several villages have been abandoned, and new ones have been built. Two villages were comparatively large a few years ago and a building (house and church all in one) was put up in each place. Now both villages are insignificant.

There are, however, some villages that have stood for many years in the same place; they are the most important of those on the coast. Such are Naporearamiut and Kasunok. If we could stay a few months every year in each of those villages, we might form a nucleus or centre of Christian life which, if once solidly established, might exert a salutary influence over the whole district. Anyway, the past twenty-seven years that are and ought to be recorded as years of heroic self-sacrifice and whole-hearted devotedness to the salvation of these poor people have taught us a lesson. Many a child is now in heaven as a result of our Fathers' labors. Since 1889, about 2,600 baptisms have been conferred, including adults. Of these latter, quite a few have been prepared for death. But of those still living, how few that have any other mark of Christianity than their baptism! I doubt if there is any family where the night prayers are said in common.

And yet, very great difficulties stand in the way of imparting a lasting, solid Christian spirit to these poor, miserable, scattered people, eking out a wretched existence on the surface of an iceberg. Undoubtedly, God in His infinite compassion will not require much of them, but *we* nevertheless have to save them.

But perhaps the school will transform the face of the country? It certainly must do good, and it does it. But how exceedingly slow is the process! For the time and effort there are not as yet, in my judgment, adequate returns. To found thoroughly Christian families we should have the boys, as well as the girls, under our training till they can settle down together in married life. But these people want their boys to stay with them; at the most, *some* of them will let their boys stay with us two or three years, and then they take them away. They come to us as children, they leave us when they are still children. There is very little strength of character in these Coast Eskimos.

They are indeed far from the sturdy, independent, lofty nature of the old-time Rocky Mountain Indians. So, when our school children return home, into a practically pagan atmosphere, into surroundings of nominal Christians, but still addicted to many of their vain pagan practices, they soon find their ideals hard to live up to. In those crowded houses, where family common prayers are unknown, the children will soon neglect their own prayers, lie down on their pallet, and say them under their blankets, then maybe leave them off altogether. The priest cannot visit the villages often enough to keep up the courage of the school children, and so it happens almost invariably that the girls will be given away by their parents on a trial marriage, according to the old custom. Many of them will thus have had several husbands before they are of the legal marriageable age of sixteen. This is the inevitable result of our not being able to keep the girls till they are of age and a suitable suitor presents himself.

But we could never hope to see a school of that kind out on this barren coast. We could *never* have a big school of boys, nor a school of big boys, for we would have *no work for the boys* in winter, except chopping wood and hauling water for the use of the school; that work is insignificant. In summer, *one* man is able to attend to the fishing; a real garden there cannot be as long as we live *in* a swamp or morass or *on* an iceberg, which must necessarily be the case out here on the coast. Now it is plain that we could have no good school for boys unless there is steady work for them. But even if our school boys and school girls should intermarry, we cannot have them in a Christian village. No such village exists. We would have to build one ourselves. Where could we build it? On this coast we are in the wilderness, with nothing here to supply a village with the necessities of life. If we want our boys and girls to settle around a mission, we would have to support them, for there would be nothing for them to do except to go out and track fox or mink. But they cannot make their living thus. The supply of game and even of fish is so uncertain and so limited, at least some years, that the Eskimo is compelled to establish himself far out and away from any one else, so he will have a large hunting ground, and also a great number of lakes, sloughs and little rivers whence to get his winter fish, for very few seldom get enough salmon in the summer to keep them for the whole year.

The supply of fish is a vital question on the coast. For the last two years we have had to *buy* most of it. The Akularak River is such an out-of-the-way slough of the Yukon that very frequently all the fish go into other channels. Up the Yukon river, at Holy Cross for instance, they can catch fresh fish all through the winter under the ice; here, partly on account of the tide from the sea, partly owing to our location, neither net nor trap is practical under the ice. If the fishing should be a failure, we should face a famine. Up the Yukon the danger of the fishing being a failure is far more remote.

The supply of wood is an equally vital question in a place so cold as this one. We have to keep all the stoves going day and night during several months. Now, for our fuel supply we depend upon the spring floods to fetch down from the upper Yukon the driftwood we need. Our Brothers have to go with four or five natives, and only in about eight or ten days will they return with a raft of logs. They must go a second and probably a third time. It does not seem at all impossible that some years the amount of driftwood will be so limited as to compel us to go and cut green brush for fuel.

As fish, so also game is sometimes very scarce. This year, for instance, there are no rabbits, no hare, no ptarmigan. Now, if we have to depend upon canned foodstuffs one may readily see the enormous expense that will be thereby entailed.

Such a school could never be self-supporting. For farming and even gardening can never be conducted on a large scale. After nearly twenty years we have not yet succeeded in raising potatoes. Only a few small turnips and rutabagas. And these few we can with great difficulty keep from freezing. We can have no cellar; we might as well try to build one inside a block of ice. In summer it would be all water; in winter it would be all ice and frost. Just a fact bearing on the cellar. For several weeks the mosquitoes are so numerous and so ferocious that our dogs are howling night and day, without our having any means to bring them relief. In some other parts of Alaska the dogs seek refuge in a hole which they dig themselves in the ground. Here they cannot scratch an inch into the ground without bringing the water to the surface.

During the thaw in spring, and before the freeze-up in fall, the ground is nothing but mud in the play-yard; and the tundra is, as usual, a swamp. Thus, for more than two months, there is no outdoor recreation possible for the children. For there is no footwear sufficiently waterproof and mudproof, and at those two seasons it is usually too cold for them to go barefooted. It is hard, indeed, to have a really good school with all these drawbacks, especially a school for boys.

When will this letter reach your Reverence? We are about 175 miles away from our nearest postoffice, St. Michael's. The Yukon, where the mail passes once a month in winter, is about eighty miles from here. At the break-up in spring, and before the freeze-up in the fall, we are sometimes one month, sometimes two months without being able to send or receive mail. Of course, we are usually two, sometimes four, months behind time with news from the States, but personally I am far from considering that a serious drawback.

Well, dear Father Provincial, I think that I have to beg

your indulgence for having inflicted such a long letter upon you. I have written its various parts at long intervals, frequently forgetting what I had already written. Hence there is likely to be some repetition. I dare say you will not have the courage to attempt the reading of it a second time. I have tried to be frank, but as I realize more and more the tremendous odds against which our Fathers have had to struggle, I cannot but admire their heroism, and I am forced to utter a prayer that I may imitate the heroic virtues of those that have preceded me.

Hoping for a visit from your Reverence, and begging your blessing as well as a frequent memento in your prayers and holy sacrifices, I remain,

Your Reverence's most devoted *in Corde Jesu,*

PHILIP I. DELON, S.J.

AN OLD FRONTIER OF FRANCE[1]

BY REV. FRANCIS P. SIEGFRIED

Science has long been studying the Niagara River. Rolling with tremendous impetuosity and unparalleled plunging and leaping the outpourings of four inland seas into the fifth, which sends the immense aggregate along the swift-flowing St. Lawrence onwards to the Atlantic, it is unique among the world's waterways. Mechanical science has weighed and measured the mighty mass of its waters and can tell in figures fairly exact of the millions of tons that hurl themselves every moment into the awful abyss of the mightiest of cataracts; while mechanical art has seized the irresistible energy of the falling flood and brought it into orderly obedience to the service of human industry. Having wrung from the heart of the river the secret of the physical power latent in its swirling waters, science has been striving to win from it the story of its past. By the records which the stream has wrought in its rocky bed and in the mountainous walls through which in the lapse of ages it has ground its channel, geologists are fairly certain that at one time, in the dimly distant past, the river, with no intervening whirlpool, made its final plunge at about the present brink of Lake Ontario, and that the giant cataract has ever since been receding year by year towards Lake Erie with whose margin it must eventually coincide. They have measured the average annual rate of this retrogressive progress, and have hit upon the inference that probably seventy hundreds of years have been consumed in the process. This, however, is rather a guess than a conclusion, since the turbulent waters refuse to have their labor measured by the exacting standards of man's industry.

[1] *An Old Frontier of France.* The Niagara Region and Adjacent Lakes under French Control. By Frank H. Severance, author of *Old Trails on the Niagara Frontier, Studies of the Niagara Frontier, The Story of Joncaire.* 2 Vols., XVII-476, XI-485. Dodd, Mead & Company, New York. 1917.

But through the long ages of its physical history what events more mysterious than the corroding of rocks were enacted upon the banks of the mysterious river? Centuries probably before the paleface looked upon this wonder of the world, had not the red man of the wilderness peered into the chasm or sped his bark canoe across the lower reaches of the river? Tribes and nations of the aborigines hurled themselves one against the other, the stronger pushing the weaker into the yawning abyss, while the shouts and cries of the battling savages and the whirrings of their deadly arrows were heard above the thunders of the cataract. For history, always a palimpsest, is never more so than in annals of the region adjacent to the Niagara. Since here, as the author of the present volume reminds us, " beneath the records of our race are dimly seen those of alien early folk whose story in its last days is involved with that of the white man, and in its more ancient periods recedes through imperfect records, through legend and myth, until it grows illegible on the parchment of time, lost in the realm of the undiscoverable " (I, p. 21).

The story of Niagara, not so much the river as the country through which it flows, and the lake region with the contiguous territory, is told in these splendid volumes whose impressive outer form is an expressive symbol of their inner worth and interest.

The Niagara Region was an old frontier of New France. A thoroughfare which linked the French settlements on the St. Lawrence with those on Lake Huron, its paths and trails were continuous with the old routes that led southwards through the valley of the Ohio and the Mississippi down to the Gulf of Mexico. The importance, therefore, from a national and economic point of view of the Niagara country cannot be over-estimated. It is not surprisng consequently that for a century and a half France and England wrangled and fought for the mastery of a territory so vital to all the interests of both nations. Nor ought it be difficult to decide to which of the two the region in justice belonged. For if priority of discovery be a title to occupancy, the French had certainly the stronger claim, since their *voyageurs* passed through the region and were engaged in trade with the Indians, and, above all, were civilizing and converting them to Christianity long before the advent of the British, who, when they did come, came not as explorers and civilizers, but either simply as traders or as warriors to dispossess by force their commercial rivals.

The first white man known to have voyaged on any of the Great Lakes was Champlain, who skirted the shores of Georgian Bay and crossed Lake Ontario. There is a strong probability, however, that he was preceded on Lake Ontario by Etienne Brulé, the guide and interpreter of Champlain. Brulé probably saw the mouth of the Niagara if not the Falls, and crossing the western end of Lake Ontario, journeyed through western New York five years before the Pilgrim Fathers landed on Plymouth Rock.

Moreover, it was this " pioneer of pioneers ", as Parkman calls him, who brought back to the Huron Missions word of the *Neuter* Nations inhabiting the Niagara peninsula—and thus led to the first visit to these wilds of a Christian missionary, the Franciscan Joseph de la Roche Dallion.

It was in October, 1626, as Mr. Severance tells us from the documents, that the Recollet friar set out from the Franciscan mission in the Huron country with two French companions, Grenolle and Lavallee, and journeyed by Indian paths six days through the forest, apparently skirting the western end of Lake Ontario and coming to the Niagara at or near its mouth. He was, therefore, within earshot of the thundering waters, but whether he turned aside to visit the falls, history does not say. Probably he did not, as the missionary was interested more in the souls of the savages than in the beauties or sublimities of nature. Mr. Severance, giving the story of Dallion's experiences, quotes the priest's own letter to a friend. He was cordially received at the various villages of the Neuters, and at one time he told the assemblage " that I came on behalf of the French, to contract alliance and friendship with them, and to invite them to come to trade. . . . They accepted all my offers, and showed me that they were very agreeable. . . . I made them a present of what little I had, as little knives and other trifles. . . . In return, they adopted me, as they say,—that is, they declared me a citizen and child of the country, and gave me in trust—mark of great affection—to Souharissen, who was my father and host." " This name, or title, of the worthy savage is the first designation in history of any individual resident in our region; and the simple barter between his people and the priest was for this region the beginning of recorded trade " (p. 15).

After Dallion, there seems to be no record of any white man's presence on Lake Erie or Ontario, or on the Niagara, until November, 1640, when two Jesuit priests from the Huron Mission came into the territory where Dallion had so devotedly labored fourteen years before. These were the missionaries Jean de Brebeuf and Joseph Marie Chamonot. Brebeuf speaks but briefly of their experience in the region, and Chamonot apparently not at all. " Self-effacement," says Mr. Severance, " characterized them both " (p. 18). Father Lallemont, completing their " Relations ", mentions " the celebrated river Onguiaahra (Niagara)," and the advantages which would accrue from the possession of the adjacent region through which passed the two routes,—one on the west, the other on the east of the river,—from Lake Ontario to Huronia. So that in this Relation of Lallement we have " the first recognition and statement of the desirability of French control over the region of the Niagara and the Lower Lakes. All unconsciously, a gentle priest, consecrated to the service of the Prince of Peace, had struck the keynote of a call to strife which was to be waged for more than a century to come " (p. 19).

Father Hennepin is usually credited with the white man's discovery of the falls. He certainly was on the river with La Salle in 1678, and ardent lover of nature as he was, he could not have refrained from visiting the cataract the thunders of which he must have heard below the rapids where he and his companions anchored their vessel and passed three days in building a store-house and palisade—the first white man's structure on the Niagara.

In his *Nouvelle Decouverte* Father Hennepin gives a long account of his revisiting the falls, where he " spent half a day in considering the wonders of that prodigious Cascade ". Perhaps it was this prolonged wonderment that led him to estimate their height as more than 600 feet, and to see back of the falling waters space " big enough for four coaches to drive abreast without being wet "; " and other equally edifying observations ", as our author subjoins. Mr. Severance is a bit severe at times on Father Hennepin. He probably does not make sufficient allowance for this enthusiastic traveler whose exaggerations are to be taken rather as signs qualitative of the big things he saw in this New World than as quantitative measurements of their spatial dimensions.

The storm centre of the international strife lay at the mouth of the river where the French, despite much protesting on the part of the English, erected Fort Niagara. Could the deep waters of the stream and the lake, which here intermingle, reflect the scenes and events that were enacted on the banks above them, what a picture they would present!

A veritable long-drawn-out tragedy it all is—a story of worldly ambitions, national hates and strifes, and battlings in which the savage Indians were enlisted now on one, now on the other side, according as the French *eau de vie* or the English and Dutch rum proved to be the more enticing

stimulant. Disease and gaunt hunger sometimes stole in
beyond the bastions and wrought havoc greater than that
which followed the bullets and arrows of the Iroquois. Mr.
Severance has told the story in a style almost dramatic.
Drawing his material from the original documents he has
woven the facts into a splendid fabric — a tapestry which,
while omitting none of the essential and few apparently of
the incidental factors, presents the whole with the freshness
and vividness of life. The story of Niagara in his pages
moves before the eye of the imagination as though it were
a pageant of yesterday. Especially is this the case with the
closing scenes of the drama — the disastrous finale to
France's tragic career in the Niagara region. One must go
to Ivanhoe to find a description equally vivid and thrilling.
It is the siege of the famous castle *sans* Rebecca.

While, however, the dominant note of the whole drama
of French life at Fort Niagara is mainly tragic, Mr. Severance is keen enough to discern here and there a rift in the
cloud where the sunshine of smiles breaks through the be-
clouding tears. One such an episode in which the tragedy
is relieved by a vein of comedy occurs in the interchange
of letters between Dongan, the English Governor of New
York, and Denonville, the commandant at the Fort which
bore his name on the Niagara, and which antedated the
more famous rendezvous of New France. Dongan had
been sent in 1683 by the British Crown to be the Governor
of New York. Prior to his coming the importance of
Niagara, either as a strategic point or as a trading centre,
seems not to have attracted the attention of either the English or the Dutch. Dongan, however, was not slow to discern this double advantage of the region, and accordingly
he opened a correspondence with the French commandant
at Niagara. There is a certain piquancy characterizing
these letters that may justify our quoting passages from
some of them in the context given to them by Mr. Severance.

Dongan fitted out two expeditions to trade with the Western Indians, one under the Dutch leader Rooseboom, the other under " a Scotch gent named McGregor ". Both passed over the Niagara portage and across Lake Erie to the Huron country, where they exchanged to advantage their wares and fire-water for Indian peltries. Both expeditions, however, on their return journey fell into the hands of the French and were made prisoners. For the time being British influence over the motley horde of Indians at the mouth of the Niagara ceased. It would be interesting, did the limits of this paper permit, to show how English ascendancy was regained and how thereby the French power in the Niagara region was eventually destroyed and New France in 1759 passed completely under British domination.

But to revert to the correspondence between Dongan and Denonville. It began with marked formality and courtesy, but soon each was accusing the other of bad faith and duplicity. The chief bone of contention was the right to trade with the Wetern tribes.

" What with the work of the missionaries, of La Salle and his companions, the French had come to look upon the Great Lakes as their own. Dongan, caring only for the region because of the beaver trade, ignored and denied these sweeping claims. He knew something of La Salle's operations on the Niagara. Now, early in 1686 word came to him by a deserter from Canada that the French proposed to establish themselves there once more; whereupon he wrote from Albany, May 22, to Denonville:

" ' I am informed that you are intended to build a fort at a place called Oh niagero (Niagara) on this side of the lake within my Master's territorys without question (I cannot beleev it) that a person that has your reputation in the world would follow the steps of Mons. Labarr, and be ill advised . . . to make disturbance . . . for a little peltree.'

" Denonville replied that the deserter's story—from which

Dongan had learned of the prospective fort at Niagara—
was 'devoid of all foundation', yet wanted it understood
that the region in question was indisputably under French
control. 'Certainly you are not well informed', he wrote,
'of all the entries into possession (*prises de possessions*)
which have been made in the name of the King my Master,
and of the establishments of long standing which we have
on the land and on the lakes; and as I have no doubt our
Masters will easily agree among themselves. . . . I will-
ingly consent with you that their Majesties regulate the
limits among themselves, wishing nothing more than to live
with you in good understanding; but to that end, sir, it
would be very *a propos* that a gentleman, so worthy as you,
should not grant protection to all the rogues, vagabonds,,
and thieves who desert and seek refuge with you, and who,
to acquire some merit with you, believe they cannot do
better than to tell you many impertinances of us, which will
have no end so long as you listen to them.'

" Dongan was not the man to let such an observation pass
without retort. He did more: he fitted out an Engish expedition and sent it up the Lakes after furs. ' It is the first
known appearance on these Lakes of any white men save
in French interest.' This was the expedition headed by
Rooseboom, the disastrous result of which we mentioned
above. Naturally enough after this failure, Dongan's temper was not likely to be any the sweeter, nor ' his correspondence with Denonville any the less forceful'. Both
gentlemen were Catholics, and the French Governor had
counted on this unity of faith for some co-operation, at
least in matters pertaining to the spiritual welfare of the
savages; but Dongan, good Catholic as he was, was ever
alert for the interests of his own king and colony. Moreover, he had the Irish gift of wit. When Denonville in-
dignantly wrote, ' Think you, Sir, that Religion will make
any progress whilst your merchants will supply, as they do,

eau de vie, in abundance, which, as you ought to know, converts the savages into demons and their cabins into counterparts and theatres of Hell ', Dongan blandly replied, ' Certainly our Rum doth as little hurt as your Brandy, and in the opinion of Christians is much more wholesome '. In due time—nor was it long, for news spread fast even in those days—Denonville learned of this English invasion. Reporting it to the Minister, Seignelay, he urged the construction of a strong French post at Niagara, to put a stop to further English expeditions " (pp. 95-97).

Thus was occasioned the construction of the famous fort which became the centre whence radiated thereafter so much activity, commercial and militant as well as religious.

It will not be necessary nor feasible to draw further upon these pages. The reader who is interested in the struggles between France and England for the mastery of the Lake region will be amply repaid for perusing these two weighty volumes. Mr. Severance treats the whole subject with an impartial hand. He metes out equal justice to both sides. Nor is this sense of justice restricted to matters national or political. It embraces no less the religious activities of the French. The heroic devotedness of the Catholic missionaries, and their service to the cause of civilization as well as religion are never slurred over nor minimized. On the contrary, they receive the measure of prominence and of praise to which they are so justly entitled. In this connection, by the way, we might call attention to the oversight in giving the title *Abbé* to Fenelon, the illustrious Archbishop of Cambrai (p. 24).

A special feature of the work is the attention given to the history of the Joncaire family which exercised so potent an influence in the latter period of French control. The author has made original research into the career of these remarkable personages, and has woven the results of his studies into the present narrative.

SAN DOMINGO REFUGEES IN PHILADELPHIA

COMPILED FROM THE ORIGINAL D'ORLIC–RODRIGUE PAPERS BY JANE CAMPBELL

(*Continued*)

In November, 1833, the car in which Dr. Aristide was journeying from Amboy met with a distressing accident, one man being killed and a number of others being badly injured, Dr. Aristide himself being among the number. His heroism on the occasion has been recorded by Tyrone Power, the famous Irish actor, in his *Impressions of America in 1833, 1834 and 1835*. The Doctor had two ribs broken, yet unselfishly assisted others before attending to his own injuries.

On Friday, November 8th, 1833, Mr. Power records in his journal that in traveling on that day an accident took place on the cars between Amboy and Bordentown.

" Out of twenty-four only one had escaped unhurt. One man was dead, another dying, five others had fractures more or less severe. . . . Never were sufferers more patient. One of them was a surgeon, a fine young fellow, who immediately set about doing the best his skill could accomplish for those most desperately hurt. D——n and I volunteered as his assistants, and with such splints as the shattered panels of the carriage supplied, the fractured limbs were bound up.

It was a melancholy task, but this gallant fellow stuck to it until he saw such of his patients as it was possible to remove, disposed of in one of the baggage cars, which had been cleared for this purpose. I had in the course of the task frequently observed him pause as though either faint, or finding some difficulty in the act of stooping, which was constantly required, but it was not until he had seen the last of his fellow sufferers disposed of to his best ability, that he examined his own condition, when it was discovered that two of his ribs were broken."

Extract from a letter from Dr. Jackson:

> NORTHUMBERLAND,
> TUESDAY NIGHT, *Nov. 13.*

My Dear Miss Rodrigue:

It was not without the sincerest grief that I read your letter of Friday, however great our reason for rejoicing and thankfulness. . . . Tho' the words " in haste " were indorsed on your letter I did not receive it till this afternoon, the unkind P. M. having neglected to send it to me.

I went immediately to see our dear friend Ann . . . I ventured to promise her that a broken rib was no very serious affair and that mere bruises were soon relieved. May this be true of my dear Doctor! Give our love to him. I hope he will be patient, thankful and obedient to his good physician's regimen.

I pray you or Evelina or Wm. to write to me immediately on the rect of this. If he is better, it will be a great comfort to us, if he is worse we ought to share in his afflictions.

I pray you present our sincere regards to your father, sister and brother.

> Your very affectionate friend
> & obt humble servt
> S. JACKSON.

Letter from Dr. Aristide Rodrigue to his sisters:

> SUNBURY, *Jan. 15, 1834.*

. . . I was suffering much from my shoulder and which is still very painful, between you and me I blame a good deal our good friend the Doct. for not cupping or leeching my shoulder in due time. I have done it twice since I've returned home & it is the only thing from which I have found relief. I got good Paddy John a rubbing it, as he calls it with comphorated spirits for a long time, but it was all in vain. I suffer at times a good deal of pain and am never without any. . . . I do not apprehend any ill consequences, time will remedy all. . . . I think I shall ever feel the effects of my accident, though it will not disable me or shorten my life any, the injury I think is in my shoulder joint, indeed I am certain of it. . . . John is a good, honest trusty fellow, I have the utmost confidence in him, he has engaged to remain with me for five years, he will return to Ireland to see his friends and then come back to me, he seems determined to stick to me, whether I will or not and I am every day more pleased with him. He is a full blooded Irishman, makes a good many bulls but no blunders, he takes good care of my horse and everything else, and withal is a perfect specimen of economy, on which he lectures me every day & I surely begin to give in to his lessons, for I find the necessity of it. No danger of his being spoiled by the people, for he does not like them, he is always at home and cannot be persuaded to associate with the people. . . . Go to Folwell's hat store on Chestnut near 3rd street, a few doors above 3, right hand side going down and ask him how long it takes to dress otter skins & whether they are fit to make a muff.

Your brother,

ARISTIDE.

Letter from Dr. Aristide Rodrigue to his sister:

June 7, 1834.

My Dear Sister Evelina:

. . . I wish you to collect all the Catholic tracts you may have as Mr. Chambers whom you saw a short time since has sounded the Tocsin against Roman Catholics in this Country. I, a few days since at the public table after a discussion on Religion, challenged him to meet me in a controversy either orally or in writing. This he shirked from, as I have already so frequently convicted him of error, falsehood and misrepresentations, he commenced the attack. Many persons have been present when what I have said above, has taken place; he is a double-faced fellow as ever lived, he is now distributing the most infamous tracts against our Religion, but he shall not escape without some exposure. Will you ask Rev. Mr. Hughes for a copy of a little agreement I gave him, which I made with Mr. Chambers by which he binds himself to prove that the same doctrines now taught by the Episcopal church are identically the same as those taught by the Church at Jerusalem, and that he can prove a regular succession from it. Tell him to keep the original and send me a copy. Rev. Mr. Levy took him in at Lewistown, when he first went there, showed him all kinds of friendship and attentions & now he turns against those who treated him well and abuses their Religion, he there circulated a tract holding forth that the Catholics give to sick hens & dogs & horses the Eucharist etc. Tell Aline she not be afraid that I shall trust too implicitly in Mr. Porter, I have smoked him long ago. I know full well the character and dispositions of those Manchester cotton spinners, & that she is very much mistaken when she says I was all English, when I was down last, whatever my dress may have been my feelings and principles never change, it is an injustice she does me in saying so, she could not have said anything more disagreeable to me.

Your brother,

ARISTIDE.

P. S. The Bishop is at Clearfield, I go there tomorrow. Monday, he is my guest at Philipsburg & I intend to ask him to preach here, I hope he will.[1]

Extract from a letter written by Miss Evelina Rodrigue to her father:

[1] "June the ninth day (1834) I delivered a sermon in the town of Philipsburg, in a house which is for the use of any of the sects. Nearly all my hearers were protestants, for aside from Doctor Rodriguez (Rodrigue?) and one or perhaps two women, there is hardly a man in the place who has the name of being Catholic." *Bishop Kenrick's Diary and Visitation Records,* p. 99.

Mon cher Papa:

Here we are about 15 miles from Sunbury with the prospect of getting there some time or other. There was a break in the canal a day or two since, which is the cause of our getting forward so slowly. The water is so shallow that we must wait until some more comes down.

Who do you think was in the omnibus with us? [car, I should have said]. Why, Mr. and Mrs. Nancrede, Mr. and Mrs. Tiernan, Father Gartland and John Savage. We parted with them at Lancaster with the exception of J. S. who went as far as Harrisburg. He was very polite. When we got to Harrisburg, I found that my trunk was missing, both he and Mr. Pleasants went in search of it and the farmer found it in one of the taverns.

I am very tired but perfectly well, and you can be certain that I have arrived safely at Sunbury, when you receive this as I will not have an opportunity of sending it before we arrive there.

The reasons for my writing on such paper is that this is the only sheet on board and I must either take this or do without. The sparks were so numerous and large that one man's baggage got on fire. . . . I have got two small holes burnt in the front breadth of my habit and many in my veil. We had either to burn or smother so we tried alternately which we liked best.

Mr. Gartland wanted to know if I was alone when we stopped at Lancaster, he bought me some cakes. I got very little sleep last night, each lock we came to awakened me, then we had a cross baby that cried much. Then we ran up against a boat which gave us a delightful jolt. When we crossed the river in the middle of the night I was almost certain that there was something amiss, for I have heard so much of water-spouts and freshets that I thought for certain there must be something amiss.

I suppose you will find some difficulty in reading this, but as Ann K. would say I cannot spell because my pen is so bad, and the writing because my brains are so muddled—every now and then we give such a nice jolt and that causes me to give such a nice flourish. . . . .

Ta soumise fille

EVELINE.

This letter was partly in French, partly in English. Dr. Aristide Rodrigue, to whom she was paying a visit at Sunbury, added a few lines to his father, announcing her safe arrival. The letter was dated June 27th, postmarked June 28th, was received, as noted by Mr. André Rodrigue on the back of the letter, on June 30th, and the postage was 12½ cents. No year is given. Probably the visit was made in 1833 or 1834, or in 1837 or 1838, as Dr. Aristide was living in Sunbury during those years.

Letter from J. H. Hopkins to William Rodrigue:

NEW YORK, *June 23, 1834.*

Dear Sir:

You may remember your intention to go over the Camden and Amboy Rail Road with me. I hope you may find it convenient to do so.

I shall leave this place on Thursday morning in the early line and stop at Amboy for a portion of a day and I shall proceed thence to Philadelphia leisurely so as to arrive there Friday evening or Saturday morning.

Yours very truly,

J. H. HOPKINS.

WILLIAM RODRIGUE,
    C. Engineer.

This same year, 1834, William Rodrigue was in Canada, his professional duties having called him thither, and charming letters were sent by him to his family, in spite of the assertion he made so frequently that he had not the " bump of letter-writing ". It may be noticed in the letter that Rev. John Hughes was often spoken of as " Uncle ".

Extract from a letter written by William Rodrigue to his sisters:

MOULINIT, *July 8, 1834.*

. . . " So you seem to have had a collection for the Poles, and uncle beat Brekenbridge all to smash. Give my best respects to him and tell him to let me know how he is. . . . We have about 6 miles from here a Church where I go on Sundays. It is a Settlement of Highland Scotch, they preach there in Gaelic. There are a good many Catholics back at a place called St. Raphael. There is a church there which it is said covers nearly an acre of ground. There are a great many Indians about here, and all Catholics, several villages of them, one near here called St. Regis, where I intend to go to church, they are very nice and quite pious. After I've been there I will give you an account. Some time ago some Yankeys went there to church and did not behave well and the Indians turned them out in great style. They are very decent people." . . .

Your brother and friend,

W. RODRIGUE.

Extract from a letter from William Rodrigue to his sister Aline :

MOULINIT, *Nov. 26, 1834.*

" I intended to give you a description of St. Regis, but have no time. You would have been pleased to see the Indians in church. They are all Catholics and have a good church. They all wear the Indian dress, and have over their dress a sort of cloak. The women keep their heads and faces covered, so that no person can see them, they are on one side of the church, and the men on the other and sing in Indian, sometimes the men and sometimes the women. They have grand ceremonies. They allow the ladies to sit below, but men that come there are obliged to go upstairs. Some of them are quite good looking but the women are so modest that you have scarce any chance to see them. The congregation is the most orderly that I have ever seen and every body that comes there has to kneel down."

. . . I hope soon to hear from you. Remember me to Mr. Hughes and all our friends & you need not expect to hear often from me for I have to work all day and as late as nine o'clock at night.

I kiss you with all my heart.

Your brother & friend,

W. RODRIGUE.

Letter from Louis Dietz to André Rodrigue:

MONTREAL, *2 June 1834.*

Dr Sir:

With the Liberty of your Son, who is just now at my house, and whose acquaintanceship is not forgotten as yet, tho' I am a stranger to yourself.   The undersigned take the liberty of making a few enquiries of you and hopes to see your answer soon as the writer of this is ready to start for old Europe with his family on or about the 16th of July prox.

The enquiry alluded to is respecting Rudolph Dietz who always was together with Lasseuv (?) Is he alive? Or if dead what does his wife do?   Hath she the children with her? Is his step son returned from St. Thomas?   Your answer of this [as you must know that the said R. Dietz is my uncle & I have not seen him for 14 years, but am well acquainted with his wife] will forever oblige Dr. Sir

Your obt st

LOUIS DIETZ.

(Postmarked Burlington, June 5, Vermont.)

Extract from letter from William Rodrigue to his sister Eveline:

KINGSTON, *16 Feb. 1835.*

. . . Tell uncle and Mr. Frenaye to look out how they improve St. John's for if they don't look out, I'll come tumbling down on them like a storm.   I suppose they have heard that I have been elected an Elder of the Church and that Bishop McDonald . . . says he will not let me go back.   I'm very much pleased to hear that the orphans are getting so well on. No doubt Mr. Hughes must be very much pleased.   I think

Mr. Frenaye is beginning very soon to get things ready. I hope he has engaged the Hall, as he may be disappointed. I wrote Papa few days ago to let him know that Mr. Mills is going to Philadelphia and that he intends to go to our house. I hope you will receive him well, and not say anything against Presbyterians. He is a great temperance man and very strict about Sunday. I wish you to take him some Sunday to St. John and show him the church. . . .

Your brother & friend,

W. RODRIGUE.

In 1835, on February 8th, Dr. Aristide Rodrigue was married to Anne Caroline Bellas, of Sunbury, Pennsylvania. It is probably in this same year that Aline and Margaret Hughes visited Dr. Aristide, who had been ill. The letters have no year mentioned and the postmarks only give the months and days.

Letter to Evelina, postmarked Harrisburg, July 19. No year given.

SATURDAY AFTERNOON,
MOST-TEA-TIME.

My Dear Sis.

I wish I had room to give you an account of our voyage. First, I decidedly prefer travelling by night. Second never give me Canal Boat until I am so ill that there would be no other way of taking me home, so as to be buried under my little tree in my dear Uncle's garden. I was near having ten thousand fits. I would say " Mag, look at that prospect! " About an hour after " Mag, do you think we have travelled fast? Look, there is that same, very same prospect still."

When I got near the landing about twelve miles from here, some person told me Aristide was very low. You may judge how I felt when I got there, not enough stages to convey the passengers. Mag and I scrambled, Mr. Gratz pushed Mag toward the stage, another pushed me. The one who pushed me did not know Mag was with me, he pushed her away. In the meantime some one else got in, but at last we succeeded and thought ourselves off. Some altercation took place with a stubborn-headed Northumberlander and the agent said the stage should not start with that man. We were wheeled under a bridge there to wait till the man got down. You may judge my suspense after being told Aristide was so low. I said if a Frenchman or an Irishman were up there, he would be tumbled over in a very little while, but finding we had waited nearly an hour, I got so distressed that I began to cry most gallantly. However at last we got off, the agent got the passengers fixed and off we started. Tell papa that I do not know if it is my love for the "ancien regime," but I would rather travel fifty miles in a stage than twenty in a canal boat. The punishment of Tantale never beat it.

Mag sends her love and says she has packed her cranium full of Aunt Judy stories for you. By the by she has got a Presbyterian Parson for a beau.

Give my love to Mary, M. A. Elizabeth, Anna and all inquiring friends. Poor Joe! I wish I knew how she is. If you see Mrs. Blight give my love to her. Remember me to Uncle, Mr. Frenaye, Mr. Gartland, what a host crowd in my mind when I think of home. I can scarcely realize the distance I am, at no more fatigue than if I had stayed at home.

Last night, although I had not slept at all the night before, I stayed up ever so long with Caro and Eliza. Mag went to bed rather earlier. She had walked out with Eliza but I would not. Aristide and Caroline send their love. Do not forget Mrs. Hughes, remember me kindly to her and to Mr. Hughes.

Aristide was much pleased with Dr. Harnor's letter. Thank him and give my respects. Tell him I had some quinine made, but it is not like his prescription in taste, and Aristide could not help laughing at my spitting it out so quick.

I must close for want of room and it would be too much postage.

Your Sis,

ALINE.

Letter from Aline to Evelina:

HARRISBURG, *July 20.*

Dear Evelina:

Mag and I fancied this morning we could see you enjoying a good sermon from our good Uncle. When we took our solitary walk after all the Churches were in, to our little Church to say our prayers,—Oh! what a difference between the faith of the Catholics and the others who go from one to the other just as they would go from one shop to another to seek what they think the best preaching. It was pleasing to us, even lonely as it was, to go and read over our Mass before the Blessed Sacrament, that was there and was dear to us. I feel thankful for the blessing I enjoy at having it in our power to hear Mass every Sunday.

When I saw the Altar lonely, no Sacrifice, no music, save every now and then the low murmur which was occasioned by the raising of the voice from time to time, of those who were joining to the best of their power in the Holy Sacrifice offered at a distance for all. Oh! what a religion is ours! As I looked towards the Tabernacle, and felt that my Saviour was there, truly then I felt a feeling of awe which contrasted with what I saw on my return in passing one of the Protestant churches. There they stood turning their backs to the preacher, with that icy coldness, which was only excelled by the coldness of him who seemed to be the teacher. Can it be that they think such cold devotion enough for a God of so much love! Every day makes me more and more thankful for the blessing of being a Catholic.

May I close my eyes, long long before I forget my faith, or even become cold and tepid in its practice. How much my dear Sister I could write to you all but time will not permit, the post will close. I have not even time to read it over. Beg papa to excuse me, if there are mistakes. I am writing in such a hurry. I put off writing so late in hopes to have an opportunity.

Give my love to all, all, particularly my dear Uncle, how is he? Tell him not to forget me in his prayers, and Frenaye too, I think I see the good soul. Father Gartland, bless him, I wish he had been here to say Mass for us. All send their love.

Your affectionate Sister,

ALINE.

Dr. Aristide was now contemplating settling in Pittsburgh.

Letter from Rev. John O'Reilly:

PITTSBURGH, *August 10th, 1835.*

My Dear Friend:

Yours of the 6th ins. received this morning and I lose no time to comply with your request. My opinion is that at this time there would be a good prospect for a good Catholic physician here. There is not one in or about the city at present, and with a population of five thousand English Catholics besides two thousand Germans, there is little doubt of success. It is true we have had already some Catholic doctors, who have failed and been obliged to retire, but I am confident their failure was from themselves.

In a city like this however there may be some difficulty in the beginning for a new physician. It will require some time before he will be able to secure the confidence of the people. This is done only by strict attention to professional duty, and integrity of character, in either of which I could have no apprehension for your brother.

There are several physicians here, but I cannot say there are any of great eminence. All I can promise is that should he think it his interest to make trial, I shall be his friend and as such I wish always to be considered by your amiable family.

Very Respectfully,

JNO. O'REILLY.

Bishop Kenrick has been here these two weeks. He is in excellent health. Tomorrow I am to accompany him to some of his country missions. Pray that we may be enabled to triumph over the enemies of the faith, who are indeed both numerous and powerful.[2]

> Kind regards to you etc.

> > J. O'R.

Letter from Doctor Aristide Rodrigue to his sister:

> > SUNBURY, Sep. 6, *1835.*

My Dear Sister Aline:

I arrived here a few days since from Pittsburgh, having travelled both ways by stages which perform the journey much sooner though much more fatiguing as no sleep can be obtained.   I arrived in Pittsburgh from Philadelphia on Thursday morning week.   After delivering all my letters but one or two and obtaining the result of my enquiry I returned to Sunbury with an old friend whom I had not seen for perhaps 12 or 14 years, one Mr. Ague who has given me a pretty tolerable welcome in a most unchristian shaking.   Finding his presence rather disagreeable I called upon his enemy Master Quinine, who though much younger than he, will teach him better manners, however don't trouble yourself about it, as I only get it every other day, and most likely will not have it tomorrow.   From all appearances I don't like Pittsburgh at all.   I do not intend to let its dirt and smoke prevent me from accepting, so far as I can perceive the best chance I have yet had of establishing myself.   Every one but two have strongly advised me to come and I have not the slightest doubt but that they will make considerable exertions for me.   I have been informed that the Trustee's of Mr. Riley's Church have passed an unanimous resolution to invite & encourage me. . . . The city is rapidly increasing, from 800 to 1000 new houses are building this year. . . . I think it undoubtedly an excellent situation though a very disagreeable one.   I found several persons who knew my father, besides Messrs. Bounet and Baand, a Mr. Beelen, Mrs. Fetterman's father, knew me from resemblance to him; he says he was well acquainted with him, as well as several others.

> Your brother,

> > ARISTIDE.

[2] See *Diary and Visitation Records,* p. 116 1 sqq.

> (*To be continued.*)

BISHOP FLAGET'S DIARY

BY REV. W. J. HOWLETT

(Continued)

MAY.

Friday, May 1. — Heard confessions the greater part of the day. Weather stormy, rainy, gloomy. Extremely important letter to Mr. B——n. God speed and bless it! T. relaxation. S. A. P. D. M.

Saturday, May 2. — Confessions part of the morning. Visit to a sick woman, 24 miles. Rain all day. From bad to worse with Mr. XX. A. D. E. O. D. F. M. C. V. S. V.

Sunday, May 3.—Weather rainy and very gloomy. The bad weather and the unfavorable disposition of my body and mind prevented me from going to Holy Mary's. I was very sorry for it. Confessions, mass, till noon. T. P. F. A. D. S. A. P. D. M.

Monday, May 4.—No guide to conduct me to Mr. Steve Hayden's. All day at St. Stephen's. Read, study. Fine weather,—wind. T. L. P. F. D. S. L.

Tuesday, May 5. — White frost; fire very agreeable. Traveled 3 miles. Alone at St. Stephen's; frequent thoughts about Mr. XX. Return towards dinner time; preparations for Thursday. R. P. F. D. D'E. P. P. V. S.

Wednesday, May 6.—Very fine weather; a little cool for the season. Retreat at St. Stephen's. Great difficulties to settle. Lord, come to my help! P. P. F.

Thursday, May 7.—Twelve hours running of ministry; God be praised! Weather a little mixed; my head and my heart are also. Tribulations and consolations go together. Oh, how good is the God Whom I serve! R. P. S. A. P. D. M.

Friday, May 8.—Confessions till 10 o'clock A. M. Tête-a-tête with Mr. XX. Situation too painful for a sensitive heart. He came to confession; I heard him. Weather rainy and very gloomy. G. R. D. G. F. D. S. L.

Saturday, May 9.—Very stormy weather; thunder; more and more rain. Hardly any confessions. Study; frequent thoughts on the affair that occupies me. Often I make acts of humility. S. A. P. D. M.

Sunday, May 10. — To St. Charles,—7 miles. Confessions, sermon, mass, till 3 o'clock P. M. To Holy Mary's, —8 miles. Rain, bad weather. R. P. F. D. D'E. S. A. P. D. M.

Monday, May 11. — Confessions, mass, sermon, till one o'clock P. M. T. heaviness of body and soul. R. P. F. Frequent acts of the love of God and of the neighbor. Frequent thoughts of XX. Confessions all the evening. R. S. D. S. L.

Tuesday, May 12.—From Holy Mary's to St. Stephen's, —14 miles. Confessions till 11 o'clock. Fine weather. Received a letter from Mr. Bruté, one from Mr. Chabrat. G. R. and G. C. traveling. D. S. L.

Wednesday, May 13.—From St. Thomas' to Bardstown; package of letters; $5 postage,—6 miles. Talk with Mr. David. Letters of Mr. Oliv. Demun to answer. Leo is going to quit the seminary. T. P. P. F.

Thursday, May 14.—From St. Thomas' to St. Stephen's, —10 miles. Interview with Mr. Chabrat; always kind. Visit of the energumen; doubts upon all that one may give to the subject. Arrival of Mr. XX. Nothing new. R. P. D. S. L.

Friday, May 15.—To St. Rose'; Mr. B—n accompanied me; very good friends exteriorly. He has not yet answered me; I do not expect any concessions on his part. T. E. R. P. F.

Saturday, May 16.—Confessions, mass, or prayer in the church nearly all day. Weather rainy and dark. R. P. D. S. L.

Sunday, May 17. — Confessions, confirmation, instructions nearly all day. R. P. S. A. P. D. M. (Pentecost.)

Monday, May 18. — Ten miles. Confessions, confirmation, till 2 o'clock. T. P. C. L. Ch. S. A. P. D. M. Rain, storm.

Tuesday, May 19. — Rain, storm; a few confessions. Visit the energumens. Nothing decisive. S. F. 3 miles. R. P. F. D. S. L.

Wednesday, May 20. — Confessions a part of the forenoon; weather cool for the season. Arrival of Messrs. David and Chabrat. Agreeable conversation. D. D. E. S. A. P. D. M.

Thursday, May 21. — Synod; present Messrs. Badin, David, Chabrat, Wilson, Fenwick, Flynn. Less important than the first. Headache; visit the energumens; nothing decisive. P. P. T. S. A. P. D. M.

Friday, May 22. — Confessions a part of the day at the house of the father of the energumens, where I said mass. 18 miles; rain part of the day. R. P. T. D. S. L.

Saturday, May 23.—Confessions a part of the morning. Interesting conversation with Mr. Nerinckx. Beautiful weather. T. D. P. F. G. F. G. C.

Sunday, May 24. — Confessions most all day. Fine weather; cool in the forenoon. Sadness, but I do not know why. S. A. P. D. M. J. M. J. (Trinity.)

Monday, May 25.—Not many confessions. Visit of two hours by the greatest of bores. Wrote letters; visited a sick woman,—3 miles. Good weather. R. P. J. V. R. S. A. P. D. M.

Tuesday, May 26.—Weather rainy and stormy. Confessions a part of the day. Et. R. P. S. D'E. A. P. D. M. S.

Wednesday, May 27.—Very stormy and rainy weather. Confessions almost all day. Violent headache. 6 miles. R. P. S. D. E. D. S. L.

Thursday, May 28.—Confessions all the morning; confirmation. Pontifical mass; Mr. David preached, I spoke, and also did Mr. Badin. The ceremony lasted until 3 o'clock; weather stormy all the evening. 9 miles. R. P. T. D. S. L. (Corpus Christi.)

Friday, May 29. — Visit to sick. Weather warm and close. Confessions the rest of the day. 16 miles. R. S. P. D. C^r. D. S. A. J. L.

Saturday, May 30. — Weather very warm and day very close. Confessions until 11 o'clock. G. R. G. F. D. B. A. P. D. M.

Sunday, May 31.—Visit a sick woman, 5 miles. Confessions, instructions, confirmation, mass till 3 o'clock P. M. To Mr. S. Hayden's, 10 miles. Very fine weather. R. S. M. M. D.

JUNE.

Monday, June 1. — Confessions, instructions, catechism, mass, till one o'clock P. M. The evening for writing, reading and resting. Weather very fine and very hot. R. P. F. M. P. F. V. M. M. D.

Tuesday, June 2. — From Mr. St. Hayden's to Mr. Ch. Hill's,—18 miles. Visited a sick woman on the way. Met Mr. Angier and Mr. Fenwick. Fine weather; warm. R. D. D. S. D. M. M. D.

Wednesday, June 3.—Went 11 miles. Spent most of the day with Mr. Dant. Slept at Mr. Burch's. Long conversation with Mr. David. R. P. P. S. P. P. T.

Thursday, June 4.—From Mr. Burch's to Mr. Vessell's, then to St. Stephen's,—18 miles. Visited Mr. Brothers,—5 miles; head worn out. D. S. L. T. C. L. S. V. D. P. S. S.

Friday, June 5. — Confessions, visits to sick, nearly all day,—6 miles. Fine weather,—heat. G. T. C. L. S. P. J. N. P. V. C. J. D. E. P. R. P. S. D. S. L.

Saturday, June 6. — Confessions from half-past four till ten o'clock A. M. Left at 11 o'clock for Holy Mary's. Conf. at St. Charles'; conf. at Holy Mary's till half-past eight P. M. R. D. P. D. S. L. 14 miles.

Sunday, June 7. — Confessions, instructions, mass, the whole day from half-past four A. M. to eight P. M., except an hour and a half. Fine weather; thunder but no rain. G. C. F. D. C. E.'D. E. G. S. R. D.

Monday, June 8.—Confessions till 11 o'clock. Returned to St. Stephen's, 14 miles. Fine weather, great heat. Re. C. P. F. D°. A. V. S. P. M.

Tuesday, June 9.—Visit the sick. Went to St. Thomas', —10 miles. fine, but great heat. G. T. C. L. S. V. D. P. S. D. H. Oh. D. A. P. D. M.

Wednesday, June 10. — Retreat at St. Thomas'. Wrote letters, passed my time heavily because of the heat. M. P. C. L. S. V. D. P. R. P. F. S. D. N. D. S. L.

Thursday, June 11. — Today posted a letter to Mr. Du-Bois; Dimissorials for Father Urbain, Mr. Dechevigne, Romeuf and Chanche.

Friday, June 12.—Confessions a great part of the morning. After dinner I visited the girls of the school,—6 miles. Received at last the letter of Mr. B—n. Not satisfactory. Weather hot. D. E. A. D'E.

Saturday, June 13. — Mass at Mr. Livers' for the poor energumens. Confessions till eleven o'clock A. M. Confessions after dinner. Weather dark. Gr. A. D'E. P. C. L. C. R. P. F. D. S. L.

Sunday, June 14. — Confessions, mass, instructions, till two o'clock. Went to the seminary,—12 miles. Weather hot and overcast. Mr. David does not wish to receive Leo. R. Fr. P. C. P. C. M. Bn. R.

Monday, June 15.—Twenty-six miles. Considerable rain. T. F. against the heat. R. P. F. S. A. P. D. M.

Tuesday, June 16. — Confessions. All day given to the ministry. Conv. R. P. F. P. A. D. E. S. P. P. M.

Wednesday, June 17.—Confessions, visits to the sick till noon. Return to St. Stephen's,—14 miles. Weather very stormy, warm. T. C. L. Ch. E. P. L. R. S. A. P. D. M.

Thursday, June 18. — Cool weather. All day at St. Stephen's. Letter to Mr. B—n, also to M^de. Stuart. R. P. D. F. S. A. P. D. M.

Friday, June 19.—Confessions part of the day. Business visit, 3 miles. Weather heavy and stormy. Study, conversation with Mr. Nerinckx. P. R. S. D. D. D. S. L.

Saturday, June 20. — Confessions all the morning. Weather stormy. Visits of importance. Passable interview with Mr. B—n. R. S. D. P. D.

Sunday, June 21. — Confessions, mass, sermon, until 2 o'clock P. M. Started for Mr. James Dant's,—9 miles. S. D. P. G. C. D. S. L.

Monday, June 22. — Confessions, mass, sermon, till 2 o'clock P. M. Stormy weather, head heavy. R. P. F. P. C. L. Ch. P. M. S.

Tuesday, June 23.—Mass, confessions, visits to sick till 1 o'clock. Went to seminary,—10 miles. Weather stormy, thunder, rain. R. S. S. A. P. D. M.

Wednesday, June 24.—From the seminary to Bardstown, —5 miles; weather warm with a little rain. Visit from Mr. Gwynn. Talked with Dr. H. upon the subject of the energumens; he thinks that the children are playing a part. D. D'E. S. S. L.

Thursday, June 25.—Returned to the seminary, where I said mass. Went to St. Stephen's, 13 miles. Visited Mr. Brothers. Spoke to Mrs. Harris about baptizing her children. Fine weather. Spoke to Mr. B—n; no answer to my last letter. R. P. D. S. L. 14 miles—hot weather.

Friday, June 26.—Employed all day at St. Charles. Violent colic during two hours. Dined at six o'clock. D. D'E. S. P. M.

Saturday, June 27.—All day at confessions. Said mass at St. Charles. 14 miles; hot weather. R. S. S. A. P. D. M.

Sunday, June 28.—Confessions till noon. Four short in--

structions, and a long procession; confirmation and communion of the children. G. S. D. P. P. F. Afterwards T. D'E. S. A. P. D. M.

Monday, June 29.—Rain, thunder from early morning. A few confessions. Wrote letters. Arrival of Mr. B—n; complaints about the marriage of F. B—ch. (vague), to tell the truth. R. P. F. C. D. S. S. M. 2 miles.

Tuesday, June 30.—Very cool. No answer to my letters. Mr. XX. treats me very lightly. Administered a sick woman, — 6 miles. Received an answer contrary to my views. God be praised! Went to Mr. Hayden's,—10 miles. P. C. L. C. E. P. L. R. S. A. P. D. M.

JULY.

Wednesday, July 1.—Confessions, instructions, mass, till one o'clock. In the evening to Mr. Quirk's, — 3 miles. Pretty warm. In the forenoon had a disagreeable talk with Mr. B—n. P. F. C. L. C. D. S. L.

Thursday, July 2.—Day of consolation. Confessions, instructions till 12 o'clock; 28 communions. Visit a sick woman,—3 miles. From there to St. Stephen's,—7 miles R. C. Visit a sick man,—3 miles. Great heat. D. S. L.

Friday, July 3. — Letter to Mr. XX. Reconciliation is from the heart, God knows. Humiliation on my part. O my God, I accept it. Very warm. Went to Holy Mary's; confessions all the evening. 13 miles.

Saturday, July 4.—Confessions during 12 hours. Storm, heat. R. P. C. L. Ch. S. A. P. D. M.

Sunday, July 5.—Confessions, instructions until 3 o'clock P. M. Great heat. Storm, considerable thunder. R. P. D. O. P. D. D. S. L.

Monday, July 6. — Went to Casey's Creek,—19 miles. Rain, thunder. A few confessions. D. D'E. C. D. L. R. D. S. L.

Tuesday, July 7. — Confessions, instructions, procession

until half-past two P. M.   Return to Holy Mary's, — 19 miles.   Very warm.   D. D'E. T. C. L. Cti. P. S. A. P. D. M.

Wednesday, July 8. — Visit a sick man.   Return to St. Stephen's, — 20 miles.   Weather very warm, and very stormy.   Letter to Mr. David; another to Mr. B—n.   R. P. I. T. C. L. P. D. S. L.

Thursday, July 9.—Visit several sick,—5 miles.   Thunder, intense heat; heaviness of body and spirit.   R. P. F. T. F. C. L. P. D. S. L.

Friday, July 10.—Administered a young man.   Confessions all the morning.   Baptized in the afternoon 3 children of a Protestant.   12 miles,—very warm.   R. P. F. P. C. A. L. P. D. D. S. D. S. A. P. D. M.

Saturday, July 11.—Administered a young girl.   Confessions all the morning, and a part of the afternoon.   Conversed with a deist, but without converting him I reduced him to silence.   Weather stormy, thunder, pretty hot.   R. S. D. S. L.   5 miles.

Sunday, July 12.—Divine services at Holy Cross.   Confessions all the morning.   Thunder; pretty warm.   Visit a sick woman.   Went to Mr. McAtee's,—18 miles.   Thunder, heat excessive, rain.   Heaviness of body and spirit. s. a. p. d. m.

Monday, July 13.—Confessions, instructions till 2 o'clock. Pretty hot.   Visited a sick woman.   Went to the seminary, —15 miles.   R. S. S. A. P. D. M.

Tuesday, July 14.—All day at the seminary.   Talked with Mr. David on the affair of Mr. B—n.   He approves my position.   D. S. L. R. P. F.   Thunder, storm, rain, heat.

Wednesday, July 15. — Visit a sick woman, — 3 miles. Intense heat.   Went to spend the night at Mr. Gwynn's,—5 miles.   Reflections upon the affair of Mr. XX.   P. F. C. L. Ch. C. P. L. C. D. S. L.

Thursday, July 16.—Returned to the seminary.   Headache, sore throat, etc.   Very hot,—5 miles.   Wrote letters, read, etc.   R. P. F. D. D. S. D. S. A. P. D. M.

Friday, July 17. — Confessions at St. Joseph's a great part of the day. Took dinner with Mr. Saunders. Visits; letter of exchange; Mr. Hite, Protestant. Returned to St. Thomas',—5 miles. D. D'E. R. P. F. O. D. A. P. D. M.

Saturday, July 18. — Returned to St. Joseph's, 5 miles. Confessions all the morning; preached. Dined at Mr. Gwynn's at 4 P. M. Office read with Mr. Chabrat; fatigued; great heat. R. S. D. D. D. S. L.

Sunday, July 19. — At. St. Joseph's till three o'clock. Confirmation with great solemnity. Great crowd present. Mr. David preached. Very hot; storm in the evening. Returned to the seminary,—7 miles. P. R. Vte. P. F. S. A. P. D. M.

Monday, July 20. — Agreeable weather. Retreat at the seminary. Wrote four letters. R. P. D. S. L.

Tuesday, July 21. — Fine weather, cool, close after dinner. Retreat at the seminary. Study. R. P. F. S. A. P. D. M.

Wednesday, July 22.—Fine weather, cool; retreat at the seminary. R. P. D. S. L.

Thursday, July 23.—Started at St. Michael's,—14 miles. Dinner at Mr. Gwynn's; visited a sick man. Pretty warm. Arrived at Mr. Gardiner's; confessions. R. P. D. S. A. P. D. M. Fine weather.

Friday, July 24. — Confessions a part of the morning. Mr. Chabrat is doing wonders. He has the confidence of all. D. S. L.

Saturday, July 25.—Confessions a part of the morning. Visited the Elder family. R. P. D. D. S. D. Weather warm, dry.

Sunday, July 26. — Confessions all the morning. Mr. David preached with much force. First communion, and then confirmation. I baptized a young woman. I saw Miss Murphy, neophyte. Great spiritual joy. S. J. V. R.

Monday, July 27.—Returned to St. Thomas',—14 miles.

Passed the afternoon in retreat. Pretty warm. R. S. D. D'E. S. A. P. D. M.

Tuesday, July 28.—Started to St. Stephen's; visited Lucy Davis, Mr. Livers. Great rejoicing at home. Very hot. Di. Con. P. C. L.

Wednesday, July 29.—Confessions in the morning. Letters to Mr. B—n; interesting talk with Mr. Nerinckx. Pretty hot. R. P. F. D. S. L.

Thursday, July 30.—22 miles. Visited the ladies of St. Charles; went to St. Thomas'; a few harsh words with Mr. David; prompt reconciliation. Pretty warm. R. P. F. D. S. L.

Friday, July 31.—Started for Bullitt County; dinner with Mr. Gwynn; visited Mr. Miles. 14 miles. R. P. T. D. D'E. T. C. L. Ch. D. S. L.   Hot weather.

AUGUST.

Saturday, August 1.—Terrible storm all night. Confessions a great part of the morning. Consolation to see the fruits produced by Mr. Chabrat. Reports against Mr. XX; he B. A. E. Tn. E. L. Ch. S. A. P. D. M.

Sunday, August 2.—Confessions, mass, preaching, confirmation, church to build. Very extraordinary crowd. Mr. David preached magnificently. Fine cool weather. P. R. D. S. L.

Monday, August 3.—Started to the seminary,—17 miles. Hardly arrived when called to the sick, 10 miles. Fine weather. P. R. T. C. D. Ch. S. A. P. D. M.

Tuesday, August 4. — The morning to write, sleep and suffer. Storm after dinner. Went to Mr. Dant's,—9 miles. P. F. C. M. XX. E. D'E. V. D. S. A. P. D. V. S.

Wednesday, August 5. — Confessions, mass, sermon, till 3 o'clock P. M. Received a letter from XX. A. D'E. Efforts to unite myself to God. Thunder, rain. P. F. C. L. Ch. D. D. P. A. D. D. S. L.

Thursday, August 6.—Visit a sick man,—2 miles. Returned to St. Stephen's, 7 miles. Met Mr. B—n; friendly salute. Fine weather. R. Pte. S. A. P. D. M.

Friday, August 7.—Confessions, mass, till 2 o'clock P. M. Visit a sick woman till 7. Storm, thunder, rain. P. T. C. M. XX. E. P. L. R. O. J. A. P. D. M.

Saturday, August 8.—Confessions, mass, till one P. M. Received visits until 4 o'clock. Started to St. Rose'. Thunder. P. F. C. M. XX. E. P. L. R. S. A. P. D. M.

Sunday, August 9.—Rainy weather. Confirmation, mass, sermon, till 2 P. M. Dined with the Fathers. Left for St. Stephen's,—9 miles. R. S. Con. C. Mr. B. E. P. R?. L. V. D. S. L.

Monday, August 10.—Stormy weather, thunder and rain. Transport of my effects to St. Thomas'. L. C. C. M. K. E. P. N. P. B. L. Ch. S. A. P. D. M.   12 miles.

Tuesday, August 11. — Weather somber and heavy; a little rain. My head fatigued. Letter to Mr. XX. R. P. D. D. P. D. S. A. P. D. M.

Wednesday, August 12.—Came from St. Thomas' to St. Stephen's; visited a sick woman on the way.   10 miles. Weather stormy, rainy. P. C. L. P. St. L. CL. E. M. P. L. R. D. S. L.

Thursday, August 13.—Visit the Sisters; rain going and coming. Great satisfaction among these poor ladies.   14 miles. P. R. D. S. L.

Friday, August 14. — Confessions till one o'clock P. M. Visit two sick persons,—4 miles. Fine weather. Letter to Mr. B—n. R. P. F. D. D. E. S. A. P. D. M.

Saturday, August 15.—All day busy with the ministry; consolations and worries. Fine weather; good health. Visit of Mr. Twyman for Leo R. P. D. P. C. L. Ch. E. P. L. R. D. S. L.

Sunday, August 16. — Confessions, preaching, confirmation till 2 o'clock. Fine weather, hot. Consolations and contradictions. D. S. L. Farewell to my D. S. A. P. D. M.

Monday, August 17.—Visit a sick man. Confessions till four o'clock. 24 miles. Satisfactory talk with Mr. Twyman and Mr. B. D. D. M. P. R. P. F. T. C. L. Ch. D. S. L.

Tuesday, August 18.—Went with Mr. Twyman and Leo to St. Thomas'. Mr. David receives Leo. Mrs. H. gives me a negro. Fine weather. R. S. Mr. Twyman a mediator.—11 miles. D. S. L.

Wednesday, August 19.—Returned to St. Stephen's with Mr. Twyman. Overtures of conciliation with Mr. B—n. T. C. L. A.

Thursday, August 20. — Rain most all day. Mr. B—n turns over several properties to me. Peace over ¾; hope for the rest. A. D. G. A. D. P. M. S.

Friday, August 21. — Went from St. Thomas' to St. Clare's, — 27 miles. Weather stormy, rain for an hour. Arrived at Mr. Wise's at half-past eight P. M. R. P. F. D. C. L. Ch. P. M. S.

Saturday, August 22.—Confessions almost all day. Short instruction. D. D. A. L. P. D. S. L. Rain most all day. P. M. S.

Sunday, August 23.—Confessions, sermon, confirmation till 3 o'clock. Confessions a part of the evening. Fine weather. Too much levity during dinner. S. A. P. D. M. D. S. L.

Monday, August 24. — Returned from Clear Creek, 17 miles, to the seminary. Fine weather. Talked with Mr. Dd. Boone. T. R. S. T. D. S. L.

Tuesday, August 25. — Fine weather. Went to Bardstown; several communications, pamphlets from St. Mary's College. Good. Returned to St. Thomas'. D. D. E. G. E. L. G. D. D.

Wednesday, August 26.—Weather dark and rainy. General sadness. Went to St. Stephen's after dinner. Everybody quiet. R. P. F. D. D. S. L.

Thursday, August 27. — Visit to the Sisters. Rainy

weather. These good ladies seem to be happy. D. S. L. 14 miles. R. P. F. D. D. E. P. M. S.

Friday, August 28. — Confessions, sermon, mass nearly all day. Fine weather. Mr. B—n is sick. D. D. E. P. F. R. P. M. S.

Saturday, August 29.—Confessions, sermon, mass, till 2 o'clock P. M. Confessions in the evening. Fine weather. Friendly talk with Mr. B—n and Mr. Flynn. R. S. S. A. P. D. M.

Sunday, August 30. — Confessions, sermon, mass, till 5 o'clock P. M. Went 14 miles; fine weather. Visit the Sisters with Mr. B—n. Friendly, D. S. L. Charity! Charity!

Monday, August 31. — Fine weather. Started for St. Rose', — 9 miles. Interview with the Dominicans, and Messrs. David and Chabrat. Letter from the Bishop of Canada. R. P. D.

The weather in Kentucky does not seem to have changed much since the days of Bishop Flaget. His record of cold, heat, rain, sleet and wind would state conditions very fairly in our own times. One matter of surprise is, that he could do so much traveling in all sorts of weather without recording any more serious illness than an occasional headache. Those old missionaries were hardy, and their work helped to keep them so. They certainly were not pampered and debilitated by fine eating. Father Nerinckx wrote to his friends in Belgium that he lived as the settlers lived, and that their main articles of diet were " cornbread and hogmeat from the 1st of January to the 31st of December, inclusive ". And to their credit it must be said that few of them ever shortened their lives by excessive drinking, although spirituous liquors were of easier access then than now.

Bishop Flaget still watched his energumens (there seems to have been several of them—children of the same family). He brought other priests to see them, and he spoke to his

friend, Dr. John M. Harney of Bardstown, about them.
Dr. Harney put no faith in the sincerity of the subjects.

Dr. Harney was an elder brother of Gen. Wm. S. Harney, U. S. army, and a son-in-law of Judge John Rowan of Federal Hill, Bardstown, in whose house Foster composed the song, " My Old Kentucky Home ". Dr. Harney became a Catholic some years later. He was a poet as well as a physician, and after he came to know Bishop Flaget intimately he composed the following lines as a tribute to him:

TO A VALUED FRIEND

" Devout, yet cheerful; pious, not austere;
   To others lenient, to himself severe;
   Tho' honored, modest; diffident, tho' praised;
   The proud he humbled; and the humble raised;
   Studious, yet social; though polite, yet plain;
   No man more learned, yet no man less vain.
   His fame would universal envy move,
   But envy 's lost in universal love.
   That he has faults, it may be bold to doubt,
   Yet certain 'tis, we have not found them out.
   If faults he has (as man, 'tis said, must have),
   They are the only faults he ne'er forgave.
   I flatter not; absurd to flatter where
   Just praise is fulsome, and offends the ear."

In 1812 the observance of Lent was a more serious business than it is now. On the Sunday before Ash Wednesday (Feb. 12) Bishop Flaget announces Mondays, Wednesdays and Saturdays as abstinence days, which, with the Fridays, made four days each week when flesh meat might not be eaten, instead of our two days now. His Holy Week services were very simple. He had his usual " confessions, sermon and mass until one o'clock " on Thursday and Saturday, and on Good Friday he notes a few confessions, no ceremony, but a day of rain and gloom spent in sadness and meditation. Nothing is said about the consecration of the Holy Oils. Easter was also a day of only the usual services, but Corpus Christi was celebrated with the greatest solemnity.

The Bishop mentioned some correspondence with the Bishop of Quebec in matters of jurisdiction. The Bishop of Quebec had charge in former times of the missions from Detroit to St. Louis. When this territory came under American control Bishop Carroll, and later Bishop Flaget, felt it a duty to provide for these missions, and especially for the many Americans who were settling in and around them. As division lines were vague, the Bishops sought to secure the validity of the jurisdiction of priests sent from either side by the mutual granting of the powers of vicars general to each other. In this way the faculties of priests sent by either bishop were approved by both. In Bishop Flaget's case this arrangement was necessary for the territory on the Great Lakes and for that around St. Louis.

Some of the glitter is taken from our commonly conceived notions of the episcopal office when we read Bishop Flaget's laments over his troubles. But bishops are men, and those over whom they are called to preside are also human. Bishop Flaget's entries here show how sensitive he was under difficulties, and some of them could serve only to recall to himself the remembrance of his troubles. They were inexplicable to anyone but himself. His diffi- •
culties with Father Badin (B—n) were known, but indications are too vague to name now with anything more than a probability the person he designates as Mr. XX or his troubles with him. The difficulties with Father Badin were partially settled through the mediation of Judge James Twyman, as we see by entries of Aug. 17 to 20. A few business interviews in a friendly way in the presence of such cool heads as Judge Twyman would, in all probability, have settled the whole matter, but these impossible Frenchmen stood apart and wrote letters to one another while looking at opposite sides of the question. Judge Twyman was a prominent lawyer of Scott county. His wife was a Miss James, a Catholic, at whose mother's house Father

Badin often said mass before any church was built there. The Judge himself was instructed and baptized in the faith by Father Badin during those early years.

In connection with this matter this diary contains the following reflections:

" May 2, 1812.—In the painful conversation I had with Mr. Badin he expressed to me his intention of leasing the greater part of the land near Bardstown. This justifies my fears that he does not intend to make an episcopal establishment of it. He complained that I had treated him harshly. I acknowledge that on two or three occasions his conduct towards me was so singular that I expressed myself in a manner strong and perhaps harsh. But he himself knows well that it was but the expression of the moment, and that my heart has always been open to him, and very wide open every time that it seemed to me he wished to come to me. My soul, in writing all this, in recalling what is past, and in looking forward to what might arrive, was sunk in bitterness, but by good luck my hand accidentally rested on one of the volumes of Père Jude. I found his beautiful meditation for St. Andrew's, on Love of the ·Cross. I blessed God for having given me similar consolation.

" At this moment I learn that Nancy Rhodes gave two or three hundred dollars for the purchase of the land at Bardstown, and that Mr. Nerinckx gave 60 or 100. Two facts to be verified.

.   .   .   .

" Nota.—Mr. Badin proposed to me to put into my hands all the property purely ecclesiastical, provided I would give him my letter of exchange to Mr. Small, without exacting security for the remaining debts,—evident proof that these debts did not worry him very much, and that it was a precaution, useless to him and insulting to me to exact, as a condition *sine qua non*, that I should be security for all debts occasioned, etc., although at this time I had agreed to give eighty dollars more than he actually asked, for I offered to pay $200 to Messrs. Porter (?) and Small.

" I said that his *conduct* towards me was *unjust,* and I do not retract it, because his conduct may be unjust without his being so himself. I acknowledge, however, that it is not without an effort that I separate the one from the other. God knows well that I value the friendship of Mr. Badin a hundred times more than all the lands.

" The 5th of May I wrote Mr. Badin under the pretext of explaining certain expressions which he used last Saturday, but really to induce him by new motives to cede me the land at Bardstown. To give him a proof of my constant friendship I sent him a letter of exchange to Mr. Small. I told him that I had some more at his service, and, although he had two commissions to send that very day, he did not deign to acknowledge the receipt of my letter. When I paid $120 for him at Baltimore he never thanked me, and he never will acknowledge such proceedings.

 . . . .

" The 2nd of May Mr. Badin went so far as to say that, if he wanted to, he could keep *all the church property* although I had asked for it. He said that he had his principles formed upon this subject, and that his conscience would not reproach him in the least. I answered that my principles were quite the contrary, and that my conscience would be entirely at ease in putting them into execution.

" When Mr. Badin advanced these principles he had not yet read my letter of the 18th of April, although it had been given to him. He would have seen in reading it that I had anticipated all his objections. I do not yet know what effect this letter has produced on his mind. As he has accepted my letter of exchange I must conclude that he wishes to turn over to me at least the Church property. God of mercies, do not permit that I should be the cause of any scandal; make me know the voice that I should follow. Death, yes, a thousand times, rather than that I should offend Thee!"

THE LIFE OF BISHOP CONWELL

BY MARTIN I. J. GRIFFIN

CHAPTER XXIX.

STATE OF THE DIOCESE AFTER THE BISHOP'S RETURN.—
APPOINTMENT OF KENRICK COADJUTOR.—HE CLAIMS
PASTORSHIP OF ST. MARY'S, AND TRUSTEES OBJECT.—
CLOSING OF THE CHURCH.—CONWELL ENCOURAGES
TRUSTEES.—TRUSTEES SUBMIT.—END OF THE SCHISM.

1830.

The diocese of Philadelphia was "really in a deplorable plight", wrote Father Hughes to Fr. Purcell. Bishop Conwell after his return from Rome and Baltimore "lived quietly and wrote to Rome by every packet". "No oils had been consecrated for two years, no one to attend to it except at the risk of being considered officious."

It seems from various allusions that the Bishop, when in Rome, had been ordered "not to return to his diocese under pain of being deprived of his faculties." Notification of the penalty he had incurred by violating this prohibition was probably the reason for his exclusion from the Council of Baltimore. At any rate when he returned to Philadelphia, he abstained from exercising episcopal authority until Rome had forgiven his act, and at the same time practically superseded him by the appointment of a Coadjutor with exceptional authority even over the Bishop. It was probably while assembled in Baltimore that the Archbishop and the Bishops recommended to Rome for this office the Rev.

Francis Patrick Kenrick, who was there present in attendance on Bishop Flaget. Bishop Conwell also is said to have approved the selection. Father Kenrick was appointed about March 13th, 1830, and the Bulls were received by Bishop Flaget on May 1st. He presented them to Father Kenrick, saying: " Behold the certificate of the cross you have to carry." (Reuss, *Biog. Cyclo.*) Father Matthews seems to have had little to do with the affairs of Philadelphia, so that from the date of the Bishop's departure for Rome, July 15th, 1828, until the arrival of Bishop Kenrick, July 7th, 1830, Philadelphia was without the services of a Bishop.

On April 29th, 1830, the Archbishop notified the Episcopate of the restoration of Bishop Conwell and the appointment of Bishop Kenrick. Here is his letter to Bishop England.

From the original document in the Catholic Archives of America, Notre Dame, Ind.

BALTIMORE, *April 29, 1830.*

Right Rev'd and Dear Sir,

I am requested by the Sacred Congregation of Propaganda to inform you and all the Bishops of the Province, 1st, that His Holiness has restored to his grace and favor the Bishop of Philadelphia, and forgives his act, done last year *minus considerata.* 2ly, that I have received and forwarded the briefs for Dr. Kenrick, appointed Dr. Conwell's coadjutor and administrator of the Diocese of Philadelphia.

That the honor, dignity and reputation of Dr. Conwell are consulted—the administration to be carried on as if it were spontaneously given by Dr. Conwell who may solemnly officiate, give confirmation in public or private, confer orders on those whom Dr. Kenrick shall approve.

It would be well to keep secret (but I fear it is already known from Washington) that Dr. Kenrick's administration and jurisdiction derives from Propaganda.

Bishop Conwell in a letter received this morning testifies to me his gratefulness, seems pleased—says he will come shortly to converse with me.

The dispatches, consisting of letters to Drs. Flaget, Conwell and Kenrick and Mr. Matthew, and a letter to me with copies of the letters to Dr. Conwell and Kenrick, were dated at Rome, 13 March and received in Baltimore 20th April, although they must have remained in England at least 7 or 8 days. The London Packet-ship that brought them arrived at New York in 15 days and 3 hours from Portsmouth.

On the 18th of April I received another letter from the same Cardinal prefect dated 27th of Feb'y—he says my letter, recommending Dr. Conwell to the Pope's benevolence and proposing (sapientes) the plan now adopted was ———— gratissima—that he would write quam primum the decision (as he has done) that he had also received the decrees and acts of our provincial council and our joint letters to His Holiness. That Propaganda will examine the decrees and acts and he inform me of the result.

The motives mentioned for appointing Dr. Kenrick are that he was petitioned for by Dr. Conwell, the Archbp. and all the Bishops, and also because he was well known and highly esteemed by the Sacred Congregation.

I hope that the above intelligence will be pleasing to you and the rest of our Brethren.

Yesterday I paid to Mr. Maguire (bookseller) five dollars, he is a poor man and asked for it frequently. We sent to you according to your order 3 doz. German Catechisms, for which he was not paid. You will be kind enough to enclose to me a U. S. note of five dollars.

+ JAMES ARP. OF BALTIMORE.

To RT. REV. BISHOP ENGLAND, D. D.

This settlement of Bishop Conwell's case, left him, practically a Bishop only in name. Bishop Kenrick, as appears from some expressions in his letters and from his subsequent conduct, took up " his cross " with two clearly fixed determinations, namely, to treat the aged Bishop with every consideration that circumstances would permit, and, should the hydra-head of revolt venture to appear, to strike at it quickly and powerfully in the hope of ending its existence once for all. In the later purpose he was perfectly success-ful, so that the first year of his administration may be looked upon as the last of the prolonged revolt. As to the former, many circumstances, the poverty of his resources, the unpopularity of Bishop Conwell, but especially the Bishop's own character, obstructed the fulfillment of his good intentions. The Bishop was very suspicious, jealous of his dignity, and obstinate in his own views. He had given evidence of these traits very often in the ten years of his episcopate, and began to manifest them towards Kenrick, even before the latter's consecration.

PHILADELPHIA, *May 15th, 1830.*
To The Most Rev. Dr. Whitfield,
Archbishop of Baltimore, Md.
My Dear and Most Rev. Sir:

I have written to Dr. Kenrick and expecting to hear from him soon, wish in the mean time to be informed when and where the consecration is to take place. It were to be wished that the Revd. Gent. passing here from Baltimore, would observe most prudence in speaking of the Coadjutor's powers (?). Such details are calculated to do him harm instead of good, which they might have intended. One of them said they had *good authority* for spreading those reports. I observe perfect silence, and hope that nothing will ever occur to raise pre-judices or unfriendly feelings among us or between us. And if left alone I am very sure that he and I will agree in every-thing, for instead of controlling him, I shall be his friend on every occasion and support his rights and his dignity as he will mine. The contrary conduct was the ruin of Mr. Mat-thews, who is without a friend or well-wisher in this Diocese, where he might have thousands by acting otherwise. Attempts at offering insults or dishonor to any dignified character must be forever attended with like results. Mr. Carberry (the Revd.), from St. Inigoes is here to have medical advice. Another Jesuit, Dogherty, is here begging money to build a church at Gettysburg. He cannot *succeed*. Mr. Jameson (the Revd.) has been here last week, and others are constantly passing.

With respect to Dr Kenrick I think that there is nothing to be said of necessity (necessitate medii) more than that he has been appointed my Coadjutor. And as to the rest ——. We shall never have any difference or altercation about rights or pre-eminence unbecoming our character, which is Rome's idea and recommendation on the subject. I trust none of my secrets to secretaries, for, if I should, the secrets might be violated, which I know by experience. Messrs. Spalding and Lancaster had letters for me which I have not yet received.

The Sacrament of Confirmation has been administered last Sunday in Pittsburg without my knowledge. I write by this mail to Mr. Maguire to be informed of it.

I have the honor to be with the greatest respect and veneration,

Your Grace's devoted and faithful friend,

HENRY CONWELL, *Bishop of Philadelphia.*

M. R. DR. WHITFIELD.

Archbishop Whitfield sent notice of the time and place of the consecration to Bishop Conwell, who set out for Bardstown, Ky., accompanied by Rev. Nicholas O'Donnell of St. Augustine's. The consecration took place there on June 6th. The consecrator was Bishop Flaget, assisted by Bishops Conwell and David. Bishop Conwell " presented the Very Rev. Dr. Kenrick to the consecrating Bishop in the manner prescribed in the Pontifical, and performed all the offices of the senior assisting Prelate. Dr. Conwell was waited on by Rev. J. Elliott, in quality of chaplain."

Bishops England of Charlestown, and Fenwick of Cincinnati, and Rev. Nicholas O'Donnell were present, while the number of people present on the occasion is set down at three thousand. At the consecration dinner at St. Joseph's College, where Bishop Kenrick had served for nine years, one of the speakers was Mr. Charles J. H. Carter, a seminarian, who was afterwards attached to the Philadelphia Diocese as assistant at St. Mary's, and afterwards as Founder of the Church of the Assumption. (*U. S. C. Miscel.*, X. 23, 28.) In his address, he said: " To you, venerable Prelate of Philadelphia, we offer the warmest congratulations that heaven has favored your declining years with such an able and efficient Coadjutor."

Bishop Conwell and his Coadjutor set out for Philadelphia by way of Pittsburg, where confirmation was administered by Bishop Kenrick. It would seem therefore that Bishop Conwell's jealousy had been deceived by a false report of confirmation a few weeks previously. On July 4th, ofter having visited the Prince-priest, Father Gallitzin at Loretto, Bishop Conwell dedicated the Church of the Holy Trinity at Huntingdon, Penna.; from thence they journeyed to Harrisburg and Lancaster, and arrived in Philadelphia on July 7th. Bishop Conwell presented the new Bishop to the pastors and people of the various churches, and visited St. Joseph's and St. John's Orphan Asylums. The latter had been lately established in Prune (now Locust) St., above Fourth, near St. Mary's Church.

The new Bishop was " exclusively invested by the Apostolic See with episcopal jurisdiction for the government of the Diocese of Philadelphia." But Bishop Conwell could not always restrain his discontent with his anomalous position, and frequently betrayed it, even going so far as to array himself on the side of the Trustees in the difference which soon arose between them and the Coadjutor.

The difficulty, and it was a momentous one in this history, arose over the question of the Bishops' support. It will be remembered that by the agreement made in 1808, when Bishop Egan was appointed, St. Mary's agreed to pay

$400, St. Augustine's $200 and Holy Trinity $200 for the support of the Bishop. The same amount was agreed to for the support of Bishop Conwell, but not paid. St. Mary's defaulted for several periods during the schism, and St. Augustine's, if we may trust to Bishop Conwell's complaints, was nearly always in arrears. There were now two Bishops to be supported, and naturally the agreement which had failed to provide for one was not to be relied on for the support of two. Bishop Conwell had eked out this scanty provision by the income of the " Bishop's Burial Ground ", by that of the mensal parish of Lancaster, and by what he managed to get out of his claim as pastor of St. Mary's. The Trustees had claimed that, as the Bishop's attention was divided between all the parishes of the Diocese, St. Mary's should contribute only to his support as Bishop, and not as a pastor of the church of St. Mary's. The question now arose, how were the two to be provided for. After the Trustees had called on Bishop Kenrick, they reported that he " disclaimed all design of connecting himself with a particular church . . . but would give his services equally to all, and depend upon all for his support." Mr. Randall, as Secretary of St. Mary's Trustees, wrote to St. Augustine's relative to increased appropriations for this purpose, and received this reply:

ST. AUGUSTINE'S, *Aug. 2nd, 1830.*

Dear Sir:

I have the pleasure to acknowledge the receipt of your note of the 18th ult., and beg to state in reply, that as I have uniformly paid to the Bishop of this Diocese the sum of one hundred dollars per annum (even whilst absent in Europe) and shall continue to do the same in the hereafter, I do not feel myself called upon to enter into any further arrangement for the support of the Episcopal dignity—and the rather as the said sum is the maximum that the existing means of St. Augustine's Church can afford.

Respectfully Yours,

MICHAEL HURLEY.

St. Mary's was willing to contribute $200 more than what had previously been allowed, but that was all that was forthcoming for the purpose. Those in charge of the inicome of the Lancaster fund, which was part of the Sir John James fund, bequeathed in 1741 for the support of religion in Pennsylvania, hesitated as to whom the amount should now be paid. But Bishop Kenrick refused to deprive the old Bishop of that income, as will appear from the following letter, which he wrote while absent from Philadelphia on a visitation of the Diocese.

LITTLE YORK, *Sept. 12, 1830.*

Right Rev. and very dear Sir:

Understanding that some pecuniary demand upon you creates considerable embarassment, I seize the opportunity of proving to you my solicitude for your honour and happiness by declaring that I am ready to sign any instrument which may be deemed necessary or advisable to secure to you the prompt payment of the Lancastrian mensal. I am informed that some reluctance to pay it to you was manifested in consequence of the appointment of an administrator; and as the same difficulty may be urged in regard to the relation in which I stand, I am most anxious to remove it. You are aware that I do this at a time when every other subsidy for the maintenance of the Episcopal dignity has been denied me, and whilst traveling with as much dependance on a kind Providence as if I were still an humble missionary in Kentucky. Could I give you any stronger proof of my regard and attachment, I should do it without hesitation.

My visit to Lancaster has been blessed with the reconciliation of Messrs. George Daly and Lynch and the Rev. Pastor. Columbia Church was blessed this morning, and confirmation administered to above sixty persons. The painting of Lancaster Church deranged my appointments. I am going tomorrow to Emmitsburgh, and mean to return here for Thursday. Conewago is said to be under repairs, and unfit to receive guests. I am therefore compelled to anticipate by a week

my visits to Chambersburgh and Bedford. When I shall reach
Pittsburgh is yet quite uncertain. Many enquiries are made
by your friends, who express great respect and attachment, in
which, however, I can assure you from my heart, that they do
not surpass

Your affectionate Brother in Christ,

+ FRANCIS PATRICK,
Bishop of Arath and Coadjutor of Philadelphia.

[From copy printed by Bishop Conwell for circulation].

This liberality leaving him, he said, as dependant upon
Providence as a backwoods missionary, Bishop Kenrick
took a step which precipitated the final struggle with the
Trustees of St. Mary's, and in December he notified the
Board that in future he would " act as chief pastor of St.
Mary's " [1] with Father Keiley as assistant. The old issue
was thus raised again. The Trustees replied that his recognition as chief pastor would " secure the salary attached to
that position ", while " your attentions are divided among
all the churches of the Diocese." This answer was followed
by many disedifying incidents, which we omit as they do
not pertain to the history of Bishop Conwell. But on April
22nd, 1831, Bishop Kenrick struck the final blow by ordering the cessation of all religious services at St. Mary's.
One would think that in a case almost identical in principle
with that for which he had so long contended, Bishop Conwell's sympathies would have been with his Coadjutor. On
the contrary, his sympathies were on the other side in regard to the measure of coercion which Kenrick had taken,
and he claimed the right of chief pastor for himself. His
letter to the Trustees shows this to have been his position.

PHILADELPHIA, *May 13th, 1831.*

My Dear Sir,

Having been recently informed that blame is attached to

[1] See Bishop Kenrick's *Diary and Visitation Record,* pp. 44 and sqq.

me for coinciding with the measure which leaves the congregation of St. Mary's Church without the benefit of clergy or any opportunity to hear mass or observe other Christian duties on the Sabbath Day, I judge it expedient to signify that I have never sanctioned the proceeding, that I regret it exceedingly, and entertain feelings of sympathy for the suffering multitude. Those sentiments are materially aggravated by the consideration that many weak minds may be led astray and prevailed on through the influence of the noxious passions, acted on by sophistical reasoning, to become apostates, or embrace some new system of religion. I add no more on that subject. The next thing which I wish to be made known to the Trustees is, that I am the incumbent of this Southern District of Philadelphia and that I possess inalienable rights in virtue of this title distinct from the rights which I enjoy as Bishop of Philadelphia. In order to make my meaning clear on this topic, it is necessary to state, that, since the building of St. Augustine's Church, and that of Holy Trinity, Philadelphia has been divided into two distinct parishes, the Incumbent of each of them separately having parochial rights guaranteed to him by the Sacred Canons. The division was made from Market Street Northwards, into which the Rev. Mr. Carr was inducted. The Rt. Rev. Mr. Egan was inducted and put into canonical possession of the Southern part of Philadelphia from Market Street as the limits of his parish. On the demise of Mr. Carr, Mr. Hurley succeeded him as parish priest. On the demise of Mr. Egan, Mr. Barth succeeded him and in 1820, I became the canonical incumbent which I possess accordingly. I have never abdicated either in the capacity of Parish Priest or of Bishop of Philadelphia, both of which I shall ever adhere to. In the mean time though I claim St. Mary's Parish as a benefice, yet I require from the Trustees no more than three barley corns yearly, if demanded; that is, in my quality of parish priest; whilst I hope to get what has been formerly allotted to me as Bishop of Philadelphia with everything else which may accrue to me in that capacity, by right, comprehending that of a clerical member of the Board of Trustees, with privilege of sitting as a member of the Board, having a vote as such, accordingly.

I have many things more to relate which it is more expedient to postpone, lest the narration might prevent the application of a speedy remedy to the disorder under which the congregation suffers extreme pain and anguish of mind, which I feel and lament exceedingly.

With best respects to the gentlemen who compose the Board of Trustees, I have the honor to be, my Dear Sir,

Your sincere and faithful friend,

HENRY CONWELL, *Bishop of Philadelphia.*

ARCHIBALD RANDALL, *Esq.,*

Secretary of the Board of Trustees.

A copy of this letter, translated " from a copy printed in Italian, evidently one of those prepared for transmission to Rome," may be read in the *Am. Cath. Hist. Researches,* April, 1887. The translation is substantially the same as the above; it is no doubt a copy of the English version sent to Mr. Randall. In the Italian version we have " one dollar " instead of " three barley corns ".

But not even the sympathy of their one time opponent could reanimate the cause for which Hogan's Trustees had fought, possibly because everyone was heartily tired of the scandalous struggle. The church remained closed until the Trustees submitted to the Bishop. It was reopened on May 28th, but Hoganism, and all that accompanied it and followed in its footsteps, was dead.

CHAPTER XXX.

DISPUTE OVER " MY ROOM ".—OVER THE PETER GILL BE-
QUEST.—LETTERS TO MOUNT ST. MARY'S, CONCERNING
HENRY MCKEON.

1831..

The points at issue between Bishop Kenrick and the Trustees were thus definitely settled. But he had a more difficult and more delicate task in dealing with Bishop Conwell. A lamentable difference arose between them. Bishop Conwell's statement of the facts of the case, and likewise the measures he would have liked to see taken, are expressed in the annexed letter, written about this time and later published by him in Latin.

" I was very much pleased yesterday to receive your letter, dated Rome, June 16th, since it informed me that the Holy Congregation is ready to grant my request regarding the promotion of D. to some apostolic seat in this Province, where many Bishops are still needed owing to the great increase of Catholics, who are widely separated. For example, one especially is needed for Michigan, where Detroit is situated, this district is now under the jurisdiction of the Bishop of Cincinnati, another Bishop is none the less needed in Indiana, where Vincennes is situated, and which is now subject to the jurisdiction of the Bishop of Bardstown, Kentucky. Where D. is beloved as much by clergy as by people, that he cannot be spoken about in the Diocese of Philadelphia, where he has incurred the hate of everyone, because of his bad management during the last two years. The good of religion, aye even due justice to me, demands that this or something similar be done by the Holy See, the sooner, the better.

Everybody knows that I never left my diocese to its fate, nor given up rights belonging to me. Yet D., while only a Bishop-elect, dared to give faculties to priests of this diocese.

I have already appealed to the Holy Father against the violation of the Sacred Canons. As with many others, indeed, no answer is given to me to this day. So much being done, now certain things, heretofore unheard must be told, which relate to D's administration. Shortly after he came to this diocese, he visited its remote parts when he expelled from their parishes, three missionaries, who bear the best of reputations, and suspended them without just cause, viz: D.McG. from Westmoreland; a D.D., a Carmelite from Ebensburg, and D.F. from Milton. As to the first D.McG., he was reduced to the necessity of working for a living, in a field which he bought with his own money. D.F. likewise did the same. Nevertheless D.D. was suspended from all priestly functions (just as if he were guilty) so that in his own defense he was forced to leave the diocese. Moreover law-suits have arisen in the Civil Courts, on account of ruined reputations and subsequent losses, which are not as yet settled. In the meanwhile D.D. is a missionary in the Diocese of New York. About this I have nothing to say, except that this reason for action on the part of D. was a great scandal as much to priests as to people.

When D. returned to the city he notified me that he wished to retain my room, and immediately took with him several workmen, whom he had hired, and ordered them to take away all my household furniture (which was done without hesitation), then to take the locks from the doors and to put in new ones, so that for six months I was excluded from my room. While in the mean time D. had opened a restaurant in my house, asking from each guest five Roman or Francesconian *scudi* per week. Wherefore I have quietly stayed, an exile, as it were, in my bedchamber, so as to avoid scandal..

(To be continued)

NOTES AND REPRINTS

Under the above heading there will appear at intervals in the RECORDS a series of short notes on current historical topics, as well as a number of interesting items culled from early Catholic newspapers and other sources.

Apropos of the return of Archbishop Dougherty to Philadelphia, we print the farewell address of the students of St. Charles' Seminary to the then Bishop-Elect Dougherty, 28 April, 1903, on the occasion of his formal visit to the Seminary prior to sailing for Rome to receive episcopal consecration from the hands of the late Cardinal Satolli. The address is as follows:

RT. REV. BISHOP-ELECT:

Amidst the general happiness and satisfaction which attended the first announcement of your elevation to the episcopate, Rt. Rev. Bishop-elect, no hearts felt more elated than those of the students of St. Charles' Seminary. It was the joy of a disciple rejoicing in the well-deserved distinction conferred on his beloved master. We looked upon it as, in some way, a personal honor conferred on us individually, for in your elevation we all felt exalted. And as we recalled that it was but lately that you had placed within our reach a new and able work in defense of St. Peter's Roman Primacy, there seemed to be a special fitness in St. Peter's successor calling you to become a successor of the Apostles. We rejoiced that the choice of Leo had fallen on one who was in every way suited to occupy and adorn that sublime office, on one whose learning was at once accurate and extensive, whose loyalty and devotion to the Church

of God and to her venerable head was generous and un-
wavering, whose love and veneration for the priesthood was
strong and exalted, and who ever strove with all the ardor
of his being that now, as of old, " the lips of the priest
should keep knowledge ".

But at the same time it was not without more than a passing pang of regret that we realized that your elevation
meant the sundering of those ties which have united us for
so many years, that the larger life which spreads out before
you entailed a corresponding loss on our part, so that in
some measure we were made partakers in the sacrifice which
you are called upon to make in assuming this apostolic
burden.

But our hearts would be callous indeed did we allow this
opportunity to go by without publicly testifying to the sentiments of joy and gratitude which fill our breasts on this
auspicious occasion. During the many years of your professorship in this seminary you have spared neither time
nor labor to further the intellectual advancement of the
students; with painstaking care you have endeavored to
help us understand and realize the doctrines of our Holy
Faith; you have impressed upon us by word and example
that thoroughness is the essential quality in all learning;
that not " how much ", but " how well ", should be our
motto in our studies; that superficial fluency of speech cannot compensate for lack of thought. Such, then, are the
lessons which you have left deeply graven on the minds and
hearts of the hundreds of students whom you have guided
and instructed during the past thirteen years, lessons which
will make you ever present to us, even though an ocean
separates us.

And now, as the time of parting grows near, as you are
about to depart for your new sphere of labors amongst a
people alien indeed in blood and tendencies, but brethren in
the household of the faith, as you go forth to devote all the

energies of mind and heart and soul to the upbuilding of the Church of God in those distant islands, we, with one accord, bid you God-speed in your new career. As a successor of the Apostles you will in very truth have apostolic labors to perform. Your new office has demanded and will demand from you sacrifices numerous and heavy, but, confiding in Him who has begun the good work, you nevertheless go resolutely forward, even as St. Paul went to Jerusalem, though he knew that bonds and afflictions awaited him there.

Finally, although the diocese of Philadelphia is losing a faithful and devoted priest, and the Seminary of St. Charles Borromeo a valued and able teacher, yet the people of the ancient diocese of Nueva Segovia are receiving a shepherd whose ability and learning will command their respect, whose zeal for souls will gain their love and veneration, and whose strong and resolute character augurs a firm and just rule.

Go forth, then, Bishop Elect, to your distant flock, bearing with you our sincerest gratitude for your endeavors in our behalf, and our fondest hopes that you will be spared "ad multos annos" for the glory of God and the good of the church in the Philippines.

BOOK REVIEWS.

THE VERY REV. CHARLES HYACINTH McKENNA, O.P., P.G.
Missionary and Apostle of the Holy Name Society. By the
Very Rev. V. F. O'Daniel, O.P., S.T.M. Holy Name
Bureau, New York. 1917. Pp. xiv-409. Price $2.00.

Biographies as a rule are interesting. The biography under
consideration is of more than usual interest, for its subject is
a popular missioner, whose activities were not confined to any
particular part of the United States, and whose friends were
legion.

The author, in a style beautiful in its simplicity, tells us in
the life-story of this saintly man, how the hardships of his
early manhood did but serve as stepping-stones to the object of
his ambition, the realization of which brought him into the
ancient and venerated Order of St. Dominic.

A few introductory chapters, beautifully written, on the
institute and scope of the Order of St. Dominic, can hardly fail
to inspire the aspirants to the religious life, and the early
struggles of the future missioner are a strong incentive to those
who would tread in the footsteps of this truly apostolic
preacher.

From his ordination to the priesthood the story is told, it
grips, it fascinates. The chapters go on, and though the
life of a virile Dominican missioner is a continuous grind of
the arduous work of the confessional and still more arduous
work of preaching, and may appear dry, the author has painted
a picture of Father McKenna at this time, with simplicity
and charm.

The interest of the American Catholic public is intensified
in members of the Rosary Confraternity and Holy Name men,
for the latter years of the saintly man's life were spent or-
ganizing and strengthening the bonds of the flower of Catholic
manhood.

The author wrote no eulogy of Father McKenna. None was needed. A monument more lasting than bronze, the increased activities of the Holy Name Society throughout the United States, which is due in no small measure to the "Apostle of the Holy Name Society" is a living monument which will ever endure. Were this the only sphere of his activity, the biography would not need a *raison d'être*, hence the sub-title as a tribute to his memory.

A memoir would indeed be incomplete if it did not give us a pen-picture of the inner life of the subject. Here we read the story of a soul. Father McKenna's life, his inner life, is laid bare; and its simplicity will not be unnoticed by priests and religious in community, to whom the work will make an inspiring appeal.

In the telling, not without interest, the principal events of this saintly life, Father O'Daniel ever takes care to show the formation of character and the spirit which vitalized unusual activity.

An extremely edifying narration of the works of a missioner as he travelled from coast to coast, will doubtless explain the appreciation of the pastors who were proud to know him well, and the veneration in which he was held by the thousands of pious souls to whom he was ever and always " dear old Father McKenna."

A span of nearly sixty years brought Father McKenna into contact, an intimate and ever increasing contact, with the visible growth of the Church in the United States. From the viewpoint of the Catholic historian, his long life of mostly missionary activity is of inestimable value.

The many years he spent, 1870-1906, travelling from place to place, gave him a wide acquaintance with the reality of the growth of the Catholic Church in this country.

This the reverend author, in the story of his life and work, has skilfully woven into the warp and woof of the biography, as a background for the unceasing activities of the great Dominican missioner.

an authoritative conception of the meaning and the method, the rise and the growth, of the popular missions as we have them to-day.

The last few years of his life he spent for the men of the Holy Name Society. The largest society in the United States, as such it is a fitting memorial to a simple priest.

Father McKenna's life is a valuable contribution to American Catholic history. Father O'Daniel had the advantage of many chats with his brother Dominican, which gave him the opportunity so desired of all biographers, of gathering many and important facts, so that his sources were as well abundant as authentic.

Taking the work by and large, it is a well-written life of an interesting man with a notably successful career.

The publishers have done their part to make the book attractive. The type is large and clear-cut. Illustrations though but few, are in very good taste and enhance not a little the beauty of the text.

The author, we are pleased to remark, has thought it advisable to annotate his work with exact references to the authorities he so frequently quotes. A comprehensive index of persons, places and things will be of assistance to the critical reader, and will render the book even a more valuable addition to our libraries.

M. B. Heenan.

Washington, D. C.

History of the Society of Jesus in North America— Colonial and Federal. By Thomas Hughes, of the same Society, Text. Vol. II: from 1645 till 1773. With six maps. Longmans, Green and Co., London, New York. Pp. 759. 1917.

One of the most important activities of the scholarship of the past half century has been the re-writing of history, the reconstruction of the past from original sources, with a resulting substitution of fact for prejudice and truth for rhetoric. A new drive on the " conspiracy against truth ", by which celebrated *mot* the witty Count de Maistre described history, is marked by the appearance of Father Hughes's *History of the Society of Jesus in North America,* a second volume which follows its predecessor after an interval of ten years. The particular sector of the hills of prejudice and the trenches of misrepresentation attacked by this really monumental work is that period of American Colonial history which extends from 1645 to 1773. We have in this volume of Father Hughes's an exhaustive history of. Catholicity in North America from the days of Cromwellianism in England to the time of the severance of the American Colonies from Great Britain. It is a history of Catholicity because missionary work in this portion of the New World was almost exclusively Jesuit enterprise.

We have not to read far to realize that being a " Papist " in British Colonial America was about as comfortable as professing Christianity under Diocletian. In Virginia, for instance, " Popish recusants " were disabled from holding any public office, Popish priests were subject to deportation within five days of their apprehension, recusants were fined £20 sterling for each month of absence from the Anglican parish chapel, and as half of the fine went to the informer there was some zest in hunting down Catholics. Massachusetts guaranteed liberty of conscience for all Christians " except Papists ". The same freedom of worship prevailed in Georgia. New York gave no toleration to adherents of the Roman Catholic religion. Pennsylvania, the most liberal of the colonies, allowed Catholics to practice their religion, but only privately; they were not compelled to attend heretical religious services but no one could hold office without taking an oath abjuring all belief in Transubstantiation, the Sacrifice of the Mass, and the invocation of Saints. It is surprising to learn that Maryland, despite its Act of Toleration of 1649, was no paradise of freedom for Catholics, and that Cecil Lord Baltimore was no hero in the cause of religious liberty. There was, of course, throughout the colonies special hatred of the dangerous "sect" of Jesuits. All the political changes in the mother country were naturally reflected in America and the days of Cromwell's Protectorate and of the Orange revolution were especially trying days for Catholic colonists.

We read that in 1679 a Catholic directory of the clergy of British North America would have contained the names of but four priests (all Jesuits), and two lay brothers. The hardships of missionary life and the rigors of the climate were so exacting that of the twenty-one Jesuits appointed during thirty-nine years to the missions in America, seventeen were carried off by death. The average term of individual service in the missions of the Society all round the world has been estimated at ten years, the limit of the stupendous apostolic work of St. Francis Xavier. Except for the chance appearance of a priest here and there, the nascent Church in English America was represented entirely by the Jesuits who had their centre in Maryland and their missionary territory in the half dozen surrounding colonies. The record of the endeavors and achievements of these heroic priests in bringing the truths of faith to the Indian and in keeping faith alive among the settlers is indeed an edifying page of history. Up to 1776 we read of eighty-four missionary martyrs within the present territory of the United States and seventeen of them were Jesuits. Other orders were represented in the Spanish colonies.

The present volume relates again the old story of the strongly contrasting treatment of the Indian by the Catholic French and the Protestant English. Historic proof is not wanting of the veneration of the Indian for the " Black Robe " who was his friend and counselor and physician as well as his priest. The French system left the Indian an Indian " fishing and hunting and fowling ", while the English practice treated the natives " to the mockery of white civilization and the reality of white depravation."

Of special local interest is the chapter (XVII) which tells of the Jesuit missions in Pennsylvania. In 1734 Father Joseph Greaton, himself a convert, opened the first Catholic chapel in Philadelphia. The congregation is said not to have exceeded forty members, the majority of whom were Germans. Later came Father Theodore Schneider and Father

William Wappeler to found the missions at Goshenhoppen and Conewago. The *London Magazine* for July 7, 1737, is quoted as follows:

" In the town of Philadelphia, is a public Popish chapel where that religion has free and open exercise and all the superstitious rites of that Church are as avowedly performed as are those of the 'Church of England at St. James'; and this chapel is not only open upon fasts and festivals but is so all day and every day of the year, and exceedingly frequented at those times when the meeting house of the men of St. Omer's (sarcasm for Quakers) is thinnest and vice versa."

John Adams, strolling into the successor of this Catholic chapel (now St. Mary's church) during the pastorate of Father Robert Harding in the year 1774, thus records his impressions: " This afternoon led by curiosity and good company I strolled away to mother Church, or rather, to grandmother Church, I mean the Romish chapel.—How shall I describe the picture of our Saviour in a frame of marble over the altar, at full length upon the cross, in the agonies, and the blood dripping and streaming from His wounds? The music, consisting of an organ and a choir of singers, went on all afternoon, except sermon time; and the assembly chanted most sweetly and exquisitely. Here is everything which can charm and bewitch the simple and ignorant. I wonder how Luther ever broke the spell? "

Between 1732 and 1763 six churches were built by the Jesuit missionaries in Pennsylvania, two in Philadelphia and one at each of the other central stations, viz. Conewago, Goshenhoppen, Lancaster, and Reading. The Catholic population of the colony in 1765 is placed at 6000, though eighteen years before the number of Catholic communicants over twelve years of age was exactly computed at 1365. In addition to the name already mentioned the roll of honor of Jesuit missionaries prominent in the spread of the faith in Pennsylvania includes the names of Fathers Steynmeyer *alias* Farmer, Settensperger *alias* Manners, Pellentz, and Frambach.

The *History of the Society of Jesus in North America* is an exhaustive and critical work on the subject of which it treats. Its rich bibliography will make it especially attractive to the student. Convenience in using the book is enhanced by the marginal headings of the paragraphs telling at a glance of the topic treated, and the arrangement by which the maps may be unfolded and consulted, whatever portion of the text of the volume is being read. An occasional humorous touch lights up the otherwise ponderous style as there is little attempt at making an interesting narrative. The frankly polemical tone of the book gives it a somewhat acid character which one would rather see absent from a dispassionate and critical history where the facts speak for themselves.

WILLIAM J. LALLOU.

Records of the

American Catholic Historical Society

| Vol. XXIX | September, 1918 | No. 3 |

AN HISTORICAL SKETCH OF THE DIOCESE OF HARRISBURG

BY THE RIGHT REV. MONSIGNOR M. M. HASSETT, D.D., V.G.

Prior to the year 1868 the territory comprised in the existing dioceses of Scranton and Harrisburg formed part of the vast diocese of Philadelphia. How difficult it was, in pioneer days, for the Bishop of Philadelphia to superintend the scattered churches of his jurisdiction is vividly revealed in the interesting diary of Bishop Kenrick who, during the twenty-one years of his administration, made frequent pastoral visitations of his widely dispersed, and none too numerous flock. The establishment of a diocese at Pittsburg for western Pennsylvania, in 1843, removed some of this burden from the shoulders of the Philadelphia Ordinary, but the rapid growth of the Church in the central portion of the State, brought about chiefly through the development of the rich coal lands, within the next quarter of a century, made another division advisable, and accordingly two new sees were erected at Scranton and Harrisburg, in the year 1868.

At the moment of its creation the Catholic population of
the diocese of Harrisburg was estimated at twenty-five
thousand souls, scattered over an area of some ten thousand
square miles.   Twenty-two priests, attending forty churches
or chapels, as well as a considerable number of stations,
came under the jurisdiction of the first Bishop of the see,
Right Rev. Jeremiah F. Shanahan, who received consecration at the hands of Archbishop Wood, July 12, 1868, in the
cathedral of Philadelphia.   Born at Silver Lake, Susquehanna Co., of Irish parentage, July 13, 1834, the first Bishop
of Harrisburg was thus entrusted with the government of a
diocese at the early age of thirty-four.   As is natural to
infer from his rapid advancement Bishop Shanahan had,
from early youth, when a pupil at St. Joseph's College near
Binghampton, N. Y., given evidence of much more than
average ability.   After a distinguished theological course,
subsequently, at the seminary of St. Charles Borromeo,
Philadelphia, the future Bishop was ordained priest by the
venerable Bishop Neumann, July 3, 1859.   A few months
later Father Shanahan received the important appointment
of Rector of the newly created preparatory seminary at
Glen Riddle: a remarkable testimony to the esteem in which
he was held by his saintly Bishop.   Nor was the confidence
thus reposed in the youthful Rector in any wise misplaced.
At this stage, indeed, his career resembles in many respects
that of the famous Doctor Doyle during the period of his
professorship at Carlow College: in both priests more than
the average of intellectual ability was united with an exalted
ideal of the sacerdotal state which won them the esteem of
their respective pupils.   Under such a Superior, endowed
with the virtues of piety, prudence, and intelligence, the
Preparatory Seminary made such notable progress that in
the nine years of his rectorship Father Shanahan was able
to send to the Philadelphia Diocesan Seminary more than
thirty subjects for the priesthood: no mean feat in the conditions of sixty years ago.

Having thus proved himself in a small, though important sphere, it is not surprising that when, on March 3, 1868, Pope Pius IX created three new sees detached from the diocese of Philadelphia, namely, Scranton, Wilmington and Harrisburg, the Rector of Glen Riddle should have been chosen to govern not the least important of these new centers of Catholic development in the rapidly expanding Church in the United States.   For, though the number of Catholics in the diocese of Harrisburg at the moment of its erection was small, yet, it must be borne in mind that the city which gave its name to the see was the capital of the second State in the Union.   This meant that the Bishop of Harrisburg would, in all likelihood, be brought into frequent contact with the members of the State legislature, a body which, under our democratic form of government, should comprise the best lawmaking talent in each commonwealth.

The capital of Pennsylvania lies 97 miles west of Philadelphia, on the left bank of the majestic, and more than ordinarily attractive Susquehanna River.   On a fine eminence, overlooking the broad stream, with its beautifully wooded shores, stood, in 1868, the old state house.   Two hundred yards to the west of this structure St. Patrick's church was seen, on State Street, between the capitol and the river, while about the same distance towards the east St. Laurence' church was situated.   The first of these churches, now to become the pro-cathedral of the new diocese, had been dedicated in 1827 to St. Patrick, whose spiritual children thus had the honor of establishing the first Catholic church in Dauphin county.   Judging from an old print St. Patrick's church was a quaint structure, of no particular architectural character, whose completion, forty-one years before, had brought great joy to the heart of its builder, the Rev. Michael Curran.   This fact we learn from a delightful sketch of its dedication, written at the time by Father Curran, in Latin, in the General Register of the parish, which, translated, reads as follows:

"On the twenty-first day of October, 1827, the church at Harrisburg was consecrated (dedicated?) under the invocation of St. Patrick, Apostle of Ireland, by the Right Rev. Henry Conwell, D.D., Bishop of Philadelphia, assisted by the Very Rev. Father Hurley, V.G., and the Rev. Michael Curran, pastor of said congregation.   There were also present four priests and three clerics from Emmitsburg, who, during the Solemn Mass, celebrated by the Rev. Pastor Curran, assisted by deacon, subdeacon and servers, admirably rendered several choice specimens of musical composition.

"After the Gospel the Very Rev. Vicar General delivered a most eloquent and powerful sermon on the text 'Because seeing they see not, and hearing they hear not, neither do they understand (St. Matt. xiii, 13)', against the errors of ancient philosophers and modern sophists.   The conclusion contained a touching allusion to the dedication and to the Real Presence.   The city of Harrisburg has never witnessed, nor, perhaps, for a long time to come shall it witness, anything so magnificent.

"TO GOD ALONE BE HONOR AND GLORY."

But the church of which good Father Curran had been so manifestly proud was, after all, a modest structure, as may be inferred from its cost of $6500.   It was, consequently, by no means a pretentious pro-cathedral.   The parish, however, had in the intervening years, grown so well, that at the date of the establishment of the diocese it numbered some two thousand souls.   The pastor, at this time, Rev. Pierce Maher, was a fine type of the middle nineteenth century missionary priest of the United States.   Zealous for souls, indefatigable in labor, and possessed of a keen sense of humor, Father Maher was highly esteemed in the capitol city.   As a young man he had, in 1837, succeeded Father Curran, and thus at the coming of Bishop Shanahan, had completed thirty-one years as Pastor of St. Patrick's. But his labors had by no means been confined to the city of Harrisburg: on the contrary he had, one time or another, attended numerous missions within a radius of fifty miles from home at Lebanon, Carlisle, Lykens, Elizabethtown, Duncannon, Millerstown, Rattling Run, Cold Springs, Rousch Gap and Gold Man Gap, besides looking after the spiritual wants of the Irish laborers engaged in construction work in his immediate vicinity.

Father Maher received his young Bishop with great cordiality, and took a prominent part in the services incident to the installation. Then, probably realizing that new conditions would arise to which an old missionary would find it just a bit difficult to adjust himself, he tendered his resignation, and retired to Norristown, where five years later he died. His successor at Harrisburg was the Rev. Richard Barry, subsequently diocesan chancellor.

The second Harrisburg parish in 1868 was that of St. Laurence, organized in 1859, for German-speaking Catholics, by Father Dryer of York. The congregation was small and occupied a church on Front Street, purchased from the United Brethren denomination for $2500.

Besides these two moderately sized congregations the only other parish in Dauphin county, fifty years ago, with a resident pastor was that of Lykens. The few Catholics of Baldwin, afterwards Steelton, a town which owed its considerable later development to the Pennsylvania Steel Works, attended St. Patrick's, Harrisburg, while the still fewer members of the fold in the neighboring town of Middletown formed a mission of Elizabethtown. Thus in the entire county, of which Harrisburg was the chief city, Bishop Shanahan found not more than three thousand persons who acknowledged his authority.

Outside the home county the status of the Church in the rest of the diocese may briefly be summarized as follows.

The counties of Perry, Juniata and Snyder had not within their limits either a Catholic chapel or mission, and to-day, with the exception of one mission, at Enola, they are in precisely the same situation. For this condition the chief cause undoubtedly has been, and is, the intense prejudice against all things Catholic entertained in certain portions of Central Pennsylvania by the descendants of the original German protestant settlers. How strong, and at the same time how absurd, this sectarian dislike of the Church was half a century ago is well illustrated by two anecdotes which 'the late Mgr. Koch used to relate with a keen sense of amusement. When pastor of Milton, one Sunday morning, in November, 1864, Father Koch was called to attend a sick person at the lower end of Snyder county. Night, dark and stormy, overtook him en route, so that he was obliged to seek accommodation until next morning in a hotel at Port Trevorton. But when the fact become known that he was a Catholic priest the traveler was told he could not be accommodated. To his indignant demand for the reason for such inhospitality the proprietor replied that his wife regarded priests as the incarnation of a certain gentleman supposed, popularly, to rejoice in horns and cloven feet, and therefore she could not in conscience permit so unwelcome a visitor to remain under her roof. Whereupon the suspected emissary of Satan assured the good man of the house that this was another case of mistaken identity, of which he would be glad to convince the landlady if she would but grant him an interview. Reluctantly this concession was made, and a venerable matron, in steel spectacles, came on the scene. Addressing her at first in English, which she appeared not to understand very well, Father Koch then in German requested the woman to convince herself, by the senses of sight and touch, that he really was not possessed of the physical characteristics of the fallen angels. Whether it was the sound of the tongue of the fatherland, or the actual evidence of a head manifestly without adornment of the kind expected, the outcome was another victory for Rome, and the previously reluctant proprietress at once became a model and friendly hostess.

On another occasion Father Koch arrived one evening at Trout Run, Lycoming county, to visit some Irish laborers in that locality. Leaving his baggage at the hotel, the missionary, as previously arranged, proceeded to hear the confessions of his people in a neighboring shanty. But, on his return to the inn, about 10.30 P. M., the son of the proprietress, who in the meantime had discovered the awful identity of the guest, handed him his belongings, and at the same time asked him to depart. Demanding the reason for such treatment, the priest was told that the young man's mother would not permit a Catholic clergyman to stay in her house. While this scene was being enacted a man who appeared to have been asleep on a couch in the room suddenly arose and threatened to make serious trouble if the management should continue to insist on Father Koch's departure. The belligerent, known at the inn, where for a dozen years he had been an employee, as Tom the Scotchman, it now developed was an Irish Catholic who, knowing the prejudice against those of his faith entertained in the locality, had long concealed his race and religion. But the ill-treatment of a priest proved too much for his worldly prudence with the result that Father Koch remained in the hotel over night, Thomas acting as a guard of honor before his door.

Such was the advanced intellectual position, fifty years ago, of the population in certain portions of Central Pennsylvania, comprised within the diocese of Harrisburg. A Catholic, at that time who, like Thomas, was rash enough to thrust himself into an atmosphere so hostile to his belief, either concealed this altogether, on the one hand, or on the other took the first opportunity of liberating himself from the influence of an environment, so dangerous from the spiritual, so depressing from the natural point of view. Those who adopted the former alternative almost invariably lost their faith. For, to retain their position they had, from the beginning, to drop all Catholic practices. Indifference was the next step, and mixed marriages, with protestant children, completed the process. In this way, in isolated localities, multitudes were lost to the Church, as is only too well demonstrated by the numerous Luther O'Sullivans and Wesley Magillicudys, in Central Pennsylvania, who, invariably, are the descendants of Catholic ancestors.

Besides the four named the diocese of Harrisburg at its origin comprised in addition the countries of Lebanon, Lancaster, York, Adams, Franklin, Fulton, Cumberland, Center, Mifflin, Clinton, Union, Northumberland, Montour and Columbia: territory extensive enough to afford scope sufficient for the zeal of a St. Paul. But the difficulties above enumerated for the counties of Perry, Juniata and Snyder operated, in a greater or less degree, for the other counties also. True, the more enlightened public opinion of the larger centers of population, such as Harrisburg, Lancaster and York, better appreciated the merits of Catholicism. When for instance, the veteran Father Maher resigned the rectorship of St. Patrick's, a leading local paper paid him notable tribute. " Those acquainted with Father Maher," said the *Patriot*, (September 12, 1868) " know his ability as a speaker and his unblemished character as a herald of the cross. By his long and consistent record in the divine service he had demonstrated that there is great efficiency in the Christian religion. By his unremitting zeal and unflagging energy he has built up the Church over which he has presided for thirty years from a few persons to a large congregation. Genial, urbane, intelligent, he has endeared himself to all who possess the elements of sociability. We could not easily over-rate the qualities of Father Maher."

This high estimate of a Catholic priest was not at all unique in the Commonwealth of Pennsylvania, but unfortunately it was confined to the intelligent minority; the majority in the cities were little if at all more liberal-minded, where Catholics were concerned, than in the country districts.

But, needless to say, if the Church took cognizance of obstacles in any sense other than as incentives to greater exertions, she would have never existed, and consequently, the Ordinary and clergy of the infant diocese of Harrisburg, fifty years ago, were not in the least discouraged at the prospect before them. Of the twenty-two priests who formed the Bishop's staff at the outset eighteen were resident pastors; most of these, however, in addition, attended from one to four missions. And although from the present-day standpoint, almost all the parishes of the diocese were small, still not a few among them had a long and interesting history. A brief survey, therefore, at this stage, of the origins of Catholicity in Central Pennsylvania, will not be without interest.

By right of priority of origin, as well as of its importance as the cradle of Catholicity in this portion of the State, the famous Jesuit mission of Conewago has here the first claim on our attention. The Conewago Valley was first settled, in the early eighteenth century, by English colonists, among whom were some Catholics from the colony of Lord Baltimore. From this time Catholics, chiefly of Irish and German origin, came in, slowly but steadily, drawn thither by the fact, which was widely known, that the Jesuit Fathers ministered, in that locality, to the spiritual wants of their Catholic brethren. Such, for example, was the inducement which attracted Samuel Lilly, who, landing in Chester in 1730, proceeded at once to Conewago, where, he understood, there was a Catholic colony looked after by the Jesuits from Maryland. This pioneer died in 1758, and his tomb may still be seen in Conewago Cemetery. By the middle of the eighteenth century the number of Catholics in the district had increased to the point that a resident pastor became necessary, the Jesuit Father Manners being the first to hold the office.

For the next fifty years the records of the Conewago mission, probably in part owing to the suppression of the Society of Jesus (1773) by Clement XIV, are scant. However, from a report of Father John Carroll, afterwards Archbishop of Baltimore, we learn that in 1784 there were at Conewago about a thousand communicants. During the first half of the nineteenth century the Church in this favored territory continued to flourish, and the Jesuits, as occasion demanded, established missions at Hanover, Littlestown, Taneytown, Bonneauville, Gettysburg, Paradise and New Oxford. A handsome church, to take the place of the original log edifice, was erected at Conewago in 1787, and this, in turn, enlarged and finely decorated, was consecrated by Bishop Kenrick, August 15, 1851. "Conewago Chapel", as in the vicinity it is affectionately designated, was the first church in the United States dedicated to the Sacred Heart. As an early and highly successful Catholic colony also, this famous Jesuit mission should prove of special interest to the social historian. For, according to a well-informed local authority, there were, thirty-five years ago, as many as five thousand Catholic descendants of the early settlers in the Conewago district. This same writer informs us that in the territory bounded by Hanover, Gettysburg, Littlestown, and New Oxford, at the same date, from half to two-thirds of the population was Catholic.

Leaving Adams county, within whose limits were most of the missions above named, we find in the neighboring county of York, in 1868, two parishes and one mission. In the year 1757, according to a report then made to the

British government, York county contained a population of 116 German and 73 Irish Catholics, who had already, in 1750, purchased the property on which St. Patrick's church, in the city of York, now stands. Up to 1819, when the parish received its first resident pastor, St. Patrick's was attended from Conewago. In 1852 a second parish, for the German-speaking Catholics of the town, was established by Bishop Neumann. This congregation at its origin contained about 100 souls, while St. Patrick's at the time of the separation contained in the neighborhood of seven or eight hundred souls. Lancaster county, probably the best represented in Catholic population in the new diocese, contained in 1868 five parishes with resident pastors, two in Lancaster city, two in Columbia and one in Elizabethtown. The oldest parish in the county was that of St. Mary's, Lancaster, ground for which was purchased by the Rev. Henry Neill, S.J. in 1742. The original log church was destroyed by fire of, it was believed, incendiary origin, in 1760. This was replaced by a stone structure which, in turn, proving too small for the needs of the congregation, gave way to the present St. Mary's, erected in 1852. According to reliable data this parish in 1785 had a membership of about 700. When Lancaster came to form part of the diocese of Harrisburg St. Mary's had as pastor one of the most venerable figures in the American ecclesiastical world of the time: the Rev. Bernard Keenan. Father Keenan, born in county Tyrone, Ireland, came with Bishop Conwell to the United States in 1820. Shortly after his arrival he was raised to the priesthood (November 21, 1820) and is said to have been the first priest ordained in Philadelphia. Three years later he was appointed Rector of St. Mary's, Lancaster, a position he continued to hold for the next fifty-four years. He was the first Vicar General of the diocese of Harrisburg, and died in extreme old age in 1877.

St. Joseph's parish, Lancaster, formed in 1850, included all the German-speaking Catholics of the city. From the beginning the congregation must have been comparatively large and in a few years it surpassed in numbers the parent parish of St. Mary's.

Probably the other most important parish in the lower section of the diocese in 1868 was that of St. Mary's, Lebanon, where a congregation, attended by the Jesuits, had existed from the latter part of the eighteenth century. A fine tribute is paid St. Mary's by Bishop Kenrick in the diary of his third episcopal visitation, for the year 1832. " Peace and piety," says this great missionary prelate, " flourish here. Sixty persons received Holy Communion on the day named above (February 14, 1832); and very many, a number not less than sixty, on the days preceding. There are about 500 souls in the congregation. Father Boniface (Corvin, S.J.) told me that, even during the week, every day, when he is here, the faithful Germans come to the church to receive the Sacraments ". One can imagine what pleasure it would have given that Apostle of daily Communion, the late Holy Father, Pius X, had he known that, more than eighty years ago, the devotion to the Blessed Sacrament he so strongly inculcated had been anticipated by the Catholics of a remote town in Central Pennsylvania. At the date of the establishment of Harrisburg, Lebanon contained about two thousand Catholics, and, as a striking proof that the faith of St. Mary's congregation had by no means diminished in the intervening years the fact may be cited that Father Kuhlmann, appointed pastor in 1869, in four years erected and paid for the fine Gothic Church of which Lebanon Catholics are so justly proud to-day.

Such were the most important centers of Catholicity within a radius of fifty miles from Harrisburg half a century ago. Besides those named Chambersburg was the only parish, in this part of the diocese, which then had a resident pastor; Center and Clinton counties, which now belong to the diocese of Altoona, had two resident pastors, one of whom, Rev. Thomas McGovern, stationed at Bellefonte, was destined to be the second Bishop of Harrisburg.

But the county of the diocese that in the future was destined to exhibit the largest and most rapid growth was one which, within its limits, possessed untold mineral wealth in the form of anthracite coal—Northumberland county. The most important town in this county, from the standpoint of Catholic growth, Shamokin, was founded in 1835, just as the anthracite coal regions of Pennsylvania were in the beginning of their development. Catholic families were among the earliest settlers in this locality and had the honor of erecting the first church within the limits of the present borough in 1836. For the next thirty years Shamokin mission was attended by various priests from Milton, Pottsville, Minersville and Danville, until in 1866 it received its first resident pastor in the person of the Rev. John Joseph Koch. Just as Father Keenan at an earlier date, in the southern part of the diocese, was a landmark of the Church, so in the northern section, from the sixties to his death, January 31, 1917, Father Koch had been an eyewitness, and fosterer, of Catholic growth. Born in 1840, in Lorraine, then part of France, at the age of seventeen John Joseph Koch entered the Grand Seminary of Nancy. Five years later the young seminarist volunteered for the American missions, and in May 1862 arrived in Philadelphia. After completing his course of studies at the diocesan seminary of St. Charles Borromeo he was ordained, February 1863. and the following May was appointed pastor of St. Joseph's parish, Milton.

The parish of Milton at that date embraced a territory one hundred miles long by forty wide, with five small churches and fifteen stations: from which it is evident the young rector's charge was not one to which a lover of ease would aspire. After three years of strenuous missionary life, spent mostly on horseback, attending to the spiritual wants of his widely dispersed flock, Father Koch was appointed pastor of St. Edward's parish, Shamokin, where, at the date of the foundation of the diocese, we find him, but relieved of all his missions save those of Locust Gap and Trevorton. Fifty years later, notwithstanding the exhausting labors of his early missionary career, Monsignor Koch, V.G., celebrated the golden jubilee of his pastorate in Shamokin, a record nearly unique in the annals of the Church.

Besides Father Koch there was, at the coming of the first Bishop, but one other resident pastor in Northumberland county — Father Stenzel of Milton, while the adjoining county of Montour, the last in the diocese to be enumerated, had but one small parish at Danville.

Such was the diocese of Harrisburg at its origin: a field not at all promising. It consisted of a large territory, with a handful of small, scattered parishes, which averaged not more than five or six hundred souls. Most of these parishes, too, carried a heavy burden of debt and, not infrequently, experienced difficulty in raising the amounts necessary to meet their annual interest. This was one of the first matters that demanded the attention of the Bishop. In numerous instances he came to the rescue of small congregations, and by means of personal appeals, mostly in the large churches of Philadelphia, he secured considerable sums which proved of the greatest service to pastors with too limited resources.

The next urgent question to be solved by Bishop Shanahan was that of securing a greater number of priests, since, without laborers, it was evident, his extensive vineyard could not properly be cultivated. With a view to supplying this deficiency he purchased the splendid property in East Harrisburg known as Sylvan Heights, where, in October 1883, he opened in the mansion on the estate a diocesan seminary.

The Bishop himself took up his residence in the seminary, the immediate direction of which he entrusted to an experienced professor, Rev. Massimo Cassini. The experiment proved fairly successful and, during the term of its existence, the diocesan theological school produced a considerable number of excellent priests. But a few years, unfortunately, demonstrated that a diocese so limited in resources as Harrisburg could not maintain an adequate teaching staff, thus rendering necessary, in 1886, the closing of Sylvan Heights Seminary, and the transfer of its students to various long established institutions for the training of priests. The property, however, was retained, and served as an episcopal residence until 1901, when, in the enlarged and remodeled mansion the second Bishop Shanahan established on Sylvan Heights an orphanage for girls.

As the supply of priests gradually increased Bishop Shanahan lost no time in establishing new parishes, for he realized that unless a priest was stationed in every community capable of erecting a church and maintaining a pastor, religion would, sooner or later, suffer serious detriment. Acting in accordance with this correct view we find that during the eighteen years of his administration he erected new parishes at Williamstown, Lancaster (St. Anthony's), Marietta, New Freedom, Phillipsburg, Lock Haven, (St. Agnes), Shamokin (St. Stanislaus), Mount Carmel (Our Lady of Mt. Carmel and St. Joseph's), and Centralia, while in addition he appointed resident pastors to the missions of Littlestown, Snow Shoe, Renovo, Carlisle, Lewistown, Locust Gap and Danville (St. Hubert's). Thus the diocese during this period was enriched with ten entirely new parishes and seven missions were elevated to the rank of parishes. The important mission at Steelton also was established about 1870 and was attended from the procathedral.

Another subject that was near the heart of the Bishop of Harrisburg was that of the religious training of Catholic children.   When one looks over the history of the Church in the United States for the past fifty years it is impossible not to admire the courage of the Bishops and priests of that pioneer age for the manner in which they grappled with the all-important question of Christian education.   For, both of these orders of the hierarchy at an early period fully realized that unless the children of Catholic parentage were carefully trained in the religious tenets of their forefathers the future of the Church in this country would, through the constantly increasing tide of religious indifferentism, be gravely imperiled.   Bishop Shanahan gave special care to this phase of his episcopal duties, and with excellent results: on his arrival in Harrisburg there were but seven parish schools in his jurisdiction, whereas, at the date of his death, September 24, 1886, his diocese possessed 29 schools, with an attendance of 4,252 children.   The Catholic population also increased under his administration from twenty-five to thirty-five thousand, and the number of priests from 22 to 51.

From the above facts and figures it is evident that the episcopate of Bishop Jeremiah Shanahan was eminently successful: all the progress that, with the small resources at his disposal, could reasonably have been expected by even the most optimistic had been fully realized when death snatched him away, at the early age of 52.   His unexpected demise was universally and deeply regretted throughout the diocese, and by his numerous friends in Philadelphia. Those who knew him intimately never weary speaking of` the charms of his personality, enhanced as this was by the added charm of ripe scholarship.

After an interregnum of eighteen months, during which Very Rev. M. J. McBride acted as Administrator, a successor to Bishop Shanahan was appointed in the person of Rev. Thomas McGovern, then pastor at Danville.   Born in

Co. Cavan, Ireland, in 1832, the second Bishop of Harrisburg was at the time of his consecration, in his fifty-sixth year. When Thomas McGovern was only a year old his parents emigrated to Bradford county, Pennsylvania. Like his predecessor Bishop McGovern received part of his classical education at St. Joseph's College, Binghampton, N. Y. In 1855 he entered Mt. St. Mary's College, Emmitsburg, Md., where, in 1859 he received the degree of Bachelor of Arts. A few months later he entered Mt. St. Mary's Theological Seminary, but completed his studies for the priesthood in the Philadelphia Seminary of St. Charles Borromeo, where he was ordained by Bishop Wood, December 27, 1861. After three years of priestly labor at St. Michael's, Philadelphia, and in Pottstown, Father McGovern, in 1864, was placed in charge of the Bellefonte mission, which then embraced three counties: Center, Mifflin and Juniata. Here, zealously performing the strenuous work of a missionary, he continued until 1870, when he was appointed pastor of St. Patrick's, York. In 1873 he was made pastor of Danville, where he remained until called upon to accept the responsibilities of the episcopal office.

Thus it will be seen that the second Bishop of Harrisburg belonged to the class of hard-working missionaries who laid the foundations of the Church in this State, and who, moreover, by their great exertions, " in journeyings often ", were, under Providence, the means of preserving the faith in their widely scattered congregations. To those who, like the writer, only knew him in later life the most marked characteristics of Bishop Mcovern were a great kindliness of manner, a calm unruffled temper, and a keen, logical mind, well stored with the salient facts bearing on the chief controversial questions which, in his early years, were so warmly debated between Catholics and Protestants. Yet, although fearless and uncompromising, as well as able, in public debate, these aggressive qualities did not prevent his having in private life many warm friends among non-Catholics. One of these at the time of his consecration paid him the following tribute: " Rev. Thomas McGovern is a man of ability, energy and executive powers. As a controversialist he is a dangerous opponent and seems to be armed at every point of battle for the Church and defence of the faith he professes. Yet he is liberal and generous, courteous and pleasant to all,. and holds an honorable place in the community."

During the ten years of Bishop McGovern's administration the growth of the diocese continued in all its phases. Among the first and most important of his works was the enactment in synod of an excellent code of laws, which, with additions and some modifications, is still in use. The four important missions at Hanover, Middletown, New Oxford and Waynesboro were raised by him to the rank of parishes, and he created six new parishes, four in Mt. Carmel and two in Shamokin, for the accommodation of the constantly increasing population of the Slavic race. Of the many problems that have engaged the attention of American bishops in the past four decades perhaps none has been more difficult of solution than that of providing for the religious needs of the enormous body of immigrants that have come to the United States from the Austro-Hungarian, the German and Russian empires and from Italy. From about the time of the formation of the Harrisburg diocese the coal fields of Pennsylvania, where work was plentiful and remunerative, began to attract Polish immigrants, and in 1874 the Poles of Shamokin took steps to organize a congregation. A census taken at that date discovered in Shamokin 35 families and some unmarried young men of this nationality, nearly all from the Prussian province of Posen. In 1876 the Polish people of Shamokin were fortunate enough to secure as their pastor a man whose memory is still held in high esteem by all of his race in that flourishing borough: Rev. Father Klonowski. The predecessor of Father Klonowski, Father Juskiewics, had purchased lots and begun the erection of a church in 1874; the edifice thus initiated was completed by Father Klonowski and dedicated in 1881. Between these two dates the number of Polish Catholics had rapidly increased in Shamokin, and in their wake came also, in considerable numbers, Lithuanians, Ruthenians and Slovaks. For the time being all of these attended the Polish church, but later, as we shall see, each nationality established a separate congregation.

About 1860 Poles began to settle in Mt. Carmel also. At that date there was no Catholic church in this borough, but in 1866 a mission was established and attended by Father Koch of Shamokin. Three years later this mission was attached to Centralia, whose pastor, Rev. D. I. McDermott, erected the first Catholic church in Mt. Carmel. For some years all the Catholics of Mt. Carmel attended the same church until, in 1878, the Polish population were authorized to form a separate congregation. Here also the first steps toward organization were taken by Father Juskiewicz and the work completed by Father Klonowski. The new congregation, consisting of about seventy families, undertook to erect a church, which was dedicated, December, 1878.

Such was the status of the " foreign " question when Bishop McGovern assumed the direction of the diocese. During the ten years of his administration it occupied no small amount of his attention. For, as the tide of immigration from Eastern Europe grew, it became a serious problem to provide priests of the various nationalities who were capable of coping with the situation. It is indeed true that this difficulty was not quite insurmountable. But at the same time experience proved that many of the clergy, who, in those days, came from Europe, were afflicted with an almost uncontrollable *wanderlust*, so that they seemed unable to attach themselves permanently to any congregation. Moreover the gift of finance, indispensable to a priest in the United States, was too frequently wanting in men who, otherwise, were worthy enough representatives of the priesthood.

In the diocese of Harrisburg Bishop McGovern had to cope with no small share of the perplexities and annoyances that were inseparable from the task of providing for the spiritual care of a large body of non-English-speaking immigrants. But his patience in this regard was inexhaustible, and he nobly did his best to meet all difficulties. His perseverance was rewarded with success, so that, not only did he continue to provide for the spirtual welfare of the two congregations existing at the time of his consecration, but in addition he established in Shamokin separate churches for the Ruthenians and the Slovaks, and, in Mt. Carmel, for the Russian Poles, the Lithuanians, the Ruthenians and the Slovaks.

In the spring of 1898 the health of Bishop McGovern became seriously impaired. Although a man of robust constitution the great strain of his early years as a missionary priest and, in later life, the cares and worries of the episcopal office, had together undermined his strength, so that when grave illness overtook him his resisting powers were feeble. At first he seemed to recover from what proved to be his last illness, but a sudden relapse, caused by the intense heat, rendered his case hopeless, and, July 25, 1898, he was called to his reward.

Under the administration of Bishop McGovern the Catholic population of the diocese increased from thirty-five to forty-five thousand, the number of parish schools from 29 to 32, and the school attendance from 4353 to 5959. The parishes already formed, too, during this decade, devoted special attention to the improvements of existing plants: churches, schools and rectories. Seven new churches were erected, some of them quite ambitious structures, in the following places: Littlestown (1892), Mt. Carmel (Our Lady, 1888), McSherrystown (frame structure, 1889), York (St. Patrick's 1895), Quarryville (1896), Columbia, St. Peter's (1897) and Renovo (1897). Thus it will be seen that under the direction of Bishop McGovern considerable progress was made, especially in the matter of organization and the upbuilding of parishes.

During the interregnum of about nine months following the death of Bishop McGovern, the diocese was ruled by the Very Rev. J. J. Koch, as administrator. On January 7, 1899 the third Bishop of Harrisburg was appointed in the person of the Rev. John W. Shanahan, then pastor of the church of Our Mother of Sorrows, Philadelphia. Born at Silver Lake, January 3, 1846, and ordained from Overbrook Seminary in 1869, the second Bishop Shanahan began his episcopal career about the age when that of his brother, the first Bishop of Harrisburg, ended. Consecrated, May 1, 1899, the Bishop a few days later took charge of his diocese, the ceremony of installation taking place in the pro-cathedral. The first few months after his arrival in Harrisburg were largely devoted by the new Bishop to the necessary task of obtaining his bearings; this he accomplished by means of extensive visits throughout the diocese, making inquiries in practically every parish as to local needs and conditions. The outcome of his investigation was the conviction (1) that the time had now arrived for the creation of many new parishes, (2) that the diocese was in need of commodious institutions for the care of orphan children, and (3) that the erection of a cathedral, if feasible, was much to be desired.

We have already seen that the six parishes created by Bishop McGovern were for non-English-speaking peoples, and that the parishes of Irish and German origin were, during his term of office, chiefly occupied in erecting or enlarging churches, schools, and rectories. This latter necessary work of internal consolidation had in most cases now reached a certain stage of finality, so that the time was ripe to take up the question of extension. Beginning with the episcopal city, Harrisburg, in 1899, with a general population of some 50,000 people, had but two Catholic churches, both located in the centre of the town, and within less than a furlong of one another. Of these two churches one, as already noted, had been in existence for over seventy, the other for about forty years. Meanwhile Harrisburg had grown from a small town to be a fairly large city, and it was quite natural that many Catholics should have selected for residence locations in the out-lying districts, where property was less expensive.

Thus, while the Catholic population was slowly growing, this growth, to a considerable extent, was in suburban districts, remote from both existing churches. For the accommodation of the Catholics thus situated in 1900 two missions, attended from the pro-cathedral, were established in the eastern and western sections of the city. Within a few months this experiment proved so successful that, in January 1901, the east Harrisburg mission became St. Francis parish, and at the same time the Sacred Heart parish was established in south Harrisburg. The mission in the west end, where also a parochial school had been opened, remained attached to the pro-cathedral until 1907, when it also was formed into St. Mary's parish. At the present time two of these parishes are in flourishing condition, with commodious churches and schools, while the third, in a less developed section of the city, has held its own. Strange to say that the pro-cathedral parish, from which all three congregations were detached, has suffered very little in consequence, although in 1901, when the first two new parishes were established, it comprised less than 2300 souls.

The Harrisburg experiment having thus, with God's blessing, proved a success, Bishop Shanahan subsequently tested
its efficiency in various other places and always with the
same good results. In Lancaster the Sacred Heart parish
was organized in November, 1900; York, some years later,
followed suit with St. Rose of Lima's (1906) and St.
Joseph's (1912), and Shamokin (1913) with St. Joseph's.
Besides these, in the more important cities, the second Bishop
Shanahan established, for English-speaking Catholics,
parishes at Midway and Locust Dale and appointed resident
pastors to the missions of Cornwall, Dallastown, Fairfield,
McSherrystown, Orrtana, Paradise and Sunbury.

At the same time, their continuous and rapid increase
in the diocese, during the previous decade and a half, even
more than at any earlier period, exacted from the Ordinary
more than the average of attention to provide for the
spiritual needs of the foreign-born population. For these
immigrants, constantly pouring into Central Pennsylvania,
Bishop Shanahan provided the following parishes with resident pastors: Berwick, St. Mary's (for Americans, Slovaks,
Magyars and Italians), SS. Cyril and Methodius (Greek-
Ruthenian); Lebanon, St. Gertrude's (Austro-German and
Italian), SS. Cyril and Methodius (Slovak); Merion
Heights (Polish, Slovak and Italian); Mt. Carmel, St.
Peter's Tyrolean and Italian); Shamokin, St. Michael's
(Lithuanian), St. Stephen's (Polish); Steelton, St. Mary
of Grace (Croatian), St. John's (Austro-German), St.
Peter's (Slavonian), St. Anne's (Italian). Missions were
also established during Bishop Shanahan's regime, at Ex-
change for American Catholics, and at Waltonville and
Harrisburg for Italians. Thus, altogether, Bishop Shanahan
founded 21 new parishes, raised seven missions to the rank
of parishes, and erected three new missions. He also established a resident chaplaincy at Mt. Alto, for the patients
at the State Hospital for tuberculosis.

The second item on the program of the third Bishop of Harrisburg, to provide adequate accommodation for orphaned children, was no less urgent than the first. Prior to 1901, with the exception of a small parish orphanage, the diocese had no institution for children deprived of parental care. The want of an establishment to meet this demand was all the greater because of the many dangerous avocations of men in this section of the Commonwealth: coal-mining, steel-working, railroading, which deprive, perhaps, an abnormally large number of children of their natural protectors. Yet, despite the acknowledged need, the important question, eighteen years ago, was: Could the diocese erect and maintain its own orphan asylums?

After deliberating the pros and cons for a year or so Bishop Shanahan, trusting in God, resolved to transform the old episcopal residence, and former seminary, at Sylvan Heights into a home for orphan girls. The clergy of the diocese heartily endorsed the Bishop's determination, and, to meet the necessary expenditure, cheerfully assumed the burden of an assessment amounting to a dollar a head for every individual in their respective parishes. While the financial difficulty was thus easily disposed of, the old mansion on Sylvan Heights was so remodeled that when opened, in 1901, in charge of the Sisters of Mercy, it housed comfortably about a hundred children. In 1910 a new wing, containing a chapel and class rooms, was added to the original structure. A few months before Bishop Shanahan's death, however, the main building was destroyed by fire, and among the latest acts of his life was the approval of the plans for the existing fine structure on Sylvan Heights, one of the best appointed orphanages in Pennsylvania.

The orphan girls thus provided for several years elapsed before any provision could be made for the boys of the diocese in need of institutional care. At length, in 1907, some generous gifts from a few philanthropically disposed persons made this project of the Bishop also feasible, and he began the erection of a commodious building at Paradise, Adams county, on a diocesan farm of some two hundred and eighty acres. The original gifts, supplemented by others which came in from time to time, carried the work on a considerable way, and a second assessment on the diocese, which, as in the previous case, was cheerfully borne, completed what is now a model Agricultural School, capable of accommodating 150 boys. The average attendance since its opening in 1910 has been about 100: the institution is in charge of the Sisters of St. Joseph.

Meanwhile, in the interval between the establishment of Sylvan Heights Home and Paradise Protectory, the third article of the Bishop's program had been undertaken and successfully brought to completion. The original St. Patrick's church in Harrisburg had been considerably enlarged and handsomely decorated in 1873. But of course even the remodeled edifice was merely a temporary expedient, intended to serve only until such time as a dignified cathedral could be erected. This time arrived in 1903 when, the debt on the church property being almost entirely paid, plans drawn by Mr. George I. Lovatt for a new cathedral were adopted. In three years the edifice was completed and dedicated with all due solemnity. Its style is renaissance and the structure presents a handsome appearance, the universal verdict being that it is worthy of a place, if even an humble one, in the splendid catalogue of cathedrals erected by Catholic genius and Catholic generosity during the past nineteen centuries. Of its cost, amounting to $185,000.00, the diocese contributed about $100,000.00, the balance being assumed by the cathedral parish. In this instance, as in the case of the orphanages, the response to the Bishop's appeal for funds was remarkably generous. St. Patrick's parish alone, consisting of about fifteen hundred souls, contributed, while the cathedral was in course

of erection, some forty thousand dollars, and since the dedication has paid all but a few thousand of the remaining
debt of forty-five thousand dollars.

After seventeen years of intensely active pastoral work
Bishop Shanahan was called to his great reward, February
19, 1916. Five months later his successor was appointed,
July 10, 1916, in the person of Right Rev. Philip R.
McDevitt, D.D., fourth Bishop of Harrisburg.

Such in brief is the history of fifty years of Catholic
growth in the southern portion of Central Pennsylvania.
Absolutely speaking, of course the progress made in this
half-century is comparatively small, yet, in relation to its
population and resources, few dioceses, perhaps, can point
to a better record. Beginning in 1868 with 22 priests and
a few, mostly unimportant churches, scarcely any parochial
schools, and a few thousand Catholics, the diocese of Harrisburg numbers to-day fully a hundred thousand souls, and
this, despite the fact that three of its original counties, including about six thousand souls, were, in 1906, given to the
new diocese of Altoona. One hundred and twenty priests
are now actively at work within its limits; every one of its
68 parishes has a handsome church, and forty-four of
them have parochial schools, in which more than eleven
thousand children receive an excellent grammar, and some
a high-school education. The diocese also, as we have seen,
is prepared to care for its orphans and the spiritual and
material condition of the various parishes is excellent.

THE LATEST HISTORY OF ACADIA.—II. THE DOOM OF THE ACADIANS.[1]

BY THE REV. JOHN M. LENHART, O.M.Cap.

This second volume of Richard's *Acadie* surpasses the preceding by its intrinsic historical value. It covers only the space of six years (1749-1755), but years fraught with momentous developments. Events march with dramatic swiftness leading up to the final climax, the deportation. Certainly, friends of justice and of the " square deal " will find it no pleasant reading to follow the author through all the infamous machinations devised to ensnare a guileless people and eventually bring it to ruin. All the foul deeds perpetrated by the British officials in dealing with the naive Acadian peasantry are presented in the dazzling light of historic truth and are branded by accents which honesty lends to indignation.

The volume under review comprises Chapters XIII to XXIX (pages 1 to 425) of Richard's original work together with seven appendices of documents published by the editor (pp. 429 to 497).

The object of Richard's work is to give us the true history of the most dramatic and, at the same time, the most barbarous episode of American History, of the "Acadian Tragedy," as it is called. Acadia had been forty years in the possession of the English and, yet, in 1749, there were not a half a dozen English colonists in the whole province. The British garrison stationed all this time at Annapolis

[1] E. Richard–H. D'Arles, *Acadie*, T, II, Depuis la Paix D'Aix-La-Chapelle jusqu'à la Deportation. Quebec & Boston. 1918. Pp. XVI, 505. On the first vol. cf. Records, Vol. XXVIII, pp. 193-201.

had been depending on the Acadians for supplies, and this was one of the many reasons the English had for keeping these French peasants in their country. In March 1749, England decided to found a British colony in Acadia. On June 27th following 2756 persons landed there and founded Halifax (Richard—D'Arles, II, pp. 9-11). At that time about 9,000 Acadians lived on British territory, while nearly 3500 more had settled in French domains (pp. 8, 62). Things had changed now. The Acadians were henceforth treated with still greater rigor. But despite ever-increasing oppressions and odious provocations perpetrated with the express intent to exasperate this good-natured people and to incite them to some rash deeds of a nature to justify their deportation, the Acadians never once committed themselves to threats nor to attempts at rebellion (p. 14). "The memorials," states the non-Catholic historian B. Murdoch (*History of Nova Scotia*, II, p. 286), "which the Acadians addressed to the Council of Halifax are all marked with a deferential moderation."

That the Acadians still inhabited Acadia in 1749 was due to the perfidy of the British officials. The Acadians were granted permission to leave the country by the Treaty of Utrecht, April 1713, and accordingly had resolved repeatedly to withdraw from the British territory. But every time they were prevented from leaving the country on various pretexts. In 1713 when Vetch, the Lieutenant-Governor of Acadia, received the warrant from Queen Anne, dated June 23, 1713, directing him "to allow the Acadians to remove elsewhere if they would choose so," he pretended that he had no authority and that they had to wait for the return of the Governor who again put them off by the pretext that he had to get further directions from the Queen. The Acadians naively had been looking for a final answer on this question during three years, but none was ever given. In 1720 Governor Philipps ordered the Acadians either to take the oath or to leave the country without carrying away anything else besides their clothes. The Acadians chose the latter alternative to the great dismay of the Governor. Since they could not leave by sea, having no ships, they commenced to open a road across the country. But Philipps proved himself master of the situation by ordering them to stop this work. And the Acadians obeyed like dutiful children. Again in 1726 the Acadians had determined to leave the country rather than take the oath and again they were ordered by Lieutenant-Governor Armstrong to stop their preparations toward emigration. Moreover, French ships were not allowed to enter the ports of Acadia and British ships would not transport any Acadians. Later when in 1749 a direct over-land route had been opened into French territory, the Acadians would not leave on account of their qualified oath of allegiance taken in 1730 (*op. cit.*, pp. 39-41).

The Acadians had refused for fifteen years to take any oath of allegiance whatever. In 1730, however, all took this oath " upon condition that it should be understood that they should always be exempted from bearing arms against either Indians or French ", as the former Lieutenant-Governor Mascarene informed the Council of Halifax on July 14, 1749 (*op. cit.*, p. 16). Later, on July 18, 1755, Lieutenant-Governor Lawrence informed the Lords of Trade that the Acadians never yet had taken an *un*qualified oath (*op. cit.*, p. 352). Even Parkman, the most thorough-going antagonist of the Acadians, admits in his latest book *A Half Century of Conflict*, (Vol. I, p. 209, Vol. II, p. 173) that the oath taken in 1730 " was qualified by a promise on the part of Governor Philipps that they should not be required to take up arms against either French or Indians ". The Acadians had not been molested after that during nineteen years. But on July 14, 1749, seventeen days after the foundation of Halifax, Governor Cornwallis issued a declaration stating that the Acadians had to take an unconditional oath of allegiance within the space of three months. The Acadians refused to take this oath and demanded permission to leave the country. Cornwallis informed the Acadians, on Aug. 1, 1749, that those who would like to emigrate could do so *provided that they do not take anything of their property away with them* (p. 21). But this qualified permission was equal to a covert injunction. The Acadians insisted on their rights guaranteed by the Treaty of Utrecht and demanded permission to sell or transport their property. This matter was still pending when Cornwallis received instructions in March 1750 that " all forcible measures to induce the Acadians to leave their settlements should for the present be waived." Now the whole situation had changed. Accordingly Cornwallis had to alter his course and to bend every effort to keep these French settlers in the country. When, therefore, the Acadians came to Halifax in April of 1750 to ask for the long-delayed leave to emigrate, Cornwallis ordered them to go back and first do their sowing. The Acadians good-naturedly obeyed and tilled and sowed their farms, apparently for the benefit of strangers. On May 25, 1750 they returned to beg again leave to retire. This time the governor resorted to another subterfuge. He told the Acadians they could not leave without his passport, as they themselves knew, and that he was willing to issue such passports, *as soon as peace would be re-established in the Province.* Cornwallis now had things well in his hands. Acadia was at peace and could not be more so at any other time. Every Acadian wishing to emigrate needed a passport which could be refused on the plea that the country was not yet at peace. The Acadians were not slow in finding out that such passports never would be granted. There was no other alternative left them than either to stay or to leave without the governor's permission. Over-conscientious as they were, they remained peacefully on their farms till the time of the deportation (pp. 14-58).

During the two years from 1750 to 1752 nothing more is heard about the vexed question of taking the oath. The Acadians worked quietly on their farms and the governor and his council at Halifax did not concern themselves with them. The despatches of Cornwallis to the home government are almost a total blank regarding these French peasants all the while. In August 1752 Cornwallis was succeeded by Hopson. The new governor had received instructions to exact an unconditional oath of allegiance from the Acadians. On December 1752 he implored the home government not to enforce these orders. " It is impossible to force the present oath on them," he wrote. " The Acadians of Chignecto or Beaubassin made it a pretext for leaving their lands. Mr. Cornwallis can inform you how useful, nay, even necessary, these people are to us. *It is impossible to supply their place if they leave.*" To his great satisfaction this most conciliating of all British governors of Acadia, received the answer, on March 28, 1753: " The French inhabitants are *not to be forced* to take the oath, although it is desirable they should do so " (pp. 171-190). Two years later they were offered the oath of allegiance for the last time and when they accepted this offer, they were not admitted to take the oath, but kept prisoners in their own country till they were finally deported (pp. 252-259, 312-315, 327-329, 353). Richard gives (p. 258) a graphic list of all the subterfuges practised upon these unsuspicious peasants from 1710 to 1755.

The exemption which the Acadians demanded was a matter of dire necessity for them as well as an expression of lofty humanitarian sentiments. The oath would have placed them invariably in the unfortunate position either to be killed by the Indians or to bear arms against their own French brothers. Their demand was not contrary to true loyalty, as the Acadians had proved repeatedly. The English government should have either let them go or accepted their conditions. When the exemption, their chief condition, had been granted once in 1730 the government was bound to respect it. Richard points out (p. 58) an analogous case, that of the Mennonites who settled in Russia under the same stipulation not to bear arms. The editor, however, remarks (note on p. 60) that the situation of the Mennonites in Russia bears only a remote resemblance to that of the Acadians in Acadia. Yet if the editor would have been better informed on the history of the German colonists in Southern Russia, he would have observed that the resemblance is very striking. From 1763 to 1820 more than 100,000 Germans emigrated to Southern Russia where they cultivated the vast steppes. The Russian government guaranteed to these colonists free exercise of religion and exemption from military service. Moreover they were to enjoy a liberal share of self-government. The majority of these settlers were Lutherans and Catholics, the Mennonites forming a small minority. The Russian government fulfilled its obligations towards those German-speaking colonists for a whole century. The Catholics were always supplied with German-speaking priests. In 1847 even a German diocese was established for these colonists (Tiraspol). These German priests and bishops could do much that was forbidden to their colleagues in other parts of Russia (cf. *Catholic Encyclopedia*, s. v. *Tiraspol*, XIV, p. 739). For more than 150 years the Russian government did not infringe on the free exercise of religion guaranteed to these settlers. Exemption from military service, however, was revoked in 1871 and a respite of ten years granted during which the colonists might emigrate without forfeiture of any property. The greater number of colonists, even of Mennonites, preferred to remain in Russia, while only a small minority emigrated to America. The conclusion which

Richard draws from this parallel case is surely unimpeach-
able, viz. that *liberal* England should have accorded to her
exempts in Acadia nothing less than the *Tsar* had been doing all along regarding his colonists in Southern Russia.

The chapters XV to XVIII (pp. 61-169) describe the
efforts made by the French to draw the Acadians over into
French territory. More than anybody else the Abbé Le
Loutre had tried, but without avail, to induce the Acadians
to go over to the French side. He is, therefore, the pre-
dominating figure of these chapters. "All historians,"
remarks Richard (pp. 66-67), " speak of the Abbés Le
Loutre, Germain, Maillard, Le Guerne, as if they had been
missionaries to the Acadians on English territory. On this
supposition, their efforts to subserve the interests of France
are interpreted as shameful. But none of these priests ever
was a missionary to the Acadians in British Nova Scotia.
All these missionaries lived in the territory claimed and occupied by France." Moreover, they were missionaries to
the Indians, and the Indians were neither British nor French
subjects, but allies of either the one or the other. In a
similar manner historians have been overlooking the broad
fact that the missionaries to the Acadians on *English*
territory from 1710 to 1755, had not been British subjects
nor under the jurisdiction of the King of Great Britain,
but had been sent *and paid* by the French government according to the terms of the treaty of Utrecht (*Canadian
Archives*, 1894, pp. 90-91. Cf. Richard—D' Arles, II,
186 sq.). Hence the patriotism shown by these French missionaries is justifiable and even deserving of credit, while
their zeal for saving the souls of the Acadians is the more
commendable.

Richard is in some points too severe censuring the conduct
of the missionaries on French soil. His strictures are on
some heads lamentably unjust. Certainly, he is careful in
exculpating them in so far as to believe that they acted in

good faith, being victims of excessive patriotism (pp. 62-83).
Richard charges Abbé Le Loutre with the burning of the
village of Beaubassin due to his ordering the Indians to set
fire to these houses and farms in order to force the Acadians
to desert their country and pass over to the French side
(pp. 86-87). But even Cornwallis, who blamed Le Loutre
for almost any act of hostility committed on the English,
expressly states that the French commandant is responsible
for this outrage (p. 87 note). Parkman charges the sen-
sational murder of Captain Edward Howe (1750) to Le
Loutre, an accusation which is masterly disproved by Richard (pp. 88-120). Yet the author is fair enough to state
that Parkman has made ample retractation in his latest work
where he admits that " this worst charge against Le Loutre
has *not* been proved " (*Half Century*, II, p. 180). The
murder of Captain Howe which " spread consternation both
into the British and French camps and by aggravating the
irritation of the British against the French brought on that
terrible after-effect, the deportation of the Acadians " (pp.
88, 120) was no base political crime. Abbé Maillard informs us that it was purely an act of religious zeal on the
part of the Micmacs who bore a deadly grudge against
Howe because he had in 1739 ridiculed their faith and particularly their devotion to the Holy Virgin Mary. He was
saved then from certain death by some Acadians who cir-
cumvented the Indians. Ever after the Micmacs had been
lying in wait for him during eleven years. He was repeatedly warned of his danger both by Acadians and the missionaries, even Le Loutre. It is only due to his foolhardi-
ness that he was killed on that fatal day. This is the most
authentic account of Howe's murder we have. Abbé Maillard wrote it in 1755 (*Lettre sur les missions Micmaques,*
published in 1863 in *Soirées Canadiennes*, pp. 388-407).
Neither Richard nor his editor were acquainted with this
important document which completely upsets what he wrote

on pages 112 to 113 and 116. Mr. Richard remarks (pp. 89-90, note 5) that Captain Howe is one of his ancestors, for his great-grandfather was a natural son of Howe through no fault of his mother. This vein of British blood or a mild atavism may be responsible for his strange British prepossessions.

Dread of the Indians had prevented England for forty years from colonizing Acadia. When at last, in 1749, Halifax was established, the course of events proved that these apprehensions had been well founded. The French, writes Richard, encouraged the Indians to commit all kinds of hostilities upon the British colonists in order to chase them away and to force the Acadians to go over to the French side (pp. 123-150). According to the English historians the Indian missionaries had been the chief agents of the French government in this Indian warfare. Even Richard charges Le Loutre and Germain, S.J. with the instigation of all the vexations and atrocities committed by the Indians on the colonists of Halifax (p. 131). This is a calumny pure and simple, as the editor points out. Regarding the few instances where Indians forced some Acadians to quit their country and go over into French territory, Richard states himself (p. 134) that those Acadians were promised complete indemnification for losses sustained. On the other hand Richard admits that the atrocities committed by the English in those days are much more revolting than those of their inveterate foes, the Indians (pp. 140-166). This Indian warfare had been going on for three years when it came to an end, at least temporarily, by the treaty concluded in Nov. 1752 between the Micmacs and the British governor of Acadia. Abbé Le Loutre and the French are almost invariably accused by the British historians of having thwarted this treaty of peace. As a matter of fact it had been of short duration, brought to a premature end, not by any machinations on the part of Abbé Le Loutre or the French, but by the treachery of the English.   Le Loutre, on the contrary, as seems probable, even had favored that new treaty (pp. 152-165, 174-175).   Breaking of this peace in July 1753 was followed by a renewal of hostilities which came eventually to an end as late as in 1759 and 1760 through the efforts of the missionaries Maillard and Manach.

Both Richard and his editor, like the host of historians in dealing with this Indian warfare, overlook completely a basic principle of international law as it was practised then. In treaties of peace between powers in Europe, *the Indians had never been included*, but had made separate treaties with the king's governors.   This principle was acted upon both by England and France throughout the eighteenth century and long after (Cf. *Canadian Archives*, 1894, p. 139).   In October 1748 peace was concluded between England and France, but this did not include the Indians who had many reasons of their own to continue the hostilities.   Their grievances against the English are set forth in: " Motifs of the Micmacs and Malseet Indians to continue the war against the English after the late peace ", a document enumerating all the foul deeds and infernal treacheries committed from 1744 to 1750 on these Indians and their missionaries (published by Bourgeois, *Anciens Missionnaires de l' Acadie*, pp. 65-69).   This document was written, as seems very probable, by Abbé Maillard, *the gentlest of all Indian missionaries* who " died in 1762 at *Halifax* and was buried by order of the Lieutenant-Governor, and his pall was supported by the President of the Council, the Speaker of the House, and four other gentlemen of Halifax."   That the Indians continued the war, was their own private affair, for which neither the French nor, still less, the missionaries, can be held responsible.   It was stating the truth when the French Governor of Cape Breton wrote to Governor Cornwallis, Oct. 15, 1749 that he had no control over the Indians, who were allies not subjects.   (*Canadian*

Archives, 1894, p. 147). It was *legitimate* warfare on the part of the Indians, a fact which both Richard and his editor overlook. The missionaries accompanied them to mitigate their savage mode of warfare. " How many deeds of savagery would have been committed," writes Abbé Maillard (*op. cit.*, p. 68 sq.) " if the missionaries had not prevented them." Le Loutre saved the lives of several English officers. Captain Hamilton, who was ransomed in 1750 by Le Loutre, esteemed this much maligned Catholic priest highly (p. 81). But there were times when the most influential missionary lost all control over the Indians. This was invariably the case when they had become intoxicated. Then the English prisoners were killed mercilessly and woe to the missionary who would have attempted to interpose! And in that way many British traders who supplied the Indians with this deadly poison were responsible for the death of English prisoners (Cf. Maillard's *Lettre*, pp. 319-320, 327-329, 335-336, 351-352, 366-368). These facts clearly prove that those charges against the French and the missionaries are utterly unfounded. The hostilities were not instigated by the French, neither was the conduct of the missionaries blamable. Accordingly everything that Richard wrote in this regard is wrong (particularly pp. 66-68, 80-81, 123-132, 269-271, 279).

The best part of Richard's work are the chapters XXI to XXIX (pp. 203-425) dealing with the administration of Lieutenant-Governor Charles Lawrence from October 1753 till September 4, 1755. In July 1754, Lawrence had already matured the sinister plan to deport the Acadians (pp. 213-218, 222, 235-236, 243), but he could realize his base project earlier than July 28, 1755 when the Council at Halifax took the final decision to expel and deport the Acadians (pp. 354-365). On September 5th, 1755, the first Acadians were arrested to be deported, precisely three months after Lawrence had attacked the French at Fort

Beausejour (June 2, 1755) while France and England *had been at peace*, thereby breaking the peace concluded in 1748 and opening that war which eventually drove the French from North America (pp. 273-289). On Aug. 4, 6, and 10, following, the priests ministering to the Acadians were arrested and carried off to England in direct violation of the treaties of Utrecht (1713) and Aix-la-Chapelle (1748) (pp. 348-350). All these pages reveal a continuous series of treachery, oppression and persecution inflicted on an innocent people for the *express purpose* of exasperating them and of driving them into open rebellion, thereby palliating the crime of deportation. But the more those tyrants tormented these guileless peasants the more submissive the latter showed themselves. The next volume of Richard's work will recount the *Tragedy of Dispersion* of this Acadian peasantry " *to which the history of the civilized world affords no parallel* " (Mrs. Williams. *The Neutral French*).

The editor has spared no pains to bring the original work of Richard up to the highest standard of accuracy. He inserted new documents (pp. 23, 27, 252, 412), substituted a fuller text to fourteen extracts of the original work, and corrected in no less than 49 different notes erroneous views of the author. Moreover, he added numerous notes elucidating certain facts touched upon in the text and an appendix of new documents (pp. 427-497). All this additional material tends to evince with all possible clearness the fact that the execution of this doubly criminal measure, deportation of an entire people, had been in many regards more dastardly and hideous than Richard had described it.

BISHOP FLAGET'S DIARY

BY REV. W. J. HOWLETT

(Concluded)

In September of that year Bishop Flaget and Father Badin started to Baltimore, partly to have this business of the church lands settled by the Archbishop, and partly to attend a council of the bishops, which for some reason, probably on account of the difficulty in communicating with Rome, was not held. During this journey Bishop Flaget kept his diary, and also wrote an account of his journey. These two should be read together.

SEPTEMBER.

Tuesday, Sept. 1.—Conference upon the distribution of the missions, upon my departure, upon the prayers in time of war, and upon Mr. Badin. Fine weather. P. C. L. Ch, S. A. P. D. M.

Wednesday, Sept. 2.—Came last night to Holy Mary's, —16 miles. Confessions all day until 9 o'clock P. M. Fine weather. F. R. D. S. J. V. R. G.

Thursday, Sept. 3.—Confessions till one o'clock P. M., mass, sermon till three o'clock; fine weather. Returned to St. Stephen's; visited the Sisters,—14 miles. P. R. S. A. P. D. M.

Friday, Sept. 4.—Large congregation; confessions, sermon, mass, till 4 o'clock P. M.; fine weather. Went to St. Thomas',—11 miles. R. D. D. E. P. M. S.

Saturday, Sept. 5.—Confessions, mass, till 12 o'clock. Walk with the students; fine weather. R. S. S. J. D. V. A. D. S. L.

Sunday, Sept. 6.—Confessions, sermon, mass, till 2 o'clock P. M. Started at 4 o'clock for Clear Creek,—16 miles. Visited a sick man. R. P. F. S. A. P. D. M.

Monday, Sept. 7.—Returned from Clear Creek; dined with Mr. Dant; went to St. Stephen's,—25 miles; fine weather. Confessions; visits. R. and D. P. F. imp. S. A. P. D. M.

Tuesday, Sept. 8.—Went to St. Charles'; confessions till one o'clock P. M. Returned to St. Stephen's; sad dinner; started to the seminary at 5 o'clock on my journey to Baltimore. Fine weather,—25 miles. Ind. S. D. P. P. M. S.

Wednesday, Sept. 9.—At the seminary. Fine weather. Preparation for Baltimore; disc. D. M. S. A. P. D. M. Slept at Mr. Saunders'. T. D. G. P. V.—3 miles. Letters from Mr. Tessier, B.

Thursday, Sept. 10.—Returned to the seminary; mass. Last preparations; fine weather; P. M. ind. for rain for the evening. Mr. Chabrat came for me; went to Mr. Gwynn's, —5 miles. D. F. M. R. S. A. P. D. M.

Friday, Sept. 11.—Rain all day. Went to St. Michael's; dined with Mr. Gardiner,—10 miles. A. M. R. S. A. P. D. M.

Saturday, Sept. 12.—Copious rain; a few confessions. H^te. (Harriet) perseveres in her vocation. Srs. Char. Started for Shelby County with Mr. Horrell,—12 miles. R. P. F. D. S. L.

Sunday, Sept. 13.—Confessions, sermon, mass, till 2 o'clock P. M. Mr. Chabrat preached twice. God continues to bless him. F. M. S. A. P. D. M. Weather warm, fine.

Monday, Sept. 14.—36 miles; fine weather; beautiful road to go to Flat Creek. Disappointment, as no one expected us. Slept at Mr. Denis O'Nan's. R. P. F. D. D. E. S. P. M.

Tuesday, Sept. 15.—No one comes. Fine weather. Six or seven confessions, mass, instruction. The good people need to be visited. Started for Mr. Angier's,—17 miles. R. D. S. L.

Wednesday, Sept. 16.—Visited Mr. Twyman; dinner with him. Fine weather. Promising district. S. A. P. D. M.

Thursday, Sept. 17.—Rain all the morning. Mr. Chabrat returned to Mr. Horrell's. L. T. L. L. ruling. D. L. M. G. K. H. S. E. S. E.

Friday, Sept. 18.—Confessions till one o'clock P. M. The confessions begin too late. The rest of the day in retreat. Sadness; weather cold and clear. D. A. E. M. E. V. D. S. P. M.

Saturday, Sept. 19.—Confessions all the forenoon; some in the afternoon and a visit. Retreat. R. P. T. D. D. S. D. D. S. L.

Sunday, Sept. 20.—Confessions, sermon, mass, confirmation, till 3 o'clock P. M. Information about land. Unbecoming mirth. D. D. E. S. A. P. D. M.

Monday, Sept. 21.—Confessions, announcements, mass, till half past twelve. Dinner with Mr. Twyman; Fine weather. R. ind. S. A. P. D. M.

Tuesday, Sept. 22.—Confessions, mass, till one o'clock P. M. Dinner with Mr. B. Greenwell. D. D. E. P. C. L. S. V. D. P. P. S. Fine weather.

Wednesday, Sept. 23.—Fine weather; very few for confession. Read and study; prayer. L3 miles. R. S. S. A. P. D. M.

Thursday, Sept. 24.—Confessions, mass, sermon, confirmation, till three o'clock. Dinner at four; fine weather; 3 miles; slept at Mr. Gough's. R. D. S. L.

Friday, Sept. 25.—Confession till 9 o'clock; mass. Fine weather. Arrival of Mr. B—n. Dinner at Mr. Twyman's. Started for Lexington. R. P.

Saturday, Sept. 26.—Lodged at Mr. Tebbatts'. Confessions; fine weather; visits. D. D. E. G. T. C. L. P. A. P. D. M.

Sunday, Sept. 27.—Confessions part of the morning, mass, instruction, confirmation. Motives of consolation; fine weather; borrow $40 from Mr. Twyman. R. P.

Monday, Sept. 28.—Mass, instructions, confessions. Fine weather. Mr. Fenwick and his nephew; letter from Mr. David; preparations for the journey; started at 4 o'clock P. M.—9 miles. D. P. D. S. L.

Tuesday, Sept. 29.—My horse seems to be sick; heat. Mr. Badin's horse is sick,—30 miles. Visited Paris and Mr. Cally. My horse is better. R. P. D. S. L. Conference, singular, L. G. G. C.

Wednesday, Sept. 30.—Rather warm. Visited the Salt works. One wagon load of wood evaporates only one bushel of salt. At 4 o'clock arrived at Mr. O'Neall's. Fine weather; Well received. D. D. I. A. L. M. H.

OCTOBER.

Thursday, Oct. 1.—After saying mass started for Mr. Mitchell's. Religion lost in this family. Distant hope if a priest could be sent there. Pride and insolence in the master of the house. L. E. E. P. C. L. S. V. D. Ch. R. P. F.

Friday, Oct. 2.—Mass, instructions, no confessions. Ennui; conversation with a Protestant lady. The son of the house uses improper language. R. En. P. C. L. S. V. D. P.

Saturday, Oct. 3.—Mass, one confession, Mr. Badin preached a long and solid sermon. Returned to Washington; fine weather. Sad. Afl. d'E. R. P. F.

Sunday, Oct. 4.—Mass, instruction, no confessions. Mr. Badin preached at the court house; the public was pleased. Fine weather; talk with the Catholics; baptisms.

Monday, Oct. 5.—Rain during the night and the morning. Dinner at Dr. Watts. Well treated by the lady. Left for Limestone; Slept at Mr. Gallagher's. Well received; fine cool weather.

Tuesday, Oct. 6.—Fine weather; baptized child of Mr.

Gallagher; I was the godfather. Slept at Mr. Allen's; met Mr. Guerin. R. P. C. L. cH. S. A. P. D. M.

Wednesday, Oct. 7.—Met two Catholic families on the road; baptized four children; fine weather; slept at Mr. Plutto's; fine farm. R. S. D. S. L.

Thursday, Oct. 8.—Fine weather; visited Chillicothe; met two or three Catholics; a reprobate of a Spaniard. Slept at Tarlton. R. P. F. D. D. E. S.

Friday, Oct. 9.—Fine weather. Met a Catholic hotel keeper; arrived at New Lancaster; several Catholics; 5 children baptized. Slept at Mr. Ditto's. R. S. A. P. D. M.

Saturday, Oct. 10.—Weather overcast. Confessions, mass, instruction; rain. R. P.

Sunday, Oct. 11.—Confessions, mass, instruction; numerous congregation. Mr. Badin preached at different times 2 hours. Rain a great part of the day. Hopes of a good congregation here. The devotion to the Blessed Virgin is unknown. R. D. S. P. M.

Monday, Oct. 12.—Weather overcast. Visit the church ground. Slept at Mr. Dean's; several confessions; Dean's son married by Mr. Badin. R. P. T.

Tuesday, Oct. 13.—Fine weather. Met several Catholics. D. D. E. T.

Wednesday, Oct. 14.—Arrived at the house of a good German. Treated well, and at cheap price. P. R. S. A. P. D. M.

Thursday, Oct. 15.—Passed through several little villages; found one Catholic family; baptized a child. Fine weather. D. D. S. A. P. D. M.

Friday, Oct. 16.—Slept 15 miles from R—stone. Passed through Alexandria, Washington; spoke to two Catholic families. Fine weather. T. P. F. D. D. E. S. P. M.

Saturday, Oct. 17.—Arrived at Mr. Guny's. Welcome. Fine weather. Read a letter to make me go back. T. D. E. mel. aig. D. S. L.

Sunday, Oct. 18.—Fine weather. Two confessions, mass, instruction, till 3 o'clock. Mr. Badin preached a long and solid sermon. Numerous congregation. D. D. E. P. T. S. A. P. D. M.

Monday, Oct. 19.—Fine weather. Mass at Mr. Touks'. Started about one o'clock P. M. for Mr. Noble's; admirable family; very pious evening. D. S. L.

Tuesday, Oct. 20.—Fine weather. Mass, visit to the farm; instruction on agriculture. D. D. E. T. C. L. S. V. D. P. S. P. M.

Wednesday, Oct. 21.—Rain about 3 o'clock A. M., four confessions; mass. Fine about 9, and left at 12 o'clock to continue our route. R. S. V. A. L. G. S. A. P. D. M.

Thursday, Oct. 22.—Fine weather, cool. Met a young lady who wished to travel with us. She embarrassed us. Snow. R. R. A. L. G. D. S. P. M.

Friday, Oct. 23.—Five or six inches of snow. Said mass with Mr. Clark Aub. Left to go to Mr. Arnold's; lost in the woods; arrived at Mr. Mattingly's; well received. T. D. E. S. D. Ot. S. A. P. D. M.

Saturday, Oct. 24.—Said mass, confessions, preached, until 2 o'clock P. M. Confessions in the evening; parish neglected. R. S. F. D. D. S. D. Mr. XX at Mr. Mattingly's.

Sunday, Oct. 25.—Confessions, mass, sermon, until 3 o'clock P. M. Mr. Badin preached; marriage; a chapel; large congregation; people well disposed but very ignorant. D. S. L.

Monday, Oct. 26.—Left Mr. Arnold's for Cumberland. Arrived at Mr. B. Carrico's. Talked with the lady—half-Catholic, part Indian. R. En. S. A. P. D. M.

Tuesday, Oct. 27.—Rain. Left Mr. Carrico's; breakfast at Mr. Slagle's, Catholic; his wife a Methodist, children Protestant. Slept at young Beaven's by favor gratis. Talked with Messrs. Escrige, Bean Dis. and Gd. Abl. and Hogin. D. D. E. R. P. F. S. P. M.

Wednesday, Oct. 28.—Breakfast at Mr. McKiernan's; well received; nothing to pay. Met Mr. Ragen; visited Mr. Goolding; stormy weather. Slept at Mr. Snider's; dispute about marriage fees, etc. P. M. S.

Thursday, Oct. 29.—Very badly received by a Catholic. Tried to see Mr. Maguire. Passed through Williamsport, Hagar's Town; slept at the house of a German, very poor accommodations but very cheap. D. S. L.

Friday, Oct. 30.—Started for Emmitsburg; arrived there at 11 o'clock A. M. Saluted by the Jordan family, visited the monastery, the seminary,—friendship everywhere; weather superb. G. C. R. S. A. P. D. M.

Saturday, Oct. 31.—All day at the monastery; edifying conversation with my dear Bruté. DuBois, Duhamel, etc. Very fine weather. R. P. D. S. L.

November.

Sunday, Nov. 1.—Superb weather. High mass, sermon; conversation upon the establishment of Emmitsburg. D. D. E. R. P. F. D. S. L.

Monday, Nov. 2.—Mass at the good Sisters'; sermon to all the little community. Left for Taney Town; fine weather. R. D. D. E. D. D. S. D. D. S. L.

Tuesday, Nov. 3.—Started for Baltimore. Mr. Badin goes to Conewago for his retreat; very fine weather. Arrive at Baltimore. Very friendly reception by my confrères. G. D. D. E. P. C. L. Ch. S. P. M.

Wednesday, Nov. 4.—Fine weather. Visited Mgr. the Archbishop. This respectable old man threw himself on his knees to ask my blessing. Other visits. D. S. L. R.

Thursday, Nov. 5.—Dined with the Archbishop; visits paid and received. Heat extraordinary; rain towards evening. D. D. E. G. D. S. A. P. D. M.

Friday, Nov. 6.—Visit the Fathers of the College. D. D. E. T. R. P. F. Rain.

Saturday, Nov. 7.—How tiresome and of little merit is this sort of life. Bad weather. T. D. D. E. S. A. P. D. M.

Sunday, Nov. 8.—Assisted at high mass and vespers; gave the benediction. Weather somber and depressing. Visits. D. D. E. R. P. T. D. S. L.

Monday, Nov. 9.—Meeting at the seminary; affairs seemed to me in bad state. Weather somber and rainy. G. D. D. E. T. S. A. P. D. M.

Tuesday, Nov. 10.—Visit Mr. l'Abbe Moranville; the ladies Trapp. house badly organized; many visits. D. D. E. S. P. M.

Wednesday, Nov. 11.—Dined with Mr. Turner; well received. Made a few visits. Weather fair. D. R. P. T. S. A. P. D. M.

Thursday, Nov. 12.—Paid a few visits; received coldly by Madame Volunbrim; interior satisfaction. Fine weather. D. D. E. R. P. F. S. A. P. D. M.

Friday, Nov. 13.—Received and paid visits. Weather cold and variable. Wrote to Mr. Garnier. R. P. F. S. P. M.

Saturday, Nov. 14.—Received so many visits that I am tired of them. I am, however, very sensible of the good will of these people. D. D. E. P. D. R. S. A. P. D. M.

Sunday, Nov. 15.—Assisted at high mass; received visits; took tea at Mr. John Welsh's. Gayety pushed a little too far, perhaps. God give me recollection. J. M. J. J. M. M. S. V. P.

Monday, Nov. 16.—Visit Miss Emily Caton; her father received me very coolly. Woe to the rich; it is to the poor that God speaks. Heard Mr. Sinnott. D. D. E. R. P. J. M. J.

Here ends Bishop Flaget's daily entries for this year, and here begins his narration of events during his journey to Baltimore. I give his words without comment, only remarking that his difficulty with Father Badin was but an episode after all. They lived many long years after this as friends, and died such, and neither of them left an enemy behind him when life was ended.

JOURNAL OF MY TRIP TO BALTIMORE.

The 8th of September, day of the Nativity of my Good Mother, I went to St. Charles' to take leave of the dear Sisters. I thought I would find them alone, but I had the entire congregation. It was three o'clock in the afternoon before I could get my breakfast. The meal that I took at St. Stephen's was said. The good women who served me were at times in tears. I tried to keep up heart, and appeared more cheerful than usual, but the effort was painful. About five o'clock I started for the seminary, and stopped a short time at Mr. Livers' place. The two girls there were very much excited over my departure. All these demonstrations prove to me that I have gained the confidence of these good people, and nothing could please me better. About nine o'clock I arrived at the seminary, and I was received with more joy because they had given up expecting me.

The ninth, after dinner, I went to Bardstown to visit Mr. Saunders, to whom I am under obligations. I spent the night there, and the next morning I returned to the seminary to say mass and make my last preparations. After dinner I gave my blessing to those dear children and the entire community, and went for a moment to recommend my journey to God before the Blessed Sacrament. Then, with the weather threatening rain, I left St. Thomas, accompanied by Mr. Chabrat, and went to pass the night at Mr. Gwynn's. The 11th, after having said holy mass and taken my breakfast, I set out with Mr. Chabrat to go to St. Michael's, where we arrived about two o'clock muddy and wet, on account of the rain which fell almost continually while we were on the road. Mr. Horrell arrived in spite of the rain, to serve as my guide and conduct me to the congregation of Shelby.

The 12th, after having celebrated mass at the house of the good Mr. Gardiner, I set out, still accompanied by Mr. Chabrat, and preceded by our guide. We still had the rain upon us, and we arrived at the home of our guide about two o'clock, where we dined and slept. To-day (13th) we said mass in his house. The congregation was considerable,— the most being Protestants, who had the patience to listen to the advice I gave them, and to two sermons from Mr. Chabrat—one on the good use of time, and the other on the necessity of baptism. He speaks with much fire and unction, and I hope that God will do much good through his ministry.

After having said our masses in honor of the Cross, having Mr. Carrico for a guide, we started for Flat Creek. The first Catholic house is about thirty miles from Mr. Horrell's. The route going there is superb, and the country is rich and well settled. We arrived at our first post about two o'clock P. M. The house was filled with young girls, and not a man to unsaddle our horses. Mr. Chabrat supplied the want, and did his work marvelously well. They guillotined three or four chickens which were getting ready to go to roost, and in three quarters of an hour they were doing the honors of a dinner for us.

We expected to pass the night at this lodge, where we would have no need of a candle to light us to bed, as the moon had free access to the room where we hoped to give ourselves to the sweets of sleep, but, for reasons which I could only conjecture, it was determined in the counsel of the young ladies with the lady of the house at their head, that two of them should act as guides to conduct us to the place where Mr. Badin was accustomed to say mass. This arrangement was so definitely made that I thought it would be indiscreet to offer any objections or observations. We then took to the road. The sun soon went down, and we found ourselves in the growing darkness. The young girls lost their way, and God knows, I found myself getting very uneasy. Fortunately, we came to a plantation where we got directions that put us on the right road, and about nine o'clock we arrived at our lodging place. Here no one expected us, and the man of the house was absent. The lady, who was a Protestant, was very much embarrassed. I tried to assure her as well as I could possibly explain, and then I said night prayers, and we went to bed. To-day, the 15th of the month, no one came until nine or ten o'clock, when a score of persons assembled,—part Catholic and part Protestant. There were seven or eight confessions, but only one communion. If I do not provide for this congregation soon the faith will be lost.

After dinner we left for Scott County, and we arrived at Mr. Angier's about eight o'clock in the evening. To-day, the 17th, Mr. Chabrat went back in a pouring rain. My stay with Mr. Angier lasted nine or ten days, and I had occasion to exercise my holy ministry with some satisfaction. More zeal for the salvation of souls on the part of him who is at the head of the congregation, and things would go marvelously well. The Archbishop, when I was leaving him for Kentucky, particularly recommended to me the visits of confirmation as a powerful means of arousing the congregations and renewing the people. The little experience that I have had of these visits has convinced me of the truth of this observation. I hope, with the grace of God, that I shall not cease to visit my flock, and that death will surprise me with my arms in my hands during one of these visits.

(Observation:—Spiritual languor in the pastor and the people. Coldness in the people about buying ground for the church.)

Mr. Badin arrived Thursday evening at Mr. Twyman's, but I did not see him until about noon on Friday. Our interview was a mixture of coolness and warmth. That same evening we left for Lexington, where we arrived about 8 o'clock, and were received very cordially by Mr. Tebbatts. Everything is languishing in this congregation for want of priests. Mr. Badin has counted more than 30 families in Lexington or in the near surroundings, and I am sure that in a couple of years there would be a hundred and fifty families if a priest resided in the town. Mr. Badin would not object to a residence there, and I myself think that he would be the one to suit best if he were to become more spiritual and interior. There were 17 or 18 communions, and as many confirmations. Mr. Badin said that this was an extraordinary number, and he attributes it to the epis- copal visit. The church is well advanced as far as the outside work goes, but the workmen of Lexington, as every- where else, make themselves extremely important, and do just about as they please.

At about 4 o'clock P. M. we left Lexington. Mr. E. Fenwick accompanied us two or three miles. He gave me some dispatches, very extraordinary on account of what they contained relative to ————. I admire the prudence of my dear friend. I am, thanks to God, much more easy in mind than he is upon the matter; nevertheless I appreciate and am thankful for the friendship he bears me. Why have I not been able to gain the heart of m. c. d. v; (? compagnon de voyage)! What good should have been done and which has not been done? I am quite content with what awaits me at Baltimore.

We slept about 9 miles from Lexington. The landlord was a very strong democrat. I talked with him for amuse- ment, and using a few Socratic arguments I succeeded in making him repudiate all that he had before said. Then an old soldier arrived, and he so monopolized the conversa- tion that there was no room to put in a word. According to the two gentlemen our young Kentucky warriors would never sheath the sword until they had pushed the Indians back to Hudson's Bay, and driven the English out of Canada, etc.

After a good supper we went to bed. The next day, Feast of St. Gabriel (?), (Sept. 29), we were not able to say mass. We started about six o'clock in the morning, but my horse appeared to be sick, and was more disposed to lie down than to set out on a journey of 600 miles.

About 11 o'clock we arrived at the city of Paris, capital of Bourbon County. Although this second Paris is much inferior to the first, it is certain that there was a time when the first was still smaller than the one where we took our breakfast. Mr. Kelly, a Catholic married to a Protestant, received us coolly but civilly. His wife was very friendly, and we talked pleasantly during the meal and parted very good friends.

Ten miles from there we found a French merchant named Vimont. His wife is a Protestant and he is nothing. He has 4 or 5 children, and not one of them baptized. I complained in a friendly manner to him of this, and he promised to have them baptized when I returned. Mr. Badin is persuaded that he is presuming on my simplicity (il fait les gorges chaudes de ma simplicite; giving me hot air). Felicity Vimont, his sister, came from France two years ago with the Ursulines of New Orleans. She appears to have some good principles yet, but if she were an angel she would be perverted in the school where she now is.

We went ten miles farther, and would have kept on only Mr. Badin's horse got very sick, which will probably retard us considerably. We are lodged with a farmer, and nothing is lacking to us but water. There has been no rain for two or three weeks, and the poor people, as well as their animals, will be exposed to die of thirst. There has been no such drought since the contry was settled. After supper Mr. Badin began a conversation with the lady of the house on religion. The prejudice of this young woman against

Catholics is beyond anything I ever conceived. We tried to destroy it, but I have every reason to think that we lost our time.

The next day, Wednesday, we continued our way, the weather being very fine, and soon arrived at the famous Salt Springs near the Leaky River. The water from these springs runs on the surface of the earth in great abundance, and the taste of it is disagreeable on account of the sulphur, which predominates in it. The director of the works told me that a wagon-load of wood would evaporate just about one bushel of salt. For 14 miles the soil is as barren as it can be, and they told me that wherever these salt springs are the land is unfit for cultivation to a great distance.

About four o'clock in the afternoon we reached Washington. Mr. Oneell and Madam, his wife, received us very civilly. The next day we had the happiness of celebrating mass, and after breakfast we left them to go and see Mr. Mitchel, near Limestone. Religion is being lost in these quarters. The blacks are in the most profound ignorance, and the whites are extremely indifferent. If there were a zealous priest at Lexington he could form a very fine congregation there, and have several stations in the settlements on this side and on the other side of the Ohio.

On Sunday I said mass at Mr. Oneell's, in a fairly large room filled with Protestants. I spoke to them on the Sacrifice of the Mass in a manner to make some little impression. Mr. Badin was requested by the men of the town to give a sermon in the court house, which he did, to the delight of the Catholics, and the very great displeasure of some of the Protestants. He preached on Baptism, and after the sermon a Catholic, who until then did not dare declare himself such, had his five children baptized.

The next day we went to dine with Dr. Watts, who the day before had put his name down as one of my sheep. He and his lady received us *à la Française*, with soup, fish, etc. I hope, from the extreme kindness which his wife, who is not a Catholic, showed me, that at my return she will allow me to baptize all their children. Towards evening we left them to go to Limestone. Mr. Gallagher, the only Catholic of the town, as well as his amiable wife, insisted that we should spend the night with him. The next day his youngest son was baptized, and I consented to be the godfather.

After breakfast we crossed the river, the only incident worthy of remark being that at bedtime in the evening we ran across Mr. Guerin. His demonstrations appeared very lively and very sincere. Upon the pretext of showing us the miniature of Jo. Daveiss he spread out before us a portfolio filled with banknotes which did not belong to him. He told me that he had read with Mr. Knox the 2nd vindication of St. Mary's College, and he had found it very well written. Mr. Knox assured him that it was by mistake that he was credited with having written the articles against the College. Anyway he was sure that the dispute would go no further.

The next day, after parting from Mr. Guerin in a very friendly manner, we continued our journey with very fine weather. The country we passed through is superb, and very well settled. It is only 20 years since the beginning of any settlement here, and at this moment there are more than 30,000 inhabitants. We took dinner with a Wm. Cassel, a Catholic himself and also his wife. We persuaded them to go and live on the farm of Mr. Badin, and I am sure they will do well there if they are not bothered. That night we stayed with a German who has a magnificent farm. His religion is to make money. He showed us a stallion which cost him over eleven hundred dollars. I never saw a more perfect animal. I saw there also a *Merino* ram.

From there we took the road to Chillicothe. The country through which we traveled, right up to the town, is among the richest of the state. The road was covered with Methodist ministers coming from their conference. The zeal of this sect is prodigious and capable of covering us with confusion.

The town of Chillicothe is situated on the Scioto river. The great floods of the river have already carried away the greater part of the first street. The inhabitants seem to be very busy and industrious. There are several Catholics, but they are ashamed to show themselves as such. Among others is a Mr. Lamb, owner of a great cotton factory. He is said to belong to the Anglican Church, but one of his former friends assured us that he had seen him go to his duties several times in his younger days.

After a rather poor dinner I had a conversation with a young Spaniard, a cigar maker in the town. I thought that, as a good Castilian, he would want to kiss my hands and feet. but what was my surprise when I found him worse than a Protestant, for his impiety was as great as his ignorance. I tried by gentleness and persuasion to bring him back, but all was to no use. We parted—he apparently very much satisfied with having shown his impiety, and I filled with sadness to see the frightful ravages that irreligion, impiety and libertinage are making every day. They told us that a new sect has established itself in Chillicothe, the name of these fanatics is *Socinians,*—Arianism. I could not learn anything about their dogmas.

We went that night to Tarlton, where we slept at the Brand's. The country is broken, the inn is good, and the woman is extremely clean. They had the wisdom in Ohio not to allow slavery. Just now hired help is costly, but with the present increase of the population this inconvenience will not last long, and they will be delivered from a race that might become a danger.

Before sunrise we left Tarlton and were on the way to New Lancaster. Mr. Badin shouted to the right and left that he was a Catholic priest, and thus discovered an inn-keeper on the way named Marquart, who was born and baptized a Catholic, as well as his wife. They received us perfectly, asked us to stop with them upon our return, and were satisfied with our prayers in payment of their bill. Their faith seems to be yet strong, but their practice puts them at the level of the most relaxed Protestants.

Some hours later we arrived at New Lancaster. This town is situated on a hill, and I was told that the air is very pure, and industry is making rapid progress. There are but three or four Catholic families here, but they are among the most respectable both by the rank they occupy and by their wealth. Mr. Badin baptized five children here.

We went to spend the night with Mr. Dittoe, an excellent Catholic who keeps an inn on the road. This faithful believer has already bought, conjointly with one of his brothers, 320 acres of land for the location of a priest. He has already built a little house on it and cleared ten acres. In three years he hopes to have thirty acres cleared. I promised him that I would try to send them a priest, at least once a year until Providence would permit me to give them one permanently. I advised Mr. Dittoe to build a house which would be at the same time a house for the priest and a chapel, and he is going to do it. This chapel could also serve as a place where the Catholics might gather together every Sunday, thus serving to draw them closer in the bonds of charity, and reminding them of their duties as Catholics. The Catholics at New Lancaster, or near Mr. Dittoe's, are in sufficient numbers to form a very respectable congregation, and with the taste that the Germans have for music, I am very sure that divine services there would be held with a great deal of beauty and dignity. All the children of Mr. Ditto are musicians, and at this moment while I am writing they are making a chorus of melody which pleases me very much. God of all goodness, send me priests!

I was informed in the congregation of the Cumberland Mountains that Mr. R. exacted one dollar for each baptism, although he receives $60 or $70 from these good people, whom he visits three or four times a year, and who are extremely poor.   Such a condition seems to me reprehensible, and for this reason I promised to give notice of it to the Archbishop.

It is almost impossible to form an idea of the Catholics who forget their religion on account of the lack of priests, or the lack of zeal in the priests who have charge of these congregations.   Not a day passes that we do not find great numbers of these strayed sheep, who, because they do not see their real shepherd, become Baptists, Methodists, etc., or at least nothingists.

To remedy this great evil it would be necessary that a priest, filled with the spirit of God, and convinced of the value of souls, should often get away from his accustomed route, and going out into the country, ask if there are not Catholics in those regions.   The discovery of a single one will lead to the discovery of ten others.   If he found only one family he could say mass there, preach, catechise and pray.   Let him show a great desire for the salvation of souls, and a contempt for their money.   With such dispositions a priest would have the consolation of bringing to the bosom of the Church millions of her children who never will enter it unless we go after them.

My sojourn in Baltimore, although in every respect agreeable to nature, became painful by reason of the dissipation which it brought.   From morning till night my room was hardly ever empty of persons who came to seem me,— some to hear of the state of religion in the country where I live; others, and these were more numerous, to get news of the good Father David.   All of his spiritual children are very strongly attached to him, and the tears that they shed in spite of themselves prove how sensible they are to the loss they have sustained. The most painful slavery is the obligation of going out of the seminary so often to eat. The news that I receive from my seminary, and the state of poverty in which I see that of Baltimore, the impossibility of being able to bring with me any subject who would be suitable,—these are real episcopal crosses. I forget them, however, when the truly singular conduct of my traveling companion presents itself to my mind. I am tempted to fly naked from my burden.

[THE END]

THE LIFE OF BISHOP CONWELL

BY MARTIN I. J. GRIFFIN

CHAPTER XXX.

1831.

(*Continued*)

In the meantime an interdict is declared against my church, the Cathedral Church of St. Mary's, by which a cleric of any degree is prohibited under pain of suspension, incurred by the very fact of so doing, from celebrating the Sacrifice of the Mass in the Church, without any just cause, so that he may have a chance to suspend, if I should celebrate, and so that he may deprive the congregation of the opportunity of hearing mass on Sundays and Holydays. This has given many Catholics a reason for joining Heretical sects. He claims all his authority from Rome. I am quietly bearing all these things with patience for sake of peace, lest the civil authorities will step in and make it an occasion for a law suit. A discussion of this affair in the Civil Courts will not leave the Holy See unsullied and is therefore to be avoided. After six months D. again went off to visit the remote churches, when it occurred to me to enter my room and to occupy it again under the protection of the civil authorities, which had ordered D,'s furniture to be removed, and to be sent protected to some other place. D. hearing of all this wrote to me, ordering that his furniture be replaced in my room, which he called his, under pain of suspension if I should refuse to obey his precept. I enclose the letters which he himself wrote. Returning after a month, he found out he could do nothing, and immediately ceased to make threats, except by demanding from the Trustees the yearly stipend which he had previously given to me. But the Trustees' not knowing to whom it was to be given refused to give him this stipend until they had the authority of the Civil Courts, therefore, the lawyers instituted an action to determine to whom it was to be given. The case was settled Jan. 16, in my favor, by right as Bishop of Philadelphia.

I pass over many more things no less absurd; it is sufficiently evident from these already mentioned that D. is not competent to govern or administrate to this diocese. Not long since I notified him that they were forbidden to act as a priest, under pain of suspension, who did not ask my blessing before preaching the gospel—however I am silent on account of reverence for the Holy See and, this affair not hindering me, I will not cease to exchange salutations with him on every occasion.

I pray the Holy See will take care lest it should consult the Archb, or may take his advice, or show faith in his relations to me, since it is supported by prejudice and ignorance of Canon Law. It is well known that the most happy P. who, when returning from Rome in 1829, and begging Baltimore that I might take a seat in the Council being held there, the Archbishop not only hindered me from occupying my seat among my colleagues and to use the vote of this Province, but even dared to suspend me from celebrating the Sacrifice of the Mass on Sunday in the presence of all the Bishops and the Congregation, as tho' I were a criminal and he the Supreme Pontiff. All these things I have concealed and borne in silence, hoping in the future that I may have a more fitting occasion for appealing to the Holy Father, Gregory XVI, as far as S.B. is forced to go to Rome and there be subjected to an examination or, at least so far as he is forced to undergo Canonical punishment, if he is called he may refuse to go to Rome. So much being said: I have not hesitated to declare the Council of Baltimore (the case in point) to be an imperfect Council and illegitimate because my seat was vacant daily during the session of the Council, and at the same time I have been compelled to hear mass, deprived as it were of episcopal dignity."

A document in the A. C. H. Society, gives an account of some of these proceedings.   ·

" Memorandum of the removal of Dr. Kenrick's furniture by Dr. Conwell during the absence of the former.

On Sunday 31st July, 1831, Bishop Kenrick, before his sermon, apprised the congregation that his duty required him to be absent for some time from the city, on a visit through the diocese, during which time Rev. Mr. Ginn would assist the Rev. Mr. Keily and would reside at St. Joseph's. Dr. Kenrick left the city Tuesday Aug. 2nd. The Rev. Mr. G. was to occupy the Bishop's apartment in the clergyhouse at St. Joseph's. On Wednesday, the day after the departure of Dr. Kenrick, Dr. Conwell entered the room in the presence of Mr. Ginn, pastor, and removed all Bishop Kenrick's furniture and replaced it with his own, declaring that the room was his. Some of the furniture was sent out of the house and some to other parts."

Bishop Conwell tells more of this incident in a circular which he had printed but " not published ".

For several months, whilst he occupied my house, for the accomodation of himself and boarders, I was under the necessity of confining myself to the use of a bed chamber. Finding myself thus circumstanced, after a long interval of silent meditation, on the state of my unparalleled sufferings, I resorted to an eminent lawyer, Joseph R. Ingersoll, for such advice, as to prevent scandal, in the first instance, and at the same time to ascertain my rights, and be put in legal possession of the same. My counsellor advised me to wait until Dr. Kenrick should happen to go to the country and then to repossess myself of what I had been unjustly deprived of—and that he should engage the protective authorities of the city, to guard me in the possession of my rights. I followed his advice as far as it related to the parlour, by removing such articles of furniture as he might claim to be his, and sending them to a place of security.

Having proceeded thus far, and reinstated myself in the possession of my parlour, I then wrote to him to apprise him of the circumstance above related, to which, I received the following ungracious answer.

(Dr. Kenrick's Letter to the Bishop of Philadelphia.)

BLAIRSVILLE, *Aug. 20, 1831.*

Right Rev. Sir,—

Your communication of the Ist. inst. has been handed to me by the Rev. Mr. Gallitzin, after I had received a circumstantial account of the scandalous and disgraceful intrusion into my rooms. Such conduct on the part of one who for seven months eat of my bread, and was waited on by my servants, and lived free of all share in the taxes and other expenses of house keeping, which were all defrayed by me, (the Rev. Mr. Hughes and Mr. O'Donaghoe paying me their board) is as ungrateful as it is dishonourable! "Si inimicus meus maledixisset mihi, sustinuissem utique, tu vero homo unanimis dux meus et notus meus, qui simul mecum dulces capiebas cibos: in domo dei ambulavimus cum consensu."

I have to request the immediate redress to these wrongs, by the delivery of the key to the Rev. Mr. Hughes, and the previous removal of your effects. Should you delay, or neglect complying with this demand, you will be surprised at the adoption of measures on which you have made no calculation.

With veneration for your dignity, respect for your age, and pity for your misfortunes, I remain

FRANCIS PATRICK,
Bishop of Arath and Coadjutor of Philada.

(Right Rev. Henry Conwell.)

This insulting letter, replete with false insinuations and concluding in derision and mockery, determined me to cut off all future correspondence with Mr. Kenrick.

Perhaps it is at the time immediately succeeding Bishop Kenrick's return to the city that the following incident is to be referred. It is related by Rev. P. A. Jordan, S. J. in *Woodstock Letters,* 1872-73. He says that:

" When Bishop Conwell was informed that Bishop Kenrick was down stairs and wished to pay his respects to him, ' Tell the boy,' said the venerable Bishop, ' to go at once to Arath, (of which he was Bishop), The Bishop of Philadelphia is old enough to mind his own business.' "

Bishop Kenrick went to live in a house on Fifth St., (now 257 S. Fifth St., next to the cemetery) and then to a house on the west side of S. Fifth St., bel. Buckley (bel. Spruce.)

Bishop Conwell gave confirmation on Sept. 4th, to 160 persons in St. Augustine's Church. On the feast of St. Augustine, Father Hurley said the Mass, and Bishop Kenrick preached, Bishop Conwell being present.

The Gill bequest was a matter of difference between the two Bishops. Peter Gill in 1797 had made a bequest in his will leaving certain sums to the " Superior of the Clergy of St. Mary's ". This was always paid to the senior pastor, and when Father Egan became Bishop in 1808, as being still the senior pastor, and so it became an episcopal rather than a pastoral perquisite. Disputes arose over it more than once during the schism. Now however there were two Bishops, each laying claim to the superiorship of St. Mary's. Bishop Conwell relates what occurred. Bishop Kenrick " called on Joseph Snyder, then Treasurer of the Board of Trustees of St. Mary's Church, and demanded payment of a certain sum bequeathed by Mr. Peter Gill to the Superior of the clergy of St. Mary's Church, and left an order with Mr. Snyder to pay the same in his absence to Lewis Ryan, his agent. I made the like demand at the same time, in consequence of which the Trustees determined to pay neither of the claimants, until it should be decided by law to whom it should be given. Application was therefore made to the courts of justice, and after a full examination of the case, an impartial jury brought in a verdict, on the 16th of January, 1832, that Bishop Conwell and no other person, was justly entitled to receive the amounts of this or similar bequests."

Here is a copy of the notice of the suit, served on Bishop Kenrick. (A. C. H. S. Case N. R. Peter Gill Estate,) Randall papers.

Endorsed: "Rt. Rev. Henry Conwell vs. Trustees of St. Mary's Church. Copy of notice to Bishop Kenrick."

Rt. Rev. Sir,

In pursuance of a resolution of the Board of Trustees of St. Mary's Church, passed August 2nd 1831 (with a copy of which you have been furnished) an amicable action has been entered in the District Court for the city and county of Philadelphia to September term 1831, No. 418, wherein the Rt. Rev. Henry Conwell is the Plaintiff, and the Trustees of St. Mary's Church are the defendants, in this action is intended to try the right of the Plaintiff to receive the amount of Peter Gill's legacy left to the Corporation in trust for the Superior of the Clergy of St. Mary's Church. It is marked for trial on Monday, the 24th day of October next, as the Trustees are mere stakeholders of this fund, and have no evidence to controvert the claim of Dr. Conwell, and the amount of the legacy having been claimed by you, I have been directed to give you this notice, and to request that you will adopt such measures as you deem expedient in relation thereto, any papers documents or other evidence, in possession of the Trustees, that may be supposed material to the issue, will be cheerfully produced at the trial if requested.

Very Respectfully,
Your obedient Servt.
ARCHD. RANDALL, *Secretary.*

RT. REV. FRANCIS P. KENRICK. *Sept. 12, 1831.*

Left the original, of which the above is a copy, at the house of Dr. Kenrick, in Willing's Alley, Sept. 13, 1831.

•   JAMES GARTLAND.

Two letters the originals of which are in the Catholic Archives of America, at Notre Dame, Ind., refer to other matters which interested Bishop Conwell at this time.

PHILADELPHIA, *Oct. 24th, 1831.*

My Dear and very Rev. Sir,

Henry McKeon who delivers you this letter, and has the honor to be thereby introduced to your notice and attention, is my grand nephew. He was designed by his parents for the Church from his early years and has been sent to me from Ireland for the purpose of getting their design carried into effect. Through my care he is considered to be a tolerably good Latin and Greek scholar, and has a most excellent moral character. He is in the 23rd year of his age.

He came to me without means of paying for his education in a college, to be prepared for Holy Orders. If circumstances rendered it convenient for me to answer his expectations, I should be very willing to pay for him. But this I cannot promise to do further than by advancing $25 at present, and engaging to remit the like sum in the course of six months from this date.

He proceeds by my order in hopes that this recommendation will suffice to procure him admission into your college, and that his conduct and readiness to be useful will entitle him to your regard and consideration. And as to myself, I shall ever consider myself under obligations to you. John O'Brien is very assiduous, expecting to receive premiums at the next examination in Emmittsburg. Dr. C. Columbus is giving him instructions daily. His grandmother was greatly displeased with his mother for taking him home. Best respects to Rev. Mr. Brute, Jameson, and all the Rev. Gentlemen and students.

And I have the honor to be with great respect, my Dear and

Very Rev. Sir, your faithful and sincere friend and servant in Christ,

HENRY CONWELL, *Bishop of Philadelphia.*
REV. MR. PURCELL,
 President Mt. St. Mary's College, Emmittsburg, Md.

       PHILADELPHIA, *Nov. 21, 1831.*
My Dear and Very Rev. Sir,

 I received your kind favor in due course. I am greatly obliged to you for your compliance with my request by taking my nephew under your protection. I am sure that he will be forever grateful to you and the Gentlemen who in conjunction with you, take a part in the management of the concerns of the college. Mrs. O'Brien desires me to say that she will send John to you in April, in the mean time she wishes that his clothes were sent on here by the first safe opportunity. She gives the use of his matrass and bedding to my nephew, Henry McKeon.

 I have received a letter this day from the Rev. Mr. Rooney No. 4 Rue Duphot, Paris near the Louvre, where he is an assistant priest in the Church of the Assumption. Paris is tranquil at present. Dr. Murphy, the Bp. of Cork has been there lately. Dr. DuBois has been there also in Sept., and remained only for a short space of time. He cannot say where he went from thence.

 An Italian priest passed through Paris on his way to Baltimore, having been invited to leave his native country for saying that civil liberty was consistent with religion. I should procure a cloak or some warm clothing for Henry at this season. Is the cheque plaid allowable for students. I give my best respects to the Rev. Mr. Brute, Jameson and all the Rev. Gentlemen,

  I have the honor to be your sincere friend,

      HENRY CONWELL, *Bishop of Philadelphia.*
P. S.—I sent by Henry $25—I enclose $10.
REV. MR. PURCELL.

Henry McKeon did not receive Holy Orders, but became a bookseller. The author knew him well and procured from him some of the documents used in compiling this history. He and his wife died, it is believed, in the almshouse.

Dr. C. Columbus (Conwell) was a nephew of the Bishop and a young man of considerable literary talent. He published *The Hymns of Homer,* and other *Poems.* In his Opera *The Knights of the Red Branch* occurs the song: "My heart's in old Ireland wherever I go." He died August 11th 1832, only 22 years of age.

CHAPTER XXXI.

DEDICATION OF ST. JOHN'S CHURCH.—BISHOP CONWELL TO BISHOP FENWICK.—TO DANIEL O'CONNELL.

1832.

On St. John's Day 1830, Bishop Kenrick gave authority to Rev. John Hughes, Pastor of St. Joseph's, to build a new church. St. John's on Thirteenth Street was therefore erected. It was dedicated [1] on 8 April, 1832, in the presence of Bishop Conwell.

Bishop Conwell to Rt. Rev. Dr. Fenwick. (Original in the Catholic Archives of America, Notre Dame, Ind.)

PHILADELPHIA, *Oct. 4th, 1832.*

My Dear and Rt. Rev. Sir,

I wrote to the Rev. Mr. Mullin some time since, requesting an answer which never came to hand. This gives me reason to suppose that he is not at home, and therefore I take the liberty of writing to your Lordship, to know if two candidates

[1] Bishop Kenrick's *Diary and Visitation Records,* p. 69.

for the priesthood, namely William Graham, and Mr. Bradley who left this near 2 months ago for Cincinnati be there, or if they have passed on to New Orleans, also another candidate, Mr. McGettigan, who left here lately for Cincinnati, I wish to know if he arrived.

I am very well pleased to hear in the public prints, that your Lordship is in excellent health. And I have the honor to be, with best respects to all the Rev. Gentlemen of Cincinnati, your sincere and faithful friend,

HENRY CONWELL, *Bishop of Philadelphia.*

The annexed letter to the Irish Liberator was printed in the *Catholic Herald*, Vol. 8, 1833, p. 11.

The Rt. Rev. Bishop Conwell and Mr. O'Connell.

We feel peculiar pleasure in recording in our columns to-day, the patriotic letter addressed by the venerable Roman Catholic Prelate of Philadelphia to the Irish Liberator. This letter with which the pious writer favored us exclusively will be regarded as the effusion of a mind deeply imbued with the spirit of patriotism, the principles of liberty and the feelings of liberality. The exalted sentiments of toleration, liberality and justice, which it inculcates, are eminently worthy the head and heart of the prelatial author.

J. R. SHIELD.

PHILADELPHIA, *Dec. 1st, 1832.*

My Dear Sir,

The blood of the martyrs killed at Wallstown and at Kilkenny, under the specious pretext of law, by hired assassins sent for that purpose as it is reported by the Marquis of Angelsea, has excited the sympathy and angry feelings of all mankind. The friends of Ireland and of humanity in this country, derive some consolation from the hope, that the time is not very remote when the cries of the widows and orphans of these murdered victims will call forth the vengeance of Divine Providence, to punish the authors of such atrocities.

The payment of tithes is the ostensible cause of the cruelties which have lately disgraced your unfortunate country, in consequence of which that system cannot be tolerated much longer. The wisdom of Parliament will at length see the necessity of abrogating that iniquitous law, when it shall appear that there is a general deeply-rooted hatred and aversion to tithes impressed on the minds of the people of Great Britain as well as of Ireland; and it is well known that this is the case at present. The man therefore who will rid and free the nation from this grievance, will deserve well of his country and merit the gratitude of posterity, as well as of the present generation.

Without praise or fulsome flattery in the sincerity of my heart I consider you to be an instrument in the hands of God for effecting that great measure as well as the repeal of the union; without which the King who is the bond and essential head of the Union, cannot properly speaking be called the King of the United Kingdom of Great Britain and Ireland, because since the period of the commencement of the interregnum, which has now lasted thirty-two years, that is since the dissolution of its national Parliament, Ireland has been reduced to the rank and situation of a province, and must continue to be so, until its parliament shall be restored.

Persevere, therefore, boldly in your bold undertaking without fear or trembling; but never let your natural courage or passion of any kind, excuse this innuendo, tempt you to be guilty of a breach of the law, which your enemies wish for. Your object is not to counteract or oppose the law, but to procure the repeal of all bad laws and bad systems. I am an Irishman by birth; America is my country by choice and adoption. As a true-born Irishman, I cannot but feel a lively interest in the welfare of my native country. Under all circumstances I conceive it to be my duty to contribute my meed in aid of your laudable endeavours to effect and accomplish the great work of real radical emancipation and reform, which you have been at all times busily employed in promoting for the good of your country; and for this purpose I send you a bill of exchange amounting to ten pounds sterling which I request you to hand over for me to the Treasurer of the national fund, and let me have the honor of being inscribed as a member of the Irish National Political Union.

The public agitation created by the election of a fit person to fill the presidential chair, has hitherto prevented the people from meeting to take into consideration the means of raising the Irish National Rent. This matter however will not be long delayed. My friend General Andrew Jackson, the present President, is re-elected. Wishing you health and long life, with every blessing, I have the honor to be, with the greatest esteem and respect,

Your most sincere and faithful Friend and Servant in Christ.

HENRY CONWELL, *Bishop of Philadelphia.*

To DANIEL O'CONNELL, ESQ. M. P.

(To be continued)

SAN DOMINGO REFUGEES IN PHILADELPHIA

COMPILED FROM THE ORIGINAL D'ORLIC–RODRIGUE PAPERS
BY JANE CAMPBELL

(Continued)

Letter from Dr. Aristide Rodrigue to his sister:

PITTSBURGH, *Oct. 31, 1835.*

We must really my dear sister Aline thank you kindly for your many kindnesses & little presents & sincerely regret that we are so far separated from such affectionate sisters. I can never think of you without your image bent over me at Harrisburg, presenting itself. I believe I feel more sensitively your affection now than ever, not that I mean you have not been uniformly kind to me, but you know such circumstances excite more powerfully at times, some who feel how superior the attachment of a sister is. We have at last got into a dirty old house, which I fear the good management of Caroline & the hard work of John & the girl will hardly keep clean. I was very happy to learn the conduct of the congregation. We have here a rumor that perhaps Mr. Hughes may be appointed bishop of Western Pennsylvania, as soon as the division can be made, which is daily expected from Rome. It would truly be a great event for this section of country, but I think very improper to remove him from such warm friends in Philadelphia. . . .

Your brother,

ARISTIDE.

Letter from Mrs. Aristide Rodrigue to Aline:

PITTSBURGH, *Oct. 31, 1835.*

Dear Aline,

As my husband has come to the conclusion that he cannot write without a subject, and as we women can write without any, I must needs take advantage of our superior powers to fill up some of the paper he has left, which it is always a pleasure to do when it affords me an opportunity of communication with my kind sister, and the anticipation of receiving one of your precious letters in return for my nothings, which serve the best purpose they are capable of by letting you know that we are alive and in health. . . . John arrived yesterday and I felt almost as if an angel had come. I have been busy giving him instructions as my master of ceremonies, commencing with hand-brush and soap, which we are obliged to use most plentifully on hands and faces as well as walls, notwithstanding which we are rapidly passing from the brunette to something of considerably darker hue, and if the darker race of mankind had first been discovered here, the difference in color might easily have been accounted for, but you really ought to see us in our little parlor and at our little table, notwithstanding the absence of splendor, which we philosophically consider only makes the dirt more troublesome, and I am a little worried for fear I might not be considered a clean housekeeper. . . . I have been castle building on the idea of Mr. Hughes being sent here to reside, as the means of bringing us all together, for I feel you could not stay behind, but I feel it is all a dream, the cruelty of separating you all from Phila., can never be practised. . . .

Your affectionate sister,

CARO.

(This letter cost 37½ cts. postage.)

Letter from Margaret Hughes to Evalina Rodrigue:

CHAMBERSBURG, *Oct. 6, 1835.*

My Dearest Evalina,

How shall I write or give expression to the feelings of delight and thankfulness I at this moment experience? Yester-

day's post brought me two dear and valued letters, yours &
one from Emily Ogden containing the delightful tidings that
my ever dear brother is not to set out on the intended voyage.
We have frequently heard of the effects sometimes produced
by sudden, unexpected good fortune. I know not how that
may be, but do know that unlooked for, and still more, un-
hoped for good news is quite sufficient to work strange things
in one's upper story.

From time to time since this morning I repeat to myself,
" Is it possible we are to enjoy the happiness our brother
so near us, when it will be in our power to hear from him
and write to him as often as we wish? The assurance that it is
so makes me so happy that I scarcely know what I say or do,
therefore my dear you must make allowance for whatever may
be amiss in this letter. . . . What in the name of wonder has
given your Papa and Duponceau the idea of going to France?
Do they, like my father, consider it a respect and duty they
owe to their friends? Is it not a strange notion? Your arrangement is admirable, particularly the part respecting
Garesché, let us go with them, and we can pull straws for him
on board, what do you say?

From your stating that your Papa had gone to D's, I infer
that he has got rid of his six month's cold. Give my love to
him & tell him from me he must be careful not to expose too
much in making preparations for his voyage to France. . . .
I am still at Michael's, as my father's house in the country
is not yet fitted up, it is about as far off as is the Court House
from 13th street. He have lived in it for the last two years
& seems quite out of his element when away from it. We
have daily intercourse with him & I hope soon to be with him
altogether, altho' M. and his wife are very kind, yet would
I prefer being with my father, as that was my object in coming. This morning I went to see how he was coming on. The
road was rather bad, as a great deal of rain had fallen lately
& I was revolving in my mind how my father could make
choice of a peace so difficult of access in rainy weather; on
reaching the house the sight that attracted my notice was
really such as to compensate for a walk twice the distance even

through mud. It was the reflection of the sun just emerging from the clouds & resting on the opposite mountains, the rich and various foliage of which appeared decked out in its innumerable tints of shade and coloring. It was most beautiful & I did not for many minutes desist from gazing upon it. It was such as I had never before beheld. . . . Rev. Mr. Hayden has just been here when I read to him that part of Miss O's leter which says my brother is not to go, I thought his eyes would start out of his head, they were like saucers. . . . Give my love to Mrs. Pleasanton & tell her I hope she will think of me sometimes, at least, when she is kneeling just behind the spot I once occupied. Give my love to Dr. and Mrs. Nancrede, Rev. Mr. Gartland and Mr. Frenaye and all friends.

Your Friend,

MARGARET.

Letter from Doctor Aristide Rodrigue to his sisters:

PITTSBURGH, *Nov. 27, 1835.*

My Dear Sister Aline,

Caroline is so busy cleaning house & fixing that she will not be able to write to you to-day, her mother has arrived. . . . You ask me for information, etc. about Pittsburg & Mr. Riley, he is well & kind to me, he does all he possibly can for me, he is for me like his countryman O'Connell for Ireland agitation, I believe he seldom if ever fails to do legally all he can for me, he has been truly faithful to his word. I have a plan of St. Paul's church for you, a view of the interior, which I will send by the first opportunity. The church will hold 2500 persons & is generally full. Miss Williams has obtained a good school, I am told & will of course remain here this winter. Her singing attracts many strangers. I have been obliged to take a pew in the church, but fear I shall not hold it long, as it is a very good one near the altar & some persons talk of purchasing it, so I shall have to go back again. I saw a few days since a number of Indians, Ottoways from Mackinaw, Michigan, all Catholics. They were on their way to Washington, all chiefs, but the principal one has been educated at Rome, quite a young man, speaks well and fluently, French, Latin, Italian & English, they were all except him dressed in their Indian costumes, each having Rosary beads & a crucifix hanging from their necks. What a pity all Catholics do not wear a crucifix & show that sign as they do to all the world. They were asleep when Mr. Riley went in, as soon as they were informed who he was, all, young & old went on their knees & asked his blessing, all chiefs, some quite young & one a very old man. After breakfast I saw them just leaving the table & as they left their lips moved a thanks & they made the sign of the cross. You have no idea how much I was delighted with them, the tribe consists of about 4000, nearly one-half of whom are Catholics and the rest becoming so. Some Evangelical Missionaries sometimes go among them and endeavor to change their faith, they invariably send them away, will have nothing to do with them, they know them well, call them imposters, they always endeavor to produce disturbance among them.

My Dear Sister Evelina you can form no idea of the difficulties we have living in this dirty place, the soot falls constantly in large flakes. It has been snowing to-day & two hours after, the whiteness of the snow was no longer visible. We have had three girls since we have been here & on Monday we change again, but for how long I do not know, without John we would be lost. I have subscribed to the Catholic Periodical, which proposes to republish all the standard works, if you & Aline would like to read it first, let me know & I will order it to be left with you first. . . . Mr. Riley desires Rev. Mr. Hughes to send him, according to promise, his review of Bishop Onderdonk's charge. I should like to have a copy. Tell Aline I left with Revd. Mr. Corcoran, to forward to her, the French work she lent me le Compte de Valmont, I think that is the name. . . .

Adieu your brother,

ARISTIDE.

Letter from Dr. Aristide Rodrigue to Rev. John Hughes:

PITTSBURGH, *Jan., 1836.*

Rev. and Dear Sir,

Rev. Mr. Mahan will present this to you, he leaves this place to-day accompanied with the sincere regrets of all the Catholics, and more particularly of those who had the happiness of his personal acquaintance, and with all best wishes for his future welfare. His conduct, both public and private, has been such as only to elicit respect and his talents, admiration. I take pleasure in bearing witness to them myself, be pleased to introduce him to my father and sisters who will endeavor I hope by their attention to repay in some measure the many kindnesses for which I am indebted to him.

Very truly yours,

ARISTIDE RODRIGUE.

PITTSBURGH, *March 18, 1836.*

Extract from a letter from Mrs. Aristide Rodrigue to Aline—about her little son:

One afternoon while he was ill Messrs. Morn and Riley came and baptized him. Mr. Morn was Godfather by proxy for William who requested the honor, and as he had no Godmother I will appoint you, confident that the character will be well fulfilled, we knew no one here who could stand for him. . . . . We have to-day been reading a new book *Impressions of America,* by Tyrone Power, he was in one of the cars at the time Aristide met with the accident, and speaks of him very handsomely in the first volume — near the beginning, tho' no name is mentioned, he is soon recognized. Aristide remembers him.

Your affec. sister,

CARO.

Letter from John Jackson to William Rodrigue:

CORNWALL, CANADA, *14 June, 1836.*

Sir,

I take this opportunity of writing you these few lines, to inform you that we are all well, thank God, and hoping that this may find you in the same. We are expecting to hear from you every day since we have received your last letter, for we are ready and willing to go to you any time you write for us. We have not taken much ·pleasure in remaining here since you have left us. We have got new engineers, they seem to be good men, but they do not please us as well as those who left us. We have applied for more wages, but it seems the Commissioners are not willing to increase our wages, so for that reason we will not remain any longer with them. You will give us notice as soon as possible and we will go to you if you can give us any encouragement at all.

Mr. Burfort's family and Mr. Crawford's family are well. All the ladies are still inquiring if we have heard from you since you left. Mr. Mills stopped here about ten days ago in good spirits. I hope he will do well wherever he goes, but I think they will have to send for you and Mr. Mills before Canal is finished yet, for your sappers understand Canalling as well as some we have known. If they do not send for Yankee Engineers as they call them, I am afraid the Canal will never be finished. The contractors think their fortune is made since you and Mr. Mills have left here, but I expect they will wish you back again. Miss Mary Ann Christy is married to John French, Miss Anderson is married to Feed, the lock contractor. All the inquiring friends are well.

I received the favor of yours with a kind of present and know not indeed at this time any other way to show my gratitude than by my hearty thanks for the same. Everything you do carries a charm with it, your manner of doing it is as agreeable as the thing done. In short sir my heart is full and would overflow in your praise did I not stop and subscribe myself

Your most obliged and obedient humble Servant,

JOHN JACKSON.

Extract from a letter from William Rodrigue to his sister:

MOUNT JACKSON, *July 10, 1836.*

My Dear Sister Aline,

I rec. your letter of the 3d instant and I learn with much pleasure that your Uncle who is my brother [I hope] has been appointed Bishop of Philadelphia. I am very much gratified by it, principally as it secures his remaining in Phila. for I was always in the fear that he would accept the See of some other city.

You mention in your letter something about the windows of the towers that are over the door. All I can say about it is that the four sides must be exactly alike [part of the letter torn out]. . . . If they have put them over the doors, I think they would do well to alter it, for the four sides of the towers must be uniform, as you can see from the sketch I make here. . . .

Your brother and friend,

W. RODRIGUE.

The " sketch " is drawn on the lower end of the page on which the letter is written.

Later in this same year William Rodrigue and Margaret Hughes were married.

Extracts from a letter written by William Rodrigue to his sister:

EDOM, 5 MILES FROM
HARRISBURG, *31 July, 1836.*
" I wish next time you see Mr. Gartland you would get him to lend you the *Catholic Almanac,* and next time some of you write, that you would send me an extract of the places and days that they have church in Virginia, and at what place Mr. Whelan resides. I wrote several times for it, but have never yet received it. I am anxious to get this in case I may be in need of it. . . . I was pleased when I learned that my intended brother was appointed Bishop. He certainly deserves it, to say the least of it, but on the other hand it will give him a great many more occupations. How does his late Controversy with Brackenridge take, what do the Protestants say about it, are the others pleased with it, do they seem to relish his giving the Presbyterians a drubbing? Let me know something about it! "

Your brother and friend,

W. RODRIGUE.

The year 1837 found Dr. Aristide settled in Sunbury.

Letter from Dr. Aristide Rodrigue to his brother William —about coal lands, etc.:

SUNBURY, *May 9, 1837.*

My Dear Brother,

I received yours of the 3rd instant from Philadelphia on Saturday and I am glad to learn of your safe arrival. We shall be happy to see and receive you and yours. We will give the best we have, we are not as well fixed as I would wish but as there is no help, we must make the best of it, still you will be comfortable and I hope pass your time agreeably.

You are altogether mistaken with respect to what I wrote on the subject of coal lands. In the first place a railroad is not to be made either as permanently & expensively as the main road; the Pottsville and Danville road from here to Stambaugh averages about $8000 per mile, that is including Bridges and all, now the facility for making a railroad from these lands is as great as can be ordinarily expected as—run descends from these common roads near Pottsville and other places without being plated with iron are made for $2000 per mile, but suppose it to cost as you say $10,000 per mile, the interest of that would only be $1,200. Now, cart as you would, 20 tons a day, I will give you all the advantages possible. I will admit that 2 horses and a driver will cost at least $2 per day and the most they could have would be 4 tons that would make 20 tons cost $10, which multiply by 300 working days would give $3000 beside the injury the coal received, etc. It is true that at this time there is too much difficulty in the money market to hope much, besides the main road has not been continued this Spring, though it is possible it may at any time.

. . . Tell my father that if coal can be purchased now at a low price to buy in his winter supply, as all the companies have very much reduced their hands and some discharged them altogether, and without doubt next winter will be one of great scarcity.

. . . I want Mr. Wright to make me a shooting coat of English —— or mole skin, white, double breasted, only 2 pockets outside, and 4 inside, the skirt not to be made too wide or very large or shaped like a cape. . . .

Your brother,

ARISTIDE.

Letter from Dr. Aristide Rodrigue to his sister:

SUNBURY, *July 4, 1838.*

My dear Sister Aline,

As we have never yet given a party, although having received many, we propose giving one next week, but there being no wine fit to drink in this place, we shall have to get the following articles. . . . We expect a good many people, the Judges of the Supreme Court will be here and of course accustomed to the best and always expect it.

1 gallon of the best Madeira.
1 gall. of best pale Sherry.
1 gall. of best Port Wine.

These may be put in demijohns.

2 bottles of best Old Madeira.
2 bottles best old pale Sherry.
2 bottles of best old Port.
1 bottle of best old brown Sherry.
1 bottle of best old Noysaix [?]
½ doz. bottles of best old Claret.
2 bottles of vin de Muscat.

These must be extra fine old wines, they are intended for the Judges.

2 bottles of orange water syrup.
2 bottles of lemon syrup.
2 bottles of orgeat syrup.
2 pineapples.
4 doz. best Oranges and 2 doz. Lemons.
300 Pickled Oysters.
3 doz. soft shelled Crabs.

The wines can be obtained good, no doubt from either Mrs. Seveliage, if my father thinks so, or from John Vaughan alias Snyder, Mr. Miller [Clement S.] is acquainted with him

and possibly will attend to it for you.   The syrups you know
where to get, oranges, etc. and Crabs, Patrick, Mary's husband
will probably take charge of them and see them on board the
R. R. cars, the whole to be directed to Amos Kapp, Stage
Proprietor, Northumberland, via Harrisburg to be forwarded
immediately.

And 2 or 3 lbs. of Mocha Coffee if that can be obtained.

2 packs of French cards (Linen) I think that is all we want.

Your brother,

ARISTIDE.

THE SILK WORM CRAZE.

Letter from Dr. Aristide Rodrigue to his sisters:

SUNBURY, *2 Feb., 1839.*

My Dear Sisters,

. . . I purpose cultivating the *Morus Multicaulis* next summer. . . . I shall also carry on the silk worm business so far
as seeing both are immensely profitable especially the former,
although I think it will be overdone in a year or two, the last
cannot for many years to come.   You may easily calculate
the profits of the first, cuttings or buds are about 2 inches in
length planted in the Spring in right ground will grow by the
ensueing fall, about 5 feet, say but four, that will give 24 buds
& the root, the buds or cuttings sell for 4 cts apiece, the roots
for 40 cts, in all $1.36, & that from an expense of 4 cts, but
then the attending will cost about ¼ & ground ¼, the highest you can possibly put it at, still you have 68 cts. profits
for each, an acre of ground will rear 15000 plants, say but
10,000 for accidents, loss etc, it will yield after all these deduc-
tions $6800, that is no exaggeration, I have it from persons
who are in the business & who have already realized the above
& it is notorious that extraordinary fortunes have been lately
made.

Now would it not be well for you if anything is received
from St. Domingo to purchase back the country seat and retire
then upon it cultivate these trees, plant out, besides cultivating

them, an acre or so in trees, raise the silk worms & reel the silk, which is a very pretty business for females, as it is light, easy & in peace and quietness earn more than a comfortable living. Think well on the above, if you have not sufficient to buy the place & engage in it, borrow the money & give a mortgage, then with what you have & may receive from France you may live well. You might beside that take a few young ladies to educate, which would without interfering with your business materially assist you. Reflect well that you are daily spending what you have without certainty of bettering yourself, and when all is gone what will you do? You could live in that place for the rent you now pay & I am very sure you could find a few young ladies to bring up. You could hire a man at $10 or $12 a month who would do everything, would cultivate garden, trees, take care of horse, etc., make all the enquiries necessary from your friends and those likely to know anything about it & remember that summer is coming on, when your school will necessarily be thinned. I think more of the silk worms & reeling than I do of the rearing, for the latter will soon be over. I am willing if you have need of any one or propose going into it to come and stay two or three weeks & get you started & make all the necessary arrangements for you. . . .

Your brother,

ARISTIDE.

Letter from Mrs. Aristide Rodrigue to Miss Aline Rodrigue:

SUNBURY, *March, 1839.*

. . . This Spring Aristide commenced the raising of Mulberry trees and silk worms, it is considered a safe and is certainly a very profitable business, and one that advances itself fast without additional capital, but on account of limited means we shall first begin on a very small plantation, but I do think that a very suitable employment is now open to us. I pray God that with it the anxiety that has so long hung over us will have an end, but our spirits once so buoyant have been too long oppressed to yield to a prospect of relief, but this business offers a variety of employments, each returning considerable profits without much expense, and the whole county is alive with it.

I suppose you have heard of ·the destruction of the Northumberland bridge from the breaking up of the ice, and nearly all communication has stopped for the present between the two places, as the ferry is not yet very well established. We commence the building of a new one immediately.

Your affectionate sister,

'CARO.

Letter from Dr. Aristide Rodrigue to his sister:

SUNBURY, *Aug., 1839.*

My Dear Sister,

. . . I have about 700 trees, mulberry to sell, I will arrange copies of two letters, the one for persons acting as agents of *Morus Multicaulis*, & the other for seed stores and gardeners, you can find out if there be any others than those I name, in order to send to each a copy; either through the postoffice or to be at their stores, you might & it would be proper to send beforehand to the different garden establishments, some persons to enquire the price they sell forest trees, such as I name, in order that I may know what prices to agree upon if they give me an order. . . . There is an establishment near where you live, running from George to Chestnut St. besides Hirst & Dreer, Chestnut near Front, Landreth, Maupay & McMahan & any others that you may know. The trees I propose to send are Linden, Sugar and other Maple, American or Yellow Poplar, Aspen, Locust, Dogwood, or any other forest trees which they may order.

You need not mind the other book from Chevalier, I put out 6000 eggs but none came out, they were good for nothing, of course a great disappointment, but all my other labors I hope will not turn out so bad, vegetables we have an abundance, more than I know what to do with, I am feeding my cow upon elegant cabbage heads, carrots, etc., piggy gets all the delicacies of the season, green peas, squash, cauliflower, etc. I have a trench of 200 feet in length of celery, which it is ten

to one, if I raise, I may feed up also.   People made great com-
plaint, they could buy nothing, now no one will buy.

To agents of *Morus Multicaulis*.

SUNBURY, *Aug., 1839.*

Sir,

I will have from 1 to 3000 of Genuine *Morus Multicaulis,*
to sell this fall, to average more than 3 feet with branches, no
leaves having been plucked to feed worms upon, which I think
a recommendation.   Will you have the goodness to let me
know if I can make a contract for their sale & what price I
can obtain for them, delivered in Phila.   I also can furnish
any quantity of the following forest-trees to be delivered in
Phila., if you can obtain any orders for them, naming the size
wanted, Linden, Sugar and other Maple, Yellow or American
Poplar [*Lyriodendron Tulipifera*] Dogwood [*Cornus Florida*]
Locus, Aspen or any other Forest trees.

Please address as soon as convenient Chestnut St., Phila.

ARISTIDE RODRIGUE.

There is nothing in the letter to indicate how the experiment in raising the *Morus Multicaulis* succeeded—but it is
altogether likely that, like the venture in Philadelphia and
other places, it was a disastrous failure, and proved the financial ruin of many who had built the most sanguine hopes on
the result.

The " morus multicaulus " or silk worm craze spread over
portions of Philadelphia, notably Germantown, at that period
an independent Township, that could only be likened to the
" tulip mania " in Holland.

Fortunes were to be made from the mulberry trees, the
multicaulus and the culture of the silk worm.   This special
variety of mulberry was said to be a perfect feeding ground
for the worm; speculation was rife, and great quantities of
trees were imported.   Silk worms had been raised, and not
unsuccessfully before this, the insects having been fed on
the white mulberry of Italy.   It is called the white mulberry
on account of the color of its fruit, which is usually white,

though it is said that since the days of Pyramus and Thisbe, the tree will occasionally bear black fruit.

The *morus multicaulus,* however, had leaves double sometimes treble and at times quadruple the size of the ordinary mulberry. Germantown was the " head centre " of the speculation. The demand for the trees was enormous and every one who could was buying and planting cuttings. Prices were steep and the owners waited hopefully for the expected fortunes.

Mr. Philip Physic was perhaps the heaviest investor in the craze. He owned about 40 acres of land in a good part of Germantown, on part of which he built a house for the proper propagation of the worm. He also dammed up the waters of the Wingohocking Creek, erected an engine and a pumping house, so as to force water into every part of the silk-worm house, the " Cocoonery " as it was then and ever afterwards called.

Every available spot on the grounds was planted with the large-leaved mulberry and everything done to foster the industry which was to make so many people rich. Most unaccountably, however, the worms did not thrive, but on the contrary died in great numbers, and the fortunes were never made.

Dr. Physic was financially ruined. John F. Watson of *Watson's Annals* fame and many another well-known citizen were involved in the disastrous loss and the *morus multicalus* craze died a sudden death.

It is only in very recent years that any intelligent explanation has been given of the apparently unaccountable mortality among the worms. It is now thought that the trouble was over-propagation of the plant by cuttings caused a disease in the leaves and the worms feeding on these infected food, naturally enough were killed.

About three only of the million or more trees that were planted during the craze survived until recent years. One of these was in Independence Square back of the Philosophical Society's building.

The " cocoonery " stood the ravages of time better than the trees.   Standing in the midst of spacious grounds it was for a number of years utilized as a boarding house but it was always known as the " cocoonery " until it was torn down a few years ago.

The next letters are from William Rodrigue who was now in Chambersburg.

Letter from William Rodrigue to his sister Evelina:

CHAMBERSBURG, *25 May, 1839.*

My Dear Evelina,

. . . I am sorry to say we have not been as good as you have been in the city, for we have been very little to church, for the very good reason that we are like a wild flock of sheep, having been deprived of a pastor, partly by circumstances and partly by the wisdom of our trustees, who are seven in number, and who when together *font de l'esprit comme quatre*.   They wanted Mr. Haiden and instead of going straight about it, they were like the Ass in the Manger, who between hay and oats starved.   They acted so well that we have no priest [1] and a great number of us have not been to their duty this year, among others, your humble servant.   It is a pity for we have a fine congregation and a neat little church. . . . I am much pleased that Papa and Sister are well and that Papa is able to go about for he must have had a tedious time this winter. How much I wish we were living in the city.   I think that Papa would be amused with sonnie, he now crawls about and looks all the world like Papa.   Tell Aline that if he was in the city he would make her run up stairs, for he is always climbing everywhere and can go up a flight of steps without stopping. . . .   Your brother & friend,

W. RODRIGUE.

[1] June 20th.   " I confirmed three persons in Christ's Church in the town of Chambersburg...there is no pastor, since the Rev. William Loughran left the place on account of the vexations of the trustees." Bp. Kenrick, *Diary and Visitation Records*, p. 175.

Extract from a letter from William Rodrigue to his sister:

CHAMBERSBURG, *June 9, 1839.*

" I find by the *Herald* that Bishop Kendrick is to be here next Thursday week, and as I think there is no suitable place for him to stop at, except the tavern, I thought it would be well to invite him to stop at our house. I have to write to Mr. Frenaye in answer to a letter he wrote me, and will mention it, but I think it will be better for you to invite him, so I wish you would invite him to stop at our house, and that I will be happy to accommodate him and the priest who may accompany him, so will you be good enough to call on Bishop Kendrick, present our respects and invite him for me, to make his home with us while in Chambersburg.

I don't know that I care very much about the chandeliers that were in the church. One thing consoles me in the change is that if the Sanctuary is to be lighted with gas, that it will smoke so as to oblige them to get the ceiling painted over again, and that they may get it done so as to correspond with the architecture of the church. . . .

Your affec. brother,

W. RODRIGUE.

Letter from William Rodrigue to his sister:

CHAMBERSBURG, *Dec. 8, 1839.*

My Dear Sister Aline,

I am much pleased with your account of Bishop Jançon, and that you were so much pleased with him, particularly as it seems our dear papa took so well with him. When I first heard of it I had been in great hopes that papa made up his mind to go to his duty, it would have been such a favorable opportunity for him. I hope yet that he will do so, and God may give His grace to him, and that he will not put off until he is older. When I first heard of his intimacy with the Bishop I had made up my mind that papa had gone to him. There is nothing on earth I so much hope for, for I see nothing that could prevent him, or make him put it off. . . . My Dear Sister Evelina · · · I am much pleased with your account of

Bishop Janço, I would have been much pleased to have been able to see him, particularly as I would have sympathized so well with him in politics. If you see him you may tell him that the little Duke has faithful subjects in our town, ready to be French, when he is King. . . .

Your affec. brother,

W. RODRIGUE.

Dr. Aristide now made another change of residence, finally locating at Ebensburg to which place his father and sisters eventually followed him.

Letter written Nov. 1839 by Dr. Aristide Rodrigue:

SUNBURY.

My Dear Sisters,

I rec. a few days ago a letter from Mr. McDonald of Ebensburg, Cambria County, informing me that he and his friends considered it a good opening for a physician. There had been two in the place, one went West, and the other has been recently elected Prothonotary of the County, and will not practice. There is no physician nearer than 17 miles. Dr. Gallitzin with a congregation of 3 or 4000 is distant only five miles. Ebensburg is on the northern route to Pittsburgh, about 20 miles from Hollidaysburg on the Alleghany Mountains, pretty much Phillipsburg over again. Mr. McDonald was acquainted and employed me in his family in Pittsburgh. I propose going next week to visit the place and if it suits to remain there this winter and not remove my family till next spring. I would wish you to get from the Bishop a letter of introduction to the Revd. Mr. Gallitzin, and at the same time enquire of him concerning an advertisement which I observed in the *Herald* about a Catholic Colony in Illinois. The place is called Postville, I have had some idea of the place for some time. . . . I have not been able to sell any of my mulberry trees, I have about 500 good sized trees and as many smaller ones.

Your affec. brother,

ARISTIDE.

(*To be continued*)

NOTES AND REPRINTS.

Under the above heading there will appear at intervals in the RECORDS a series of short notes on current historical topics, as well as a number of interesting items culled from early Catholic newspapers and other sources.

Through the courtesy of Mr. Joseph A. Weber we are permitted to print the following transcript of the official attestation of the episcopal consecration of the Rt. Rev. Michael Egan, O.S.F., together with an official note of the consecration of Rt. Rev. John N. Neumann, C.SS.R. The originals, in the handwriting of Archibshop Carroll and Archbishop Kenrick, respectively, are contained in a manuscript Record of Ordinations in the Library of St. Mary's Seminary, Baltimore. The complete publication of this unique and authentic record of early American ordinations and consecrations would be an invaluable contribution to our knowledge of early Catholic American History.

I.

1810. Hisce Ego infrascriptus Archiepiscopus Baltimorensis testatum facio Rev^m Patrem Michaelem Egan, Presbyterum ex Ordine D. Francisci Recollectorum designatum ad cathedram episcopalem Philadelphiensem, noviter a Sua Sanctitate erectam, lectis litteris Apostolicis apud S^m Mariam Majorem datis sub annulo Piscatoris die 8^a Aprilis an, 1808 et praestito prius ab ipso electo, juxta Pontificale Romanum, paucis mutatis ex Sedis Apostolicae concessione, juramento, assistentibus RRsmis DD. Joanne Cheverus (electo) Sacerdote et Episcopo electo Bostonien., et Benedicto Josepho Flaget, pariter Sacerdote et Episcopo electo Bardensi, die 28^a Octobris, an, 1810 in festo SS.Ap. Simonis

et Judae, et in templo Bmi Apostoli S. Petri, in civitate Balti-
mori a me ad Sacrum Episcopatus ordinem rite fuisse con-
secratum. Die et anno suprascripto, 28ª Octobris, an. 1810.

JOANNES ARPUS BALTSIS.

TRANSLATION. By these (letters) I, the undersigned
Archbishop of Baltimore, testify that Rev. Father Michael
Egan, O.S.F. Recollect, appointed to the episcopal Chair of
Philadelphia, lately erected by His Holiness, after the reading of the Apostolic Letters given at St. Mary Major's un-
der the Fisherman's Ring 8 April, 1808, and the oath ac-
cording to the Roman Pontifical, with a few changes by the
concession of the Apostolic See, having been first taken by
the Elect, was by me properly consecrated in the sacred or-
der of the Episcopate on 28 October, 1810, on the Feast of
Sts. Simon and Jude in the Church of the holy Apostle St.
Peter in the city of Baltimore, assisted by the Rt. Reverend
John Cheverus, priest and Bishop-Elect of Boston, and
Benedict Joseph Flaget, likewise priest and Bishop-Elect of
Bardstown.

On the aforesaid day and year, 28 October, 1810.

JOHN ARCHBISHOP OF BALTIMORE.

II.

1852 Martii 28 die consecravi Joannem Nepomucenum
Neumann, Episcopum Philadelphiensem quartum, in ecclesia
S. Alphonsi in hac urbe, adsistente Bernardo O'Reilly, epis-
copo Hartfordensi et Francisco Lhomme Vic. Gen. Baltim.
Ex Bohemia oriundus, annos natus 41, ipso die natali con-
secratus, ex Ordine SS. Redemptoris, in Dominica Passionis.
. . . Obiit subitanea morte 5 Januarii 1860; vir pius doctus
zeloque insignis.

TRANSLATION. On 28 March, 1852, I consecrated John
Nepomucene Neumann, fourth Bishop of Philadelphia, in
St. Alphonsus' Church in this city, assisted by Bernard

O'Reilly, Bishop of Hartford, and Francis Lhomme, Vicar General of Baltimore. Born in Bohemia, aged 41, consecrated on his birthday, Passion Sunday; a member of the Redemptorist Order. . . . Died suddenly 5 January, 1860; a pious, learned and very zealous man.

III.

The first Ordination ever held in the Diocese of Philadelphia and the first and only one by the Rt. Rev. Michael Egan, O.F.M., D.D., the first Bishop, was on the Rev. Denis Carroll, when he received the four Minor Orders and the Subdiaconate from Bishop Egan, 1 June, 1814 in St. Mary's Cathedral, Phila. He received first Tonsure 14 March, 1812 in Balto. and Deaconship 29 Sept. 1815 also in Balto., both from the Mt. Rev. Archbishop Carroll.

The seminary records of St. Mary's Seminary, Balto., say that he received priesthood in Phila., in 1815, date and prelate not given.

BOOK REVIEWS.

THE LIFE OF JOHN CARDINAL MCCLOSKEY. By His Eminence John Cardinal Farley. Longmans, Green & Co. 1918.

Disappointment will come to him who opens this volume with the anticipation of finding a critical biography, rich in original sources and furnished with ample bibliography. The reader, however, will be rewarded by the perusal of a book written in attractive literary style telling the history of one who lived a tranquil life in the midst of great events but who as a prominent Churchman could view from the inside all those changes which marked the growth of the Church in America during the three quarters of a century which was the extent of his life. The eminent biographer of America's first Cardinal, his successor both in his metropolitan see and in his cardinalitial title, evidently found it a labor of love to employ his scanty leisure in recording those impressions of Cardinal McCloskey which are dear memories of his own early days in the priesthood when he served the Metropolitan of New York as secretary.

John McCloskey, the child of Irish parents, was a native of Brooklyn, where he was born March 10, 1810. An alumnus of Mt. St. Mary's, he received both his collegiate training and his theological course at the Mountain. He was raised to the priesthood by Bishop Dubois in 1834 in old St. Patrick's, Mulberry Street, New York, where ten years later he was to receive episcopal consecration. The future Cardinal had the then rare privilege of continuing his studies in Rome for two years after his ordination. Association with Perrone the great theologian, with Cardinal Weld, and with Lacordaire, did much to fit the young man for the prominent rôle which was to be his in the American hierarchy.

On his return from Rome, Father McCloskey became rector of St. Joseph's, New York, where he had an unpleasant experience of one year with a board of trustees to whom he was not welcome. It is curious to learn that one of the recalcitrants was the Patrick Casserley well known to students of Latin prosody. The patience and pacific disposition of the young pastor finally won over his persecutors. "He will not fight but he will conquer," said of him by an intimate friend, describes the tactics of his entire life. For one year Father McCloskey was president of St. John's, Fordham, the preparatory college to the diocesan seminary, but poor health compelled his return to St. Joseph's.

Bishop Hughes consecrated Rev. John McCloskey as his coadjutor by whom he was served for three years in this capacity. It is interesting to know that Bishop Hughes was not a *persona gratissima* when he came to govern the diocese of New York and that the diplomacy of his coadjutor did much to soften the feeling against him. When in 1837, the dioceses of Albany and Buffalo were divided from New York, Bishop McCloskey was named first Bishop of Albany. The first years of the seventeen years of his episcopate in Albany were years of difficulty with trusteeism and of struggle with debt and of the hardships of a missionary bishop. Imagine the diocese of Albany receiving regularly assistance from the Leopoldine Society of Vienna and from the Propagation of the Faith in Lyons and this within the memory of men of three score and ten. "An unmistakable sign of the intolerance of the times" was the passage in 1855 by the Legislature of the State of New York of the Church Property Bill, which practically made it impossible for the Church to hold property except by trustees. Happily the bill remained a dead letter and was repealed seven years after its enactment.

When Archbishop Hughes died in 1864, the name of the Bishop of Albany appeared first on the list of candidates for the vacant see. With characteristic modesty, Bishop McCloskey shrank from the appointment and wrote at least one strong letter to Rome to prevent the designation which nevertheless came to make him second Archbishop of New York where he was enthroned as metropolitan Aug. 27, 1864.

The opening of the new provincial seminary at Troy and

the completion of the great cathedral begun in New York by Archbishop Hughes were among the tasks which confronted the new archbishop. The Seminary was blessed on Dec. 1, 1864, but the erection of the cathedral meant fifteen years of incessant collection.

In justice to the memory of Cardinal McCloskey his biographer calls attention to the fact that the Archbishop of New York at the Œcumenical Council of the Vatican voted *non placet* on the question of the expediency of the definition of papal infallibility but that he cast an affirmative vote at the Solemn Session.

The Roman purple came for the first time to the Church in the United States when on his sixty-fifth birthday Cardinal McCloskey received the news that he had been created by Pius IX a member of the Sacred College. The conferring of the scarlet biretta on the new Cardinal was naturally the occasion of a brilliant ceremony. The first of American churchmen to have the right to vote for the election of the sovereign Pontiff arrived in Rome too late to participate in the conclave which elected Leo XIII from whom he received the cardinalitial hat.

The crowning work of Cardinal McCloskey's episcopate as metropolitan of New York occurred on May 25, 1879 when the magnificent Gothic cathedral on Fifth Avenue was dedicated. It was the third cathedral which it had been his work to build, having completed the pro-Cathedral in New York and the present edifice in Albany.

Unable to attend the Third Plenary Council of Baltimore, Cardinal McCloskey was there represented by his Coadjutor Archbishop Corrigan. As a young bishop he had sat in the First Plenary Council in 1852 and he had taken an active part in the second of these assemblies in 1866.

The Cardinal's strength had been failing for a decade before death came to close his long career on Oct. 10, 1885. Those who knew him have a memory of an ecclesiastic of princely bearing and of saintly disposition, of a prelate " kind and gentle and fatherly." The story of his life is interesting as the record of one who lived to see Catholicity grow in his native state from pioneer missionary conditions to the queenly proportions of an important metropolitan see and whose part in its history though not a commanding one was yet an effective though gentle influence in the shaping of this stupendous growth.

WILLIAM J. LALLOU.

THE PHILADELPHIA THEOLOGICAL SEMINARY OF ST. CHARLES BORROMEO. A Record of its Foundation, Charter, and Career: comprising a list of the trustees, members of the faculty and of the priests therein ordained: 1832-1917. With illustrations. Philadelphia: Printed for His Grace, Most Rev. Edmond F. Prendergast, D. D. MCMXVII.

The Rev. Augustine J. Schulte had already issued two editions (1890, 1905) of his history of Overbrook Seminary before the present greatly enlarged one was desired by Archbishop Prendergast. It had proved its value in many ways, not perhaps the least important being the condensed information given in the List of Priests ordained for the Diocese of Philadelphia. Not only does the present edition add a large number of entries to this list, of priests ordained between 1905 and 1917 (June), but the whole previous list has been gone over with most painstaking minuteness of research, with the result of valuable emendations. Only those who have engaged in such research can surmise the labor, the patience, the diligence required for the compilation of such a list (pages 124-158). It contains 919 names and gives the date and place of ordination and the ordaining prelate. As in the edition of 1905, the names are numbered in the order of time of ordination; but one feature of the present edition which is newly added and which cannot fail to be justly appreciated is the table of contents giving the names arranged alphabetically together with a reference to the number affixed to each name in the List itself. In this way immediate access to the table and the list is furnished to an inquirer. All the other tables (e. g. of priests connected with the Seminary who studied in foreign colleges or at the Catholic University of America; of priests attached to the dioceses formed ·out of the original diocese of Philadelphia; of priests who, coming from other dioceses, labored for some time in the diocese of Philadelphia) have similarly been revised and brought up to date. It is clear, also, that the History itself has been carefully revised throughout in its text, and a number of pictorial illustrations have been either withdrawn or replaced with more suitable ones. The new illustrations include the Escutcheon of the Seminary (in colors) ; a front view of the Seminary, showing the beautiful addition of the Archbishop Ryan Memorial Library; an autograph letter of St. Charles (recently acquired for the Library of the Seminary) ; the Drexel Memorial Altar and the Drexel Monument; the new addition, St. Edmond Hall; the Service Building (now in course of erection), etc.

These new illustrations remind us of the immense enlargements which have been made in very recent years and of the uninterrupted process which has been going on in respect of the artistic enhancement of the Seminary. One might easily fancy, in the three editions of Father Schulte's invaluable History, a compendious illustration of the progress of Catholicity in the United States. But it needs no flight of fancy to recognize, from the interesting text of the History itself as well as from the greatly enlarged table of priests which the volume furnishes, the scarcely believable progress of Catholicity in the Diocese of Philadelphia. The History is thus something of a sermon, although not so intended, on the parable of the mustard-seed. Bishop Kenrick inaugurated his diocesan seminary in the upper rooms of his own modest residence, with a class of five students, in 1832. The History exhibits to our wondering gaze the rapid growth of the tender plant, signalized by the names of Glen Riddle, Eighteenth and Race Sts., Overbrook; and at Overbrook itself, by the constant additions of new buildings. The text for a sermon to any timid Catholic of the early decades of the nineteenth century, as he witnessed the first planting by Bishop Kenrick, might well be the words of Christ to the timid Peter: " O thou of little faith, why didst thou doubt? "

He is a poor reviewer who cannot find something to quarrel

with in his author or who cannot suggest desirable additions to the author's volume. The present reviewer candidly confesses his poverty.

H. T. H.

THE CONVERSION OF TWO LUTHERAN MINISTERS TO THE ROMAN CATHOLIC CHURCH IN 1863. By Rev. Ignatius Zeller. Published by J. Schaefer, 23 Barclay St., New York. 1918. Pp. 79. Price, 25 cents.

This pamphlet, translated from the German by Joseph P. Brentano, relates in an intimate way the steps which led Christian Charles Schnurrer and Ignatius Zeller from the Lutheran ministry into the Catholic Church. The former became editor of the Ohio *Waisenfreund* and the latter a priest of the Brooklyn diocese.

THE EARLY LIFE OF PROFESSOR ELLIOTT. By George C. Keidel, Ph.D., Washington, D. C. 1917. Pp. 10.

In this reprint of a paper read before the Romance Club of the Johns Hopkins University, 12 October, 1916, Doctor George C. Keidel, late associate in Romance in that University, draws with a friendly and reverent pen a very readable sketch of the early life of Aaron Marshal Elliott, Professor in Johns Hopkins 1876-1910. It is probably intended as a prelude to a more ambitious sketch of the life of Professor Elliott.

THE INFLUENCE OF THE CATHOLIC CHURCH AND HER PEOPLE UPON THE HISTORY OF ILLINOIS. By Arthur J. Hughes. Pp. 40. University Press, Notre Dame, Ind. 1917.

This study obtained for the author both the Mgr. O'Brien prize and the degree of Master of Arts from the University of Notre Dame. · In a readable popular style it shows the part which Catholics, past and present, have played in the upbuilding of Illinois.

RECORDS OF THE

AMERICAN CATHOLIC HISTORICAL SOCIETY

Vol. XXIX.   December, 1918.   No. 4

JOHN KEATING AND HIS FORBEARS

BY J. PERCY KEATING, ESQ.

Some years ago the late Martin I. J. Griffin called upon the writer seeking information regarding John Keating's connection with an early land settlement in Pennsylvania which was known as the Asylum Company; and in the course of the conversation he expressed his surprise that no member of the Keating family had ever taken the trouble to " write up " so interesting a personality. In his article subsequently published in the AMERICAN CATHOLIC HISTORICAL RECORDS he has this to say: " Of John Keating, much could be said but little has been published concerning this foremost and most venerable old-time Philadelphian. The name is familiar and a household one in our city. It is to be hoped that his descendants will soon make public recognition of the worth of their progenitor, a truly representative Catholic. . . . Just read the tribute of Liancourt to his worth and then wonder why more has not been given in recognition of it by those who could do so."

Unfortunately John Keating did not leave many papers from which to gather the details of his career in America.

For a few years he kept a diary, but almost solely for the purpose of recording the virtues of his beloved wife whom he lost after a short married life. The death of his two sons and his son-in-law during his own lifetime, and the subsequent busy professional career of his only grandson, which left little time for leisure pursuits, precluded the usual course of transmission of the many passing incidents of his daily life which might now be of interest to his own and possibly to other people of this day and generation. There are, however, old documents and papers having reference to the earlier history of his family and to his own career before his emigration to America which are not without interest, and to the facts as thus derived have been added herein such scraps of information as could be gathered here and there from copies of his own correspondence, if only with a view to discharging as far as possible at this late date the duty which Mr. Griffin's words would seem to impose.

As regards the old family papers referred to, it can hardly be doubted that if all the buried and forgotten personalities and associations of earlier days were brought to light and submitted to inspection from our more modern point of view, there would be found in every family history, however obscure, characters, incidents and associations which would excite human interest. And so it is with these old papers of John Keating. Through them his forbears and their doings are traceable farther back than is the case with many families laying legitimate claim, according to the usual tests of popular distinction, to greater importance than his own. And their contents would seem to possess sufficient interest to warrant a fuller and more detailed reference to John Keating's antecedents than is usually made in short biographies such as this paper is intended to cover. The collection and preservation of these papers was due in large part to the emigration of the Keating family from Ireland to France in the eighteenth century. At that time it was of importance, owing to the deference paid to caste in that country, to supply the proper authorities with particulars as to origin gathered from the public offices and the private registers then extant.

It thus happened that upon the arrival of John Keating's father in France in 1766, in order to establish his social status in the land of his adoption, he brought with him proofs of his paternal and maternal ancestry for ten preceding generations, and these in part have been preserved, though some were destroyed as a measure of protection during the French Revolution. Thereby he not only gained official recognition of his rank from the Crown, but, what is of more interest at the present day, confirmed the racial origin of his particular family line as traced in its own traditions. The purely Gaelic families of Ireland, of course, need no such proof, nor indeed do some of those of Anglo-Norman stock whose names alone indicate their origin, such as the Eustaces, Cruices, Purcells, Montgomerys and Graces; but the Keating name, because of its Irish derivation, might prove misleading, especially as all who bear the name in our day are not, as it seems, of the same race.

It was through this means, therefore, that it was established that John Keating's family is of Anglo-Norman descent, by which are indicated those families of Norman stock who preceded or accompanied Henry II of England in his invasion of Ireland in 1169, or who followed him, once his rule was established. These families, traceable to the County of Wexford, where the expedition landed, while retaining in part the traditions of their race and living to a large extent within what was known as the English Pale, intermarried not only within their own race, but also with those of pure Irish blood, and though intermediate between the native Irish and the English of the Pale, gradually became identified with the Irish people in their later struggles, especially because of their adherence to the ancient faith, thereby giving rise to the popular expression that they were " more Irish than the Irish themselves." At their head stood certain great families, such as the Kildares and the Desmonds of the Geraldine line, being descended from Maurice Fitzgerald who accompanied Richard de Clare, Earl of Pembroke, surnamed Strongbow, in the advance guard of Henry's expedition. The history of these families is imperishably associatetd with the struggle for Irish freedom against English oppression.

The Keating family is of this stock, and its tradition, as set forth in an ancient narrative still in possession of the family, traces the name to an incident occurring during Strongbow's Expedition. A young man in charge of a detachment was sent ashore on the coast of Wexford, with orders to light fires in case he should land unopposed. In effecting his purpose he put to flight a wild boar which lay hid in a laurel bush. In commemoration of his successful adventure he afterwards assumed the name Kiadtinneh (soon after modified to Keating), which is said to be the Gaelic for many, or a hundred, fires, and quartered his arms with four laurel leaves surmounted by a wild boar as a crest. The family tradition makes him one of the Fitzgerald clan. As to the meaning of the name, it can only be said that it was so interpreted at least as far back as the time of Queen Elizabeth; for when certain members of the Keating family were driven by the religious persecution of that day to seek refuge in Spain and Portugal, they translated their name into Spanish and became known as the family of Cienfuegos, which has the same meaning, their coat-of-arms being also the same as that of the Keatings of Ireland, to wit, the four laurel leaves surmounted by the boar. And as regards the descent, it may be noted that in O'Hart's *Irish Pedigrees*, vol. 2, p. 216, the Keatings of Wexford are stated to be descended from Griffin or Griffyth, son of William de

Carew, who was a brother of Maurice Fitzgerald above mentioned. At all events, the name in its Anglicized form appears in the chronicles of the times shortly after the invasion of Ireland as identified with the County of Wexford, where the Keatings appear to have held high rank among the Anglo-Norman settlers, though certain Irish families afterwards, in assuming Anglicized forms of their own Gaelic patronymics, took the name of Keating, and are therefore not of the same blood.

The stock from which John Keating descended, however, is clearly traceable in the family record before mentioned to the Wexford Keatings and is always associated in the histories of the times with the Geraldines as represented by the Earl of Kildare, of whom they were devoted adherents. The first of the name who appears on the beautifully illuminated old genealogical tree drawn up in 1767 and still in possession of the family, is Henry Keating, Knight, of Wexford, who lived in the fourteenth century and from whom John Keating was tenth in direct descent. Those were the days of Edward III and the Black Prince — of Crecy and Poitiers. The king drew largely from Wexford for his army at that time, and it would not be improbable, though there is no record of it, that Henry Keating, a knight of English descent, should have participated in the taking of the little city which four hundred years afterwards received his direct descendant as an exile.

The most interesting, though perhaps not the most devout, member of the family of that period was James, the grandson of Henry and brother of John's eighth ancestor. He was Prior of Kilmainham, a priory of the Order of St. John of Jerusalem, afterwards known as the Order of Malta, and subsequently Grand Prior of the Knights Templar of all Ireland and one of the Thirteen Knights of the Order of St. John, a military confraternity instituted by the Irish Parliament about the year 1470 for the defence of the

English Pale against what were termed the "wylde Irish".
In the Wars of the Roses, Keating sided with the White
Rose, or the House of York, whose cause was espoused by
the Earl of Kildare, then Lord Deputy, and was involved in
the great struggle with the House of Lancaster. More than
this, he was accused of being unfaithful to his trust and
deposed from the office of Grand Prior. According to
Webb's *Compendium of Irish Biography*, upon the appointment of Lord Grey as Lord Deputy in place of the Earl of
Kildare, Keating, who was then Constable of Dublin Castle,
broke down the drawbridge and defied the new deputy with
his 300 archers and men-at-arms. He was finally subdued
and stripped of his offices and honors on the accession of
Henry VII of the House of Lancaster, and died in poverty
and disgrace. Inasmuch as the then Archbishop of Dublin
and the Chief Justice of Ireland both suffered with him, it
may charitably be supposed that he was not as black as he
is painted in the quaint chronicles of the times, and especially
in Sir James Ware's *Antiquities of Ireland*. Nicholas
Keating, the oldest son in the seventh generation preceding
John and nephew of the recalcitrant James, was summoned
to the Irish Parliament as a baron of the realm—the only
way by which barons were created in those days—but lost
his title and possessions for rebellion under Queen Elizabeth in company with several others of his kinsmen. It was
this claim of title, which had reverted to the line from which
John sprung by reason of failure of descendants from
Nicholas, which Louis XVI recognized when John's father
sought recognition from the French Crown on his arrival in
France. The younger brother of Nicholas, William by
name, who was John's direct ancestor, seems to have also
been a person of note in his day. By letters patent from
Henry VIII he was constituted Guardian of the Marches or
waste lands lying between the English Pale and the territory
of the native Irish. The Pale, wherein the English rule and

system of land tenure prevailed, consisted at that time of the seaport counties of Louth, Westmeath, Dublin, Kildare and Wexford. The rest of Ireland was unequally divided among sixty Irish chiefs and thirty chiefs of English origin living under the Breton or tribal law which recognized no land titles save those of the tribe or clan. Many Irish, of course, lived within the Pale and many Anglo-Irish lived without; and the intervening waste land, which served as a protection to the inhabitants of the Pale, had to be guarded and policed. The Guardians of the Marches were vested with this duty, Keating's force of light armed infantry being known as the Keating Kerne. His sense of allegiance to the Crown did not at times, however, press very hard upon his conscience, for in Bagewell's *England under the Tudors* he is referred to as having sided with Lord Ossaly, the son of the Earl of Kildare, in 1534, in a rebellion which originated in a rumor which spread through Ireland that the Earl, as Lord Deputy, who had been summoned to England, had been summarily executed on his arrival. The rumor was unfounded, however, and Keating with his whole force was captured, but suffered to return to his allegiance; and his office was continued in his descendants until the time of the great rebellion under Charles I.

In Queen Mary's reign King's and Queen's Counties were formed out of districts acquired from the Irish lands, and Queen's County was divided — the Irish under their tribal law being assigned to the western half and the English to the eastern half. A few natives whose services as captains of Kerne had deserved recognition were accorded grants of land out of the English section. Queen Mary died, however, before the transaction was completed, and it was not until shortly after Elizabeth's accession that William Keating's son, Thomas, became vested under royal patent with the estates of Crottentegle and Farraghbane in the parish of Killabin, Queen's County, which became the family domain and remained so until their forfeiture by Cromwell upon his invasion a hundred years later. It is not to be supposed, however, that their enjoyment of their possessions was altogether undisturbed. William Keating's direct descendants intermarried with families of both Norman and Irish stock, the O'Dempsies, Hoares, Purcells, O'Regans, Eustaces, Fitzgeralds, Quins and Creaghs, all devoted adherents of the ancient faith. And from the time of Elizabeth the one aim of the English crown was to stamp out the Roman Catholic religion. For a long while the priests were the special object of attack, because the loyalty of the laity in the English section was a great asset in subduing the native Irish; nor was it in the power of a handful of Protestants, as Lingard tells us, to deprive a whole people of their religion. It was perhaps fortunate also for the Keating family that the scion of their house was for the greater part of the reign of James I a minor. Then came Charles I, and it might seem surprising that he should have seen fit to confirm by letters patent dated May 15, 1636, unto another Thomas Keating, John's great-great-grandfather, the privilege of holding his own land. The explanation lies in the fact that Charles was much pinched for funds, and Lord Strafford, his then Viceroy, seized upon the pretext of flaws in the titles to Irish lands in general to compound with their owners under threat of forfeiture. And the very flattering terms made use of in describing the Keating family in the letters patent would seem to indicate that Thomas paid a pretty high price for his peaceable possession of his own.

But it was not to be for long. The headstrong King in pursuance of his shifting policies was alienating both sides in the fierce struggle which was then impending, and losing his hold upon the affections of the Irish people upon whose fidelity, despite their past treatment, he could have relied. Both within and without the Pale they stood for him as long as he showed any inclination to yield to them the free exercise of their faith; but his vacillating conduct in making promises in return for their support, only to be broken to suit his purposes, gradually forced them into a position where religion took precedence, and this resulted in the King's undoing as well as their own. Thomas Keating naturally sided with all his kin and suffered with the rest. His eldest son, a lieutenant of horse, was killed in the first uprising. His second son, Redmund, John's great-grand-father, raised a troop of horse at his own expense to assist the King. Then as the situation gradually developed into a religious war, the Anglo-Irish drew towards their Celtic compatriots and upon Cromwell's invasion they were swept away. The Keating lands were forfeited and turned over to one of Cromwell's generals by name of Gale, the family being suffered during the reign of Charles II to occupy a small portion of the old estate. And this was all the recompense they had upon the restoration — a fate which befell thousands of their countrymen besides. Here they lived until the close of the reign of the unhappy James II. When William of Orange invaded Ireland Redmund Keating, John's great-grandfather, who in 1653 had married Elizabeth Fitzgerald, a direct descendant of the great Earl of Desmund, was still living in the small section of his ancient patrimony above referred to. He had many sons, all of whom were in King James' army. One was killed at the battle of Aghrim, another at the battle of the Boyne, but Geoffrey (or Jeffrey), the grandfather of John, survived, and his history is sufficiently interesting and romantic to warrant mention here. After the battle of Aghrim, as captain of horse he retired with King James' army to Limerick, where they made their last stand. Before withdrawing into the city itself, Geoffrey was stationed with his company at Adare, situated about seven miles from the city, where dwelt Thadeus, or Thady, Quin, the possessor of a fine estate—the site of an old abbey the ruins of which are still extant. He had a daughter •Mary by his first wife—who was a Rice, of the family now represented by the Spring Rices. She was about 16 and he 22 years of age. Her father insisted upon Geoffrey's taking up his lodgings at Adare House, with the usual result that the young people found that neither could live without the other. A proposal of marriage was accepted and the situation admitted of no delay. The marriage had no sooner taken place than the General, being apprised of the approach of the enemy, called in all the outposts, including the young captain, and Limerick was besieged. The world-renowned capitulation followed, when almost the entire Irish army, being given the option whether to enlist in the English army or accept exile abroad, chose the latter, and rendezvoused for the purpose on the Quin Estate. Captain Keating then bade good-bye to his young wife, and neither of them saw nor heard of the other for six years. The Irish army was incorporated into the famous Irish Brigade, which gave such a good account of itself for years on the continent under Louis XIV.

The vessel in which the young captain sailed for France was wrecked off the coast of Denmark; his troop was dispersed and separately sought their way as best they could through the low countries to France. He relates in his own narrative that being reduced to great distress and having spent the last penny he had and sold all his effects, " even his silver buckles," and walking carelessly on the high road he stumbled upon something which he discovered to be a purse which contained enough money to defray his expenses to St. Germain, where he found King James and his family established. There he learned that his regiment was in garrison at Bapaume (the scene of such terrible strife in the present war) and had taken the name of the Dorrington regiment after its colonel, a custom prevalent in those days. It was the same regiment in which John Keating served a

century later. The regiment was then sent to reinforce
Marshal Catinat's army in Italy in its campaign against
Prince Eugene, and on St. Francis' day, October 4, 1693,
Captain Keating was made major of his regiment on the
field of battle at La Marsaille in Piedmont for valor in rush-
ing into the midst of the enemy and rescuing a standard of
colors which had been taken at the beginning of the battle.

In 1696 he obtained leave to return home. In order to
secure entrance to England he disguised himself as a Flem-
ish merchant, but was arrested on entering London and
thrown into the Tower. After some six months' imprisonment, nothing suspicious having been discovered on his person, he was visited by an old companion in arms who had
entered the English service and was then under-secretary
of state, who besought him to abandon the Stuarts and
accept an equivalent rank in the English service. This he
refused to do, asking only that he be allowed to visit his
wife in Ireland, and the permission was secured. And the
old narrative states that upon his altogether unexpected
arrival in 1697, she " fainted away and was some time
without giving signs of life." He then quitted Louis XIV's
service and received a grant of land for a hundred years'
duration from his father-in-law, which was supposed to
represent his wife's interest, through her mother, in the
Rice Estate, and which was called Baybush.

Thady Quin remarried, and his descendants by his second
wife subsequently became Lords of Adare and Earls of
Dunraven, from whom the present earl descends. Geoffrey
settled down at Baybush and had three daughters and two
sons—Redmund and Valentine. Owing to his Stuart lean-
ings he was under constant suspicion, and was once tried
for high treason on a trumped-up charge, but was honorably
acquitted. The circumstances, as narrated by his grandson
in a paper still extant, are sufficiently interesting to warrant
insertion here. " Sitting by the fireside with his wife and

children, then very young, on a winter's night he heard a
great rap at the door. Surprised at a visit at so late an hour
he went himself to know who the stranger was, and received
for answer that he was come by order of the Government,
and summoned him in the King's name to open the door;
which having done, he saw a young officer, who told him in
the most polite manner that he was very sorry to be under
the necessity of executing the disagreeable order he received
from the Governor of the City of Limerick—that he had
thirty soldiers under his command, that the house was surrounded, and that all resistance or attempt to escape would
be vain, and that he must conduct him immediately to that
city. Major Keating begged he would not alarm his wife
and family, gave him his word of honor that he would
follow him the next morning, and invited him to supper and
to take a bed at Baybush. The offer was immediately
accepted by the Lieutenant who commanded the detachment; all the soldiers were invited to enter the house and to
eat and drink, and the day following the Major and his
servant, an old soldier, set out with the escort for Limerick,
where they were confined for some days and thence transferred to Dublin. There he learned for the first time that
he and his servant were accused of high treason for having,
with many other persons all unknown to him, entered into
a plot of subverting King William's Government, and he
was, moreover, particularly accused of being commissioned
to raise 60,000 men for Louis XIV's service. They were
all brought to trial, all the facts were sworn to, and the jury
was about to deliberate, when one of the witnesses, struck
with remorse of conscience, rose up and declared publicly
that they were all suborned; that their accusation was false
and dictated by a spirit of revenge and hatred against some
of the prisoners; that the names of Major Keating and his
servant were added to the list in order to give more probability to the indictments, and that all the papers concerning

this affair were deposited in a press or closet in a certain house in Dublin. These documents having been found and laid before the Court, the prisoners were discharged, the false witnesses punished; but the instigators of this foul plot were so powerful that their names were not even mentioned."

Geoffrey died in 1741. His eldest son, Redmund, studied for the Bar, and acquired a good practice in Dublin. Valentine, the second son, after being educated with his brother in France, married Sarah Creagh, of an old Irish family whose estate, Tiervon, on the banks of the Shannon in the County Limerick, had been forfeited during the rebellion. They lived at Baybush, where all his children, including John, were born. The penal laws against Roman Catholics were strictly enforced in those days, and the prospect for his children, all strictly reared in their ancestral faith, was most discouraging. His elder brother Redmund, who had never married and was devoted to his brother's family, finally abandoned his practice and agreed to join him in emigrating to France, where the Irish had always met with a favorable reception from the Crown and the people and where the Catholic faith prevailed. Accordingly in 1766 they relinquished their holdings at Adare and embarked at Cork for Havre, proceeding thence to St. Germain, whither old Geoffrey Keating had directed his steps some seventy-five years previously, and where several Irish families were still living to whom Louis XV, after the example of his ancestor Louis XIV, had assigned apartments in an old castle.

The Keating family had no need of support or assistance from their new-found friends upon their arrival in France, as Redmund Keating had acquired what was considered a handsome property from the practice of law. After a short stay at St. Germain, therefore, they moved to Poitiers, where the sons had formerly attended the Jesuit school.

There, Redmund having relinquished his right by primo-
geniture, letters patent of nobility were granted Valentine
by Louis XV in recognition of his rank in Ireland.   They
purchased an estate in the neighborhood of the town, known
as Cicogne, and there Valentine and Redmund lived and
died.   The family consisted of nine children, five boys and
four girls.   The oldest, Geoffrey, upon whom, at his father's
death, the title devolved, followed a mercantile pursuit,
married into an old French family, lived with his wife on
her estate in Poitou, and died childless.   The second son,
Thomas, entered the French army, was given a commission
in the Walsh (formerly Dorrington) regiment of the Irish
Brigade — the same in which his grandfather had served.
John and William, twins, born September 20, 1760, were
sent to the College of the English Benedictines at Douay in
Flanders, and the daughters in time were suitably married
to scions of the French nobility.   After graduating, both
John and William obtained commissions in the same regiment of Walsh, and finally, after France had declared war
on behalf of the American Colonies, the youngest son, Redmund, secured a like commission.   So there were at the
same time four brothers, officers in the same regiment.
Count Walsh Serrant was the colonel of the regiment, himself of an old Irish family and ever afterwards John Keating's intimate friend.   The battalion in which the brothers
served was included in a fleet of 150 vessels which sailed
for Martinique under Count de Guichen in January, 1780.
Thomas took part in three engagements with Admiral Rodney, was captured and afterwards exchanged, while Redmund and John were engaged in the capture of the Island
of Tobago.   Soon afterwards preparations were made for
an expedition the object of which was kept secret.   Several
detachments of different regiments were ordered to be
ready.   Twelve hundred men were put on board three frig-
ates and smaller vessels, John's being among them, and the

fleet sailed under command of M. de Bouillé, it being the general belief that the destination was North America. After they had proceeded some distance they were met by a sloop-of-war sent by Count de Grasse, to inform them of the taking of Yorktown and surrender of Cornwallis. Thereupon they changed their course and made for the Island of St. Eustatius which had recently been taken from the French by Admiral Rodney. This they stormed and captured, taking 700 English prisoners. John's description of the fight is interesting as indicating the primitive mode of fighting as compared with ours, in those days. It is as follows:

" The Irish detachment were to pass themselves for British troops sent for the benefit of their health from the Island of St. Lucy to St. Eustatius. We were provided with mattresses to throw upon the thorny, prickly pears that grew in the ditches that surround the fort, for the escalading of which we had ladders. All seemed well calculated. Our information, however, proved false to the last degree. The bay we landed in was crowded with rocks; every boat was stove in; the men had to wade in the water; our cartridges were wet; we were surrounded by high mountains and no means of getting up to the top but by a ravine formed by the rains. We fortunately had two or three ladders with us without which we could not have reached the top. We had taken them to escalade the fort. About four o'clock in the morning of November 25, 1781, M. de Bouillé mustered the troops, gave no sign of dismay and only said, ' Le vin est tiré, il faut le boire.' He marched at the head of the Irish. We had to pass in view and under a high hill called Panga, where a watch of a few men were stationed to keep a lookout, and by firing of guns give signals of the approach of vessels. One or two of them had slept in town, contrary to orders, and the others were seized asleep by surprise. To this may be attributed the success of the expedition. We continued our march and at sunrise we got a view of the town and of the troop that was going to mount guard. The road was imbedded in thick and high hedges; our arms were carried horizontally to prevent the sun shining on them. We ran along bent almost in two till we came to an opening into the field where the British troops were parading. We immediately drew up in battle and marched towards them. Our poor and scanty firing was the first signal of an enemy—unprepared and astonished, they fled in every direction.

" The Governor, Col. Cockbrun, who was distinguished for his bravery in North America, having seen vessels far out at sea, and nevertheless no signals made, galloped for his usual ride to the parade ground and addressed himself to us to know what was the matter. Being told by one of our officers, Mr. Trant, that he was a prisoner, he made off, but, being fired on, surrendered. The fort was immediately attacked; the pont levis was not drawn up, there was a hard struggle there, but some French officers bore it down and opened a passage to their men. The fort was then surrendered. The English troops, amounting to about 600 or 700 men of the 13th and 15th Regiments that had served in North America, were taken successively; they were quartered with the inhabitants, had no general place of rendezvous, were so bewildered on seeing an enemy of whose landing or approach they had not the least idea and whose numerical force was announced to be some thousands, whereas there were not above 400. . . . I remained on the island. There was a considerable sum of money remaining in the hands of the Governor, the proceeds of sales of prizes made by Admiral Rodney. This sum was divided amongst the fleet and army, the first instance of land forces receiving any prize money. All other moneys found in the Governor's house in bags with the owner's names were restored to them, as also the keys of their cisterns; every kind of vexation was done away with. The island was held by the French for the Dutch, for whom a civil governor, M. Chabert, was named. The garrison was commanded by Captain Fitzmaurice of Walsh's regiment."

In the meantime Thomas Keating became aide-de-camp to the Governor of Tobago and Redmund was sent to a port where three of his predecessors had died of fever, and he soon succumbed himself. Thomas at this time must have seen service in the United States also, though there is no mention of it; for he was afterwards elected an honorary member of the Rhode Island Society of the Cincinnati, which could not have been the case had he not been associated with the Revolution. Then in 1783, after peace was concluded, the two brothers returned with their regiment to France and in 1788 the regiment received orders to sail for Mauritius, otherwise known as the Isle of France, in the Indian Ocean. John and William were included in the orders, John sailing aboard the Penelope, a fine frigate of 44 guns. She ran ashore at the Cape of Good Hope and became a total loss, thirty-five men and the second in command being lost. The remainder continued the voyage in another frigate. After a year's stay on Mauritius, the regiment was ordered to return to France.

In the meantime William Keating, John's twin brother, being stationed with a detachment in the District of Grand Port on that island, met with the daughter of a prominent planter by name of Rochecouste, a native of France, and fell in love with her. He resigned from the army, married her, settled on the island, and left a numerous progeny, many of whom still survive in France and in the island of Mauritius and in the United States. His eldest son, as will later be seen, was sent to Philadelphia to his uncle John to be educated, and there married John's daughter, his cousin, and from him are descended the present Keating family of Philadelphia. John Keating sailed from Mauritius with the regiment. They were driven out of their course by contrary winds, and through failure of provisions were forced to land in Martinique in the West Indies, but not without being put into peril by fire which broke out amidships and came near destroying the vessel. There at Martinique they got their first news of the outbreak of the Revolution and took the tri-color cockade. There, too, John Keating was introduced to Madame de Beauharnais, the future Empress Josephine, who it will be remembered was a native of Martinique and had not as yet entered upon her wonderful career. Sailing thence to France, after a voyage of six months from Mauritius, they found the most extraordinary change to have taken place since their departure. John describes it in the following words: " We found the country in a great state of consternation and confusion and were astonished to see and hear all that was going on. We had to yield to the impulse given and to submit to the dictates and caprices of demagogues scarcely known before the Revolution. Our own station was in Britany, and of course close to the seaport; we received orders in the end of 1791 to embark for San Domingo where the greatest troubles were threatening that fine island with desolation and murder. Previous to my departure I received the cross of St. Louis by commission dated November 27, 1791."

Thomas Keating did not accompany the regiment. He had been promoted to the colonelcy of the 87th or " Dillon " regiment of the Irish Brigade. From that point his subsequent promotion was rapid until he became a general of brigade. He participated in the whole campaign in Belgium in 1793, in command of a portion of the Army of the North which acted as advance guard under La Marlière, in the taking of Antwerp and in the battle of Nerwingham, and he was temporary commandant at Ruzimonde, Boulogne, Montreuil and Mesdin. Then, as might well be expected, owing to his family affiliations, notwithstanding the universal testimony of his brother officers of his loyalty to the army, he began to be suspected of monarchical sympathies. He was removed from his command and thrown into the prison of La Force, where he remained eighteen months during the Reign of Terror, and but for Robespierre's downfall would have been guillotined with the other victims. The testimonials of his brother officers are among the family papers and indicate his great popularity in the army. He died at the family home at Cicogne in 1795 at the age of forty-two, a victim to lung trouble brought on by his imprisonment.

John's trip with his regiment to San Domingo was anything but pleasant. Meeting with contrary winds, and compelled to seek the Canary Islands for shelter, obliged to seek another ship on account of unseaworthiness, confronted with mutiny among the soldiers owing to their having imbibed the principles of the Revolution, their progress was slow, and it was six months after their departure from France before they reached their destination. John's experience on his arrival and his subsequent actions may be best explained in his own words. " I soon perceived from what I witnessed and from what I learned from the officers who had been for some time on the Island that it was impossible that the military and civil commissioners Polverel and Santhonax, sent by the Convention, could agree, and that some great blow was unavoidable. The moment was at last come, the military seemed to predominate, and determined at the end of September (1792) to seize the Commissioners and send them to France. In less than half an hour, when all the military corps were under arms, they turned their backs on their officers, sided with the commissioners and forced all their officers to embark for France. Amongst them were the Governor, Lt. General Count d'Esparbes, M. de Blancheland and M. Tousard, well known in the United States. At the demand of the 92d Regiment,.

backed by the Commissioner Santhonax, I had to take the
temporary command of the Regiment. I'was resolved, however, to give it up as soon as possible and leave the Island."
And in another place he says: "A few days were sufficient
to convince me that there was nothing to be gained by a
stay on that Island owing to the divisions prevailing among
its inhabitants and the troops. The blacks were in full insurrection. The whole country was in their power. The
plantations had all been burned, the whites and the troops
were confined to the town; there was no union, no confidence. The whole population divided into parties and factions, and all complaining and condemning one another.
The arrival of a large body of troops did not allay the discontent. The 92nd Regiment insisted upon my remaining
to take the command, which I complied with by order of the
Civil Commissioner, but on condition, as my commission
mentions, that it should be but a temporary act, as I could
not acknowledge any right in troops to dismiss and name
their officers at pleasure. All my efforts now tended to
facilitate my departure. I obtained permission from M.
Santhonax and from General Rochambeau, who had succeeded to the Government of the Island, to go to France or
to the United States. I preferred the latter. . . . My reason
for preferring the United States was that I was very doubtful, notwithstanding the opinion of many, whether the
Prussian army under the Duke of Brunswick had reached
Paris and put an end to the Revolution. Though the Civil
Commissioner Santhanox has been universally looked upon
as a very bad character and as having been the greatest pro-
moter of the misfortunes which have befallen San Domingo,
I must say that during the five or six weeks in my official
capacity I had to do business with him directly I found him
much better disposed than I had any reason to expect; he
granted me everything that I called for. He promoted those
that I represented as victims of insubordination of the sol-

diers and facilitated to some the means of leaving the Island. As respects myself, he rendered me every service I asked for."

John Keating was at this time thirty-two years of age, a captain in the French service, placed in temporary command of the troops in San Domingo, but on the eve of dissociating himself for good from his past environment and entering upon an entirely new career in the land of promise. " I sailed," says he, " from Cape François at the end of November, 1792, on board a frigate with M. de Blacons. We got up to Philadelphia the eve of Christmas, which was then kept very strictly. We were received at the widow Papley's the day after Christmas." The widow Papley's was a well-known boarding-house in those days, and a resort of many of the prominent emigrés fleeing from the horrors of the French Revolution. " I must add," he says, " that when I landed in the United States all my means of support did not exceed $280 and all my recommendations or introductions were two letters: one from General Rochambeau to General Washington and another from M. Santhonax to M. de la Forest the French Consul at Philadelphia. My only acquaintance was my fellow-traveller the Marquis de Blacons, by whom I got acquainted successively with the emigrants of note from France, especially with M. de Talon and Vicomte de Noailles." General Washington was, of course, at the time President of the United States and the capitol was at Philadelphia; so it is to be assumed that the letter of introduction from the son of his old associate in arms, Rochambeau, was duly presented to the President, though John Keating makes no reference to the incident. As to de la Forest, the letter of introduction was the beginning of a friendship which became closer and closer with the lapse of time and descended from father to son for three generations.

Inasmuch as the association with Messrs. Noailles and

Talon had much to do with John Keating's subsequent career, a brief metion of them may not be out of place. Noailles had come to America with his brother-in-law, Lafayette, and was the officer designated by Washington to receive on the part of the French the sword of Cornwallis at the surrender.   After our Revolution he returned to France, was a deputy of the nobility in the States General in May, 1789, and as a member of the National Assembly on August 4 of that year proposed the acts whereby the whole feudal system was swept away.   Falling, it is said, under the displeasure of Robespierre, his estates were confiscated and he was sentenced to death.   He escaped to England and thence sailed for the United States, where he lived for a while in Philadelphia, having formed a partnership with William Bingham.   After the Revolution he returned to France, served under Napoleon and lost his life in a naval engagement off Havana.   Omer Talon was just John Keating's age.   He was a royalist member of the National Assembly in France, escaped to Havre, where his friends put him in a cask and took him aboard an American vessel bound for Philadelphia.   There he became an American citizen and kept open house for his exiled countrymen.

Talon and de Noailles at the time of John Keating's arrival in Philadelphia were interested in projects having to do with the acquisition of large bodies of land in Pennsylvania and elsewhere, and the settlement of refugees then arriving in large numbers from France and San Domingo.   They asked John Keating to join them, though he was of course without means, and, as he says, they had never known him before.   The Asylum Company was the project then in hand, and inasmuch as Mr. Griffin's article and the very interesting book of Mrs. Louise Welles Murray entitled "Azilum" give the fullest particulars as to its origin, management and outcome, only a word need be said about it here.   Robert Morris, the financier of the Revolution, and John Nicholson owned enormous tracts of land in the eastern section of the United States which they desired to develop. With these two Frenchmen, for the purpose of attracting foreign settlers, they formed in 1794 the Asylum Company, of which Morris was made president, and proceeded to secure a large tract on the North branch of the Susquehanna River, now part of Bradford County; and John Keating was made one of the three managers and the intermediary between the owners in Philadelphia and those on the ground, dividing his time between the two places. Many colonists resorted thither and for a time it was a thriving settlement. It was generally supposed that Asylum was planned for Queen Marie Antoinette, for some of the houses were known as the " Queen's houses." But the poor Queen was guillotined late in 1793, long before her accommodations were in readiness for her. The project finally failed, not only for want of financial backing, but because, as I apprehend, the emigrés were not an agricultural people and could not therefore adapt themselves to a life in the wilds of Pennsylvania. Accordingly, when Napoleon invited the emigrés to return to France, the days of Asylum were numbered.

De la Rochefoucauld, in his most interesting *Travels through the United States in 1795*, a book which was in everybody's hands a century ago, referring to the settlement, speaks of John Keating as one of the managers in the following terms: " Mr. Keating is an Irishman and late Captain of the regiment Walsh. At the beginning of the Revolution he was in San Domingo, where he possessed the confidence of all parties, but refused the most tempting offers of the Commissioners of the Assembly, though his sentiments were truly democratic. It was his choice and determination to return to America without a shilling in his pocket rather than to acquire power and opulence in San Domingo by violating his first oath. He is a man of uncommon merit, distinguished abilities, extraordinary virtue and invincible disinterestedness. His advice and prudence have proved extremely serviceable to M. Talon in every department of his business. It was he who negotiated the late arrangement between Messrs. Morris and Nicholson, and it may be justly said that the confidence which his uncommon abilities and virtue inspire enables him to adjust matters of dispute with much greater facility than most persons." Alexander Grayson, in his *Memoirs of his own Times* (1846) gives us a little picture of the social side of the project, as follows: "A letter from Major Adam Hoopes of about the year 1790 or 1791 introduced me to Mr. Talon, then engaged with the Viscount de Noailles in establishing a settlement on the north branch of the Susquehanna, to which he gave the name of Asylum. In the course of this business he several times passed through Harrisburg, and never failed on these occasions of giving me the opportunity of seeing him. Mr. Talon fully justified in my conception the favorable idea that is given by Lord Chesterfield and others of a Frenchman of rank. I have seldom seen a gentleman with whose manners I was more pleased. . . . On one of his visits to Harrisburg he was attended by not less than ten or a dozen gentlemen, all adventurers in the new establishment from which they had just returned on their way to Philadelphia. Of these I only recollect the names of M. de Blacon, Captain Keating and Captain Boileau. My brother and myself, who had waited on them at their inn, were kept to supper, and I have rarely passed a more agreeable evening. The refreshment of a good meal, coffee and wine had put in motion their natural vivacity, and the conversation, carried on in English, which many of the company spoke very well, was highly animated. Captain Keating was, in fact, an Irishman, and Captain Boileau had been among the troops which had served in this country. . . . The French Revolution being touched upon, it came into my head to ask Captain Boileau how it happened that he and the other gentlemen who had been in America, and must of course have been foremost in circulating the doctrine of liberty in France, were now so entirely in the background. His answer was interrupted by a loud and general laugh, and Talon, who had probably been averse to the Revolution in all its stages and modifications (as he was the person on account of whose courteous reception General Washington had been roundly taken to task by the citizen Genet), enjoyed the thing so much that he thought it worth remembering, and put me in mind of it in an interview with him a long time afterwards. This gentleman did apparently stand high in the confidence of the King, as on once dining with him at his lodgings he, at the instance of a French lady from St. Domingo, who was present and had observed that I was infected with the regicide mania, showed me his picture on the lid of a box studded with diamonds that had been presented him by his Majesty."

John Keating became a citizen of the United States January 20, 1795. The land speculations of Morris and Nicholson afforded a very tempting bait to the French emigrés, and in one way or another Keating became associated with various enterprises of the kind besides the Asylum project, so that his time was entirely absorbed, and this became the business of his life. People who came over for purpose of temporary residence only until the reign of the guillotine was over, would purchase wild land and vest the title in John Keating, leaving it to him to manage and sell according to his best judgment. A transaction with his friend Noailles gives us a little insight into his doings in those days. John's twin brother William, as we have seen, was settled as a planter in the Isle of France, known as Mauritius, and rearing a large family. Viewing the situation in the French dependencies as precarious owing to the Revolution, he determined to settle his eldest son, Jerome, born in 1792 and then a child of four or five years of age, in

America and sent him in charge of a colored nurse only, consigned to Thomas Fitzsimmons of Philadelphia under care of Captain Meany of the brig *Rose*, to be brought up and educated by his uncle—a long voyage, it must be admitted, for so young a hopeful; but he arrived safely none the worse for his trip. His father desiring also to remit funds to his brother for the benefit of the son, Noailles informed John Keating that his friend Nicholson had an agent in the Isle of France, and Nicholson agreed to honor any drafts that might be drawn on him in this way. When the draft was presented, however, Nicholson was in financial difficulties, but Noailles, with whom he had business relations, agreed to assume the draft and accept in payment either certain lands in Tennessee or shares of the Asylum Company at his option. Nicholson and Morris were in such financial straits at the time that they were obliged to shut themselves off from their creditors by occupying a little house on the Schuylkill River; and thither John Keating journeyed on several occasions in arranging the particulars of the transaction. Noailles decided in favor of the Tennessee lands and gave Keating his personal bond for the draft. He also engaged Keating to go to Tennessee to record the deeds, look up the title and acquaint him with the situation generally. For this service Keating was to receive approximately 2,600 acres of the land and his expenses. Keating started from Philadelphia September 11, 1797, and was back in Philadelphia in the following November, having accomplished the mission entirely on horseback in 54 days to the entire satisfaction of Noailles. The bond was paid, but Noailles himself became financially embarrassed, sold the land without notice to Keating, and left for San Domingo without giving him his share or answering his letters, or even repaying him the expenses of his journey, which included the pay of a servant and the keep of two horses. Keating takes pains to say in his diary, however, that he freely forgave him, though he thinks it would have been more honorable for him to have frankly explained his condition. He feels sure, however, that it would have been a pleasure for Noailles to have satisfied his debt, as he was most generous and did not care for money for its own sake.

Previous to this time Keating had made the acquaintance of Pierre Bauduy, the son of a planter of an old French family in San Domingo. His brother, Baron de Bauduy, afterwards became a general under Napoleon. Bauduy had married the daughter of M. J. Baptiste Bretton Descha- pelles, of a noble family in France, who had also owned a large sugar plantation in San Domingo, but had been forced to emigrate to America owing to the insurrection, and was living in Wilmington, Delaware. Another of M. Descha- pelles' daughters had married Marquis de Saqui, an admiral in the French service; another the Marquis de Sassenay of Paris, whose descendant was a most devoted adherent of Napoleon Third and of the Empress Eugenie in her lonely widowhood. Eulalia, the youngest daughter, was at that time twenty-two years of age and lived with her sister, Mrs. Bauduy, in Wilmington, their parents being dead. She was tall and handsome and of a most engaging personality. Bauduy, who had taken a great fancy to Keating, asked him down to Wilmington to dinner, and there he met the sister-in-law and fell in love with her. Some of his friends in Philadelphia favored the match, but, as he says in his diary, having no fortune he hesitated to address her. But he naïvely adds, " having learned that another proposed to do so " he hesitated no longer. He wrote Bauduy, asking him to be the bearer of his wishes. The letter was mailed the day of Keating's departure for Tennessee on the Noailles mission. Returning home by way of Washington and Bal- timore, he arrived in Wilmington, having had, of course, no answer to his letter and not knowing how he would be re- ceived. " There was company present and Eulalie, in her timidity, shrank from seeing me, lest my visit should occasion remark." So he left for Philadelphia, but returned occasionally for short visits. The old French mode of courtship was far different from that of the present day. For awhile she gave no answer, and they never spoke of it and were never alone. Finally the occasion presented itself. He was as much embarrassed as she was. She consented, however, and he kissed her hand, without however, as he says, taking her glove off, for he was " not used to the situation." The family received the news with delight and the usual French formalities were observed. A paper setting forth the consent of the Deschapelles family and friends to the union is a typical example of the old French custom and interesting as a relic of the "Ancien Régime". It declares it to be the unanimous opinion, after due deliberation, that the marriage is in every respect advantageous to the young lady and that provisions are satisfactory. The " provisions " were contained in a marriage settlement executed at the same time, which only goes to show upon what modest means people began housekeeping in those days. By this settlement she contributed her small interest in the family patrimony, her clothing and jewelry and a few shares in the Bank of Pennsylvania and Insurance Company of North America; and he contributed his intetrest in the estate at Poitiers in France, his rights to a commission in the agency of the Asylum Company, " which though certain, cannot be determined as yet," also the 2,600 acres in Tennessee which he expected to have, but never got, from Noailles, and 10 shares of the Asylum Company. The marriage took place December 11, 1797, at 6: 15 p. m., before Abbé Faure at the Bauduy house in Wilmington, there being no Catholic church in Wilmington at the time. The young couple took up their residence in Wilmington. Three children were born of this marriage, John Julius Geoffrey Keating, born September 16. 1798; Hypolite Louis William, born

August 11, 1799, and Eulalia Margaret, born September 24, 1801. Besides these John Keating, as has been seen, had adopted his nephew, Jerome, the son of his brother William. Their married life, alas, was very short, as we shall presently see. In the diary to which I have already referred, written in French, and which is so taken up through many long years with the one engrossing thought of his wife's virtues as to neglect the details of his own career, he portrays her as follows: " She was large and stout, of a pretty figure, with dignity and reserve, beautiful eyes, a large mouth in which a few upper teeth were wanting, which however did not disfigure her countenance; she had a noble bearing and a fine memory, was well read and endowed with good judgment, but was modest and retiring. She disliked dressing, though it became her. She was absolutely devoid of vanity. She loved the domestic life with her children. She disliked compliments and never paid them. She had remarkably fine hands and arms." Her portrait, painted by Bonnemaison in Paris, bears out these physical attributes.

In the same year of John Keating's marriage the Ceres Company, which was to form the principal occupation of his life, took definite shape. Omer Talon had agreed to purchase 297,428 acres of land, composed of about 300 patents issued to William Bingham, situated in what was then entirely Lycoming County. By reason of the subsequent division of the county, the lands came to be located for the most part in McKean, Potter and Clearfield Counties. While the title was taken in Talon's name, it was purchased on behalf of a syndicate composed at that time of seven individuals residing abroad and two in America, and they in turn were represented by the two well-known Dutch banking houses of Raymond and Theodore de Smeth, and Condere, Brants and Changuion with whom Talon had his dealings. By the advice of Mr. Peter S. Duponceau, concurred in by Jared Ingersoll and A. J. Dallas, names universally regarded as the choicest ornaments of the Philadelphia Bar of those days, in order to meet the obstacle occasioned by diversity of interests and the provisions of the law limiting alien legal ownership, the title was vested in three individuals in joint tenancy with a secret declaration of trust vesting the disposition of the proceeds of the land in the foreign houses. John Keating, through whom the negotiations as regards title, etc., had been conducted, was named trustee together with Richard Gernon, a merchant of Philadelphia, and John S. Roulet, a merchant of New York; and Keating was constituted manager of the whole enterprise for the sale of the lands in small parcels to settlers. As each trustee died, another replaced him, at the selection of the foreign houses. The business gradually expanded, local agents were employed, and the towns of Smethport (in McKean County), named after the head of one of the foreign houses, and Coudersport (in Potter County), named after the head of the other house, became the county-seats of their respective counties. The town of Ceres was named after the company, and I am led to believe the town of Keating after John Keating himself. The business was finally wound up in 1884 by Keating's grandson, the late Dr. William V. Keating, after having realized upwards of a million dollars. In addition to this, John Keating personally, as we have said, held title to, or had the management of, thousands of acres in the same region on behalf of individuals, among them M. Pearron de Serennes of Paris, Messrs. Patrick and Richard Gernon, formerly residents of Philadelphia, Vicomte de Neuville, formerly French Ambassador to Washington, Cornelius C. Six, of Amsterdam and New York, Peter Provenchere, Comte d'Orbigny, both French emigrés, and the Deschapelles family. In all these relations, extending over a period of sixty years, neither his word nor his judgment was ever questioned. And in this connection it may not be out of place to quote the following passage from Mr. A. H. Espenshade's book on *Pennsylvania Place Names.* " According to a prominent citizen of McKean County, it is due to the memory of John Keating to say that from the earliest settlement of this County to the time of his death his watchful care over it and anxiety for its progress, his sympathy with the sufferings and privations of the settlers, and his readiness to help in every possible way partook more of the character of the care of a father over his children than a capitalist over a business enterprise." It is only proper to add in this connection that his choice of agents largely contributed to the success of the enterprise and the good-will it enjoyed from the settlers. Francis King, the pioneer surveyor of those regions, John S. Mann and Byron D. Hamlin are all names held in the highest veneration in that section of the country, and the Ceres Company, otherwise known in that region as Keating and Company, owes much of its local repute to their association with it.

Some four years after his marriage, while he was living in Wilmington, certain differences arose between Talon and the proprietors regarding Talon's profit in the transaction. Keating, of course, was familiar with the entire matter, and with the knowledge of all parties had been paid a commission by Talon for his services. He was prevailed upon by both sides to act as arbitrator in the dispute, despite his reluctance owing to his own connection with it. The employment involved a voyage to Amsterdam where all the facts were to be submitted and the decision rendered. He went alone, leaving his little family in Wilmingon and sailing September 5, 1801, by the ship *Felicity*, Captain Reed, bound from Philadelphia for Liverpool. A trip abroad was managed differently in those days from what it is now. He was seated at dinner in his Wilmington home when the ship was sighted in the Delaware, and he imme-

diately proceeded to Newcastle, where the *Felicity* hove to
in order to take him and his luggage aboard. The parting
must have been trying, for his wife was about to be confined of her third child. After her death he found in her
drawer a letter written to him in his absence in the belief
that she would not survive the child's birth. The premoni-
tion was prophetic, for she did, indeed, afterwards die in
his absence (though not on this particular voyage) under
similar circumstances. Proceeding to Amsterdam after a
voyage of six weeks he met the bankers, and being assured
of their entire confidence reviewed the evidence and, after
long deliberation, gave his decision, which met with the
entire satisfaction of all parties. In the meantime he had
joined his relations in Poitou, where his elder brother,
Geoffrey, was living, and renewed all his old associations.
It was during the Napoleonic régime and there is no record
of his doings. The family suffered by the Revolution, but
to what extent does not appear. He sailed for home July
14, 1802, on the *Atlantic*, Captain Chew, arriving in New
York September 3rd, met his wife at Frankford, Philadelphia, whither she had gone to greet him, and reached home
the day following to see for the first time his little daughter.

After his return home from abroad John Keating occupied himself assiduously with his landed interests. In a
letter to the Dutch bankers written in 1822 he explains that
the settlers are people practically without means. They
usually arrive, men, women and children, afoot with a horse
to carry their effects and sometimes with a cow; they stop
near the rivers and creeks in places least wooded; and there,
with the aid of a neighbor, build a miserable cabin, plant
corn and rely on the chase and some jobs for others for
their sustenance. They were of French, Irish, English and
German stock, and furnish a strong contrast with the immigrants of a later day who crowded our cities instead of
planting themselves upon the soil and reaping the fruits of

industrious tillage. John Keating would make annual trips to the lands and report his doings in elaborate letters to the bankers, every one of which he copied in letter books, according to the custom of the day. In those days journeys of the kind involved weeks of laborious travel, cut off almost entirely from communication with the world and attended by privations and even danger. Horseback was the principal mode of travel, and while the hospitality of the settler could always be relied on, yet where no settler was to be found the bare ground proved to be the only available resting place. He always insisted upon meeting the settlers personally and interesting himself in all the enterprises whereby to develop the country. The churches, schools and roads form the main subject of his correspondence with the agents. The Catholic Church of St. Eulalia in Coudersport was built principally by his help and named after his wife, and all the other Catholic churches and settlements throughout the company's possessions had his active interest, encouragement and assistance. He would sometimes enter the lands by Williamsport and Jersey Shore and sometimes by Bellefonte and thence to Karthaus, and he was appointed in 1823 one of the commissioners to organize the Jersey Shore and Coudersport Turnpike Company. It may seem to us, in this era of rapid transit, somewhat amusing to read in one of his letters to the bankers: " I cannot give a better proof of the happy results which will accrue from the completion of the turnpike than to say that on the fifth day after leaving Philadelphia (via Williamsport and Jersey Shore) we slept fourteen miles from Coudersport. Had the road been built, we would have gone the entire distance in a carriage in four days and a half." Today a single night accomplishes the journey. He further cites as an indication of the marvelous progress of the times, that that year the mail was to be carried by wagon from Philadelphia to St. Louis. He rarely failed, while

on these visits, to extend the journey to Geneseo, the home
of his old friend, General James Wadsworth, who maintained a regal establishment there on the finest farm in
western New York and dispensed a generous hospitality.
The two families were on terms of the closest intimacy.
It was on the Turnpike Road above referred to that Ole
Bull, the great violinist, at his own expense, about the year
1832, settled some 250 Norwegians. The settlement was
not a success, however, and Mr. Bull admitted that he had
been a loser by the transaction by about $60,000.

It was while he was making one of these periodical trips
that the tragic event occurred which marred his whole life
and happiness during the remaining fifty years of his existence. He relates the incident in substance as follows:
He had quitted his wife, who was in the best of health,
Monday, July 18, 1803, at 5 a. m. to go with her brother-
in-law, Pierre Bauduy, to Cerestown. Having accomplished
his visit, he arrived in Williamsport August 28. On his
return journey he was surprised to receive no letter from
her, but instead one from Mr. Provenchere, a relative of
hers, advising him that she was sick. At Lancaster he received another letter advising him that she was no better.
Traveling all night on horseback by moonlight, they arrived
September 2nd at Wilmington, having traveled 170 miles
in three days. He rushed into the house by the back door
and ran upstairs, entering her room only to find it vacant.
She had expired August 4th and was buried in the Old
Swedes burying-ground, there being as yet no Catholic
church in Wilmington and a section of the churchyard having been allotted to Catholics. From that time forth his
thoughts were always with her, and it is stated by an eyewitness that fifty-three years afterwards, when about to die,
he turned his eyes toward her portrait and expired while
gazing at it. The diary to which I have referred, which
was kept for many years solely for the purpose of recording

her virtues, abounds in the most tender and passionate expressions of love, admiration and regret. It manifests also the deep religious faith which sustained him in his terrible grief and never wavered till the day of his death. He was thus left alone with the charge of three infant children and the nephew, a boy of about eleven years of age. Mrs. Keating's relative, Mr. Provenchere, was a French refugee of an old and distinguished family. He had been the tutor to the Duke de Berri, second son of Charles Tenth, and was in constant correspondence with the Duke himself and afterwards his widow and the Duc D'Angouleme, heir to the Bourbon throne, during those Napoleonic days. He lived with his widowed daughter, and being desirous, on his daughter's account, of moving to Philadelphia, John Keating, who found himself for the most part in Philadelphia on account of his business, joined the Provencheres in 1808 in taking a house there, No. 183 S. 5th Street, then in the best residence district. There the children passed their childhood in an atmosphere wherein culture and piety were combined in such way as the French knew how to unite them without exaggeration or ostentation. Jerome, the nephew, upon arriving at a suitable age, was sent to St. Mary's College, Baltimore, then known as one of the best educational institutions in the country, to which the Protestant community had recourse as well as the Catholics of our city. Among the leaders of our Bar who afterwards were educated within its walls may be mentioned Mr. George W. Biddle, Mr. Pemberton Morris and Mr. W. Heyward Drayton. The two sons received their education at the University of Pennsylvania. John Julius studied law and was admitted to the Bar in 1818. That he soon attained distinction is evidenced by the fact that in the unhappy controversy which arose in 1821 between Bishop Conwell and the priest Hogan, which is so fully and ably treated by Mr. Griffin in the pages of the AMERICAN CATHOLIC HISTORICAL

RECORDS, Keating, young as he was, represented the Bishop. He was soon afterwards elected to the State Legislature and gave promise of a most enviable career as a lawyer and a citizen. On May 19, 1824, he married Elizabeth Hopkinson, daughter of Judge Joseph Hopkinson, the Federal Judge in Philadelphia, and granddaughter of the Signer, one of the most attractive women of her day, who lived to be ninety years of age and whose memory is a blessing to those who knew her. Within six weeks after this most happy marriage the young husband was taken with a fever and died in his twenty-sixth year, to the infinite distress of his father and the regret of a large circle of friends. In his most interesting diary, happily preserved among the records of the American Catholic Historical Society, Father Kenny, the parish priest of Coffee Run, about six miles from Wilmington, who had known the Keatings intimately in Wilmington — their house being for years before their departure the Catholic Church of Wilmington—makes the following minute: " July 28, 1824, Funeral of Julius Keating in Wilmington—melancholy scene indeed, William and Jerome supporting John Keating, the visibly overwhelmed father."

His hopes and pride then centered upon his second son, William. After graduating at the University of Pennsylvania in 1816, he was sent to Paris to study mineralogy, metallurgy and kindred branches to which his talents were inclined. There he roomed with his cousin Valentine, the second son of his uncle, William Keating, of Mauritius, thus keeping in touch with his nearest relatives living at the other side of the earth. Returning home, he became professor of Chemistry and Mineralogy as applied to the arts at the University of Pennsylvania from 1822 to 1827, after which he was sent to Mexico to pass upon certain mining enterprises. In the meantime he had employed a summer vacation accompanying Major Long in his expedition through Wisconsin and Canada, tracing the source of the St. Peter (now the Wisconsin) River, as the mineralogist and historian of the party. His book on the subject is the authorized history of the expedition. He then studied law, was admitted to the Bar of Philadelphia, May 3, 1834, acquired a considerable practice and was elected, and re-elected, as his brother had been before him, to the Pennsylvania Legislature, and was solicited to run for Congress but refused, as he was not "thirsting for public life." His energy was insatiable; he was one of the founders of the Franklin Institute, and recording secretary of the Academy of Natural Sciences from 1821 to 1825, a director of the Board of City Trusts and member of the Philosophical Society. In company with his intimate friend, Moncure Robinson, he was one of the projectors of the Philadelphia and Reading Railroad Company, was a manager from 1834 to 1838 as well as counsel for the company, and was sent abroad in its behalf to negotiate its first loan in London, where he died after a short illness May 17, 1840. He was a great linguist. He married Elizabeth, daughter of J. Eric Bollman, a man of international prominence, who enjoyed the intimate friendship of Lafayette and made all the plans and furnished the means for his attempted escape from his prison at Olmutz. Bollman took an active part in South America in movements having for their object the extension of the principles laid down in our Declaration of Independence. In addition to all his other activities, William assisted his father in the management of the Ceres Company and was till his death one of the trustees in whom the title was vested; and the untimely death of this only remaining son was a blow to the old father at the age of eighty-one, which can be better imagined than described. William Keating left surviving him but one child, a daughter. In the meantime Jerome Keating, the nephew, completed his education at St. Mary's College and returned home in the flush of manhood, a handsome young man endowed with high intelligence, great ambition and most exemplary character. In the diary to which I have referred, wherein John Keating bares his own deep religious faith and dependence upon our holy religion, he refers constantly to his efforts to surround his children with a Catholic atmosphere, and associates his wife with all their religious practices. On April 28, 1810, his little daughter, Lalite, made her first confession and the two boys their First Communion, offering it for their mother; and having the day before read them the letter she wrote him after his departure for Europe in 1801, he then makes this entry in the diary: " I picture my dear Eulalie accompanying her children to the foot of the altar today where they have received their God. How much this Communion would have stirred her soul, what thanks she would have shown her Creator. . . . While the world scoffs at religion, what does it believe of the body and soul—a mystery. Its system and conjecture do not explain the secrets of Providence. Examine the duties prescribed by religion. Is there any that is incompatible with reason and happiness? Compare the religious man with the scoffer; which inspires the more respect and confidence?" And so he urges his children not to blush for their religion but to be worthy of it in following it. " If people see you are attached to your duties, not by habit but by conviction, they will esteem you the more." Again on May 23, 1812, the little Lalite makes her First Communion, and he says: " I hope the next Sacrament she will receive will be that of marriage. May Heaven grant her the happiness I enjoyed. I often think of it. I wish for her a husband sweet and sensible, industrious, well brought up and of the same rank as herself. I want him to be of an agreeable presence and that he shall have as much talent and spirit as is needed to assure him of the friendship, esteem and consideration of the world. I want him to have religion and the same religion as hers; that they should have between them sufficient income for indulging their simple tastes without ostentation. Nothing is more conducive to the happiness of a marriage than for both to have principles of a solid religion which makes it a duty for them to love, sustain and console each other and work for their mutual happiness. Independently of that, I am convinced of the truth and superiority of the religion in which my daughter has been reared. I hold that she should only marry a Catholic."

In expressing these sentiments he little knew that he was actually describing the character of his future son-in-law, whom he, himself, had reared in his own household. The young people were naturally much thrown together, and an attachment sprung up between them. Though first cousins, the father saw no obstacle in this circumstance. In his diary he states that after several separate interviews he learned the sentiments they entertained for each other, and approved of the match, assuring them they were entirely at liberty to contract it. Jerome had, however, been offered the post of supercargo on a ship owned by Robert Ralston of Philadelphia, bound for China, and the opportunity for thus starting out in life was not to be gainsaid. They determined to be married before his departure, and the wedding took place August 12, 1818. Jerome then set sail and was gone a year. On his return in 1822 he formed a partnership with Messrs. John J. Borie and Peter Laguerenne for the manufacture of cotton goods at Manayunk, and as managing partner he took up his residence there, the mills being located on the river bank as they are today. There he lived in a house now occupied by the Sisters adjoining the present Church of St. John the Baptist.

At the time of Eulalie's marriage her brother, William H. Keating, was a student in Paris, her elder brother, John Julius, was just entering upon the practice of law and resided with his father and Mr. Provenchere and his daughter, both sons being still unmarried. After his daughter's marriage and removal to Manayunk, John Keating would spend his summers with them. They had several children, only three of whom lived to maturity—Amelia, who afterwards married her cousin, Peter Bauduy, William V. Keating, to whom I shall later refer, and Mary, a posthumous child, who married James M. Willcox, of Delaware County, Pa. The young couple identified themselves with the Catholic interests in Manayunk and were beloved by their neighbors, many of whom, of course, were employed in the mill, and Mrs. Keating became a little mother to all the children. An account of Brother John Chrisostum, otherwise Francis Michael Barret, which appeared in the Parish Register of St. John the Baptist Church for March, 1909, gives a little insight into the origin and life of the parish in Jerome Keating's day. The church was begun in 1830 and dedicated by Bishop Kenrick, then coadjutor Bishop of Philadelphia, in 1831, Mr. and Mrs. Keating conducting the choir, he also teaching the boys and she the girls in the Sunday school. One of the pupils, Eugene Mullin, curiously enough, afterwards shipped as a sailor for the Far East and was wrecked off the coast of Mauritius, where he was rescued and most hospitably received by the Keating family. Jerome and his partners presented the diocese with the site for the church and helped to build it. It still stands, though dwarfed by the magnificent edifice since erected through the munificence of Bernard Kane, a later parishioner. Jerome in 1819, shortly after his marriage, was elected to the Board of Managers of the Philadelphia Saving Fund and was solicited to run for Congress but declined.

In May, 1827, Mrs. Jerome Keating suffered impairment of health and was advised to go abroad. Her father accordingly invited her and her children, together with the widow of his son John, to accompany him on a voyage to

France. There they were most hospitably received in the circle surrounding Charles X, who was reigning at the time. John Keating's rank and his family connection and old associates must have all contributed to make him feel at home in his father's adopted country. On his wife's side his brother-in-law, Comte de Sassenay, who was the secretary of the Duchess de Berri, gave him access to the court circles; and his nephew, de Lyonne, welcomed him with open arms. On his own side there were his sister's children, the Comte D'Orfeuille and his sister, and his own remaining sister, Mme. de Tussac, as also his elder brother, Baron Geoffrey Keating, living at his place de Plessis in Poitou. Then there were friends whom he had known in America, among them Comte Hyde de Neuville, who had been Minister at Washington from 1816 to 1821, and who in a letter to John Keating still extant says, "My family know through me that Keating is the synonym for loyalty." De Neuville is the subject of an interesting biography by Frances Jackson entitled "The Memoirs of Baron Hyde de Neuville, outlaw, exile, ambassador." He was Minister of Marine in the Martignac Cabinet in January, 1828, while the Keatings were in Paris. There he met also the Comte de Noailles, son of his old associate, and his old commander, Count Walsh of the Irish Brigade. A little incident in this connection which occurred half a century afterwards may not be without interest. When the late Dr. John M. Keating, who accompanied General Grant on his trip around the world, was passing through the Red Sea he found himself sitting at table beside a young French officer by name of Walsh who had charge of the mails on the steamer. This officer, upon hearing the name of his neighbor, remarked that it was a name ever revered in his family because of a life-long friendship existing between an ancestor of his and a Keating formerly in the French service. Upon comparing notes they found that the friends he referred to were

Colonel Comte Walsh, Serrant of the Irish Brigade, and Captain John Keating, of his regiment, the respective great-grandfathers of the two travelers.

There were also several of John Keating's own clients then living in France who owned lands in Pennsylvania the charge of which they had entrusted to him, among them his life-long friend Comte D'Orbigny, formerly a general in the French service, M. Pearron de Serennes, whose son in after years was to write to John Keating a letter, still extant, describing his experiences during the Reign of Terror, when his mother and he came to Paris in the hope of being less conspicuous than in the provinces, and from the window of their home saw Charlotte Corday, Camille Desmoulin, Danton and others carried in the tumbril to the Place Louis XV for execution. In this letter he also dramatically describes their own narrow escape when agents of the Revolution searched their house for incriminating evidence, and by the merest chance overlooked some Louis d'or, which, because they portrayed the head of the King, would have sealed their doom. Mme. du Cayla, the daughter of Talon, who was a very prominent personage in the circle of Charles X, was also on intimate terms with the Keatings during their stay. Mr. Keating was also the bearer of communications from Mr. Provenchere to the Duchess de Berri, with whom, as I have said, he was in frequent correspondence, and in his letters home John Keating speaks of his reception by the Duke D'Angouleme, the then Dauphin of France, who was in command of the army and from whom John Keating solicited a higher post for his young nephew, Philip Marquet, an officer in the service. It was shortly after John Keating's return from France that the second Revolution occurred and the older branch of the Bourbon line were swept from the throne forever.

After a visit to Amsterdam to confer with the foreign bankers, Keating repaired to London, where he had an interview with Mr. Baring, the English banker interested in the Bingham lands, on the subject of their mutual interests. The family then returned to America, having been abroad for almost a year. They were accompanied by Mr. Adolph E. Borie, son of Jerome Keating's partner, who had been living in Paris completing his education. Mr. Borie afterward became Secretary of the Navy during General Grant's administration and his sister became the second wife of John Keating's grandson, the late Dr. William V. Keating. Mr. Provenchere died in 1831, after which event John Keating broke up housekeeping and boarded in the city, making protracted visits to his daughter's house in Manayunk. An interesting little incident is recorded in one of his letters to Baron de Neuville, who, as has been said, was then Minister of Marine in the French Cabinet, to whom he reports that in conformity with the Baron's instructions he had received M. Pierre Gregoire Reynaud, "Ancien Superieur des milices de St. Domingu," as "Chevalier de l'ordre de St. Louis." What the ceremony consisted in is not disclosed. This was perhaps the last time the order and decoration were ever conferred.

But a terrible affliction soon befell the family. Jerome Keating, the beloved son-in-law, was stricken with an affection of the heart and died at Manayunk, January 28, 1833, at the age of forty-one. Thus was the second male member of the family, upon whom his hopes were built, to part with him in his declining years. Nor even yet were his sorrows at an end. After that John Keating lived for the most part with his daughter at Manayunk, maintaining an office only in Philadelphia for the transaction of his business. In 1836 his granddaughter, Amelia, married her cousin, John Peter Bauduy, and removed to Cuba, where her husband engaged in the practice of medicine. Thereupon the family moved from Manayunk to 111 South Fourth Street, Philadelphia, which became the family residence and favorite resort of all their connections until John Keating's death. His son, William, was at that time practicing law, and a member of the Legislature, and was his father's right hand, accompanying him on his annual visits to the lands. They never failed on the occasion of these visits to bring home with them a bottle of Seneca oil, as it was called, as a cure for rheumatism, bruises, etc. This oil was collected by the Indians of the Seneca tribe, who occupied that region, by dipping their blankets in Oil Creek upon the surface of which the oil flowed, from what source no one ever thought to discover. Little did John Keating realize that in that bottle lay a secret which would suddenly, as the Civil War came to an end, reveal itself and revolutionize the world. The Keating lands were but slightly within the oil belt. Had they been located but little farther west and south they would have associated their owners in the public eye with the modern term " Bonanza ".

In 1832, while the Keatings were still living at Manayunk, the cholera visited Philadelphia in aggravated form, and Mr. Keating writes that in one week in August, out of a population of 160,000, there were 370 deaths from the disease in Philadelphia; and in September of the same year, out of 2,300 cases there were 800 deaths. Prior to this time he had taken part in the maintenance of the St. Joseph's Orphan Asylum, the oldest Catholic asylum in Philadelphia, and from that time forth until his death it was an absorbing source of labor and interest. He notes in one of his letters that throughout the entire epidemic there was not a single case in the institution. The Asylum still stands where it stood in his day, a monument to the devotion of the Good Sisters of Charity, by whose labors it has increased and multiplied its benefactions a hundredfold.

The loss of his second son in 1840 completed the sum of his sorrows. He bore it with the same patience and resignation that characterized his entire life. Writing to Mr.

Labouchere of Amsterdam soon afterwards, he says: " My poor son is much regretted, and now it is permitted me to say that I know no one who combined intelligence, judgment, exactitude and probity to such a degree. In my affliction it is a consolation to hear it so often said that it is the lot of few parents to mourn the death of such sons as I have lost. But it is our duty to resign ourselves to the Will of God, who knows better than we do what is most salutary for us." His sole reliance then rested upon his grandson William, the son of his daughter by her union with Jerome, the beloved nephew, and the reliance, be it said, was not misplaced. Having studied medicine at the University of Pennsylvania, William soon acquired a large practice, assuming in addition the charge of the Ceres Company, which his grandfather, by reason of his great age, was no longer able actively to continue. His life and achievements are not, however, the subject of this sketch.

In 1845, at the age of eighty-five, John Keating made his last trip to the lands in company with his grandson, making the entire circuit of the company's possessions, and following it up with a letter to the bankers explaining at length the entire situation. He had been elected to the Board of Trustees of the University of Pennsylvania in 1832 and to the Board of Managers of the Philadelphia Saving Fund Society in 1841, and while he resigned the University in 1852, he remained with the Saving Fund until his death. He was actively interested in all matters pertaining to the well-being of the Church in Philadelphia, and seconded Bishop Kenrick in all measures affecting its growth and development. He held pews in St. Mary's, St. Joseph's and St. John's churches —the last being then the Cathedral Church—but attended services at St. Mary's. In politics he was a Whig and strongly sympathized with Nicholas Biddle in the matter of the removal of the deposits of the United States Bank.

The last sacrifice he was called upon to make was when

his daughter, after long contemplating the step, determined to enter the Visitation Convent at Frederick. Her daughter had become a widow and returned to her grandfather's house in 1844, thus enabling her mother to accomplish her purpose. She afterwards became Superior of the House, and from there was moved to Georgetown, where she died in 1873 in the odor of sanctity.

The Bauduy family and their descendants had continued to reside during all these years in Wilmington. Their place at Eden Park, outside the city limits, was a great resort of all the family connections, and they in turn looked upon John Keating, who had outlived all his contemporaries, as the head of the family. One of Pierre Bauduy's daughters married John Garesché, of an old French family, who had formerly represented the United States as Consul at Matanzas. He succeeded to the family residence, where he and his charming wife and daughters became widely known for their hospitality and benevolence. They had a numerous family whose descendants are now distributed throughout this country and elsewhere.

As John Keating advanced in years, his tall, erect and venerable figure, striking countenance and snow-white hair, and his courtly manners won for him marked deference and respect from all, friends and strangers alike. At his elder brother's death the title of Baron devolved upon him in France, and while he never, of course, assumed it here, he was always known and affectionately termed the " Old Baron ". In a letter written in 1855, the year before he died, addressed to his old friend Labouchere of Amsterdam, he had this to say: " In 1783 Napoleon was a lieutenant of the 2nd battalion of the Regiment de la Frere, artillery, and I a captain of the 2nd battalion of the 92nd Regiment of Infantry. Two years afterwards I was captain, and I had the cross of St. Louis given me by Louis XVI. I am, perhaps, the only surviving chevalier created by that unhappy prince. Napoleon, for years master of Europe, but ending his astonishing career on a rock exiled from his country and family, dies immortalized by his triumphs and his misfortunes, and I live in the midst of my children without any ills, manager of a large land Company."

On February 12, 1851, his grandson William married the daughter of Dr. Réné La Roche, the eminent authority on yellow fever, whose father himself, a prominent physician of Philadelphia, had emigrated from San Domingo and was John Keating's old friend and medical adviser. And thereafter to the end of his days John Keating's home life was gladdened by the voices of children and the sweet companionship and filial devotion of a perfect woman.

Having contracted a cold in attending a meeting of the Philadelphia Saving Fund, he gradually lost strength. Receiving the last Sacraments with entire composure, he expressed himself as perfectly resigned to the will of God, and died May 19, 1856, in the 96th year of his age. He was buried in the family burial lot at St. John's church, Manayunk, Archbishop Kenrick performing the services and delivering a beautiful address expressive of his own estimate of the deceased's character and personality. The Archbishop also composed the epitaph on his tomb in the old churchyard, which reads as follows: " To the memory of John Keating. Born in the year 1760 in Ireland. Educated from childhood in France. Captain in Walsh's regiment of the Irish Brigade. He passed the last sixty-three years of his life in the United States, having settled in Philadelphia. He died at Philadelphia, May 19, 1856, at the age of 96 in full possession of his faculties, with lively faith and hope in God. His long life, distinguished by integrity, honor, refined manners and unaffected piety. May he rest in peace."

FOUR EARLY CATHOLIC NEWSPAPERS

The year 1833 is a memorable one in Catholic periodical literature in the United States. At the beginning of that year " The Catholic Herald" of Philadelphia made its appearance for the first time. In September of the same year " The Catholic Journal " of Washington sent forth its prospectus, and within a month " The New York Catholic Press and Weekly Orthodox Journal " was ready to make its bow to the public. In the meantime, from Boston came the announcement that its Catholic weekly had resumed the title of " The Jesuit," instead of the " United States Catholic Intelligencer."

It is interesting at this date to read the " Prospectus " of the three weeklies first named. They are here given as found in different issues of " The Catholic Herald" during its first year of issue.

I.

THE PROSPECTUS OF " THE CATHOLIC HERALD."

Since the period when the art of printing was first brought into general use, the Press has been found to exercise a mighty influence over the public mind in all civilized countries. It is to be lamented, however, that its power has been often shamefully abused, to the great detriment of pure Morality, Philosophy and Religion. But if it has been made the most efficacious means of disseminating principles and scattering the seeds of error and impiety, it may also be employed to correct in a great measure the evils thus produced.

Our Catholic Brethren, generally, cannot be ignorant that even in this country, where our free institutions have wisely placed all denominations of Christians upon the same political level, there still, unhappily, exists strong and deeply-rooted prejudices against our Holy Religion. The unjust and cruel persecutions in Europe, from which, after a long series of years, our Church has but lately emerged; the calumnies, misrepresentations and obloquy with which she has been assailed, and the consequent ignorance of our real principles, which still prevails among those who know our doctrines only from the report of our enemies, fully explain the origin and cause of those groundless prejudices which many honest and well-disposed persons entertain against the " Church of all ages and nations."

It is much to be regretted that the spirit of mutual forbearance and Christian Charity is not more generally cherished and encouraged in this land of civil and religious liberty. There are in this city alone several periodicals pubished by our Dissenting Brethren of various denominations, to advocate and defend their peculiar views of doctrine and Church Government, as adopted by the sect or party to which the Editors respectively belong. If these sectarian publications had been content with maintaining the system .of doctrine which they have severally embraced, we would have continued, as heretofore, silent spectators of their controversies, and confined ourselves to the publication of those standard works which we are convinced present a satisfactory demonstration of the truth and purity of the Catholic Church. But when we observe in several of these religious journals false statements of facts reflecting upon our Religion, and doctrines ascribed to us which our Church condemns; when we know that our silence is assumed as an admission of the truth of the charges, and that thereby uncharitable feelings are created and prejudices confirmed, we deem it expedient to establish a regular periodical journal, through which we may be enabled from time to time to lay before the public temperate vindications of our doctrines, according as the unprovoked attacks of our adversaries may appear to us worthy of notice.

To enable us to effect this object we propose issuing "The Catholic Herald," and look with confidence to our brethren for support, assured it will not be wanting on their part, to an undertaking which has the greater glory of God, in the propagation of Divine Truth for its object and the blessing of Christian Charity for its reward.

Besides the explanation and defense of Catholic Doctrine, " The Catholic Herald " will contain Biographical Sketches of Saints and others who have been eminent for piety or learning.   An account of such occurrences as may tend to show the state of religion for this and other countries.

Original and approved Essays on Religion and Literature.

Occasional Reviews of Religious Publications.

Chaste Poetical Productions, original and selected.

The present interesting State of Ireland and France will receive particular attention in our columns.

The " Herald " will carefully abstain from domestic party politics.

It will attack the doctrines of no sect or party, except in cases of wanton aggression, and at all times it will be as mild and dignified as may be consistent with truth and independence.

The proceeds of this paper, if any surplus should remain on hand after defraying the necessary expenses of publication, will be appropriated to charitable purposes.

TERMS.   " The Catholic Herald " will be printed on good type and paper at three dollars per annum, payable half-yearly in advance.

Eugene Cummiskey, Catholic bookseller at 130 S. 6th St., was agent for " The Catholic Herald."

The paper was printed by M. Fithian, N. 6, corner of Sansom and George Streets, between 6th and 7th and Walnut and Chestnut.

(*Catholic Herald*, January 3, 1833.)

II.

Prospectus of "The Catholic Journal,"

In offering this paper for the patronage of the public, the Editor is actuated by a sincere desire of promoting knowledge, and to give the people a cheap medium by which they may obtain information. He will be governed by a principle of strict neutrality with regard to the great political parties which at times agitate this country, but will give a faithful synopsis of every event that may affect the public interest in any way. Being established at the seat of government of the Union, it will not necessarily be his province to become the partisan of any man or set of men, as the citizens of this district are debarred from the privilege of legislating in the councils of the nation.

"The Catholic Journal" will calmly, but strenuously, support the cause of truth, and give a clear and lucid exposition of the doctrines and principles of the Roman Catholic Church. The *Religious Department* will be conducted under the advice of the Catholic Clergy of this District, and will receive the contributions of the Clergy of all parts of the country.

For the promotion of *Literature* and *Science*, the Editor will avail himself of communications from friends of the "Journal," and such other articles as may meet his eye, which he may think of sufficient importance and usefulness to be re-published.

The *News Department* will be composed of a faithful history of events as they occur in our own district, and a judicious selection of foreign and domestic intelligence, interspersed with interesting anecdotes and lively incidents.

The oppressed situation of Ireland, which occupies our heartfelt sympathies, claims and will receive our decided and constant attention.   The* earliest information will be obtained, and circulated through the columns of the " Journal " among the people of this country, and original and selected essays will always be found calculated to arouse our fellow-citizens to aid unhappy and shackled Erin in regaining those rights of which her citizens have been deprived by a most unjust and unnatural union.

Having thus briefly stated the manner in which the " Journal " will be conducted, and the principles by which it will be governed, little remains, by the Editor, to be said. The " Journal " will be established here, that the mild and gentle rays of the Catholic religion may diverge, as from a great centre, and penetrate every portion of our happy country.   To enable him to accomplish this object, it is necessary that the friends of the cause, in all places, should exert themselves in increasing its circulation, and yielding it support.   Trusting that such will be their desire, the Editor thinks it unnecessary to urge its importance upon their minds.

" The Catholic Journal " will be printed upon an imperial sheet, fine paper with handsome type, and delivered to subscribers at *Three Dollars* per annum, payable on receipt of the first number.

A. F. Cunningham.

Washington City, September, 1833.

(*Catholic Herald*, Sept. 19, 1833, p. 152.)

III.

Prospectus of "The New York Catholic Press and Weekly Orthodox Journal."

In compliance with a usage long established, at the commencement of a new Journal, we come before the American public with the reasons which have induced us to offer to their notice a weekly paper.   In no country, perhaps, is the newspaper department more adequately supplied with all local and general information than in these United States. Here, indeed, there is scarcely room for competition. But among a very numerous and annually increasing class of our fellow-citizens—the emigrant population—the sources of information and improvement are too limited and defective. These are facts so notorious as to require no proof. Here, then, there is ample room both for competition and improvement. The imperative necessity for establishing a creditable, an able and a convenient medium of information and instruction has been long felt and acknowledged. To attain an object so desirable, and withal so comprehensive, as to render it at once useful and agreeable to every class in this great Republic, the " Journal " will be as large, as cheap, and as well executed as any in the United States, and will be arranged under two separate departments: the *Religious* and the *Secular*.

The Religious department will, under four general heads, contain every thing necessary to edify and confirm the Catholic, or to inform and enlighten the Protestant, in the principles and grounds of the Catholic belief and worship.

1. Will contain proofs that Catholicism, in all its bearings, is perfectly compatible with civil and religious liberty.

2. Will contain a clear and lucid exposition of the Catholic doctrines as taught by Christ and his Apostles, as handed down to us by their legitimate successors, and as maintained by the Holy Fathers and General Councils.

3. Will present a weekly Review of Religious and Controversial Publications which may have a tendency to misrepresent the Catholic Faith.

4. Will exhibit a connected view of the present state of the Catholic church in various parts of the globe, with much interesting and miscellaneous matter, &c.

The Secular Department will, under the same number of heads, comprehend everything calculated for the instruction and amusement of the citizen and the emigrant in the different walks of society.

1. In Politics, a faithful synopsis of every important national question and political event which may affect the public interest will be given.

2. In Literature, a suitable selection will be made from the most eminent literary productions, both foreign and domestic, which may interest the man of learning.

3. In History, will be given a succinct view of the most eminent personages who, in ancient or modern times, have distinguished themselves in the Church or State.

4. In Morals, an occasional lesson will be selected to promote the advancement of virtue and increase of charity—the great sources, certainly, of human happiness.

To accomplish all these great objects and fully redeem our pledge of making the " Journal " of the most interesting, and the most instructive on this side of the Atlantic, no labour, no pains, and no expense shall be spared. To ensure the consummation of these views and promises, the place from which the "Catholic Journal" will be issued contains in itself every possible advantage; need we name New York? — which, for celerity of communication, extent of opportunities and abundance of resources and means stands unrivalled. We, therefore, respectfully invite and earnestly solicit the learned theologian, the man of letters, and the pure patriot to throw into this great channel of varied information a portion of the fruits of their knowledge and talent.

The oppressed condition of Ireland, which has the strongest hold upon our heart's-core sympathies, claims, and will, in each successive number, receive our decided and special attention. From Catholics, therefore, and from Irishmen, who will constitute the greatest portion of our patrons, we anxiously look for generous co-operation. The duty which they owe to themselves and rising families, the obligation which they owe to their native or adopted country, and, above all, that reverential regard which we must ever feel for the maintenance of our Holy Religion, imperatively call on their prompt and liberal support for this much-desired auxiliary in the cause of Religion, Knowledge and Humanity.

CONDITIONS.

" The New York Catholic Press and Weekly Orthodox Journal " will be published every Saturday morning. It will contain 16 closely printed pages, or 48 columns, on fine paper and in good type, in quarto form, so as to admit of its being bound into one large or into two handsome volumes of 416 pages each.

TERMS.

Four Dollars per annum, payable half-yearly in advance, in all cases, on the delivery of the second number.—To be Edited and Published by an Association of the Members of the Catholic church of New York.

All communications of Remarks (post paid) will be directed to " To the Editor of the New York Catholic Press and Weekly Orthodox Journal, New York."

* Letters on business or remittances of payment, &c., are to be directed to the Rev. J. A. Schneller.

J. Cooney, General Agent.

In consequence of the difficulties to be encountered in preparing for the publication of so extensive a periodical, it is contemplated not to issue the first number until the first Saturday in October.

(*Catholic Herald*, Sept. 26, 1833, p. 159.)

IV.

" THE JESUIT."

We are pleased to announce to our readers that the Catholic paper published in Boston, formerly under the title of " The Jesuit," and subsequently under that of the " United States Catholic Intelligencer," has resumed its former name.

The first number of the fourth volume, in an abridged form and at the reduced price of two dollars, has appeared.

(*Catholic Herald*, January 17, 1833.)

FIFTEEN YEARS OF CANADIAN CHURCH HISTORY
(1775-1789).[1]

BY J. M. LENHART, O.M.CAP.

The history of the Catholic Church in Canada has not been a neglected field of study hitherto. Yet it is invariably bound up with the political history of the country. There are some very useful monographs on certain phases, it is true, but a general Church history of Canada on an extensive scale still remains a desideratum. The Abbe Auguste Gosselin has undertaken the task to fill partly the existing gap by treating the modern period: the Church of Canada after the Conquest (1760). The second volume comprises the eventful period from 1775 till 1789, and is of the highest interest to the American students setting forth the attitude of the French Canadian clergy to the War of Independence.

In 1760 Canada had become a British possession. At that time the Catholic population of the extensive territory scarcely numbered 70,000 souls, all of French descent. When the American colonies had been threatening revolt, the British Government was forced to conciliate the Catholic Canadians and granted them by the Quebec Act of June, 1774, many liberties hitherto withheld. In the following year began the American Revolution. Its leaders tried to make the revolt continental, and invaded Canada (May, 1775), hoping that the French would join them. When Carleton, the British Governor,

[1] Aug. Gosselin, L'Eglise du Canada après la Conquete. II. Partie. 1775-1789. Quebec 1917. 8o pp. VI, 365.

heard of the surrender of Ticonderoga to Allen and Arnold, he appealed to the Catholic bishop of Quebec, John Oliv. Briand, for support. That prelate sent immediately a mandate to the parishes, to be read by the pastors after divine service (May 22, 1775).

Abbe Gosselin opens this volume with this momentous event (pp. 1–14). The Catholic bishop addresses his circular to "all people of this colony," Catholics and Protestants as well as Indians, exhorting them to defend the country and to remain faithful to England. "A group of subjects have rebelled against their Legitimate Ruler who is likewise ours. The singular kindness of King George, still more your oath and your religion oblige you absolutely to defend your country and your king" (pp. 2, 3). The Bishop lays the greatest stress upon the fact that they themselves or their parents had taken the oath of allegiance in 1759 and 1760. It was a great crisis for the Church of Canada. The vast majority of the people were favoring the American cause, as the Bishop himself admits (p. 9), and the Governor and the priests corroborate (pp. 11–14). The clergy, however, the nobility and the gentry with a few exceptions remained firm in their loyalty to the King. Governor Carleton wrote Sept. 21, 1775: "In spite of the efforts of the clergy, nobility, and gentry the Canadian peasantry refused with few exceptions to march" against the Americans. When the Bishop had been apprised of the first act of resistance against the orders of the Governor, he wrote to the pastor (June 4, 1775): "Let the people know that they do not only commit the sin of violating their oath but also expose themselves to the greatest punishments" (p. 13).

During these troubled times Bishop Briand made his third episcopal visit of the diocese (June 24–July 11) (PP. 15–25). Not a word was said about the burning

American question, because "the minds were not in a
proper state to receive my instructions with due respect
and submission" (Bp. Briand, Sept. 20, 1775) (p. 14).
The "infatuation of the Canadians" was increasing still
more after the Rebels had overrun all the country and
were in many places joined by numbers of the "perfidious Canadians" during September and October, 1775
(Guy Johnson, Oct. 12, 1775, in *Canad. Arch.*, 1904,
p. 346, 351). It was at that time, Oct. 9, 1775, that the
Vicar General Montgolfier wrote to Bishop Briand: "All
those who violate their oath of allegiance taking up arms
against the King, cannot be saved, can receive neither
sacraments nor Christian burial" (p. 25). But those
Catholic rebels tried to palliate their disloyalty by specious reasons. As early as Sept. 20, 1775, Bishop Briand
complains about those "casuists who know better than
the priests" (p. 13) what is right. "We did not take
the oath," they argued, "our parents did so." And how
did they take the oath? "Without proper reflection
and morally compelled" (p. 25sq.). It is quite evident
that the pastors had a hard time with those turbulent
spirits" (p. 27). During his visit the Bishop had given
his instructions regarding these rebels and soon after all
the pastors of the diocese uniformly refused the sacraments to such disloyal Catholics. Celebrated preachers
meanwhile went from one place to another to inculcate
on the faithful people their obligations towards the King
(p. 28–29). Even more troublesome to the pastors were
the American sympathizers who did not actually go so
far as to take up arms. Everywhere these formed the
majority in the parish and naturally were opponents to
the pastors vexing them in many ways (pp. 29–40). In
many places the women were even worse than the men
in this regard (pp. 34–35). The Bishop even dreaded
very much that they would turn Presbyterians before

long (p. 37). Nevertheless, he gave explicit orders to the pastors on Oct. 25, 1775, to refuse also both all sacraments and Christian burial to those violent American sympathizers (pp. 37–40); orders which were carried out as long as the troubles lasted.

By this time the invasion of Canada by the Americans was well under way. At many places the invaders were greeted as friends and liberators. Fort St. John and Montreal were captured (Nov. 3 and 12) and Quebec besieged (Dec., 1775–May, 1776). May 6th, 1776, however, the siege was raised and early in July following the Americans had evacuated Canada (pp. 41–69). During those dark days of the siege the Bishop and his clergy supported the Protestant Governor Carleton as valiantly as they had aided in 1690 the Catholic Governor Frontenac. The distinguished Prelate did not hesitate to ascribe the happy turn of events to the miraculous intervention of Mary Mother of God (pp. 55, 92).

Quebec had been still besieged by the Americans when Congress commissioned Franklin, Chase, and Charles Carroll to invite the Catholic Canadians to join the federal union. John Carroll, later Archbishop of Baltimore, accompanied his brother in the vain hope of moderating the opposition of the Canadian clergy. The commissioners left New York April 2, 1776, and arrived in Montreal April 29th. They discovered on their arrival that the public opinion had turned meanwhile against the Americans, and left partly May 13 and partly June 10(pp. 69–72). Their mission had proved a failure.

On Oct. 25, 1775, Bishop Briand wrote: "I should impose the interdict upon all churches and almost the whole diocese. But I will wait yet hoping that the people will open their eyes" (p. 39). Six months later, May 12, 1776, he penned these words: "May heaven grant that the deliverance of Quebec, this signal favor of

Divine Providence, open the eyes of our brethren that they come back to the path of truth, listen to the voice of their pastors and submit to the Powers established by God" (pp. 65 sq.). But God had heard the fervent prayer of that Prelate; the people were disillusioned and prepared to make their peace with God and the Church. For the time being, however, "nothing can be done for these disloyal subjects before the King has granted amnesty," ordained the Bishop May 11, 1776. And there were numerous parishioners who could not make their Easter in that year. Towards mid-June the Bishop issued a mandate against the rebels. On the banks of the St. Lawrence the French regime had never been extolled in such unqualified terms by a French Prelate as Bishop Briand praised the British government. This Catholic Bishop and naturalized British subject reproached the disloyal Canadians that they revolted "against the most mild and least sanguinary government" (p. 79), committed sins of disobedience and violation of oath, were abettors of theft, assassination, arson, and persecution of priests" (pp. 82–83), and "will be debarred from the reception of the sacraments till the King will have granted amnesty" (p. 82). Gradually the Canadians returned to their sense of duty within the following year. Yet long after we read of "annexionists" who persevered in their obstinacy and were denied accordingly Christian burial (pp. 77–93). The clergy stood firm with the Bishop against the Americans. Yet there were exceptions. Such a notable instance was the Jesuit Floquet at Montreal, peremptorily suspended in June, 1776 (pp. 72–76). Another "Americanist," Father La Valinière, was finally deported to France in Oct., 1779 (pp. 100–103).

But a new scourge invaded Canada, the German auxiliaries. On April 7, 1776, the first regiments sailed under Burgoyne for Canada. These foreign troups spread all over the country under the plea of pacifying the people. Their exactions and extortions exasperated the peasants very much, teaching them at the same time a very salutary lesson. Then those farmers who had two or three years before treated their pastors in the most shameful manner remembered who their true friends were. They quite often had no other protector against these oppressors than their pastors (pp. 94, 95, 103, 104). Among those German "yagers" there were two unfrocked ecclesiastics who were eventually reclaimed to their duty (pp. 95–100).

Meanwhile England had been preparing for the invasion of America. On June 16, 1777, Burgoyne advanced from St. Johns into the hostile country, where he was forced to capitulate Oct. 17th following. In this campaign all Canadian detachments had their Catholic chaplains whose names, however, are not known save that of John MacKenna, an Irish priest (p. 105). Excepting those comparatively few Canadian volunteers the great majority of the Catholics of the country observed strictest neutrality. Even the Bishop never exerted any influence on the people towards enlistment in the army. This time it was the question of invading a hostile country and not of defending their own. The clergy also was neutral with the exception of a few priests who were active in the interests of England. On December 17th, 1777, France determined to support American Independence, and on April 10, 1778, a French fleet sailed to the United States. Yet the prospect of returning under French dominion did not tempt the Canadians. The impassioned appeal of their mother country and particularly that of Count Estaing dated Oct. 28, 1778, to join with the United States could not shake their resolution; they remained either neutral or defended the

British cause. Not a single priest abetted the French-American alliance. This loyalty to England is the more commendable since both the Bishop and the most influential clergymen of Canada had been born and educated in France; they remained Catholics and French under the British flag (pp. 104–110).

Though somewhat disjointed in the manner of presentation, this part of Abbé Gosselin's book presents the best account we have of the attitude of the French Canadians to the American Revolution. It evinces with all clearness what we knew already that it is mainly due to Bishop Briand that Canada was lost to the United States and not to Jay's anti-Catholic utterances.

The next chapters of Gosselin's Church history contain a mass of miscellaneous matter about the Quebec Act (pp. 111–117), Abbé Bailly (pp. 124–134), Seminary of Quebec (pp. 135–139), Instructions of the Bishop (pp. 131–133, 142–149), Abbé Hubert (pp. 139–151), and encomiums of Governor Carleton (pp. 117–123, 142).

One of the best arranged chapters of the whole work is that dealing with the Missions of Acadia (pp. 152–168). After Abbé Maillard's death (1762) there remained only one priest in the extensive territory, Bonav, Carpentier, who resided at the northern border line at Chaleurs Bay. The Catholics living in the south had no priest to minister to them. "Manach who had passed over to France dreaded Protestant fanaticism and did not return" (p. 152). This statement of the author contains a gross injustice done to this intrepid missionary. Abbé Manach did not leave Acadia on his own accord, as the author would have us believe, but was apprehended and sent out of the country by the English in April, 1761. He so little dreaded Protestant fanaticism that he tried already in 1763 to return to his mission (*Canad. Arch.*, 1894, 242, 243, 247), but was kept out

by the English.   In May, 1765, he was sent by the King
of France to St. Pierre and Miquelon with the aim *to go
to Acadia* (*Canad. Arch.*, 1905, Ip. 367).   Yet three
more years elapsed till the Catholics of Acadia eventually
received the ministrations of a resident priest.   In 1764
no less than 1,762 French Acadians had been living in
Nova Scotia (*Can. Arch.*, 1894, p. 252).   What they
could not obtain their powerful friends, the Catholic
Micmac Indians, did extort from the British Government, a resident Catholic priest.   After Abbé Maillard's
death the Indians applied to the British Governor for a
priest.   However, the home government informed the
Governor that Protestant missionaries would be sent to
the Indians who "may wean them from their prejudices,"
but no priest (May 8, 1764).   The Governor of Nova
Scotia in turn notified the British rulers Oct. 9, 1765,
that "any attempt to convert the Indians by Protestant
missionaries will only exasperate them and may be fatal
to the settlements."   But the Indians would not brook
any more delay.   On Sept. 3, 1766, the new Lieutenant-
Governor wrote to London: "The Indians are determined to have priests, whether permitted or not.   They
had assembled, threatening to destroy the out settlements, but dispersed on the arrival of a Canadian priest
from the Bay of Chaleurs.   A rupture with the Indians
would have destructive effects" (*Canad. Arch.*, 1894,
248–272).   This threatening attitude of the Indians determined the English government at last to send a priest
to Acadia.   In July, 1768, the Abbé Bailly arrived at
Halifax "to officiate only to the Acadians and Indians,
receiving a salary of fifty and later of one hundred
pounds" (*Canad. Arch.*, 1894, p. 288).   The Abbé
Bailly is *the second Catholic priest that drew a salary
from the British Government, the first having been the
Abbé Maillard*.   At that time there lived about 1,500

Catholic Indians, of whom 550 were fighting men in the Province (*Canad. Arch.*, 1894, p. 270). The Government officials were highly pleased with this polished Catholic priest. Letters singing his praises were pouring into the Colonial Office at London, a strange thing in those days. Abbé Bailly, however, remained at Halifax no longer than four years. He left that city in May, 1772, on account of the violent opposition of the Protestant ministers and the common people. "Your Lordship can form your own judgment," he wrote to the Bishop, "looking over the Boston newspapers what they have written against me" (p. 154). At that time Abbé Bailly was a young man of not quite 32 years. The British government paid his allowance for a year and a half after his departure to Quebec in the hope that he would return (*Canad. Arch.*, 1894, pp. 320–321).

Five months after the departure of Abbé Bailly from Halifax a Scotch priest James MacDonald arrived at Cape Breton with a considerable number of Catholic Highland emigrants. The next year (1773) a French priest, John Bourg, commenced to minister to the Catholics of Acadia proper. Father MacDonald died in 1785 and Abbé Bourg was left the only priest in this vast territory for some time (pp. 155–159). But the year 1785 had not yet drawn to an end when two new missionaries had made their appearance in Acadia, the French priest Le Roux and the Irish Capuchin John Jones (pp. 159–166). Abbé Bailly, we heard, was permitted to officiate only to the French Acadians and the Indians. But there were other Catholics also at Halifax who could not receive the ministrations of a Catholic priest, viz., *Irish Catholics*. We are informed in February, 1763, that 850 parishioners of Halifax belonged to the Church of England, including 250 French and Germans, and *250 suspected Roman Catholics* whose children are brought up in the Church of England, and many of whom would go to that church. In June, 1864, we are told that the 900 members of the Church of England at Halifax include 250 *Irish* suspected Roman Catholics (*Canad. Arch.*, 1894, pp. 239 sq. 254). When the Penal Statutes had been repealed in 1783, the Irish Catholics of Halifax applied for a Catholic priest to the Bishop of Quebec (July, 1784) who appointed Father Jones definitely as their pastor in October, 1785. The new Catholic pastor of Halifax was a splendid preacher, gaining much prestige among the Protestants by his oratory. Father Jones wrote to the Bishop that there was a need of priests who *could speak the Irish language*. Before long a group of excellent *Irish* priests were working in the Acadian missions (pp. 166–168).

Meanwhile a change had taken place in the government of Canada. Carleton was replaced by Haldimand in June, 1778. The new governor was born at Yverdun, Switzerland, of Huguenot descent, and subsequently naturalized as an English citizen. This French-Swiss never learnt to speak or write English well. The relations between the Catholic clergy and Haldimand were not as cordial as under the administration of Carleton (pp. 169–212). But we cannot lay the blame for these rather strained relations wholly on the governor, as the author does. Haldimand has incurred extravagant strictures from French-Canadian historians, but a close study of his voluminous correspondence has been revindicating his political measures of late. Likewise Canadian Church History will have to reverse its verdict on his ecclesiastical policy. What are the charges against Haldimand? He sent back two French priests who had come to Canada *un*authorized by the government (pp. 192–197). But Haldimand executed simply his "Instructions," as the author admits (p. 188). Why blame him for it?

Carleton had received the same anti-Catholic instructions but he quite often disregarded them in favor of the Catholic clergy (pp. 116–117). Carleton, the Englishman, was powerful enough to act contrary to the letter of his orders. But could Haldimand, the naturalized citizen, have ventured to follow the same humane policy? I think not. Accordingly there is some truth in the author's statement that "Haldimand's great misfortune was that he was *no Englishman*" (p. 174). Moreover, Haldimand is blamed for the perfidious insinuations against the loyalty of the Canadians, particularly the clergy. He is "afraid that the Canadians will revolt" since France has joined the rebels, "he apprehends a general insurrection," he perceives a "change on the minds of many of the priesthood" since the French-American alliance (pp. 174–179). Yet Haldimand is frank enough to admit that "the clergy behaved well." These apprehensions Haldimand entertained time and again must not be regarded as malicious insinuations. He was of a very distrustful disposition and had many Canadians imprisoned on mere suspicion, as the author states (pp. 179–180). Yet he never molested any priest except the troublesome "annexionist," La Valinière, whom he sent to Europe to the satisfaction of everybody (p. 176). Then again not every apprehension is perfidious. The author himself relates an instance of this kind. On October 20, 1787, Bishop Desglis of Quebec wrote these words: "The nomination of a *Protestant* Bishop at Halifax is a real misfortune for our religion. I think we must be continually on the alert since the Government seems to regard the Catholics with an evil eye" (p. 270). Nothing proved more unfounded than these insinuations of the Catholic Bishop. Why does the author brand Haldimand's insinuations as "perfidious"? They were no worse than the Bishop's appre-

hensions. The author harbors still another grievance
against Haldimand: he tried to force French-speaking
priests from Savoy upon the Bishop. Since the British
government excluded priests from Canada who were
subjects of France, Haldimand formed the project to re-
cruit priests in Savoy which at that time did not belong
to France. The government finally approved his plan
and six priests were sent who somehow or another never
reached their destination (pp. 188–192). But neither
the Bishop nor the clergy were in favor of these "*foreign
priests,*" and the author approves of their view; they
would have priests either from France or none at all.
And the Savoyards had been equally as good Frenchmen
at that time as they are nowadays. But Bishop Briand
was of a different opinion. He wrote June 30, 1784:
"These foreign priests from Savoy will always remain
mercenaries who will return to their country as soon as
they will have made enough money to live upon. The
diocese has no need of foreigners for parishes. The
clergy would not like it that priests would come from
Europe to be pastors, because they would fear that these
Europeans would be placed upon the most lucrative parishes" (p. 207). This language surely sounds strange,
to say the least, and more so considering that these
words were addressed by a Catholic Bishop to a Protestant gentleman, the former Governor Carleton. "The
diocese has no need of foreigners for parishes." And
yet it is a fact that one priest had sometimes charge of
three and four extensive parishes at the time when
Bishop Briand penned these words (p. 310). Bishop
Briand's successor Desglis acted differently. Since he
could not have priests from France, he applied for such
in Ireland (pp. 162–168), and was well served. Haldimand was recalled in 1784 and was succeeded by Carleton. But Carleton who is so much idolized by the

author did no more than Haldimand to give free access to French priests; they remained excluded till 1793 (p. 199).

´ In 1784 Bishop Briand resigned (pp. 246–258). His successor was Desglis, the first *native* Canadian Bishop (pp. 259–274), who died in 1788 (pp. 322–325). He in turn was succeeded by his Coadjutor Hubert (pp. 275–292, 298–303, 308–333).

The *internal* history is neatly dealt with in two separate chapters (pp. 213–245). Additional material, moreover, is scattered all over the work. The Bishop was in touch with both clergy and people (pp. 213–214), instructions to priests (pp. 131–133, 142–149), conversions (p. 215), number of priests (pp. 217–326), tithes (p. 218), schools (p. 219), pastors (p. 220), and troubles in the parishes. The greatest and most frequent dissensions of the parishes were caused on account of building churches (pp. 221–228, 233–239, 271–273, 289, 299, 332–333). There are mentioned exceptional cases of great crimes committed (pp. 239–243) as well as extraordinary manifestations of piety (pp. 243–245, 311). We read of foibles of the clergy (pp. 291, 308–312, 327) and dissensions between the Bishop and his Vicar General (pp. 298–303), ordinations of priests and extraordinary faculties (pp. 268–270, 330), good qualities of Bishops and priests (pp. 229–233, 245, 250).

Even this cursory survey will reveal the fact that Gosselin's Church History is rather disjointed in the manner of presentation of facts. The material is not well digested nor neatly grouped, a drawback caused by his working method. He constantly quotes the documents verbatim, filling whole pages with extracts. This procedure naturally is attended with frequent and needless repetitions. Interspersed are many digressions not fitting in the framework of the particular chapters what makes reading somewhat tedious.

The documents are mainly taken from the archives of the diocese of Quebec and are *published here for the first time*. This is the *great merit of Gosselin's work*. The British state papers are made use of but sparingly. This is the weakness of Gosselin's book. The nature of documents is attended with the ulterior feature that the Bishops are kept in the foreground, the priests and people being either mentioned as far as they had dealings with these Prelates, or completely ignored. This causes a certain one-sidedness which eventually will be offset by material supplied from the various parish archives. This defect is the least noticeable in the first part (American question) where the Bishop really was the soul of everything. But even there many gaps can be pointed out. Not a word is said about the Catholics in the Maritime Provinces which politically were separate provinces at that time. Only an allusion to the Catholic inhabitants of Illinois is found (p. 139). The Catholic Indians of Canada as well as of other provinces who played such an important part during the war are not mentioned a single time. The Catholic Acadians in the Maritime Provinces unlike their French brethren in Canada remained loyal to the British government from the very start. In 1775, *no more than twenty years after they and their parents had been exiled by the English in the most barbarous manner*, the Catholic Acadians rallied to the defense of that government which had perpetrated on them the most foul crime recorded in history. They did not need any instructions from their Bishop; they knew what their oath implied and faithfully kept it. And the sons of Erin were loyal like their co-religionists, the French Acadians. Many a secret British correspondence was *written out in the Irish language* to insure safer transmittal during these warlike times. In Illinois even that strong man who kept Canada to the British Crown had lost all control over the Catholic Canadians; Illinois was lost to the United States. The author passes over all these facts in silence; they are not mentioned in Bishop Briand's correspondence. Yet in spite of gaps and deficient presentation of matter Gosselin's work is the best Church History of Canada (as far as it goes) which we have at present.

CHAPTER XXXI

(*Continued*)

1833-34

RESTORATION OF ST. JOSEPH'S TO THE JESUITS. — THE
NEEDS OF THE " OLD BISHOP."—HE ATTEMPTS TO AP-
POINT A SUCCESSOR TO FATHER KEILY ON HIS RETIRE-
MENT FROM ST. MARY'S.

Bishop Conwell was aging rapidly, and in August, 1832,
he became blind, and so stricken " he never afterwards
said mass." But the vigor with which he held on to the
shadow of the crozier he fancied to be still within his grasp,
did not wane with his years. He still laid claim to the per-
quisites of the offices he could no longer discharge, and
imagined some of Bishop Kenrick's powers and even his
acts to be his own. In the document, " printed but not
published," in which he states his complaints against the
" usurpation of his rights," he declares: " It became necessary for me to invite Rev. Mr. Kenny (the Jesuit) to take
possession of St. Joseph's Church and the property there-
unto attached, which belonged to the Society." What he
had to do with the transfer does not otherwise appear. On
April 9th, 1832, Father Dzierozynski, Superior at Georgetown, wrote to Bishop Kenrick about the matter. On June
29th, 1832, Bishop Kenrick wrote to Father Kenny, Provincial at Georgetown, in reply to proposals made to him

on June 25th, saying: "I shall with great pleasure see the successors of the venerable men who founded the Pennsylvania mission reoccupy the first church of this city," but desired that "the intended measure should not be executed before Spring." The next Spring the measure was consummated, and on April 12th, 1833, the Jesuits "took possession of the house and church." Father Kenny wrote to Father Beschter, at Abbottstown, York Co., Pa., that "the old Bishop remains, his rooms having been secured to him for life." Yet the "old Bishop" had no quiet. He had so many relatives about the house that the Jesuits came to object, as we shall see later. In June, 1833, he received information of the death of Bishop James Yorke Bramston, one of his consecrators.

What provision was made for his support beyond the securing to him of his rooms is not in evidence. It would seem, however, from the letters given below that the Trustees occasionally voted him a subsidy in lieu of the salaries as pastor and Bishop, which had been "usurped." But as these were uncertain and irregular, he no doubt found himself in frequent need of money, especially as his printers' bills must have consumed considerable. Though constantly professing "silence," he did not fail to keep his grievances before the public, and especially before the Trustees.

PHILADELPHIA, *March 10th, 1834.*

My Dear Sir:

No man could be more delighted than I was on receiving the agreeable news of your honorable promotion. I waited up to this date to congratulate you on that occasion because I had reason to fear you must have been perplexed with friendly visits, and my affliction prevented me from waiting on you personally. Rev. Mr. Keilly tells me that your situation does not prevent you from continuing to be the Secretary of the Board of Trustees; this gives me additional pleasure.

I request you to remember me at the next meeting of the

Trustees and procure the usual grant of a subsidy by an order directed to the treasurer.

With best wishes for your welfare,

I have the honor to be your sincere and faithful friend,

HENRY CONWELL,
Bishop of Philadelphia.

To ARCHD. RANDAL, ESQ.

Give my best respects to the Trustees and advise them to keep together and be unanimous.

(Mr. Randal had been appointed Judge of the District Court.)

PHILADELPHIA, *3rd September, 1834.*

My Dear Sir:

Excuse the liberty I take to call to your recollection the $50 expected in the month of May last; my wants require it, else I should forego the mention of it.

I have the honor to be, with great respect, yr. sincere and faithful friend,

HENRY CONWELL, *Bishop of Philadelphia.*

MR. FRENAYE.

———

PHILADELPHIA, *Sept. 18th, 1834.*

My Dear and honble. Sir:

Please to lay my case before the Board of Trustees, with your influence and recommendation to obtain from them an order directed to the Treasurer to pay me the usual amount of subsidy, which never has been more needful than at the present time.

Wishing you and them health and every blessing, I have the honor to be, Yours most Respy.,

HENRY CONWELL, *Bp. of Philadelphia.*

N. B. A year has elapsed since any grant of this kind has been made.

HONBLE. A. RANDALL, ESQ.,
Secty. &c.

PHILADELPHIA, *Oct. 20th, 1834.*

My Dear Sir:

I wrote to you at the last meeting of the Board of Trustees, but had no answer, owing probably to the circumstance of your not being present on that occasion. More than a year has elapsed since I received a moiety of the annual subsidy formerly voted for my support. My wants increase, and must continue until the usurpation of my inalienable rights and that of the chartered privilege of the society of Roman Catholics worshipping at St. Mary's Church shall no longer exist. I still trust in God that these grievances, however long and inveterately persevered in, shall and will be at length completely redressed.

Please to lay this my application before the Board this evening, with my best respects to every member of it, whom I know to be well disposed towards me. If at any time you should happen to stand in need of my presence to make a quorum, send for me and I shall be among you without any delay.

Please to appoint persons to move and second this application.

I have the honor to be, most respectfully,

HENRY CONWELL,
Bishop of Philadelphia.

HON. JUDGE RANDALL,
Secrty. &c.

These appeals grow more frequent and more urgent as the Bishop's need of support is drawing to a close.

In November, 1834, Father Keily of St. Mary's withdrew from that charge. The reasons appear in his farewell sermon.

" When, some years since, I came to your city, it was not with the view, intention or expectation, to be pastor of this Church; for you had, then, those among you who were far more capable of discharging the pastoral duties of this congregation.

I came, through the invitation. of the venerable Bishop then charged with the spiritual jurisdiction of this Diocese, the encouragement of the clergy, and several of the laity, to establish in this city or neighborhood a Catholic college for the literary and religious education of youth. The very week of my arrival, and when about to secure a place for the accomplishment of this object, the Pastors of this congregation were called to another sphere of usefulness, and your church left without a clergyman to discharge its duties. The Very Rev. Gentleman then charged with the administration of this Diocese insisted on my taking the pastoral charge of this church. I did so in obedience to his wishes, but with peculiar reluctance; not from any aversion to the situation, for I considered then, as I do at present, the situation of pastor in this church as highly enviable and respectable; but from the knowledge I had of the respectability of the congregation, the eminent qualifications of the pastors whom I had to succeed, and from a consciousness of my own humble qualities to discharge the pastoral duties of your church. For some years I had, however, to perform alone, as you are aware, all the duties of the pastorship. At length the zealous and indefatigable Prelate, now before me, was invested with episcopal jurisdiction over this Diocese. Since then I felt neither the same responsibility nor the same necessity for exertion, and only sought a favorable opportunity to carry the object which I had in view on first coming to your city into effect. That opportunity has recently, and to me quite unexpectedly, presented itself, though, in a great degree, the kindness, friendship and Christian liberality of a gentleman of this congregation, now before me; and I feel now that I can leave you in peace, union and happiness, and all their concomitant blessings smiling around you—that my humble services can be easily dispensed with."

Father Keily, therefore, being about to retire, Bishop Conwell asserted " his rights " by appointing a successor, Rev. Charles Constantine Pise, D.D., of Washington, whom he named to the Trustees in this letter :

(Not private.)

HONBLE. JUDGE RANDALL.

PHILADA., *November 5th, 1834.*

My Dear Sir:

Since I learn that Mr. Keilly, my Senior vicar, is determined to abandon the charge, It is my duty as Incumbent of the Parish of St. Mary's to appoint a fit person to succeed him. The Rev. Dr. Pise is the first object of my choice, and the best calculated to promote the good of religion in Philadelphia; tho' my rights have been usurped these many years past, I have invariably observed a religious silence for the sake of peace, in hopes that God will requite my patience and ultimately deign to favour the justice of my cause, well knowing that those who put their trust in Him shall never be disappointed. It is the duty of the Board of Trustees to manage the temporal concerns of the church with scrupulous exactitude and attention to the interests of the Body Corporate, considering that usurpation is but a temporary evil. It is not expedient to say more at present, whilst in the mean time I recommend the consideration of my state of privation to the benevolence of your associates in the trust, to whom you will present my best respects, and I have the honor to be, with affectionate regard,

Your sincere and faithful friend,

HENRY CONWELL, *Bishop of Philadelphia,*
and Incumbent of St. Mary's Parish.

N. B. Please to present this to the Board of Trustees this evening. The retirement of Father Keilly took place on the Sunday following November 9th.

But Bishop Conwell's appointment of Dr. Pise was not recognized, the power of appointment not being among those which Rome had left to him.

CHAPTER XXXII

1835-1842

BISHOP CONWELL TO BISHOP DUBOIS.—NEW CHURCH OF
ST. JOSEPH'S.—THE BISHOP IN NEED.—HIS DEATH AND
BURIAL.

Though he found that he could do nothing by his mandate, Bishop Conwell still thought he might accomplish something by his counsel, as the extract from his letter to Bishop Dubois, here given, shows.

PHILADA., *Dec. 9, 1836.*

My dear and Right Rev. Sir:

I write to you in the spirit of a true friend to give you my advice, which, perhaps, may not agree with your present feelings; but I am certain that the adoption of it would tend ultimately to your comfort, and to the interests of religion in the city of New York. In a word, it is to go further than to comply with the late advice, which (I am informed) has been given to you, to allow Mr. Levins to say Mass, that is, to take him under your own protection, and restore to him the faculties which you had formerly granted to him, "*Sat prata biberunt.*" After this generous act on your part, he may be depended upon to do his duty towards you and the public more than any other Priest you could find qualified for the service of the Cathedral: therefore make this effort in opposition to your own will and present feelings. Your friends and the public at large will consider this act as proceeding from the dictates of a good heart, and a sound understanding, and you will be rewarded by the consequences of it, in the peace which it will produce in your own mind, and your enemies will be disappointed and be sorry, whilst your friends will rejoice and applaud your conduct. There is no time to be lost: act promptly, and without weighing the matter too seriously, or taking time to consider of it; for this would defeat the object I have in view for establishing your happiness and comfort, towards the future peace of your mind, and laying the foundations of a perfect good understanding between yourself and the public. Despatch is necessary.

" Qui cito dat, bis dat
    Qui tardat munera, nil dat."

After begging to be excused for the liberties I have taken in giving you the above advice, without being asked for it, I take the liberty to give you another advice, on another important occasion, relating to Dr. Power. This gentleman is very popular abroad and at home; and your character suffers not a little for postponing him to less popular and less efficient individuals, whom you have preferred to him in your postulation for a Coadjutor. There are gentlemen at Rome who may be disposed to put an unfavourable construction on these proceedings, which may create more trouble, "*Melius est prœvenire quam prœveniri.*" I entertain a project which might supersede the necessity of calling for a Coadjutor for some years to come; because if this project were carried into effect, it would give you the benefit of a Coadjutor without having one under the title of that character. The good of religion requires New Jersey to be created into a new See, where an active Bishop could do much good, and bring thousands that are astray there at present into the fold of Christ. New Jersey is divided between the Diocese of New York and that of Philadelphia; the co-operation, therefore, of these two Bishops is necessary for the canonical appointment of a new Bishop in that new See, which might be called the Diocese of Trenton, because that city is the capital of both East and West Jersey. Nothing is required to obtain from the Holy See the appointment of this new Diocese but the spontaneous relinquishment and resignation of the two aforesaid Bishops to their rights respectively in that part of their diocese which lies in the State of Jersey. The Holy See would concur in this measure, and appoint the Rev. John Power if an application should be made for him to that effect, whilst, in the meantime, you might make him your Vicar General, and appoint him to the station which he now holds in your diocese. If you think proper to join with me, I shall resign and abdicate my rights in the State of New Jersey, that there may be no canonical impediment to its being created into a new See. All your enemies would lie prostrated and silent for ever by the accomplishment of these measures specified above.

I remain your Brother in Christ,

✛ HENRY CONWELL,
Bishop of Philadelphia.

The Provincial Synod assembled at Baltimore, to whom the consideration of the above letter is referred, will give their opinion on it, and act accordingly.

In the report of the Provincial Council held at Baltimore, 1837, appears the statement, " Absent Prelate, Rt. Rev. Henry Conwell, retired from active duty, having lost his sight."

The two letters annexed are preserved at St. Joseph's. The writers, possibly relatives of the Bishop, are unknown.

LIVERPOOL, *November 8th, 1837.*

Right Revd. Sir:

With grateful affection I return you my sincere thanks for your great kindness to Me while under your hospitable roof. I had a pleasant passage of 23 days. My Brother in law received your letter, so he had a look out for Me. I gave my sister Rose a pleasant surprise as My Brother Thomas has gave me this morning after his arrival in Liverpool to see Me; it is as I think so strange he wishing me to go home that I have not the most distant thought of home (or house) is for ME.

Hanna stopped one night. Mr. McKenna has the picture, as she would not wait one day for it. Please let Mrs. Donnelly know I walked through paradise street at length but has not seen Mrs. Heart. Remember me to Mrs. Johnston and also Henry. I remain, my Lord, with love, regard and esteem,

Your humble servant,

JANE DONAGHEY.

Address (torn)

........L ∴Revd

..........onwell

.....adelphia

78 Dale St., Lpool., *Nov. 8th, 1837.*

Right Rev. Sir:

I take the present opportunity of sending these few lines to your Lordship, hoping you will receive the same in a short time; together with the small parcel enclosed, I send you 12 of Riley Catechisms, also two of the English Laitey's Directory and Brown's union Dictionary; the other part of your order I shall send early in Jany 38. Jane was 23 days on her passage. the present you sent to your native parish has been committed to my care; it has cost me about £2 & 3 days Labour, & if I was not up to the Custom House Laws & I will say a little bribery it would be little short of 100 duty, but, thank God, I have it safe. I have sent the Rev. C. O'Brien's a letter & told him he must find some trusty friend to take it home. I am sorry to hear your Lordship has lost the Use of your sight, but pardon me if I humbly crave your prayers in the old Irish fashion, viz. your beads for my Dear Wife & little family, also for your obedt Sert,

Patrick McKenna.

Addressed

To the Right Rev.

H. Conwell, *Bishop of Philadelphia.*

The Rev. John McGill, afterwards Bishop of Richmond, gives us a glimpse of Philadelphia and the " Old Bishop " about this time. While on his way to Rome he wrote to his father from New York on June 13th. He describes his visit to Philadelphia, where he was born, Nov. 5th, 1809.

" Bishop Kenrick has removed to St. John's, although St. Mary's is still the 'Cathedral, old Bishop Conwell having his see there. The old man looks quite broken and is afflicted with blindness, but nevertheless comes every Sunday to St. Mary's from Willing's Alley where he resides."

The following letter was written to a priest in Ireland, but possibly never sent. It is in the A. C. H. Society.

PHILADELPHIA, *July 18th, 1838.*

Rev. Dear Sir:

when you receive this, go to Ballyriff and give the Bill of five pounds to young Hugh Conwell. My Merchant will give him the cash for it. His mother and all the Samsons arrived here safe. Tell him to go to Belfast without any delay, and from there to Liverpool by the steamboat. There is a packet which sails every week from Liverpool to New York. let him come out in the packet as a steerage passenger, provided with sea . . . for the voyage, and when there he will come here in one day by the reail road. his mother has a bed and pillows of the best feathers, in a new tick. She desires Hugh having this bed here with him, and to put all together in old ticks, and then to cover whole with an old tick to save it on the passage; he can put this on his berth to lie on. Betty his aunt will keep possession of the house and property, and manage for herselfe in the calm way that mother did under your protection and care. she will not sell the place. If William Samson can come with him to Bellfast, you will be so good as to advance to him ten shillings, out of the fund in your hands, & place it to my account, but let no other person go with him except William Samson, you know what I mean. When at Belfast buy 1 Dozen of Reilly's Catechisms, and a London Almanac, get a score of meal maid by Mrs. Campbell, Bread the same she maid for his mother, with my compliments to her and to all . . . . . & Conwells in Ballyriff, give my love and respects to Anthonony, & his family, tell him to write to me & give me all the news he can. I sent an emblem of the Church as a present to every Bishop in Ireland, many of them in north, many of them did not acknowledge the receipt. inquire what was the reason. I am greatly pleased with the account I have of the Castle and its situation. Dear Sir, I fear hugh has not anuff of money to bring him on here, therefore tell my nephew Anthony to give him one pound sterling, and I will send him two pound for it when the boy arrives here. write to me by post, and your letter will be here with me before Hugh, & let know the balance in Yr hands.

I remain Yours Affectionately,

HENRY CONWELL,
Bishop of Philadelphia.

St. Joseph's Chapel had long been too small for the accommodation of the people. A new church was determined upon. On Monday, May 7th, 1838, Mass was said in the old chapel for the last time. Doubtless the old Bishop was present. The corner-stone of the present edifice was laid on June 4th by Rev. James Ryder, D.D., in the presence of Bishop Conwell, who in the record placed in the corner-stone is designated " Bishop of Philadelphia." Bishop Kenrick was at that time absent on a visitation of the Diocese.

The incident referred to in the annexed notice may have been the doing of an imposter, or perhaps it was the echo of another attempt of Bishop Conwell to assert his right to act for the Diocese. *The Catholic Herald* of January 3rd, 1839, has this:

" We are called on by the Boston Pilot to state whether the article which has been copied into the daily papers concerning an appeal made by the Rt. Rev. Henry Conwell to the British nation for funds for the Missions of Pennsylvania be authorized. We are without any knowledge of such an appeal; and we must presume that the name of the aged Prelate has been used by some imposter, as misstatements contained in the article are glaring. As the administration of this diocese has been for more than eight years solely vested in Rt. Rev. Dr. Kenrick, no appeal could be made without his sanction, which we are authorized to state was never given."

A diligent search in the Philadelphia papers of the time for the appeal referred to was without result. Possibly the Boston papers were the ones that printed it. No copy of the article can be found in the *Pilot* itself.

Another instance of the aged Bishop's urgent appeals for money is furnished by the circular here given.

PHILADELPHIA, *June 17, 1839.*

Henry Conwell, Bishop of Philadelphia, returns thanks to

the Ladies and Gentlemen who have contributed to his natural support, and requests John McGuigan, No. 19 Powell Street, to receive subscriptions for the same purpose, and to record the subscribers' names until a meeting of the friends of order shall be convened, by public notice, before the end of this year, at a proper time and place, to confer on the subject of the contents.

The above is from a circular seemingly designed for a collection book. No evidence of the " meeting of the friends of order " is to be found; so it is to be supposed that his " natural support " was otherwise provided for, at least for the time.

Bishop Conwell's time was drawing to a close. The feebleness noted by Father McGill in 1838 steadily increased. In April, 1842, it was seen that the period of his dissolution was not far distant, and on the 20th of that month Rev. Felix Barbelin, S.J., administered the last Sacraments. Two days later Bishop Conwell breathed his last. While he lay upon his death-bed, the *Catholic Herald* of April 28th announced in its mourning columns the passing away of Bishop England of Charlestown, which took place on April 5th. Here is an extract from the account of Bishop Conwell's funeral, as given by the *Public Ledger* of April 27th :

FUNERAL OF BISHOP CONWELL.

The obsequies of the Right Rev. Henry Conwell were solemnized yesterday noon at St. Joseph's Chapel in Willing's Alley. For the last three or four days the body has been lying in state, habited in his mitre and pontifical robes, in the aisle of the church, just before the altar, with his hands clasped as if in prayer, &c. &c. &c.

At the appointed time all the Clergy of the Catholic Church of this city and a number from New York and Baltimore entered. High Mass was then performed and an impressive sermon, commemorative of the worth of the deceased, was delivered by Rt. Rev. Bishop Kenrick. The ceremonies were concluded about one o'clock, when the body was placed in the hearse, followed by a great number of people and a long line of carriages, was conveyed to the place of interment, the "Bishop's Ground," near the corner of Passyunk Ave. and Prime St.

This deeply lamented Prelate was a native of Ireland; he had been 22 years a Bishop of the Diocese of Pennsylvania, and at the age of 94 he is gathered to his fathers. For the last 9 years he has been totally blind, and as a consequence has been shut out from the intercourse of mankind. From 9 o'Clock in the morning until the deceased was interred, the bells of all the Catholic Churches were tolled, and the Churches themselves were shrouded in mourning.

The following account is from the *Catholic Herald:*

The solemn office of the dead and pontifical requiem Mass took place on April 26th at St. Joseph's Church. The Rt. Rev. Dr. Kenrick officiated, assisted by Rev. Dr. Sultzbacker, Canon of St. Stephen's, Vienna, as Assistant Priest, Rev. C. J. Carter, as Deacon, and Daniel F. X. Devitt, as Subdeacon. The Deacons of honor were Rev. Messrs. Burke and Pancoast. The clergy of the various city congregations occupied the sanctuary, whilst the Seminarians of St. Charles Borromeo took their places beyond the railing of the sanctuary, and, forming an outer choir, assisted most effectively during the solemn chant of the Office and Mass. The Church was crowded to excess by the faithful, and the solemn prayer and absolution pronounced aloud by four assistant priests in stole and cope, previous to the closing prayer of Rt. Rev. Dr. Kenrick, was truly impressive.

The body of the venerable prelate was then borne by four priests to the front of the church, and placed in the hearse to be carried to the graveyard at the south end of the city. The faithful followed in crowds; the body was also preceded by the numerous and interesting members of St. Joseph's Orphan Asylum, and the religious sodalities attached to St. Joseph's Church. The body of seminarists and the clergy followed, and the vast concourse moved in order and strict regularity.

CHAPTER XXXIII

The Contest over Bishop Conwell's Will.—Was the
" Bishop's Ground " Personal Property?

Bishop Conwell's life, at least during the twenty-two years he spent in Philadelphia, was a peculiarly stormy one. Now his body rested in the grave, and crowds of the faithful and the clergy prayed for his soul's eternal rest. An anniversary mass was celebrated for him yearly at St. John's. But his name continued to be a storm center for many years. From the time when, in coming to America, he acted as tutor to the nephew whom he brought over with him until the time when he wrote the last letter of his which is of record, concerning the coming over of young Hugh Conwell, he was perpetually entertaining or otherwise caring for an interminable succession of nephews and other relatives. At his decease he left very little personal property. The appraisement of his personal effects showed ten cases, containing 1,080 books, valued at $177.76; one likeness of Bishop Conwell, $5; and an oil painting, " The chaste Susanna." But there was the " Bishop's Burial Ground," and around the possession of this the storm raged for many years, the nephews claiming it as the Bishop's personal property, and denying the validity of the will by which the Bishop had sought to continue it in possession of the church, and the use for which it had been bought.

On May 2nd, 1842, John McGuigan presented to Wm. Piersol, Esq., Register of Wills, a certain writing purporting to have been made 5th Nov., 1839, which he avers is the last will and testament of Bishop Conwell. Hugh Conwell and John McKeon objected to the probate of the paper, " that it was procurd by fraud and imposition, that the Bishop was totally blind for years and never executed the writing with knowledge of the contents." Conwell and

McKeon requested a trial by jury to test the validity of the said writing. The will was admitted to probate. Register John Painter so certified 22nd' July, 1845.

On Oct. 6th, 1842, Nicholas Donnelly, brother-in-law of the Bishop, was appointed administrator, *pendente lite.* Hugh Clark, of the County of Phila., and Denis Murphy, of the city of Phila., were sureties to the amount of $1000. (Book P, p. 228, No. 296.)

On Jan. 6th, 1844, John McKeon, a nephew, by affidavit before Alderman Binns, required John McGuigan to give security for money received from the cemetery.

On Jan. 1st, 1845, John McGuigan began suit against Hugh Conwell and John McKeon for $50 they had promised to him if Bishop Conwell's will was genuine. They resisted suit, declaring that it was not the true will.

On March 25th, 1845, Mr. N. Donnelly " was discharged from the duties of his appointment " as administrator, on his application to the Orphans' Court for such release, and was directed to surrender to new administrators " the property in his hands."

On March 31st John McKeon, 203 South St., and Hugh Conwell, 214 South St., Administrators (*pendente lite*) of the Estate of Bishop Conwell, gave $800 security by themselves and John Lavry, Master St., between Germantown Road and Cadwallader, and James Sherry, Germantown Road above Master. (Book P, p. 317.)

On June 9th these administrators applied to the Orphans' Court for leave to sell the real estate in the name of Henry Conwell. This meant the cemetery, which the will of 1839 had bequeathed to Rev John Mullady, S.J. John McGuigan, by his attorney, B. Newcomb, Esq., opposed the application on the score that the real estate in question was held by the late Bishop in trust. The Writ was made returnable on the Third Friday of June.

On July 1st Bernard McNeill began another suit against

the nephews, John McKeon and Hugh Conwell, on similar grounds to that of John McGuigan of Jan. 1st.

On Jan. 17th, 1846, in the District Court the issue from the Register's Court of Dr. Bernard McNeill against Hugh Conwell and John McKeon was called, on suit instituted Nov. 26th, 1845. On Feb. 14th the jury returned a verdict in favor of the defendants.

HUBERT CONWELL testified that he began living with the Bishop in 1838, and was with him until his death; that he saw the paper and read it several times, signed by Donahoe and Smith, as witnesses. The Bishop told him to get the Will from Father Donahoe. I recollect there was some things about the cemetery, something about leaving it to Mr. Mulledy. It was about a year before his death he asked me to get the will from Donaghue,—something in it he did not like,—heard him say repeatedly that one of the clergy of St. Joseph's was giving him a little trouble and he was not satisfied with him,—it was Haverman,—heard Bishop say he would never give back the will to them,—got it two years about from F. Donaghue before he died. Bishop said Mrs. Johnson destroyed the will. After her death I am positive I heard the Bishop say Mrs. Johnson had lost or destroyed the will. His not being able to find it I expect was the reason he so said. I expect that he said it was lost or destroyed; he set me to look for it. He never was dissatisfied at not finding the will. Haverman wanted the Bishop to leave the rooms he had in the house, and go into a house in Willing's Alley. The Bishop said he was not satisfied with the will because of the annoyance. Heard him say that he believed Mrs. Johnson had destroyed it. She died 10 or 11 months before the Bishop.

JOHN MCGUIGAN was offered as a witness, but objected to, on the ground that he had an interest in the will. Court sustained the objection. Counsel excepted to the opinion of the Court.

MARY DONAHOU never saw the will, never heard of its destruction, never heard defendants speak of the destruction of the will.

ANN SCHOOL lived with the Bishop the last 18 months of his life; closed his mouth after the last breath. One night Father Donahue came into the Bishop's room; when he came out, I went in. The Bishop said he had had a long conversation. Bishop said, " He is in trouble about that paper he had from me; it is no matter anyhow; Mrs. Johnson has thrown it by." One day Mr. McGuigan came in. Bishop said that McG. was uneasy about that paper that is lost. McG. told the Bishop he had a copy of it and wants me to make a will by it. The Bishop said, " I know McGuigan; now he can wear a better coat than me." I nursed the Bishop " as a mother a child; he was perfectly blind." Mrs. Murray was the housekeeper for the Jesuits. Mrs. Johnson for Bishop Conwell. Mrs. M. said to Mrs. J., " You must leave this house, and all the Bishop's people, for the Society at Georgetown considers that the Bishop and his people occupy too much of this house." Mrs. J. told the Bishop. Bishop said " He would be Bishop of Philadelphia as long as he lived, that he would have his own people about him as long as he lived, for what do I know but that they take me out, for I am blind, and leave me standing at the corner. I will hold my possessions as long as I live, and keep up my own dignity, for they shall not get what I have. It was me who sent for the first of the Jesuits, &c."

On Feb. 19th Dr. McNeill applied for a new trial on the ground that Judge Parsons had erred in deciding that John McGuigan had an interest in the will because of the power of attorney given him in June, 1828, by which he was entitled to a fee for interments in the cemetery.

On Sunday evening, two days after the verdict in favor of the nephews, Bishop Kenrick sent the following letter

and Pastoral Warning to Rev. F. Barbelin, then pastor of
St. Joseph's :　　　•

Rev. and Dear Sir:

I send you a document, of which you may make such use as
you deem proper. As it is only directed to protect the rights
of the people, I do not deem it necessary to put any restric-
tions as long as the graveyard has not passed into secular
hands, which I trust will never take place.

　　　　　　　Yours in Xo,
　　　　　　　　Francis Patrick Kenrick, *Bp. Pha.*
Phil., 21 Feb., 1846.
　　Rev. F. Barbelin.

On reverse, in pencil, "About the Burial Ground known as
the Bishop's Grounds.

Pastoral Warning.

To all whom it may concern:

Whereas some persons are devising measures whereby the
Catholic Burial Ground commonly known as the Bishop's
Burial Ground, in the district of Moyamensing, may be con-
verted into secular purposes, and to the emolument of private
individuals, contrary to the purposes for which it was originally purchased and consecrated as a Catholic Cemetery and
to the trust reposed by the faithful in the late Bishop of Philadelphia, and to the engagements made and entered into with
the purchasers of lots, and others who have purchased the
right of burial in said Cemetery.

We therefore, in order to protect the rights of all interested
and to preserve the said cemetery for its original purposes,
conformably to the laws of the Catholic Church, do publicly
warn and admonish all persons concerned that, by a decree of
the Sacred Council of Trent, all persons who by violence or
strategem, or other means, under any pretext shall presume to
convert to their own use, and to usurp ecclesiastical property,
or the revenues and emoluments arising therefrom, incur by
the very act the anathema of the Church, that is, the censure

of excommunication, from which they cannot be absolved, unless by the authority of the Roman Pontiff, after they have made restitution of the property so usurped, and the revenues and emoluments therefrom arising. In the mean time, and until full security shall be had for the maintenance of the said cemetery as a Catholic Burial Ground, we warn the faithful of the risk which they incur by purchasing lots or burial right therein, lest by any device or strategem said cemetery might be withdrawn from its original use and applied to profane and secular purposes; but, we at the same time declare that it is not our intention or wish to interfere with the rights of persons who have already purchased lots, or whose near relations have already been interred in said cemetery, or with the privilege of gratuitous interment granted to the poor by our predecessor. Given under our hand and seal, at Philadelphia, the twenty-first day of February, in the year of our Lord MDCCCXLVI.

FRANCIS PATRICK,
Bishop of Philadelphia.

Dr. Neill's application for a new trial (made on Feb. 19th) was refused on Feb. 28th.

On March 10th, B. Newcomb, Esq., Attorney for McGuigan, applied to the Supreme Court for a writ of error, alleging the same reason. Dr. Neill also appealed.

Immediately on the rendering of the verdict in favor of the nephews, a meeting was called for the following evening to organize the people and collect funds for defending the title of St. Joseph's Cemetery. James M. Smith was elected Treasurer. He collected up to Oct. 26th, 1849, a total of $499.81, of which Father Mullady is credited with $381.89.

In March, 1847, Nicholas Donnelly and Ann his wife assigned to Jas. M. Smith, Wm. Whelan, Cornelius McCauley, Michael McGeoy and Joseph Dimons all right, title or interest in the cemetery. These gentlemen were acting in the interest of Fr. Mullady. Ann Donnelly was the niece of the Bishop. Her interest amounted to one-seventh. But she would not be a party to the suit to establish the Bishop's private ownership of the cemetery.

The following is the decision on the competency of McGuigan as a witness.

DECEMBER TERM, 1847, SUPREME COURT OF PENNA.

'Testator directed a lot should be used as a grave-yard, except a part intended for the erection of a church, of which he appointed M., the sexton, and to have the care of it " as he now has during life." M. had been acting during testator's life under an authority from him, which directed certain charges to be made for interments, including a compensation to the sexton; and after testator's death, M. received fees from interments. He is not a competent witness to support the will on an issue directed, although he may have released to the executors all interest under the will.

IN ERROR FROM THE COMMON PLEAS OF PHILADELPHIA.

Feb. 9, 10. This was a feigned issue from the Register's Court to try the validity of a paper purporting to be a will of Conwell. In this instrument the testator directed that a lot of ground should be and continue for ever as a cemetery for persons certified to be entitled to interment according to the rules and discipline of the Roman Catholic Church, except a certain part of the lot set apart for the erection of a church; and I hereby appoint John McGuigan, sexton of the same, to have the care of it as he now has during his natural life. By a separate paper, testator had appointed Hughes and McNeill, the plaintiff, executors. McGuigan had been originally named as the plaintiff, but, on motion, McNeill was substituted.

On the trial the plaintiff called McGuigan to give testimony in support of the will. It appeared that in 1828 he had been appointed by the testator to manage the burying ground during the testator's absence, with directions to charge certain fees for interments, &c., among which was a sum as compensation to the sexton and grave digger. The defendant proved that, since the testator's death, there had been some interments, and that McGuigan had received some money. The witness then released to McNeill, the plaintiff, all right and title to any property or benefit arising to him, or that he might be entitled to under the will. The court rejected the evidence; and this was the only error assigned. Omitting the arguments of the Counsel, Justice Burnside decided:

It is clear that the Common Pleas was right in rejecting McGuigan. He entered under a written license, and obtained possession under the Bishop. The license expired on the death of the Bishop. The will he is called upon to establish makes him sexton of the cemetery as he then held it during his life. But it is contended that his release, executed for the consideration of one dollar, on his trial, to the supposed executor, of all his title and interest (if any he has) to any property or benefit arising to him or that he is or may be entitled to under the will of the Bishop renders him competent, because they say he is equally liable to both parties. This is not so. He has received money for interments since the death of the Bishop, which the heirs at law may call him to account for. He has a clear interest in making and establishing this professed will and defeating the heirs at law. There is no executor until he creates one by his evidence; his release is to his friend, Bernard McNeill, and does not render him competent to testify on his feigned issue. Judgment affirmed. (Barr's Pa. State Reports, Vol. VII, p. 368.)

On Mar. 16th, 1848, the Supreme Court affirmed judgment against Mr. McNeill, Chief Justice Gibson, presiding.

On Mar. 23rd the Sheriff cried on Dr. McNeill's personal property, 136 S. Fouth St., for a debt of $299.38 in suit of Hugh Conwell and John McKeon.

On July 5th, 1846, Hugh W. Tener, Esq., Attorney for Hugh Conwell and John McKeon, notified B. Newcomb, Esq., Attorney for John McGuigan *et al.*, that at the trial of the case in the District Court a verdict of $30,000 would be demanded.

But the gathering of the eagles over the body was not yet complete. Here is an inquiry on behalf of another " relative and legatee " who wished a share in the banquet.

.BOSTON, *August 1st, 1848*.

Dear Sir:

I take the liberty to write to you to enquire about the Estate of the late Bishop Conwell; the reason why is this: there is a man in ·this city whose name is Hugh McFlynn or McFlein who claims to be a relative and legatee of the late Bishop. Whether such is the fact I am unable to tell; he is an ignorant Irishman and I can learn from him no particulars, and I should give but little heed to what he says were it not for the fact that there are one or two of the gentry called Brokers, who have got hold of him, and one of them has been to your city to examine into the matter, all in a private way, and I find they are very thick with him and dont hesitate to advance him money, and they are very suspicious least some one should make enquiries—this induces me to think there may be something in it. His wife, who is comparatively an intelligent woman, has induced him to give me a full power of attorney to act in the matter — I learn that he has a relative living in your city somewhere in Cedar St., of whom information may be obtained—his name is James McFlynn. If you can without much trouble look to the matter and think there is anything worth looking up, I shall be glad of the information, and also in that event I shall be glad to obtain your assistance. In the meantime if you will look a trifle to the matter, Records, &c., I shall be most happy to reciprocate the favor should opportunity offer. Of course I do not wish you to put yourself much out of the way, as 'tis perhaps a bootless affair. If it should be otherwise, or there be a fair prospect, I will transmit to you a Retainer and have the affair thoroughly investigated.

Very Respectfully Yours, &c.,

GEO. D. WILMOT,

20 Court St., Boston.

J. DEVEREUX, ESQ.

The Committee of the meeting " for defending the title of St. Joseph's Cemetery," besides assisting in the various suits affecting that title, went more deeply into the root of the matter than the Courts had as yet done, inquiring into the right of the deceased Bishop to dispose of the cemetery ather by will or otherwise. They wrote to Father Cummiskey for his evidence on the subject and received this nswer:

Dear Friends: Sept. 26th.

I received your letter of the 23rd Inst., yesterday, and I hasten to answer it. I recollect distinctly that at the time the property was about to be purchased it was to be got for the double purpose of providing a support for the Bishop and clergy of St. Joseph's, who were for some years previous living without any fixed salary and to deprive the Trustees of St. Mary's of the benefit of interments in their graveyard, and for this purpose it was proposed by the Bishop that the city should be divided into four districts. He would take one, the Rev. Mr. Harold another; the Rev. Mr. Ryan take a third; and myself take the fourth; things went on in this way for some days, in the interim the Bishop went about among the congregation and found the project to be a popular one. He told us at dinner one day shortly afterwards that he had changed his mind, that he thought he would collect all the money necessary to make the purchase himself. After a few weeks the purchase was made. If I remember well, in the name of Mr. C. Johnson and some other of the congregation, who thinking it was intended for the general support of the clergy, advanced as much money as was necessary to secure the purchase. In the mean time the Bishop was busy collecting, and finally got as much money as Mr. Johnson and his friends advanced and got the deed conveyed to himself. The property was consecrated, interments commenced in it. But that was the last the poor clergy of St. Joseph's heard of its benefits.

I left the Diocese shortly after, but I recollect having gone to Philadelphia some years afterwards, & when visiting the Bishop in his own room he told me that he had made a will and bequeathed the graveyard to the Jesuits. I remember to have remarked that I was glad that it would be continued for religious purposes.

If what I have said above be of any use to you, I am willing to testify it in any court in the U. S.   I am sure the Bishop will have no objection to my going in as far as he as well as myself would be unwilling that any . . . . given for religious purposes should be alienated to any other.

Gentlemen, I remain Respectfully,

Your obedient servant,

JAMES CUMMISKEY,

St. Columba Church.

To MESSRS. JAMES SMITH &
the rest of the Committee.

On Mar. 15th, 1849, the depositions of Rev. Joseph Cretin (afterwards first Bishop of St. Paul) and others of Dubuque were ordered to be taken, B. Newcomb and Francis Dimond appearing for J. McGuigan.

[THE END]

INDEX

LIST OF ARTICLES

LIST OF CONTRIBUTORS

BOOK REVIEWS

ILLUSTRATIONS

INDEX